People's Witness

People's Witness

THE JOURNALIST
IN MODERN POLITICS

Fred Inglis

Yale University Press
New Haven and London

For information about this and other Yale University Press publications, please contact:
U.S. Office: sales.press@yale.edu   yalebooks.com
Europe Office: sales@yaleup.co.uk   www.yaleup.co.uk

Set in Minion by Northern Phototypesetting Co. Ltd, Bolton
Printed in Great Britain by Biddles Ltd, Guildford and King's Lynn

ISBN   0–300–09327–6

Library of Congress Control Number 2002101098

A catalogue record for this book is available from the British Library.

10 9 8 7 6 5 4 3 2 1

For Richard Hoggart

Contents

Preface

The history of journalism is a thriving and productive realm of academic history. I have of course learned much, indeed everything, to begin with, from such classics in the form as those of James Curran and Jean Seaton, or Michael Schudson, or Stephen Koss. In addition there are shelves full of biographies of the best-known stars in the journalistic firmament and I honour these in my dependence on them as cited, chapter by chapter.

All the same, there is not, I believe, anywhere to be found a book such as this one: one which offers to reorder a galaxy of starring and not-so-starring, more dimly significant names in a new historical constellation. Our historical epoch begins, let us say, in 1914; it then splits open in a sensational rupture in 1989; since that date journalists and historians alike have been at pains to puzzle out what on earth is going on. During that epoch, some of our deepest values, the allegiances which give lives shape and fulfilment, which embody such signal meanings as success and achievement, have been made visible by the performance of celebrity. As never before, fame is the spur of human motivation, at least in the richest nations of the world.

Accordingly, to tell the many tales of journalistic success, the winning of fame and fortune whether meritoriously or contemptibly, is to paint a huge fresco of brief lives which, taken together, constitute the grand historical narrative not of journalism but of journal*ists*. In so far as it has been politics by any means which has comprehended our lives for us in modern times, it has been political journalists who have been our best-known, even our leading, storytellers.

This being so, the figures in this book, inevitably a selective group – choices made for the author by fame and reputation, time and chance, but choices which would surely have varied a lot in other hands and on other tongues -- together *constitute* the big story of how to be a (political) journalist. They exemplify the innumerable ways there are to be such a thing, so that the young men and women troop off to do things likewise and differently.

In making of themselves what they can, getting on and going off, each generation of journalists acquires the ethics of what, as Max Weber tells us in the second chapter of this book, is a highly ambiguous profession, now admired and applauded, now criticised and disparaged. In either condition and in both, the next generation – and there are at least four of them represented here – finds it in itself to match its character to its opportunities and, in doing so, to live well or badly according to the virtues and vices of that inescapably public figure, the journalist.

Hence this parade of biographies. Even at a time when the published biographies of individuals chosen by writers more or less according to their fame in the fame-defining walks of life – politicians, artists and writers, sportsmen and -women, actors and all those who go on to the stage and the screen to dance and sing or to pretend to be somebody else not famous at all, millionaires, scientists and even journalists – at such a time of the widespread popularity of biographies, biographic histories are still not quite the thing for those practising correct social history. A biography, on this hostile view, is too individual, too personal, to show us the past as it generally is as well as really was. Social history, even in the hands of the old masters, of G. M. Trevelyan and Alan Taylor, or in the hands of new-old Marxists, of Edward Thompson and Christopher Hill, pays only passing attention to individual biographies except in so far as they personify and calibrate the clash of classes and the march of time.

A biography is a matter of life and death. It is the readiest way we have in everyday life of getting a grasp on our history, and understanding who has been responsible for it. A good biography, however brief, signifies matters which go well beyond an individual life.

We live our lives by entering the stories open to us. We understand our society by listening to the narratives telling us how to fill those other social roles, whether this person or that has conducted themselves well or badly. When a new speaking part appears on the stage of history we attend to the character as it sorts out its duties and its field of action; we watch it grow into its story.

The twentieth century is just over; much of it was hideous, and almost as much was happy and glorious. The terrible combination of death technology, ruthless profiteering, ideological bigotry, and human monstrosity caused millions of avoidable deaths and thrived on a revolting diet of hatred, cruelty, insatiable greed and vindictive envy.

The same century saw the scientific intelligence that brought the world the fulfilment of nuclear weapons bring also the extraordinary physical redemptions of modern pharmacology, dietetics, bodily repair. On a good day, economist and politician together could provide honest work, decent food and waterproof shelter for everybody. A little later, consumer capitalism reckoned to be able to keep the promise of some such happiness as was to be found in the joys of abundance and the ease of leisure. Pitched opposite the consumer markets until the day before yesterday, old socialists held out the possibility of something even better by way of natural emancipation, uncompetitive fulfilment, equality of plenty and the unimaginable delights of a world without oppression by class or money. This was 'the short twentieth century: the age of extremes' (both phrases gathered into the title of Eric Hobsbawm's classic *Age of Extremes: The short twentieth century, 1914–1991*) and its grotesque asymmetry towers over the new millennium.

This book tells the story of that shadowy figure always to be found on the edges of the century's great events, offering to tell ourselves about ourselves. The journalists mostly start from murky origins and their outline remains murky enough for a hundred years. Yet during those years it was they to whom people turned for news and explanation of news. Whether they found the truth, of course, depended not only on the wits and disposition of the journalist on hand, but also on the extent to which governments or generals or other practised liars had got in the way. (For one answer see Phillip Knightley's pioneering and canonical work, *The First Casualty: The war correspondent as hero, propagandist and myth maker*.) Either way, the journalist had also to bear up beneath the interest taken in things by the always self-seeking and, it seems, reliably deranged owners of news organs determined to tell their newshounds what to say.

Whatever the impediment, the century's journalists were appointed to be the people's storytellers; while they were widely treated with incredulity, scepticism or derision, they were also met with admiration, with eagerness to listen and learn, as well as with, at times, the deference due to a celebrity so unevenly aligned with merit. A journalist's fame, nicely adjusted to the prominence given to his or her byline as well as to the relative authority of the newspaper or TV channel in question, could turn a story into history. Whether as first-on-the-scene or as judicious opinionator back home on the editorial floor, the right or the wrong journalist took on the task of turning meaningless events into meaningful experience. One Damn Thing

After Another became a story with a plot; a beginning, middle and end; human characters, some heroic, some villainous; a range of historical causes and human purposes; time and space with shape to them; consequences, motives, explanations.

It is time to thank and honour those who helped me find the news and shape the story of the stories. First to troop on is a group of those who have practised the trade with distinction, been, in some cases, famous in it, and figure perhaps in the pages which follow. They have each acceded to my request not so much for an interview, which they have themselves so often requested of others, but rather for a tutorial: they taught me history and, if I have proved an apt pupil, the credit is theirs, and their only reward such pleasure as the book may give. They include Ben Bradlee, Walter Cronkite, Joan Didion, Bob Douglas, Gloria Emerson, Harry Evans, James Fenton, Katherine Graham, Christopher Hitchens, Godfrey Hodgson, Peter Jennings, Bill Webb, Hugo Young, and my two cherished friends, Victor Navasky and Phillip Whitehead.

The last two carry me over to the second group of those whose help was indispensable to my hunting-and-gathering of stories, and then to the writing of them. All, I'm proud to say, are my friends, and I claim that the implicit framework of all storytelling, of pointing the moral and adorning the tale, is the circle of the writer's friendships.

Jim Hunter did so much, going so far beyond the duties of a friend and with such an exasperated affection, that he must have a sentence to himself. A better writer by far than me, he repaired my prose and reduced my pomposities, page by page, and made, I believe, a much better book of it as a result. John and Kate McAndrew, presently rising to the crest of the latest generation of broadcast journalists at the BBC, gave me readily of their experience, their savoury humour, and their time. Nancy Williams was help and hostess in Arkansas, Kathy Williams the same in Brooklyn; Wolf Lepenies was similarly hospitable to me in Berlin, as well as giving me precious advice and at least one crucial lead; Laurie Taylor and Boyd Tonkin provided powerful insights, good gossip, and – a theme of the book – were prompts to laughter. Quentin Skinner, as always, was the absent companion of all my writing, in his work as in his life an example to teach all those still trying to hold together the intellectual virtues and the idea of a university, how best to go about it. On biographical detail, Nick Jones gave me indispensable help and Lynn Guyver did the same for the index. Carol Marks took away an impossibly dense, double-crossed and compli-cated manuscript and turned it into order, and the result is as much hers as mine. Bill Hamilton proved the best and most effective of agents, Robert Baldock the kindliest of editors. Finally, I thank and pay tribute to Henk Wesseling and Wouter Hugenholz and their incomparable librarians, all at the Netherlands Institute of Advanced Study, in the quiet and comfortable surroundings of which, as Fellow-in-Residence, I started my researches for this book in 1999, and was generously received back again by them to finish it off in a last headlong four weeks in 2001.

Richard Hoggart, my dedicatee, was, I believe, the first to conceive of the serious study of newspapers and news broadcasting; in any case he has been far and away their most intelligent critic. Not only that, his public services have been such, I guess, as to make more possible that serious-minded, civic-spirited and reflective news gathering and news commentary we have to have if, in this dangerous world, we are to combine caution, resolution and longevity. I cannot think there is an Englishman of the past half-century who has done more than he has to connect the life of the moral imagination to the common good of society, and the only way I have of emphasising the heartiness with which I say this is to place his name at the front of the book.

Fred Inglis

First Lady: Martha Gellhorn

The three bright primaries of television – red, blue, yellow – flicker and coalesce in the close-up image of a face. It is the poised, handsome, rather haughty face of an American woman of uncertain age, bright blonde hair, a strong beaky nose, well-shaped mouth, nice receptive blue eyes, the left lid drooping very slightly, a long graceful neck. We never see her hands.

She is speaking of her life's work to an interlocutor we don't see at all. She says, 'It was the worst thing I saw but it wasn't hard to write. You wrote what you saw, it's not very difficult.' Then she pauses and reviews what she has just said. 'Are these horrors impossible to describe? I didn't catch how it was. Your shock makes you less observant than you ought to be.'

The date is 1994 and the woman is Martha Gellhorn, American journalist and novelist, eighty-six years old – you'd *never* know it – and the week's protagonist for the lateish inquisition show, *Face-to-Face.* Jeremy Isaacs, her genial, sincerely reverent inquisitor, has asked her about her arrival as one of the first journalists into Dachau immediately after Germany's unconditional surrender in May 1945. It is her worst memory, she says calmly: 'the worst of everything, the organised reduction of human beings, planned, repeated, steady cruelty. When I got there they were all still there, piles of dead stacked like wood, naked yellow skeletons and the living stood around numbly, all with typhus.' She had hitched a lift on a C-47 taking American prisoners of war on the first leg home out of Regensberg. One soldier supposes Martha Gellhorn to have been a prisoner as well.

'Where were you captured, miss?'
'I'm only bumming a ride; I've been down to Dachau.'
One of the men said suddenly, 'We got to talk about it. We got to talk about it, if anyone believes us or not.'[1]

She was thirty-seven, had been to the wars in Spain, in Finland, in China, before the whole world joined in and she went with her people to liberate Europe. But neither she nor anyone else had ever seen anything like this. It was lucky for America, and anyone else reading *Collier's* magazine in 1945, that hers was the prose they found through which to learn of the latest instalment of humankind's antique inhumanity.

She sat in the doctor's office at the camp while he talked to a man who had been found alive under a pile of dead. The good journalist teaches us to see the world, looks on our behalf at what it is, in this case unendurable to look at. This great journalist teaches us to look at a man who has since become familiar, even been made much of and featured in feel-good movies. This man doesn't feel so good. He weeps. Good that he can …

> He was a Pole and he was about six feet tall and he weighed less than a hundred pounds and he wore a striped prison shirt, a pair of unlaced boots, and a blanket which he tried to hold around his legs. His eyes were large and strange and stood out from his face, and his jawbone seemed to be cutting through his skin. He had come to Dachau from Buchenwald on the last death transport. There were fifty boxcars of his dead traveling companions still on the siding outside the camp, and for the last three days the American Army had forced Dachau civilians to bury these dead. When this transport had arrived, the German guards locked the men, women and children in the boxcars and there they slowly died of hunger and thirst and suffocation. They screamed and they tried to fight their way out; from time to time, the guards fired into the cars to stop the noise.[2]

She likes the doctor and he has plenty to tell her. He had been a prisoner in Dachau for five years. In her report at least, he shares Martha Gellhorn's gift for controlled understatement. It may be that she filled his style with hers, for hers – bare, plain, 'objective' if that means telling a story with few adornments, scarcely any descriptive detours, few adjectives, fewer adverbs, simple vocabulary – is as quick and vivid and clear to see as scenes in great literature should always be.

> The doctor spoke with great detachment about the things he had watched in this hospital. He had watched them and there was nothing he could do to stop them. The prisoners talked in the same way – quietly, with a strange little smile as if they apologized for talking of such loath-some things to someone who lived in a real world and could hardly be expected to understand Dachau.

'The Germans made here some unusual experiments,' the doctor said. 'They wished to see how long an aviator could go without oxygen, how high in the sky he could go. So they had a closed car from which they pumped the oxygen. It is a quick death,' he said. 'It does not take more than fifteen minutes, but it is a hard death. They killed not so many people, only eight hundred in that experiment. It was found that no one can live above thirty-six thousand feet altitude without oxygen.'[3]

She listens to more from her doctor about a similar experiment in which six hundred people died while the Germans placed them in vats of ice-cold water, varying the temperature in order to establish the compelling statistic that a human being will live for two and a half hours in water temperatures of minus eight degrees Fahrenheit.

'"Didn't they scream or cry out?"' He smiled at that question. '"There was no use in this place for a man to scream or cry out. It was no use for any man ever."'

In tiny ways Gellhorn shapes the prose so that it tells. Maybe the doctor really did repeat 'scream or cry out' and 'it was no use' but however it was, the dual assonance of the phrases is chillingly effective.

When she has given them their say, she finally bursts out with hers. It is of course honest and eloquent, hard to better as the response of those our people sent to tell them what they found in the heartlands of the hideous enemy as that enemy reached the end of his tether.

We have all seen a great deal now; we have seen too many wars and too much violent dying; we have seen hospitals, bloody and messy as butcher shops; we have seen the dead like bundles lying on all the roads of half the earth. But nowhere was there anything like this. Nothing about war was ever as insanely wicked as these starved and outraged, naked, nameless dead. Behind one pile of dead lay the clothed healthy bodies of the German soldiers who had been found in this camp. They were shot at once when the American Army entered. And for the first time anywhere one could look at a dead man with gladness.[4]

Collier's was a good place to read Martha Gellhorn's article, journalism which does so exactly what journalism should, is truthful, faithful to the facts, bearing witness of human actuality to those who could not actually be there, and then matching the story with adequate feelings and moral judgement. Doing so, it becomes art, and Martha Gellhorn's plain report-ing alongside the plain reporting, some of it also art, of dozens of other correspondents, takes on the power and solemnity of the books of wisdom and teaches us how to feel about one of the most terrible things in history.

She was born in 1908 in St Louis, Missouri to a comfortably-off but dedicatedly overworking doctor and his intelligent, cultivated, musical and travelled wife. Her father died of an exhausted heart in early middle age and Martha remained on close and loving terms with her mother all her long life.

The two parents taught her that painfully keen social conscience which led her, as it would for so many generations of idealistic young men and women between, say, 1929 and 1979 or so, straight to the political left. Goodness knows where she learned her blessed restlessness, but her demon together with her political allegiance drove her to seek out every war she could find in that most war-torn half-century of Christendom's two millennia.

Writing was then the only way to reconcile her ceaseless passages about the globe, finding and feeling for the devastated victims of war, and the incorrigibly cheerful and steady young men doing what they could to defend them, to defeat their oppressors, to repair the wreckage of poor and ordinary lives.

She travelled without stopping as soon as she was a woman and had left Bryn Mawr after reading enough English literature to fire her own writing.

She was long-legged and beautiful and fair-haired and reckless, generous about sex, acerbic about male bullying. She went to England and fell in with H. G. Wells 'because if you were young and a writer you had to sponge'.[5] Wells, as usual with him, knew best what was best for everybody and told her she must write every day from nine until one. She didn't like getting up and 'early breakfast was a torture but one day, to show off, I went into the garden and wrote "Justice at Night". Wells took it away and sold it to the *Spectator*, which he shouldn't have done.'

The piece appeared in August 1936. It described in Gellhorn's bare, withheld style, the lynching of a negro in Mississippi, without trial or evidence, for alleged rape. In the article she and her boyfriend have hitched a lift in a pick-up with a couple of half-drunk drivers on the way to the 'useful-looking elm' which will serve as a gallows. The horrified young man and woman make a few timid objections and are told it's none of their goddam business. Nineteen-year-old Hyacinth is hanged, soaked in kerosene, blazing on the rope. Martha and her young man Joe resume their lift.

It wasn't quite how it happened.

It was what Truman Capote would have called 'faction' – facts and fiction mixed – the two guys were coming from the lynching not going to it. Then I met a black whose son had been lynched. The whole thing happened before I got there. They were boasting and then they said 'shut up, lady' when I asked how they knew the negro was guilty. I was frightened.[6]

Fiction and journalism lie close together. Gellhorn was a novelist although her journalism is better known than her novels. In the annals of journalism, as we shall see, she is joined as a novelist, of course, by her husband-to-be, Ernest Hemingway, by John dos Passos, Sinclair Lewis, Norman Mailer, John Hersey, George Orwell, John Gregory Dunne, Tom Wolfe and Joan Didion. The principles of fiction are capacious; they take in James Joyce and Isabel Allende as well as the school of plain facts. But they are constant in their rendering of everyday life, their faithfulness to *things* in all their intimacy as well as to people in all their inwardness. Novelists follow their characters to the bedroom and the bathroom; they see them naked and they see them die. Their vocation is to make the reader see what happens, to show rather than to tell.

All these purposes apply to journalists also. These are the methods of a sociable social science: the disciplined observation, discussion and classi-fication of human oddity. The neologism 'faction' marks the uncertain territory between record and rhetoric.

Much heavy breathing is expired across this ground. The sacredness of facts is counterposed to its alleged opposite, succulent but mere opinion. It is certainly true, as Michael Schudson documents,[7] that journalism fought an unfinished war with itself over the supremacy of facts versus the power of the story, the energy given it by revelation and sensation. Lincoln Steffens complained that when he was first a reporter on the *Evening Post*: 'Reporters were to report the news as it happened, like machines, without prejudice, color, and without style; all alike. Humor or any sign of person-ality in our reports was caught, rebuked and, in time, suppressed. As a writer I was permanently hurt by my years on the *Post*.'[8]

The battle remains running. The naïve notion of a sacred factuality was soon criticised by the simple argument to be put, among others, by Walter Lippmann, that interpretation and opinionation are inseparable from the selection of the facts and that value preferences soak all the way through to the very names language bestows upon the world.

The dispute is easily understood, impossible to conclude, reanimated by any serious piece of reporting.[9] Martha Gellhorn would not have written her report on the lynching as she did if she had known Wells was going to take it away and sell it. But she shapes the report of her visit to Dachau and gives the rhythm of noble poetry to the halting descriptions of the horrors described to her by doctors and guards so that what she has written makes for the best kind of writing: true, beautiful, excellent because intense, thereby causing what is abominable in her subject-matter to become such that we can look upon it and bear up against its terror.

This is to test Gellhorn's journalism by the highest standards and it may be that it is only worth applying these when a writer finds momentous subject-matter. At a normal pitch, it wouldn't be worth it. Gellhorn, however, went so frequently to war that she lived pretty well at full pitch all the time, so we can judge her accordingly, and be grateful.

She left the States in 1929 and never lived there for very long again. In France, at twenty-one, she discovered French student life, the thrill of listening to the café intelligentsia, the true righteousness of the old Left and of pacifism. She began on the first of her eleven novels, went to visit the playground of the rich on the Côte d'Azur, took up in Cannes with the stepson of the writer Colette to edit an insurrectionary magazine called *La Lutte des Jeunes*, dropped in at the casino one night and 'saw those claws coming out covered with rings and I thought thank God I'm young and poor'.[10]

When it came, 1929 was the biggest date of the century in the American calendar. The Wall Street stock market collapsed, the great depression began and the country lay supine while the men of the working class begged, and their families hovered on the edge of starvation. In 1932 Roosevelt came to office, vilified by his many enemies on the right of the populist press as a crypto-socialist. He appointed his old ally Harry Hopkins, who was to serve him faithfully throughout the period of his reign in divers offices, head of the Federal Emergency Relief Administration. Hopkins knew the bright and beautiful traveller-writer and asked her to follow him and report on the agency work in relieving the misery of the poor.

Martha worked at her commission for two years, completed her report and started on the collection of four short novels, *The Trouble I've Seen*, which she based on what she found.[11] The work confirmed her in the allegiances, the strong frame of feeling and the way of seeing which impelled her writing for the rest of her long life.

She was lucky in this. She learned, from her parents' honest principles of liberal reform and then from her work, an immutable sympathy for the victims of human maiming and a direct, simple way of identifying the causes of human misery. This is one of the best, most necessary lines of news reporting and her sixty-odd years of work along that line are one of its finest commemorations.

London was Martha's first and last love among the innumerable cities in which she fleetingly dwelt, and it was there she was entertained by the small and knowable literary community of the Left which revolved about the weeklies and had as its leading lights and her friends Wells, Stephen Spender, Cyril Connolly, Vera Brittain. But it was in Berlin that she met the future in the uniform of fascism, and in Stuttgart read about a 'blood-thirsty Red rabble attacking the forces of decency and order ... The Nazi papers had one solid value: whatever they were against, you could be for.'[12]

So she went to Spain and its Civil War, where the legitimately elected socialist government was opposed by Franco's rebel military, openly aided by the weapons, bombs and aircraft of Fascist Italy and Nazi Germany. She took with her a sort-of certification as a journalist provided by her friendly editor at *Collier's*, as well as by her experience with Hopkins, followed a meandering route by car, truck and train to Valencia and, on 27 March 1937, arrived at a blacked-out Madrid.

She had by then stopped being a pacifist and become an anti-fascist. She had also paused in her novel-writing and become, by permission of *Collier's*, who printed her first speculative contribution and thereafter, thanks to Charles Colebaugh, never cut or altered anything she wrote for the next eight years, an eye-witness journalist. At a moment when the London *Times* was judicious and abject in its affirmation of the appease-ment of Hitler's every desire, and the New York and Washington papers were tucking Europe into the inside pages, Martha Gellhorn was, courtesy of *Collier's*, saying this sort of thing:

An old woman, with a shawl over her shoulders, holding a terrified thin little boy by the hand, runs out into the square. You know what she is thinking: she is thinking she must get the child home, you are always safer in your own place, with the things you know. Somehow you do not believe you can get killed when you are sitting in your own parlor, you never think that. She is in the middle of the square when the next one comes.

A small piece of twisted steel, hot and very sharp, sprays off from the shell; it takes the little boy in the throat. The old woman stands there, holding the hand of the dead child, looking at him stupidly, not saying anything, and men run out toward her to carry the child. At their left, at the side of the square, is a huge brilliant sign which says GET OUT OF MADRID.[13]

The bite and dryness of the prose were already part of the almost-finished style of the twenty-nine year old; the solidarity with avoidable suffering, stiffened by her researches for the Relief agency, had struck deep roots in her character; the laconic diction, the American understatement, the domestic sympathy ('you are always safer in your own place'), the fierce jokes and the admiration for everyday bravery are all distinctively hers.

Exactly the same qualities transpire in the best writing of Ernest Hemingway, nine years older than Martha, the literary star of his generation who had already made the triumphant transition from journalist to novelist by way of two marriages and some penurious years in Paris. Of course he also had his awful propensity to a mendacious boastfulness, his ludicrous overassertion of manliness, his gusto for competition, but Martha Gellhorn didn't know this when she and her mother first took the bus to Key West one December afternoon in 1936 and blew into Sloppy Joe's bar downtown.

They made a noticeable pair, the Gellhorn women: the mother, nicknamed Omi, then in her stately fifties, her daughter striking, tall, with a bold gaze and a swaying, sashaying walk, her high-heeled footsteps set precisely in a straight line like a catwalker, overmatching her handsome mother.

Martha was an adventuress, she loved sex and good wine and, though with one caustic eye, men. Hemingway was, with Beckett, the best-looking writer of the twentieth century; he had a terrific zest for life and, when sober, no less terrific charm. He had his ill-judged, gallant taste for danger and warfare and, balanced by her political commitment, so did she. Their love of love affairs made them made for each other, and Martha had no scruples about setting herself, quite without realising it, to prise Ernest away from Pauline who had prised him in her turn and with his enthusiastic complicity away from stately, plump Hadley Richardson.

She stayed for a month with the Hemingways in their Key West house, joined Ernest on the New York train out of Miami, followed him to the Madrid battlefront and, a short time afterwards, was steamed out of his bedroom in the Hotel Florida by a shell from the rebels besieging the city which exploded in the hot water tank. As they escaped hand-in-hand down the stairs to the basement, they passed Antoine de Saint-Exupéry, another writer-journalist addicted to warfare, gravely distributing fresh grapefruit to the distressed gentlewomen as they passed him.[14]

No one could say what effect each of these two heroes had on one another's writing or on one another's way of feeling-and-seeing. Martha must have read Hemingway plenty before she met him. She arrived at Bryn Mawr as *The Sun Always Rises* came out. I don't suppose he had read *The Trouble I've Seen*. Both of them had drunk in the literature which had made alike the journalism and the novels, let alone the policy of American social reform between the wars.

However it was, her journalism and his are at times indistinguishable, and set a standard – a diction and tone – which still cannot be bettered and is very hard to break away from. Hemingway filed this report two weeks after Martha arrived in Madrid.

At the front, a mile and a quarter away, the noise came as a heavy coughing grunt from the green pine-studded hillside opposite. There was only a gray wisp of smoke to mark the Insurgent battery position. Then came the high inrushing sound, like the ripping of a bale of silk. It was all going well over into the town, so, out there, nobody cared.

But in the town, where all the streets were full of Sunday crowds, the shells came with the sudden flash that a short circuit makes and then the roaring crash of a granite-dust. During the morning, twenty-two shells came into Madrid.

They killed an old woman returning home from market, dropping her in a huddled black heap of clothing, with one leg, suddenly detached, whirling against the wall of an adjoining house ... A motor car coming along the street stopped suddenly and swerved after the bright flash and roar and the driver lurched out, his scalp hanging down over his eyes, to sit down on the sidewalk with his hand against his face, the blood making a smooth sheen down over his chin.[15]

The ripped silk, the whirling leg, the pendant scalp are facts which the journalist must honour. The details show and tell, as such journalism counts on them to do. They tell of the violation of ordinary bodies, the outrage of dismemberment, especially the dismemberment of anonymity, the decent old crone in her black dress, icon of any street close enough to the Mediterranean littoral.

War journalism worked this plain style for half a century. It is the style, the American style, of Ernie Pyle and Ed Murrow; it was to be the style – the only feasible style – in which John Hersey met with the ruins of Hiroshima and reassembled the events of the morning of 6 August 1945. The Hemingways fixed the style together with the character and way of life part of it as surely and permanently as do all great poets at their maturity. What and how they wrote defined a school of writing for five or six decades.

Martha added something of her own which Hemingway's boyish vanity caused him to miss. His brave bravado kept him where the bombs were falling; her compassion sent her to find out what happened afterwards. She saw how destiny pinched faces and shrank stomachs; she reported how political cruelty, cowardice and indifference made military versions of the same human horribleness much worse. She could not match the packed immediacy of *For Whom the Bell Tolls*, but she dramatised on a world scale that powerful American melodrama in which little people are destroyed by the giant machinery of corporation or politics, and turned it into tragedy.

After her love affair with Hemingway started she treated him, a friend said, with 'humorous indulgence'[16] and accompanied him on his dangerous trips to the Loyalist frontlines along the high Sierra de Guadarama. Hemingway was helping John Dos Passos, then a communist, to make a propaganda film about the war, *The Spanish Earth,* and when it was finished in early May 1937, Hemingway left for Paris. The film was to be shown at a special screening at the White House obtained by Martha's previous intercession. She now had Eleanor Roosevelt's regard and then her lifelong friendship for her work for Harry Hopkins.

All the same, apart from a trip home to see the movie and eat the Roosevelts' awful food, she stayed in Spain. She collected Ernest from the Café de la Paix in Paris and the two of them were the first correspondents to trek round the wide arc of the Loyalist positions on the Aragon mountains in early autumn as the first snows fell. Fred Keller from the American machine-gun company in the International Brigade became fast friends with Martha. Keller was tough and funny, he travelled light and when the Loyalists were forced to retreat across the River Ebro he swam the broad, rapid, grey-brown river time and again, wounded himself, helping the wounded across. He died aged eighty in 1993 and Martha wrote him an epitaph in the *Los Angeles Times*, an epitaph also on the place where they first met, in Spain 'where fascism must be stopped'. She ended: 'Then the war, our war, ended in defeat and none of us ever got over it in our hearts.'[17]

Pauline Hemingway came to Europe to fetch her straying husband home. He went back to Key West to write and to chafe against the bonds of the marriage to which he had pledged himself in all the ardour of remorseful self-vindication ten years before. But he couldn't deny himself the blaze of excitement that came alike from the love affair and going to war. In April 1938 he returned to Martha and the Civil War.

The war was nearly lost. The Republican militia had, Martha thought, 'become an army and looked like an army and acted like one'[18] but the enemy was armed by the fascist Axis and the Loyalists were split between factions and the ruthless but incompetent manoeuvrings of the Russians. Hemingway and Gellhorn stood by their men, but they were retreating down the east coast. Hemingway's occasional reports for the *New York Times* predicted another year's fighting from May 1938 (he fancied his grasp of strategy) but by November, when she left, Martha Gellhorn was speaking a threnody over *la causa* ('never forget your manners, walk do not run,' Martha Gellhorn was the journalist with the most beautiful manners).

Like any other writer, every political journalist has one experience issuing in one key story which fixes the frame of feeling for him or her in all subsequent reporting. It becomes at once a moral measure and a narrative form. All subsequent events are discovered to have shape and meaning as they are fitted to this form. Occasionally, a writer (or any other kind of artist) reaches the limit of its usefulness and has to invent a new form, or stop writing.

No doubt everybody goes through the same process in their personal biographies. Each person tries to fit event into the story they tell themselves about themselves. The better the fit the more accomplished the style. In the management of newspaper production a particular paper defines its style in terms of just such a standard narrative. The newspaper also matches events to form, and makes its political stories accordingly.

Spain was such a story for Martha Gellhorn. It had a bold plot: democratic and legitimate revolution against illicit and atrocious old reaction. It had a simple hero – the people – against gigantic villains – Franco, Mussolini, Hitler. Like all great political drama, its action caught up the past, present and future of the continent and of her continent, its population made up so largely of immigrants from the countries now at war, herself the child of the former Austrian Dr Georg Gellhorn.

Spain made up Martha's mind about the world and its political future. The story of the world was one in which armed and wealthy capitalist bullies exploited, oppressed and murdered poor, resolute, courageous but helpless peoples.

Nobody could say that such a form fails to fit the century, and Martha Gellhorn remained faithful to it. In Spain, admittedly, the story wears a bit thin at times, as George Orwell's dispatches suggest. The acronym POUM wasn't the only thing comic about the proletarian militia arguing for democratic decision-making in the trenches, while their vicious quarrelling with both native-born and Moscow communists was fatal in all senses. But it was still one hell of a good story, effective enough even in defeat and when it found a happy ending eight years later in Germany, overwhelming, the story of the century.

Martha travelled to world war by way of liaison and, later, marriage to Ernest Hemingway, a part of her life which later she could so hardly accommodate that she threw it right out. (When I met her for the only time in Chepstow, Monmouthshire in 1990 the only advice given me by others was don't mention Hemingway.)

As much as anything there was probably rivalry in this. Ernest wrote the great novels but she wrote the great journalism. In 1939 he was publishing repellent articles in American weeklies[19] explaining how his country must make money and keep out of the war. Once it started, although he couldn't remove his genius completely from his writing, he grossly indulged his propensity for exhibitionism and lying self-aggrandisement, both in action and in his reports.

Even then his charm, his infectious high spirits, his gift for turning every situation, even a burned-out farmhouse, into a fiesta were all as irresistible as his third wife-to-be found them in Spain, Cuba and Sun Valley, Idaho.

Theirs was always an arm's length marriage. In December 1939 Martha could no longer sit still listening to 'the patriotic fervor of the Johnny-come-lately anti-Fascists' (her FBI file described her, ineffably, as a 'premature anti-Fascist') so she got a commission from *Collier's* to see what might be going to happen in Finland. She looked the country up in an atlas, learned it was the right side to choose, landed one night and woke to the sound of bombs falling on Helsinki.

After Spain, she thought, the war could only be *against*, 'too late to be a war *for*',[20] and what she judged fine were those qualities of understated courage (here most seriously at odds with her husband's overstatement of his own), dogged endurance, quiet good manners, bitten-off, bitter jokes, devotion to duty and to those near you, which she discovered alike among Spanish peasant volunteers, English bomber crews, American GIs and the Finnish President.

She came back to Cuba from Finland to find *For Whom the Bell Tolls* well on the way and Ernest punctuating sessions of intense composition with no less intense sessions at the wine, the daiquiri, the vodka and the whisky in the company of some promising Basque exiles.

The drink, the mess, the profanity, the sheer damnable maleness of it all got her down while it lasted, but they were pledged; she enjoyed her own drink, shooting, hunting, writing, and their time in bed; her steely hauteur was more than a match for his hot temper; above all and for a season she *liked* him, he was funny and fun, she travelled light, they were (goodness knows) free spirits; in November 1940, she married him. After four years of the affair, she couldn't protest that she didn't know what she was in for.

They went together on a kind of honeymoon to see the war in China, moving easily between the generals of the Kuomintang, the peasant soldiers and tumultuous jags, sustaining something strong in both of them which turned life into a rhythmic timetable of travel, writing and boister-ous parties, a life entirely without the ordinary domesticity of most people, of going-to-work-and-coming-home-again. It was a life lived in spurts, spurts of heavy work, heavy drinking, the burden and the joys of ceaseless travelling, and spurts of passionate loving to match. These are the rhythms of the always-working observant and sympathetic tourist, and they presage the way of life of all those journalists whose special stamp of authenticity was eye-witnessing.

Once the United States had joined the war Hemingway invented a little cloak-and-dagger action. He kitted out his big fishing boat, the *Pilar*, with enough weapons, barmy Basques and radios to satisfy his braggart fantasy of U-Boat hunting round Cuba. Martha became irritated beyond measure by her husband's posturings on the *Pilar* and proved as accomplished a marital combatant as her husband – once, when he had slapped her in ungovernable rage,[21] deliberately driving their big car into a tree, leaving him pie-eyed inside and walking home with icy composure.

She harried him to go to the war and went herself, back to the England she always loved better than anywhere else, to find that 'amazing nation' whom 'nothing becomes like catastrophe' turning its stolid, often negative and obdurate qualities into the virtues – 'endurance, a refusal to panic … pride, the begetter of self-discipline' – which would, once the Americans arrived, win the war.

For its last nineteen months she 'followed the war wherever [she] could reach it' which meant, first, on a Lancaster bomber station on operations nights where 'you wait for them to go and then you wait for them to get back.'[22] While you wait, you reckon up in a laconic, decorous, unbearably affectionate prose the local embodiments of the national character to be seen and heard at the station in the poised, neat girls of the Women's Auxiliary Air Force, coolly guiding the aircraft in, the comradely little jokes, in the saved-up choc bars and, when two bombers are unwarrantably late, in the group-captain who 'remarked without emphasis that he would stay up here [in the control tower] for a bit until the chaps got in'.[23]

It is one of her finest pieces, all the more affecting for its eventlessness, and it is pretty well equalled by every one of her dispatches from the terrible last months of world war: from one Pole talking of the forced labour on his own farm and another of his work as an underground observer of the practice of Nazi local government; in February 1944, from Northern Italy where she hitched a flight and joined the Free French battling up the harsh mountains towards Cassino; in June from a hospital ship, talking to the nurses as they followed the inconceivable vastness of the battle Armada going to the Normandy landings, then watching, feeling for the wounded, praying for them to be healed by miracles and some were, all of them on 'a safe ship no matter what happened', until at last 'the air of England flowed down through the wards and the wounded seemed to feel it';[24] in July back in Italy, the beautiful American journalist bathing in her underclothes with the Carpathian armoured cavalry and being shelled while they picnicked on charred duck; in September in the northern Apennines as the colossal, multicultural Eighth Army of liberation, Canadians, New Zealanders, Indians, British, Africans, flowed unstoppably on; in October with the American airborne in Nijmegen as the Allied advance stalled across the river in Arnhem, passing the time by listening to the gentle Dutch describing the occupation by the gentle Germans; in January with her countrymen in the sharpest point of the Ardennes where the Germans threw everything into their last desperate fling and the Allied line bulged and quavered and held, and a little drama she attended in which a cow was wounded and three Tiger tanks were left blazing by Thunderbolt rocket-fighters turned into the long, hard advance into Nazi Germany by way of a night bombing sortie.

All the time, as she zigzagged over Europe, she saw her duty, I would guess, as being close to that of the Quaker's *bearing witness*; Martha Gellhorn bore witness to the endurance and heroism of ordinary men-and-women-become-soldiers, and to the conduct, mostly admirable, of those they had come to save from the most abominable and evil enemy history had ever seen. She named for what they were the objective manifestations of good and wickedness as well as the legitimate expressions of revenge, and if some crazy priest of journalism[25] were to criticise her for so clearly reporting from one side (difficult, of course, at that time to report on the other) and failing to take the high view from nowhere, one could only rejoin on her part that such a precept was and remains morally mad, cognitively unfeasible, and humanly repulsive. For then she came to Dachau, where we began.

There cannot be a journalist's file of reports to match Martha Gellhorn's from November 1943 through to May 1945. She brought from Spain and from Czechoslovakia and Finland the keenness of her sympathy for victims, and she brought her hatred of crude and cruel power especially in its peculiarly modern and Fascist uniform; she brought also her tender heart and her excellent truculence in the face of the nastier sides of human behaviour. But these are values the decent among us all share; what we lack is the exact correlation she could craft between her feelings and her prose.

She gave the purest expression possible to the values she found being lived by nurses, pilots, tankmen and refugees, and in doing so stands as a kind of custodian statue to the historical charivari which follows.

In her lifetime, she professed a horror of being venerated or hero-worshipped (although she didn't actually shrink from limelight), but I don't see why. No doubt she hit lucky. Her canonical work was done when eye-witnessing was what her whole nation wanted in order to learn what their sons and husbands were doing, and doing it for. There was a lovely balance between her truthful exactitudes and the receptivity of her audience. A writer cannot ask for more.

So it is worth making a statue of her, tall, beautiful, with brilliant blue, very slightly glaucous eyes and the proud curved beak of her nose lifted in scorn or in watchfulness. She went on writing the same way, turning up at the war in Java in 1946 though nobody much wanted to hear about it, before going to Rome and Naples to see how the children who had survived the fighting were getting on. It was badly. She had found and lost Hemingway in Paris at the Liberation; he was holding literary-military court in his war correspondent's uniform in the Ritz. There were lashings of champagne and cognac. Hemingway was impossible, turning every occasion into a mixture of rapturous celebration, oafish and competitive games, and ostentatiously strategic briefings while he twirled the cartridge chamber of his revolver. Martha had looked at it all drily, and looked even more drily at the extremely pretty Mary Walsh well on her way to becoming the fourth Mrs Hemingway. She had friends to visit elsewhere in Paris. Thereafter she and Hemingway met only with bitter acrimony.

So in 1947 she bought a little house in bomb-damaged London and then, wandering as ever, joined her mother on a drive across Mexico, settled in Washington just in time to report on the hatefulness of the House Un-American Activities Committee as it followed Senator McCarthy's strident and bullying pursuit of the communist enemies within the nation. Disgusted, she quit town and went back to live for four years in Mexico, paying for her trips with freelance journalism and occasional sugary little stories written to cover the rent.

She pottered on in this quiet way, earning travel money with an essay or two here about life in Cracow behind the iron curtain, there on general elections in her beloved London, living in Italy for eighteen months, turning up in the Israeli lines during the Suez debacle to cheer on those she chose to regard as victims and decry the Arabs.

This was the first case of her narrative framework failing to fit the facts. Her October 1961 report to *Atlantic Monthly* on life in Palestine and the Gaza Strip during the United Nations protection brings out a certain splitting in her dependable schema.

For one thing those who were called refugees or displaced persons in Palestine didn't fit her experience of such people in the dreadful camps of Europe at the end of the war. The Palestinians weren't starving, their children were cheeky, in any case they were Arabs and surrounded by the Arab nations. They had millions of allies, for God's sake; what was the matter with them? For another thing, they were unyieldingly vindictive towards the Israelis, who really were the world's victims but would have been able to escape their unspeakable victimisation in Nazi Germany if only there had then been the state of Israel to escape to. And finally they breathed out hate, unconciliable hate, denied even the facts of the Final Solution, spat on common justice and swore by revenge.

Martha tried to but couldn't stand them. She spoke some truths which cannot nowadays be spoken, about the mad rage and crazy credulity taught by some versions of Islam, and about their hate-filled and hateful intransigence utterly incompatible with the tolerance essential to any conception of world peace. But by the end of her enormous essay[26] she counted on her authority as a journalist to allow her simply to lose her temper, become 'as beastly minded as an Arab myself' and blame it all on Arab factiousness, the meanness of capitalism, and the Cold War.

In 1966 she went to bear witness in Vietnam. She was fifty-eight and still her presence, her natural command and good looks, stopped conversations in bars, restaurants, headquarters and embassies when she entered. She went to Saigon with no brief from any magazine or newspaper and set herself to check against the actuality the plump little propaganda essay which was handed to every American soldier or official sent to Vietnam. It ended as follows: 'To really and truly and finally win this war, we must help the Government of South Vietnam win the hearts and minds of the people of South Vietnam.'

She inspected the hearts and minds of the Vietnamese patients in a civilian hospital and found them silent and enduring unto (frequent) death, flanked by filthy sheets and shit-jammed latrines, tended by a handful of New Zealand staff, with one meal per day for half their patients and no one but their families to look after them at night. With her scrupulous and unsparing grimness, Gellhorn looks at the napalmed children and the amputees, 'innocent bystanders' as crime reporters used to write, and goes on to a Catholic orphanage in the suburbs, finding, as she always does, the quiet, loving heroines and heroes of war in her terrible century, nuns this time, chronicling the biographies of this orphan blinded and that one deranged, the babies 'tiny, wizened soft skeletons ... too weak to move or cry',[27] all of them unknowing orphans of the war. Soeur Jeanne speaks her mind and it is the same as Martha Gellhorn's. The Americans bring ports and roads; what use are they to the masses sick with cholera, tuberculosis, starvation?

It had been a long and a short road for Martha Gellhorn from the Ardennes and Dachau to these wretches in Saigon. Even at home in St Louis tending her dying mother, her dearest friend, in the fall of 1965, the Vietnam news of television 'was disturbing the balance of my mind' and the long odyssey from Spain, the absolute commitment she had learned in war and class war to the downtrodden and to social justice made her at the last feel disgusted with her own country, 'killing poor people called commies in Vietnam, maltreating poor people called niggers at home'.[28]

She concluded, characteristically and in spite of being sick to death of death itself, the corpses, the ruined villages, the hideous aftermath of it all, that Vietnam was 'the urgent business of every citizen'. She bore witness to the sick, mad, burned and orphaned; she heard the stories of the killing and saw the holes left by the carpet-bombing; she visited the camps for the forcibly deracinated and she reckoned up the lies of American propaganda. All these things she did, as she said, not for political but for humanitarian purposes, and she also discovered that her mighty nation's most eloquent values, its great freedoms from want and fear, the self-evident truths about human equality at the heart of its noble Constitution had been dishonoured and defiled.

When she said so, nobody in America except the *St Louis Dispatch* (with the two mildest articles) and, it is a pleasure to note, the *Ladies' Home Journal* (with one) would print her. The reports, pungent enough and painful but nothing like as harsh as she could have written (or as strong as we have since become familiar with), finally appeared in the *Guardian* (London and Manchester). As soon as they came out, Martha Gellhorn was officially barred from any return to Vietnam. One of the most painful things she said was that the soldiers she met in Vietnam and the GIs she followed in the Second World War in Europe might have come from different countries; perhaps, she goes on, 'this is how you can tell a just war from an unjust one.'[29]

It is thirty-odd years since Martha Gellhorn came back with three full notebooks from Vietnam, and over twenty-five since the Vietnam War ended. Her visit turned her status a little: from writer-journalist-heroine and star of the press to lonely dissenter, one of America's diminutive intelligentsia who saw early which way the stupendous power of the nation was tending after it emerged as the prime superpower in 1945.

I had tea with her in her plain Anglo-Welsh house near Chepstow while writing about the Cold War. She had urged me to believe that she had nothing to say, but when I turned up, anxious simply to meet the great lady whatever she said, she spoke then of her solidarity with those few writers who stood out against Cold War, the fearful risks that the United States was still taking with world safety. She said:

> The best people in America now are those who try to call the country back to its own best principles. Such a call couldn't be heard in 1937 [we had been talking about Spain]. The country was completely absorbed in itself. It couldn't even see what Japan was up to. Then suddenly once we were in the war it was easy. Everybody invoked our national principles quite without cant. It was *natural* to say the Germans must be defeated unconditionally in defence of our freedoms. The language was never pompous. The GIs didn't talk about freedom much, but they did say 'we got to beat the bastards' and meant much the same.
>
> After the war people got indifferent or they got to feel they couldn't do anything and then there was only a minority – a good large one, mind you – to say 'Listen, America, you can't act like this. It's not how you are supposed to be. You're supposed to be the strong nation which protects the weak.'

Then she smiled a bit grimly. 'For some people that's how we got into Vietnam. That's when everything went wrong. Not Korea. Vietnam is the low point of the Cold War.' She looked away into the distance. 'And people say we won it ...'

She followed her principles, this citizen-journalist, wherever they took her. She had been, in 1983, once again to see for herself what America was doing. This time she called on what her President called the country's own backyard, which was to say Salvador and Nicaragua.

Salvador was as lovely as a rivered garden, and corrupt. Elections were a swindle, run for a tiny elite of the very rich clad in heavy jewellery and designer jeans; run against a landless poor, fifty thousand of whom died at the hands of their own out-of-control security forces. Hired vigilantes and trained torturers ran an underground terror and protection racket with exemplary lynchings and rapes of anybody who complained, refused cooperation or was merely dubbed a subversive. The civil war was national, the necessary support American. This was a minor Vietnam after 'Vietnamisation'.

There is something about modern governments which the best journalists whose lives are celebrated in this volume have brought to visibility, and once or twice a society has been roused. It is the blind unimaginativeness of those in power who order dreadful things to be done to people somewhere else. Imagination is a necessary adjunct of moral sympathy; to be without it is to be stupid; stupidity is closely allied to evil.

In Salvador and Nicaragua the easy-to-grasp fixities of Cold War taught that anybody who was not on the side of the United States was on the other side of Cold War, which was to say communist. The people who took the cheques-in-aid and gave parties to US advisers, ambassadors, CIA agents and assorted minor killers were never communists, so their enemies were. The hosts took the money from the blind, obtuse, generous, extravagant superpower, and either stuck to it or spent it on lavish gifts to themselves, of helicopter gunships, Mercedes and the like.

These were circumstances which lent themselves readily to the habits of observation and explanatory narratives which Martha Gellhorn found to work so accurately when she wrote her letters to Harry Hopkins in 1935, when she carried the same eye for mute suffering and ear for political hypocrisy to Spain two years later.

She looked at Salvador, reckoned up the statistics on the ownership of land and money, saw that elections were a fraud, ballot boxes stuffed by soldiers to suit those in charge, and listened as faithfully as she always did to the grisly tales of rape and mutilation told by the very poor or the slightly disobedient about the cruelty, cold or hot, of the regime's police. Not much glimpse here of Graham Greene's regretful, wise, witty and courageous Colonel Perez;[30] these not-very-ironic keepers of the social order dealt in red-hot branding, electrode attachments to erectile tissues, unparachuted ejections at five thousand feet, and punctual immersions in baths of shit.

Gellhorn looks at these appalling records, sets them down in a sort of calm anguish, and then, America being the vast, crazy and divided power it always is, pays her tribute to the 'gentle, intelligent and heroic kids of the Human Rights Commission',[31] most of them American, come to chronicle the wrongdoings of their nation.

Not surprisingly she had a large place in her heart for dissenting Americans, the majority young and students, shaggy, sometimes stoned, insubordinate, fired by their country's founding ideals to charge their country with its crimes against humanity. The best and worst of American journalists were in those days out in the streets of Washington, Chicago,

Oakland, Madison, Atlanta – oh, every great city of the great nation – during the protest marches against the war. Her own contribution was the only piece of writing Gellhorn completed after she returned with her brief-case of hard-to-place, at-times-calumniated, politely ignored articles from Saigon and Qui Nhon. The war throttled her until the helicopters lifted with the last officials from the roof of the US embassy in 1975, desperate Vietnamese clinging to its skis.

She was sixty-eight. She never let up. Patriotic to a fault, Anglophile to England's credit, she bought a flat just off the King's Road in London with views of the city skyline, and wrote about Mrs Thatcher's England just as the ideological union with President Reagan was consummated.

The American patriot and honorary Englishwoman went to see how her two peoples expressed a certain objection to the two governments she thought of as hers. To do this, she made a trip some forty miles west of London to take the temperature of Cold War in what are called England's Home Counties.

Cold War was very cold indeed just then. At the end of 1983 the Soviets withdrew from the arms limitation talks; Cold War relations were freezing harder than at any time since 1962. England witnessed its biggest political demonstrations of all time. Before Christmas the United States began to uncrate the new weapons that the disarmers had vowed to send back.

Some of these were to be set up in little nests in Sicily, others in Holland and West Germany, and some in an airfield outside Newbury, a modest English market town with its own smart race course. The airfield was sited on a sandy, wooded stretch of country known as Greenham Common, and in England common land is exactly that: land commonly owned by the people of England.

So it came to pass that a group of freeborn English *women* came to camp at Greenham Common beside the grim wire and its high concrete posts. They too had come to bear witness against the evil weaponry being uncrated inside the big green bunkers, but they came speaking a strange idiom. They contended that the filthy weapons were the product of the politics of *men*, and they spoke for a womanly politics that refused the steel phallus and its poisonous ejaculation of old militarism. They lived by a communal, even, for their enemies, communist sisterhood of values of which love, mutuality and a welcome to strangers would be the signatures.

The women built temporary bivouacs, long polythene sheets slung over the plentiful hazel and larch of the common. They fastened tokens to the wire – flowers, broom, dolls, baby clothes – and from time to time they implored the guards and the police to join them in order to renounce their guardianship of death. Their tongue was ancient, magical, pentecostal.

Occasionally the law-abiding burghers of Newbury dispatched bailiffs to evict the women for trespass or to hose them down for obscure offences; but the women of Greenham Common took their stand on ancient statutes and legal customs and always came back.

As before, as always, Martha Gellhorn made warmly common cause with those of the generations after her in England, Wales and North America who *opposed*, opposed by their bodily presence, their natural grace, their peaceful intransigence, the deadly arrogance of state and government. The Greenham women were not exactly her kind of folk – too scruffy, for one thing – but she admired them, liked them too, found in their serenity, openness, gaiety, seriousness, all that is best in a new world politics struggling to be born.

Her journalism and her character were one; that is what is meant by integrity. Moreover, she was a war-and-peace correspondent in a fuller sense than that of the straight reporter who files a few hundred words for a byline on the first two pages. Her strength is bedded in her integrity and her certainties. Those certainties are central to her definition of humanity.

We ask of a journalist that he or she tell us the truth. But whatever 'objectivity', 'impartiality', 'the separation of facts and opinions' may mean (and for all that has been done to erode them by arguments about the relative nature of truth, we have to stand by *some* criterion of detachment), they surely should not demand of those who hold to them that they extinguish those human emotions and judgements which express themselves in any turn of phrase or fall of a sentence?

Journalism is a form in literature; literature is reasonable, literature is rhetorical. We try a writer's rhetoric against what we know and what we believe. The best writers match the magic of their gift for words against the vast possibility of what may be made from those little fictions, the facts. When the writers win, the match is a draw. This is called balance.

Martha Gellhorn looks at us at the entrance to this book. She looks, as Jeremy Harding with a touch of affectionate exasperation tells us:

> her head [rising] slightly, following obediently the upward motion of her eyes, which, whenever she was at odds with you, would gaze momentarily at a point above and behind your head, blink slowly, and then return to fix you with a look of condescension and faint concern, as though you might be about to throw up.[32]

She stands here as a moral example against which to measure the men and women to follow. As another journalist once said, the end is where we start from.

CHAPTER TWO

Cautionary History: Lords of the Dance

In 1918, at the University of Munich, Max Weber gave one of his grandest and most comprehensive lectures on contemporary society. 'Politics as a vocation'[1] was written as his country ground slowly and terribly towards defeat in a four-year war which left the supposedly victorious nations, in Europe at least, in no better case than the defeated. Politics had failed utterly in its business to bring reason and reconciliation to nations in a condition of high disagreement and dudgeon. Once the politicians had allowed things to drive themselves over the edge into warfare, they had proved even less courageous and imaginative in allowing matters to become worse and worse, betraying the trust of millions doing the fighting and about to die, and stoking the self-righteous hatreds of patriots and militarists who were safe at home and would go on living.

As Weber spoke, revolution had taken place in Russia and was inconclusive in Germany. Yet he addressed the condition of politics with an impressive calm as well as authority. He announced the advent of a new social part to play, that of professional politician, and he weighed up the differences between the different versions of such a figure, among them the boss-figure, the *condottiere*, the public-spirited, class-interested wealthy man, and those people passionate for politics whose very propertylessness put them outside the pull of self-interestedness in the economic order of things.

Democracy itself teaches every politician, in each of these guises, to be a demagogue, and each must therefore be at least a sufficient orator; the practice of politics in 1918, yet more so throughout the rest of the century, was formalised as an endless succession and exchange of *speeches*: speeches written before they were spoken, spoken in order to be summarised, analysed, criticised by journalists, that other section of the political class without whom the clamour of speechifying under bright lights and in order to do and win the deals cannot be carried on.

The conductors of this endless relaying, broadcasting, negotiating and (in a strict sense) posturing are the political journalists. Weber salutes their entry on to the stage of modern politics.

> In common with all demagogues and, by the way, with the lawyer and the artist, the journalist shares the fate of lacking a fixed social classification. The journalist belongs to a sort of pariah caste, which is always estimated by 'society' in terms of its ethically lowest representative. Hence the strangest notions about journalists and their work are abroad.[2]

It remains true that journalists have no very settled place in the social structure. A handful – those whose tales are told in this book – attain celebrity and the colossal rewards that celebrity won for itself by the century's end. Mostly, however, journalism is the name of a profession celebrated less for celebrity and more for a unique mixture of raffishness and glamour, drunkenness and the kind of knowledge usually classified as being on the inside, cynicism and the caustic freedoms it confers, reckless-ness, discretion, strange working hours, even stranger friends, courage and cowardice.

Yet Weber goes on to say, lightly but firmly, that

> A really good journalistic accomplishment requires at least as much 'genius' as any scholarly accomplishment, especially because of the necessity of producing at once and on order ... It is almost never acknowledged that the responsibility of the journalist is far greater, and that the sense of responsibility of every honourable journalist is, on the average, not a bit lower than that of the scholar, but rather, as the war has shown, higher. This is because, in the very nature of the case, irrespon-sible journalistic accomplishments and their often terrible effects are remembered.[3]

It is a striking tribute as well as a quite new formulation of this novel social role, set to become at once magnetically attractive and repulsive to four generations of young men and (after 1970 or so) one generation of young women.

Weber speaks warmly of the discretion of political journalists and the 'incomparably graver temptations' which beset them in the way of their work, as opposed to those who live along the lines of more accustomed, clearly marked and much trafficked social levels. Journalists may be bribed, with money or with access; they may be flattered by audience with the mighty; they may be incited to mere boastfulness and puffed up to a terrific vanity by the secrets they know and the grandees to whom they must toady; responsible to an uncertain ethics with a loud but veering commitment to truthfulness and duty, they are exceptionally open to the persuasion of powerful enemies armed with the weapons of dismissal and, it may even be, of liquidation. Often knowing too much, they do not know whom to tell or how to make it tell.

The strains in such a role have found canonical expression in a century of novels and movies about political journalists. Journalists are uniquely usable by the writer of fiction or the film director. They are, as Weber tells us, classless, yet they have access to the mighty at the same time as they can move more or less easily between very varied social groups, including the down-and-out and the demi-monde. Their working hours take in night and day; their locale is equally the street, the city, the airport, the bar and the bedroom; they work in quick dashes and long delays; they can make leisure open up out of the most crowded schedule.

Such is the rich mythology which the novel tale of the political journalist has seeded and multiplied in the short century of its life. The professionals themselves may smile at it, the public relations officers fertilise it, the social imagination at large utilise it in order to stoke up those theories of conspiracy which best explain the world to itself and make sense of a figure in its midst, now indiscernible, now monstrous, always obscure, whose sudden switches from hero to villain, from liar to truth-teller, from trivial scandalmonger to tribune of the people, leave everybody baffled, applauding, contemptuous.

In all this, there is a likeness between the political journalist and the full-blown politician, similarly deferred to and despised. Weber points this out, but he also notes: 'that party leaders would emerge from the ranks of the press has been our absolute exception and one should not have expected it'.[4] This, he says, is because the practice of politics urgently needs the journalists it has. Each office works to sustain the business of good government, the politicians using the journalists as mediators, translators, interpreters, megaphones, the journalists using the politicians as princelings, patrons, hosts, abject dependants. Each vilifies the other as moral impostor; neither understands their mutual indispensability.

Weber is not quite right to argue that the exceptions to his rule are so absolute. On the uncertain terrain occupied by the twentieth-century man or woman of letters, more than a few made the transition from writing about politics to acting powerfully upon it. Moreover, if not the journalist dogsbodies then the owners, the lords of the press-dance, much preened themselves upon their own influence and efficaciousness in the domain of power. Weber pointed out that the journalist worker counted for less as the capitalist press-master counted for more, and three of the direful names of Weber's moment – the Lords Northcliffe and Beaverbrook, and in California the colossal figure of William Randolph Hearst – testify to just how momentous such people were and are.

The smaller names of those writer-journalists who made it to a sort of political eminence – Mario Vargas Llosa, Vaclav Havel, Willy Brandt and Michael Foot spoke some such part during the epoch of Cold War – remind us of another social role which came to birth more or less at the beginning of the short twentieth century.[5] It is the role of intellectual.

The intellectuals have a mixed provenance. Their early versions were played, with absolute sincerity, to the galleries of revolutionary Europe in 1830 and 1848. In France, Blanqui and Proudhon, in England the expatriates Marx and Engels spoke up in a new theatrical diction of the complex inter-twinings of voice, ideas and the rough beast of public opinion. Thereafter all aspirants to national power, whether ex-Bourbons, parliamentarians or Communards, would have to train and tame it into a kind of acquiescence. Baudelaire and Courbet respectively tied another knot between the people and a doctrinaire version of an art which would one day belong to the people. Until then it could show them what to fear and what to hope for.

A new politics came out of the insurrections, street riots, mass demon-strations and impromptu urban festivals which turned first a few cities and then a few nations upside-down between 1789 and 1947. Its fantastic set-piece was the revolution and one of its leading figures was the intellectual, whose writings were intended to incite or sedate, enrage or exhilarate the crowds which swirled both inside and outside the gates of power.

The twin vehicles underneath the intellectual were the newspaper column and the chariot of art. After Courbet and Zola, Ruskin and William Morris, then Bukharin, Gorky and Trotsky could go to war in uniform, armed of course with revolvers but also with literature and ideas. The intellectuals wrote out their act in newspapers and the periodicals which were the rendezvous of argument and allegiance. They fastened art to the vanguard of history, and the artists joined more or less gleefully on the ride.

This crazy cavalcade clattered along the political horizon of the nine-teenth century, gazed at with more or less contempt by the professional politicians. They could not, however, ignore it. Indeed, as far as the necessity of winning support and obedience went, they were in thrall to it. Only terror, and an absolute servitude on the part of the official means of violence, could vouchsafe power to the ruler without his having to entertain artists and intellectuals, most of them journalists, in state palaces while the crowds[6] outside waited to see what excitement could be contrived out of the clash of high ideals and low cunning.

This has been the technicolour silhouette of urban politics since revolution as well as world war became everyday concepts and since public opinion, expressed by journalists and embodied first by crowds and later by polls, became a huge and unignorable force in politics and civic affairs. Its bold outlines pick out journalist and intellectual as quick and daring figures easily followed through in the action of the story.

Naturally, the historical storyteller and story-listener in all of us loves a hero and, hardly less, thrills to a villain. The journalist and the intellectual coincide sufficiently often in the politics of the short twentieth century to be available for casting in any of its best-known political dramas. This is what modern myth is: a swift, vivid cartoon catching up the large, obscure forces which blow along the course of destiny, giving them a name, a face, a character and the responsibility for having made things happen.

The journalist and the intellectual, sometimes of one body and mind but always and caustically divided against one another, began to assume a mythic role round about the middle of the nineteenth century. They were first firmly identified as distinctive characters for whom the author of history had found a good part by Max Weber, after he noticed how well it had played in the First World War.

However, as Weber continues ominously:

> The relations of the press to the ruling powers in the state and in the parties, under the old regime [Weber is referring to the Kaiser] were as detrimental as they could be to the level of journalism ... These conditions were different in the countries of our opponents. But there also, and for all modern states, apparently the journalist worker gains less and less as the capitalist lord of the press, of the sort of 'Lord' Northcliffe [Weber's inverted commas] ... gains more and more political influence.

'All modern states', Weber contends. But with his amazing prescience he also foresees that exactly because newspapers feed off and on politicians, a newspaper owner cannot pursue an independent political policy. Even a chain of newspapers has no political base – no party, no institutions or location – it only has a readership. Profits follow, they cannot precede politics. Northcliffe, Beaverbrook, Hearst or the barmy Colonel McCormick, editor of *The Chicago Tribune*, certainly had their craziness, their capricious political preferences and a greed for power, but their power reposed in their profits, and the profits came from selling newspapers not from directing political events.

What is more, as Weber observes, already in 1918 selling newspapers was turning into the business of selling advertising space; the commodity form of the just-emerged mass media was not ten or a dozen pages of newsprint upon fibrous paper but the audience of readers which could be promised to the baying hounds of the new advertising agencies, hunting down profits for the horsemen of capital.

Along the bloodthirsty ride for money the political journalist is only a trace of the scent. Weber concluded that such a figure could hardly be on the way to political power. Maybe things would change if the principle of anonymity were to be dropped, but he observes distantly that when signatures began to be appended to wartime reports, sales may have increased but not the sense of responsibility. 'The publishers as well as the journalists of sensationalism have gained fortunes but certainly not honour.'[7] Celebrity rather than power beckoned to journalists in 1918 and Weber concluded his detour around journalism by emphasising its importance to professional political life and activity, and its dangers to those who practised the trade. They would live in a condition of rulelessness unknown to their step-sibling the scholar, who had at least clear social status and the conventions which go with it to give life and career a shape. Worse, the 'inner demands' of the job, the daily paltering with the vanity and mendacity of the great, the daily requirement to have prompt and convincing opinions on every topic under the sun and moon, could only diminish one's self-respect and assail one's dignity.

> It is not astonishing that there are many journalists who have become human failures and worthless men. Rather it is astonishing that, despite all this, this very stratum includes such a great number of valuable and quite genuine men, a fact that outsiders would not so easily guess.[8]

Thus and thus a new character enters world political drama.

The character, played in those days by men only, had been made into the complicated thing it was – like everybody else everywhere – by the grinding and fashioning of productive forces, including that force of nature, the boss.

In Britain the simplest way to see that fashioning process is as part of the titanic struggle between capital and labour which drove the nineteenth century forward until it ended in European war. The same goes, near enough, for France and Germany, and northern Italy.

In America in 1919, as we shall see, the big cities fairly throbbed with news and newspapers. The galloping development of capitalism in that one nation since Edison and Bell turned old and new worlds into one globe by means of the telegraph left it poised, as the big press owners saw, to take over the world. It did so, of course: the American era began at that date, and is far from over. But the crowds which packed Times Square on election night in 1900 to watch news flashes reporting President McKinley's victory projected by way of glass slides on to huge stereopticons faced Europe as the source and generator of news. They were nearer London and Paris in that respect than they were to their fellow Americans in the Badlands of Montana or in the dust bowls of the Great Plains, whose only newspaper would have been a hand-set broadsheet thinly sprinkled with local titbits and a single national headline picked up from the nearest telephone relay. Morse transmission cost money and a direct phone call could only reach a hundred miles.[9]

In Britain there was for many years a wistfully self-serving history of press development in which a gallant struggle is won by private citizens on behalf of public opinion. Assorted heroes battling for free speech – Fox, Wilkes, Cobbett, Hazlitt and company – prise open the grip of the authoritarian British state and its ruling class proprietors so that the combined armies of reforming middle class and newly self-assertive artisans sweep into the forum and take over civil society for themselves, with a newspaper to speak for every section of the debate.[10]

In this happy tale of liberal freedom, the market defeats the old regime when the demand for sales information brings first advertising revenue and then, as a consequence, economic independence to the press. Journalists became better paid, bribery less effective, governments less awe-inspiring. But in point of fact the liberation by advertising did not confer independence on the press; rather, it brought commerce and politics together into an intimate reciprocity.

Things need not have worked out like this. In Britain, at the vanguard of capital and industrialisation, and therefore of the new kind of class politics, a radical press flourished as the multiple platforms of the unenfranchised. Various governments came down heavily on radical journalists with trumped-up charges of libel, sedition and blasphemy; but juries proved surprisingly disobedient, charges failed to stick and certainly failed to deter, and the government tried to tax these insubordinate voices into silence. The stamp duty on paper, publications and advertising was intended to confine both ownership and purchasing power up the social scale.

The tax went up by 266 per cent over its first twenty-five years up to 1815,[11] but it failed in its task. The working-class readership clubbed together to share their copies, and the underground press simply dodged the tax altogether. In 1836 2 million people read unstamped newspapers. In spite of the increase in coercive powers which the government awarded itself in the 1850s, and which at last closed down much of the unstamped press and committed more of the editors to jail, the legitimate radical newspapers, led by *Lloyds Weekly* and *Reynolds News*, saw their joint circulations soar beyond 200,000 by 1856. Owners and editors (often the same people) were themselves radicals committed to a journalism which was also a political pedagogy; their independence had to be sustained by sales and not by advertising (the advertisers nervous of the taint of revolution); they defined, by precept and example, that ideal conception of journalism as the voice of a people teaching itself what it knew for its own emancipation and enlightenment. It intuitively grasped that objectivity might have decidedly subjective definitions, and that the accurate separation of facts and opinion, editorialising upon which was to become such an occasion for sanctimony, was almost always a matter of opinion.

The British radical press, as a range of publications, more or less failed. It survived, however, as a series of traces in the best lives of the tradition of British free-thinking and dissenting journalism. That same tradition had to renew itself in the face of general agreement, even among libertarian opponents of stamp duty like Francis Place or Richard Cobden, that the role of political journalism is to win the consent of a whole society to its present, comfortable injustices and its preferential arrangement of absolutely everything. So stamp duty was repealed as a 'tax on knowledge', and in the sacred name of free trade anybody with the money could start a newspaper. Instead, in 1870, official social control was handed over to the new state institution of mass education, and British newspapers agreed on their obligation to encourage general approval of how things were and upon their common, unspoken propensity to work up obloquy against anybody who thought otherwise.

That tacit agreement has proved a lasting inheritance for readers of the British press. But no easy identity of attitude and value existed then or exists today between owners, editors and journalists, let alone as between that trinity and their readers. For one thing, by the 1860s new print technology designed for much larger print-runs had become well beyond the financial reach of small craft producers. After the invention of the telegraph the demand rose for world news with expensive journalists to go looking for it. Cut-throat price competition forced lower circulation newspapers into bankruptcy. The so-called run-in costs of a new publication before it broke even became ever higher and longer (Northcliffe put half a million pounds into setting up the *Daily Mail* in 1896; multiply by five hundred or so for today's price[12]).

The bravery one needed to sustain a daily newspaper in this new world really did turn on the presence of the advertisers. Once upon a time, in the right political company, it was a commonplace to say that advertisers and the manufacturers who commissioned them chose those organs whose readership would not only approve their product but the (inseparable) views of the world which went with them. For some time now, however, it has been necessary to point out an unsurprising complicity between editorial position, the politics of the ownership, and the sympathy or otherwise of leading advertisers. Even today, in the climate of vociferous free-marketing in the United States, editors will look uneasily over their shoulders at advertisers with handgun interests or zealous membership of the World Trade Organization. Things were starker in the earlier days of the newspaper industry and as the phenomenon of the mass daily came into being. The advertisers put their money in the papers whose readership could afford to spend.

Matters were a bit easier for weeklies and occasionals. At the beginning of niche marketing advertisers were looking for specialised fractions of the public which could not be precisely targeted in a daily. Hence the steep rise in magazines poised on the hinge between political views and the entertainment of opinion, fantasy, whimsy or distraction from boredom. In thirty years between 1866 and 1896 15,000 new magazines started, some – *Titbits, People's Friend, Weekly Telegraph* – lasting the better part of a century and carefully addressed to the habits of life and domestic assumptions of a conversational, gossiping and thoroughly settled working class.[13] In the United States, W. E. B. Dubois launched the new century in 1900 with the left-wing *The Crisis*, and between then and 1925 *Forbes, Reader's Digest* (with no advertising), *McClure's* (with Lincoln Steffens to the fore), Hearst's *Cosmopolitan, Collier's*, the *Saturday Evening Post*, Luce's *Time* and Ross's *New Yorker* had cleared a large space for the kind of serious and extended journalism at which the Americans have always far excelled the Europeans. Each of these journals, some retrieved from terminal decline (the *Post* by George Lorimer), most founded in the first quarter-century and joined soon afterwards by *Newsweek*, *Fortune* and *Life*, spoke up in honest prose and with a proper regard for the canons of evidence and truthfulness of all that was wrong as well as right in this unprecedented kind of nation. They cherished, for better and worse, the values of small-town America and if this meant pious paragraphs of Episcopalian admonition, it also took in Steffens's famous malediction 'The shame of the cities', later to become a book, Lewis Hine's photographs of child miners on thirty-five cents a day, and the short stories of Ernest Hemingway, F. Scott Fitzgerald, Sinclair Lewis, John Steinbeck, Theodore Dreiser, Sherwood Anderson, the flower of modern American literature.

Literary London had of course always had its socially conscientious periodicals – its *New Statesman*, *New Age*, *English Review*, *Westminster Review*, *Blackwood's*, and so forth – but these had nothing like the range and popular appeal of the American ones. In any estimate of what political journalism has meant in our time, these journals and their many allies and competitors – *Atlantic Monthly*, *Harper's*, *Vanity Fair* – must occupy not only an honourable but a formative position.

Their advent brings out a timely truth about the economic contexts of cultural life, especially with regard to print journalism. This is that woodenly determinist accounts of what is or is not possible at any moment of cultural production will be false. Radical dailies foundered or went in search of a more placid readership in 1900, but radical argument could still find a home in the new or the old journals on either side of an Anglophone Atlantic. As has been firmly pointed out by political economists,[14] the peculiarities of the cultural industries – press, television, movies, books, as well as the shoals of smaller trades swimming behind these great whales – are such as to leave plenty of room for risky innovations and the creation of new little organs of entertainment and even subversion. Daring and vanity have always retained autonomy of a kind. Radicals, dissidents and licensed fools start and persist with publications to which no one gives a chance, and sometimes they survive and thrive to everyone's astonishment, voicing a few of the essential objections to such antique targets as ruling classes, the philistinism of the bourgeoisie, the deadly rule of money. Meanwhile wealthy men of a mind to cut a dash as public figures pay to prop up money-losing newspapers for the sublime gratification of hearing their opinions broadcast to the hundreds of thousands still buying them.

All the same, when all has been said and done about the indestructibility of the individual spirit and the always audible voice of the independent journalist, the fact remains that the history of newspapers in Britain is a tale with a classically capitalist moral. A new kind of cultural expression is devised and developed out of the political commotions of the nineteenth century and the debate on democracy which impelled them. As a sort of political class-compromise emerged, and public dissent petered out, new technology and old corruption pounced upon the welter of newspaper disputation and turned it into an industrial product.

This magic confection, they saw, possessed ideal qualities for the proliferation of capital. It lent itself to mass production and distribution also, especially by way of the amazing new railways. Its contents were made obsolete and replaceable within twenty-four hours. It filled a new opening in the armature of regulated time required by industrial society. The opening was called 'leisure' and the boredom which would otherwise fill it up would be occupied and transformed into benevolent idleness by sampling a daily concoction of terse news, local gossip and bright little conversational titbits nicely adjusted to the wandering attention due to triviality.

The Sunday paper became the richest such cake in the confectioners, for nearly everybody had Sunday off, even in the 1890s, and the manufacturers of leisure pastimes had plenty of experimental room to play with. Sex, violence and human grotesquerie didn't fail then and don't now. The dailies borrowed enough of these ingredients to flavour their briefer, working-day product and between 1860 and 1890 the *Daily Telegraph*, at a penny per copy, commanded the new field, rising to a circulation of 300,000.[15]

It seems odd, nowadays, to give the stolid old *Telegraph* its due for inventing the popular press and its immutable table of contents, when for thirty years it led the way to the suburbs. But as all historians unite in agreeing, the true begetter was the astonishing and extremely dislikeable Alfred Harmsworth, later Lord Northcliffe, who made his way by way of his good luck, his enormous personal fortune, his acuity in spotting what a halfpenny newspaper looking vaguely like *The Times* but in fact the *Daily Mail* might do to carry him to a knighthood, ennoblement as Lord Northcliffe and finally to the role of insane autocrat, limited philanthropist and reckless if ineffectual gambler in the affairs of state.

Northcliffe founded the *Daily Mail* in 1896. From the *Daily Telegraph* he took the recipe of politics, sex, crime and a judicious editorial manner balancing disapproval against prurience. From the raucously pioneering *Pall Mall Gazette* and the 'yellow press' journalism its owner-editor W. T. Stead had imported from the USA he took bold headlines, short sentences and paragraphs, a bright newsy manner. From the new evening daily the *Star* he took brevity in any article, ephemerality on every topic, the obliteration of the never-very-certain distinction between privacy and publicity, and the celebration of that publicity as the key embodiment of social success. The *Daily Mail* did not so much report news as manufacture celebrity.

The contents of a mass circulation daily in Britain were fixed in 1896. The success of the formula introduced a new commodity. Henceforth newspapers and their rivals and successors in radio and television broadcasting measured productivity in the size of the audiences they could hold and sell to advertisers. In the local case of what came to be called 'public service broadcasting' the size of the audiences, after an initial period of comparative freedom from commercial pressure, came to be used as a measure with which to justify or withhold state subvention.

In its first ten years the *Mail* doubled the British newspaper-buying public, and it doubled it again by the beginning of the First World War.[16] Over the same period, however, the Sunday papers outsold the dailies by two and a half times, and the Sunday news-and-views diet matched the reassuring amplitude of Sunday dinner: filling, safe, comfortable and pretty well the same from week to week. It is no wonder sharp, tart and indigestible journalism failed to make much of an impression upon a diet so powerfully shaped by lifelong experience of English Sundays.

It is entirely understandable that in Britain the noble Lord Northcliffe still dominates newspaper history. By 1921 he had bought *The Times*, still owned the *Mail*, the *Sunday Despatch* and the (London) *Evening News*, had founded the *Daily Mirror* as a picture paper and then sold it to his brother, also on his way to a peerage as Lord Rothermere, and as joint owner with Rothermere of Amalgamated Press owned a long chain of neighbourhood papers across the south of England.

The brothers Harmsworth, with Northcliffe as senior, did much to define the popular myth-figure of the arbitrary, arrogant, choleric and abruptly generous Lord of the Press still so telling a narrative in the grand mythology of politics. They did much, indeed, to counter the usual semantic distinction between myth and history. They were close enough in actuality to Evelyn Waugh's immortal press baron, Lord Copper, in the face of whose dogmatic and ignorant beliefs and assertions his editor could only manage, by way of contradiction, 'Up to a point, Lord Copper.' Northcliffe sacked editors and subeditors not just for disagreeing mildly with his proposals but simply because the whimsy took him so. The accounts in the usual biographies and memoirs[17] tell stories in varying degrees of sycophancy and hatred, of endless bullying of staff, of casual and callous dismissals at lunch and dinner tables, of dozens of instructions and countermandings every day, and of a predictably ardent taste for exactly the kind of horror stories, grisly speculation ('How long can a baby live in the womb after the mother dies?', 'What does a murderer think of while being led to the gallows?') and details of sexual perversion in which the new popular press came to specialise.

He took the same delicate attributes, of personality and imagination, into his persistent meddlings in political affairs, as well as in the absolute political control over his editors upon which he insisted. When he bought the *Observer* in 1905 the articles of agreement reserved his right 'to direct and control all articles or comments of a political character',[18] and as his wretched editor J. L. Garvin learned, by God he held to it.

Radically inconsistent in his commitments and convictions, his only theoretic device was to divide the world into his friends and enemies while frequently transferring the membership of one list to the other. His only, but deep-seated, regularity was to insist upon his own way and the primacy of his own view, whatever it was. When Geoffrey Robinson, editor of *The Times* for two stints and a total of twenty-seven years, first bent before the mass of Northcliffe's will, over the Irish crisis of 1912 and *The Times*'s loyal support of the Unionists, his predecessor recalled for him in vain that 'the independence of *The Times* is the basis of its authority';[19] Robinson spoke faithfully with his master's voice.

Northcliffe was only predictable in his devotion to himself and to those hard, small, ungeneralisable values which affirm the rightness of wealth for those who have it, the immutability of those arrangements which provided it, and the necessity of attaching to it the privileges, status and obedience which together will ensure that it cannot be taken away.

As one would expect, these treasures went along with the certainty that he had himself the vocation of statesmanship and that its historic form was the raucous nationalism with which the *Daily Mail* supported the South African war and with which, as one would expect, Northcliffe greeted August 1914. *The Times* conducted its private war with such an erratic hand that Churchill wanted to commandeer it and run it as an official organ.[20] Northcliffe first regarded as his own achievement the promotion of Kitchener to the War Office, then in 1915 was as determined to use his papers, against the run of public opinion, to get him the sack.

He failed and stormed about, saying of the coalition government, as the Prime Minister's wife herself reported, 'that he made it ... and can smash it whenever he likes'.[21] But eighteen months or so later the *Mail* ('the Paper that is combing them out') was assigned to gloat over Asquith's resignation and Northcliffe hugged himself at the power he possessed, free entirely of any responsibility to exert it wisely; as Baldwin's famous *mot* put it (given him by his cousin Rudyard Kipling), 'the prerogative of the harlot throughout the ages'. Far better sit in Printing House Square saying what he liked than assume Cabinet duties and share the killing obligations of winning or losing a war.

So when Lloyd George, the new Prime Minister, offered him a job he turned it down and continued, as all men of his kidney were to do on behalf of their old country down the century, to huff and puff about the desirability of dissolving political parties and professional politicians with them. Their replacement would be, naturally, 'a Cabinet of the Talents', 'a Business Government' – these the words of the loathsome Horatio Bottomley, sometime MP, swindler and editor of *John Bull*, a million-circulation chauvinistic rag.

Tales of Northcliffe are legion. They are the stuff of nightmares. He hovered behind the Prime Minister's shoulder, willing to wound, afraid to strike, first flouting then currying popular favour by way of his newspapers, coming and going in the corridors of power with hints of criticism of Lloyd George and evidence of toadying, all without any certain proof that such dallying *did* anything palpable beyond swirl with and around the eddies of a public opinion utterly bemused about the point and conduct of the war, and sure only of a desire to end it without dishonour. There is rough justice in the fact that Northcliffe died, only three years after the war of which he had done much to derange the progress, completely off his head. His funeral was in Westminster Abbey. Crowds lined the streets to watch the procession to Marylebone Cemetery.[22]

His significance for this book, by way of this glimpse of his scheming passion, is, however, momentous. For different classes and at different moments, his newspapers effected the formal severance of parties from press, and established the primacy not of strictly commercial interests untainted by politics (whatever those would be) but of a politics of Business itself, massive, unignorable, gorilla-shaped, and invincibly certain of its prior claims to all attention, its superiority to any principle.

Northcliffe's demon-partner in bringing about this transformation was of course Max Aitken, later and inevitably Lord Beaverbrook. Immigrant-Canadian with another private fortune, he was looking for rewards on a higher, more crowded social scale than were available north of the forty-eighth parallel.

Beaverbrook corralled the three dynamic, atavistic urges of British print journalism for the rest of the century: business, chauvinism and a durable politics of anti-politics. Politicians and political journalists alike would have to work within this stifling force-field for a very long duration. Not that Beaverbrook himself was ever anything other than the businessman's politician and he played the part with an effrontery as well as stamina which went well beyond Northcliffe's dotty vagaries. He rose vertically in the newspaper industry (much later, he boasted to the first Royal Commission on the Press that he ran the *Daily Express* 'merely for the purpose of making propaganda and with no other motive'[23]). From his arrival in England he established himself beside Northcliffe as that new kind of figure, the political press-owner-with-no-party; but naturally, the Tory Party was extremely anxious to secure his never-quite-dependable support. So with a cynicism unusually candid even for the day, he was provided with a vacant parliamentary seat in the nondescript Midland market town of Ashton-under-Lyne until such time as he might have to defend it before the electorate, when Lloyd George, not wholly without embarrassment, promoted him to join Northcliffe in the House of Lords.[24] Beaverbrook (like Northcliffe) believed himself to have been instrumental in displacing Asquith as Prime Minister in the war crisis of 1916 and putting Lloyd George in the job, and he had indeed much busybodied about while the change was made.

The lessons to the history of journalism taught by the careers of Northcliffe and Beaverbrook are that political meddling on the part of newspaper owners and even the expression of their political convictions do not always sort well with commercial success. Vanity may prove at odds with profit. Not that any such consideration would stand in the way of the effortless arrogance of a very rich man armed with ample newspaper proprietorship. It would hardly be believable were it not that that is how these things are done, but when Northcliffe died, still raving non-stop at his editors by way of telegrams to the office, his just-as-unappealing brother Rothermere took over his properties and in a trice the *Daily Mail* was foaming with simulated rage at the newly empowered British Labour Party.

In particular, the party's deplorable intelligentsia had not only attended the meeting of the Socialist International in Hamburg, thereby becoming creatures of revolutionary, worse, continental communists, they were in any case and irremediably 'notoriety-hunters, bookworms, "high-brows", discredited professors and dons, professional atheists … and haters of their fellow men'.[25]

It is a juicy manner, and for those dismayed by the tone taken today, three generations or so later, by the inheritors of the Rothermere tradition, it may be a reassurance to recollect that things used to be just as bad.

The liturgical occasion for such spittle-flecked delivery was the notorious case of the Zinoviev letter, when the *Daily Mail* passed off an obvious forgery, devised by white Russian emigrés and ratified by the Foreign Office. Released at the time of the 1924 general election (called after only nine months of the first Labour and Liberal coalition government), the letter purported in vague terms and over the signature of Zinoviev, Secretary of the Communist International, to encourage its brother communists to stir up the masses with a view to the achievement of full-blown socialism.

Whatever its origins, the letter expressed mere doctrine and wasn't in any case addressed to the Labour Party. But off went the *Mirror* into its delirium with a headline 'Vote British not Bolshie', and the *Mail* led with blunt mendacity, 'Civil War Plot by Socialists' Masters: Moscow Order to Our Reds'.[26]

At the election, the Labour Party lost power but its vote went up. It was the Liberal vote which shrank. At the time, as Curran notes,[27] a majority of the working class didn't read a daily (only a Sunday), and in any case there is a patent gap between what one might call the hysteria index of daily newspaper rhetoric and the day-to-day feelings of the readership. The everyday structure of feeling,[28] so hard to talk about, is a more modest, sceptical, accommodating instrument than the four-square passions of tabloid or broadsheet. The front page will tell you things about the feelingful state of the nation, but it cannot serve as a moral thermometer as to the nation's health. Press competition, the manufacture of news, editorial regulation and contempt for and ignorance of the readers, all presided over by the autocracy of ownership, serve not merely to distort the imaginable responses of millions of readers, but to make it impossible to enclose such responses in so temporary a framework.

What a public reads is not a measure of its quality of life. No society gets the press it deserves. The press happened that way, like it or not, and we have to read it. We read it as best we can, which at times means (I trust) in a doubtful, an incredulous or a simply inattentive way. Those (like me) whose lives are spent with print overestimate the importance of print in other people's lives.

The press came to the Americans rather differently from the way it came to Britain. But it came as a blessing spoken upon capitalism as well as an object of consumption. So it came with owners in many cases as vain and horrible as Northcliffe, as arrogant and power-hungry as Beaverbrook. The Americans were similarly to enjoy the company of Joseph Pulitzer and

William Randolph Hearst, but they did things differently. To begin with, the development of an American press had to encompass the mere facts of geographical vastness and demographical multitude. There were not only competitive ethnicities to speak to and for, there were the rival interests between Chicago and Los Angeles, New York and St Louis. In a vaster land, the capital had nothing of the centripetal pull of the old European capitals.

In these circumstances, the city newspaper remained strongly local in both form and content. Gunther Barth sees the central relationship of all big city history in the nineteenth century as being not between graft and order, or politics and capital, or even blacks and whites, but as between the city and its press.[29] The biggest story is the story of the city itself, and that story is told, retold, compounded and enlarged by the penny press.

This press is commercial from its inception, the more so in a country whose political parties had and have no class identity. It turns away from factions towards the news of its urban world. The definition of such news at that date put a high premium on novelty itself. As Barth remarks, in both function and substance, its news is the stuff of small-town gossip, bright-eyed, up-to-date, eager – 'You won't believe this, but ...', 'Have you heard ...?'

Walter Benjamin, himself part journalist, part historian of a longed-for past, always poet of the city, was shaking his head over these changes in Germany in the 1920s. Quite unable to decide whether he was chronicler of the lost past or herald of an unvisitable future, he wrote:

> The art of storytelling is reaching its end because the epic side of truth, wisdom, is dying out ... with the full control of the middle class, which has the press as one of its most important instruments in fully developed capitalism, there converges a form of communication which ... never before influenced the epic form in a decisive way ... This new form of communication is information.
>
> Every morning brings us the news of the globe, and yet we are poor in noteworthy stories. This is because no event any longer comes to us without already being shot through with explanation. In other words, by now almost nothing that happens benefits storytelling; almost every-thing benefits explanation.[30]

And he continues, meaningfully, 'Modern man no longer works at what cannot be abbreviated.'

One sees what he means while wanting to call out in objection that *of course* storytelling is still to be found and heard, and read in newspapers as well. But what he suggests is the distinction between myth and history, oral and print memory, even between traditional wisdom and objective science.

Benjamin makes the same point himself when he says that the novel since *Don Quixote* has been a source of views not counsel, and it was Ian Watt who first pointed out[31] not only that a journalist, Daniel Defoe, was the first great English novelist, but also that his kind of prose and its ideal of faithful and factual reportage in unadorned prose matched very closely the principles as set out in the hornbook of the newly established Royal Society, whose sole purpose was the propagation of science. Certainly, as my curtain-raiser shows, many of the leading characters in this book move continuously between journalism and writing novels.

The new city press in America took its subject-matter from the amazing city itself, and it was a feature of those cities to be utterly distinctive, a distinction conferred partly by the characteristic production of each – timber, meat, grain, money, movies – and partly by the clamorous friction of its ethnic neighbourhoods. In this clamour, which so scared the Londoner Charles Dickens, the new newspaper reported, and at times explained, the city to itself. The headline had to be noisy enough to catch attention over the din of the street; the vendor's ritual shriek and, until quite recently, his own shouted version of the headline, had to cut through the same clatter and racket. The American paper shone with the glittering novelty of all that cities promised.[32] Its pace ('the latest news', 'stop press'), its compression of big events into simple headlines and brief reports, its ease of access, its dependable dismissal of boredom, its putting-you-in-touch and its mastery over the force of circumstance all commended themselves to the (mostly) men for whom success in the city was the acquisition of these qualities. In Europe and the United States, *men* went in hats and out to work and filled the streets, and men first adopted the habit of reading the daily newspaper.

If that newspaper were to contain such a jostling and scattered plenitude of facts and fictions, it would have to classify specialisms for its reporters. Sense of it all had to be made in time for the next edition.

This was a messier and more urgent matter for the American than for the European editor. In Europe, the recognisable stories would be tied to politics, even if politics were to be turned into commercial packages. In America nobody had very much idea how to wring any sense out of this extraordinary new society, but if they were going to sell newspapers they would have to do so every day and with sufficient consistency to keep the readers happy.[33]

To bring off this balancing act, editors and reporters between them had to improvise a variety of ways of doing the job, which was to say, ways of working and writing which would match the mixture of voices needed to fill the saleable list of contents in each daily. No wonder that those doing the improvisation in the city and then in the columns, and doing it in a way which would keep the peace between owner and editor, looked a shifty bunch and could find for many years no fixed abode in the social structure. They had to hunt out the news and the news had to be new. Novelty-as-value is a creation of the novelist and journalist alike, and both as city-dwellers. The legendary 'nose for news' of the reporter meant having the gift to sniff out those situations which would fuse briefly into an event capable of shock. Such an event, shaped by the reporter's way of seeing, must be brief, encompassable in a single silhouette, dramatic, 'humanly interesting', at once recognisable *and* exceptional.

It's a tall order to find such contingencies every day. The only way one could anticipate such a sequence of necessary surprises would be to have to hand a pretty straightforward set of narrative classifications: of place, time, plot and character. Exceptionality and abnormality as framed by 'newsiness' became the speedily spotted signals of what the journalists were looking for. Since such attributes turned up frequently in the law courts and the police stations, then those became the haunts of journalists and lent them at the same time their air of raffishness. Lawyers, with their high tone, manner and handedness, commanded such places; policemen in the uniform of the state patrolled them; journalists hovered and sneaked in them, looking neither for retribution nor for justice but merely for that low thing, a story, a story to sell outside as cheaply and brazenly as possible.

So the offices of law and order became classified by the news industry as places which provided the facts for its fictions, and the 'assignment' system began.

The second absolutely dependable source of stories was money and those who were known to possess it, the more so if they also displayed it and became thereby that quite new sort of character on the city stage, the celebrity – a creature partly self-made in eager response to the celebrity-making machinery of the city, partly made out of nothing much by that same machine in order to feed the insatiable, clattering presses.

Power is one source of celebrity, although some of the powerful are at pains to avoid it. In any case, power works in mysterious ways and our attempt to catch it in action, whether we are journalists or citizens, isn't helped by the crude way we have of understanding power either as 'the great beast' of coercion, or a bad smell ('old corruption'). Power for journalists is mysterious and alluring. The journalist hovers as close to it as possible but even at those points at which he (and, as I remarked, in the late nineteenth century it was almost entirely 'he'[34]) unmasks the ordinariness of the powerful, their power is enclosed by an estranging, glamorous, unanalysed aura.

Power attracts and repels. In the manufacture of news it first drew the reporter to itself to celebrate itself. The owner-barons encouraged journalists in this. But they also encouraged them in the exposure of power not their own. This sorted happily with those strong drives in American life and Constitution which counterposed power to freedom and independence and for which one way of keeping power down was to show up its quotidian frightfulness and cruelty.

Hence the journalism of revelation, exposure and 'muckraking' (the new term supposedly coined by Teddy Roosevelt in 1906[35]). If American journalism had no party politics, and started out as strictly commercial, it came to politics by way of exposing the mighty on behalf of the ordinary, putting down their pretensions to probity and philanthropy by raking through the muck of their money and showing how inherently dirty was the business of making so much of it.

Muckraking went along with what came to be called reportage, which meant a plainly factual but humanly sympathetic storytelling about all those singular neighbourhoods, districts and downright slums in which the new Americans battled to make themselves the life they couldn't make in old Europe. These pieces, often series of articles in journals such as *McClure's*, *Everybody's* and *Collier's*, carried such classics as Lincoln Steffens's *The Shame of the Cities*, in which one of the big, flaring names on the staff documented the graft, corruption and worker exploitation he found in St Louis, Minneapolis, Cleveland, Pittsburgh and Philadelphia as well as in the great wens of Chicago and New York. At more or less the same time, *McClure's* ran Ida Tarbell's influential series on John D. Rockefeller's Standard Oil. The stories she told, after four full years of her investigation, undercover and above ground, into crookedness, bullying, murderous brutality in the workforce, bribery and venality in the topmost circles of American fame and power, fuelled the successful campaign for anti-trust legislation. In a similar vein, *McClure's* had printed Josiah Willard's 'True Stories from the Underworld' and 'In the World of Graft' (Willard's own coinage, they say) which, like Steffens's work and Lewis Hine's remarkable photographic exposure of ten-year-old children working in coal mines, combined reportage with *outrance*, careful social-scientific objectivity with a social conscience to match.

Muckraking lasted only ten years in its original form, although there were over two thousand essays in the genre.[36] But it set a seal on the constitution of journalism, and however differently they wrote up their revelations, later journalists felt that old radical energy running through their bloodstream, earthing itself in their own lives. Muckraking gave its practitioners and the history of their profession a populist and progressive politics. It provided the profession with one of its most unkillable superstitions: the honest, small-town reporter who, in simple pursuit of the facts, mortally wounds the enemies of the people, city bosses, robber barons, king gangsters and such. In truth, the muckrakers won reforming victories. As a question in the uses of literacy it may be that revelation of big graft on the part of Mr Big did him no harm at all, and that the local readership enjoyed the local gossip without drawing either progressive or reactionary morals. Maybe Mr Big himself thrived on publicity and maybe even the cleaning up of city shame would have come about without the press. However all this may be, the crux for us is the journalist-investigator and the powerful biographies this character added to the stock of livable narratives in the trade.

The American journalists shared with the European ones a decidedly unsettled social position, but they did a good deal more about it, not without some press-baronial help. The two American baronial biographies to hand are that of Hearst alongside that of Joseph Pulitzer, whose contribution to purifying the language of his tribe went rather beyond Northcliffe's endowment of the chair of English literature in his name at the University of London, and well beyond the great prizes through which his name is still known around the world.

Joseph Pulitzer came to the USA from Budapest without any advantage as to fortune, served for the sake of the wage the last year of the Civil War as a Union soldier, and then got a job in St Louis on the German language immigrant paper, the *Westliche Post*, burning to do well, to get in and on, chilled by loneliness and the experience of rejection.

He did well and married well, was one of the earliest muckrakers, was elected to the Missouri legislature, bought two bankrupt newspapers, merged them with the mildly profitable *St Louis Post-Dispatch* and in the fashion of American dreamers was a millionaire at thirty-five. A year later, in transit through the capital, he heard that the *New York World* was for sale, borrowed against bonds and the *World* became his for $346,000.[37] Within a year he had quadrupled circulation and after ten more he had taken the figure past all national rivals to half a million or so on both weekdays and Sundays.

He fashioned tone, manner and diction for the American daily. The day Brooklyn Bridge opened, the *World* ran the story below a broadsheet-wide front page picture, and many stories of its construction were adjusted to the scale and detail of those who had built it, died while building it, and those who now lived to cross it every day, local inhabitants of the biggest neighbourhood in the world. His journalists picked up the first criterion of American reporting as it became conscious of itself during the 1870s and 1880s: 'eye-witness' fidelity to what was seen and heard. They then made eye-witnessing into a strikingly vivid and actualised tale, one in which 'colour' and 'personality' were as important as those man-made treasures, the facts. Led, as one must think, by the very best of the bunch of Atlantic press lords, Pulitzer's editors campaigned on behalf of their readers – in the case of Brooklyn Bridge, successfully forestalling a toll on those using it.

Always well ahead of rivals in the United States and imitators in London, Pulitzer invented the modern front page and the hierarchy of news that goes with it. Once print technology provided the big cylinders of copy type which replaced the old-fashioned bed of hand-set type, he could order a front-page layout with its own patterns of prominence, major and minor headlines, big or small items.[38]

It followed from this system not only that the bottom half of the front page took less important news than the top, but that inside pages took in their turn items of diminishing weight, until later portions of the paper were assigned to particular subject-matter and the distinction between news and editorial matter was firmly embedded in format.

Given the Pulitzer combination of racy drama in reporting style and evaluative presentation in the mosaic of the newspaper form, what he had effected was, in Michael Schudson's happy phrase, 'to turn news into a structure of crises'.[39] The paper ordered news into a hierarchy by trans-forming human exchanges into events, and, then, by lending events themselves an interpretive framework of plot and character, dramatised them as crises. Thus history became news, deliberative argument was stripped down to bald assertion, process turned into individual action, and efficacy measured in terms of immediacy.

This is the heaven and hell of modern news representation and the figures of speech of our everyday politics. Pulitzer and Northcliffe contrived the diction, the narrative form, the swiftness and readily under-stood applicability of news drama, together with its simple allegiances to 'ordinary people' and its wilful dedication to conservative feeling and values its very own methods made obsolete. Form and content together made for a new kind of social and political education. It may not have supplanted the experience of state education, but it certainly came first in readiness, accessibility and usefulness. You can say, as you must some of the time, that a newspaper education betrays the best hope for an informed publics and rational democracy. You can also say that without some such framework as these men devised, a runaway world with its cartloads of explosive and dangerous debris would be utterly unintelligible to everybody.

This book pulls between the dark judgement and the hopeful vision. It is, of necessity, historical. Things may have got worse or better since Pulitzer died in 1911 and the *World* foundered with the world economy after 1929. Either way, such were the large, heavy and disobliging contexts within which, once the industry was thoroughly established, journalists would have to work.

The American story of the coming of a national, daily and popular press is thus far a much more creditable one than the British version. Northcliffe, Rothermere and Beaverbrook debilitate diction and rhetoric in the name of a yellow populism that still thrives in the present. At the same time they find that the press has, because of them, won a new powerful position for itself much closer to the political centre than press owners have ever been before. They use this power unscrupulously and capriciously, for their private ends, and without anybody trying to stop them.

Pulitzer's press comes out a good deal better in the historical reckoning. At the turn of the twentieth century the *World* led one of the justly most famous anti-trust campaigns in pursuit of corruption in the gigantic insurance industry. The battle was conducted under the banner of individual protection and business ethics, but these are far from contemptible values and even the yellowest journalism may do its bit to stand up for them. In any case, the consequence was that business ethics assumed a new sobriety and the ideological keystone of big American capitalism, the small business, acquired the strong reassurance of mutual assurance.

The Pulitzer house journal had helped solidify the Constitution. In doing so, Pulitzer (like Northcliffe) had given public opinion new weight and volume. At the same time, he had so shifted the centre of political gravity that governments could no longer ignore that public in their reckoning. The voice of the people would speak through the press and the elected government would listen. The voice might be, at times, chauvinist, hysterical, hate-filled, or it might be sentimental, idealistic, generous. But in either register, it would be heard.

Its intelligence was of a quite new order. This new newspaper thought was quick, highly emotive, rushed to judgement, particulate. It improvised swift schema with which to enclose the births of a runaway nation and a world to match. The conditions of economic action and the urgency of connection to profit left no time for reflection. Once Pulitzer and company had devised the broadsheet front page and its montage of stories, it prefigured a way of world-making. The reader's eye-and-brain scanned a compressed, stylised but (the new word) 'sensational' headline, caught enough of the story to get the point, and then moved veeringly and in no predictable order up and down, from side to side, settling itself in relation to this chancy little map of the imagined world.

The most important fact on the front page is the date. The reader is told the time, 'the steady onward clocking of homogeneous, empty time. Within that time the world ambles sturdily ahead.'[40] Characters and their narratives appear on the empty page of time, some with a bigger part than others. They disappear for a few days and come back. They vanish for good. They are unknown to the reader except by way of the stories the journalist tells, either at the behest of the owner or out of that same journalist's sense (the 'nose for news') of what the audience would read. They stand for something, unknown but knowable: they stand for this or that value or villainy, precious to the audience. They stand for it, simple, silhouetted, cartooned. They connect with hot little flames of human belief and allegiance. They earth them.

This vulgar picture of the way we learn to think and locate ourselves vis-à-vis the turning world starts out from the fashioning of the front page sometime between 1880 and 1910. It was given explosive vigour and craziness by the First World War. Even the war, however, was only a symptom of the world just brought to its modern birth; forming and framing the news was the immediate response of the entrepreneur on behalf of baffled, anxious millions. Awful as the owners so often were, mixed as was the bag of journalists, things might have been worse.

It has been argued[41] that Woodrow Wilson was a President who matched his methods and, indeed, his very character to this new presence in politics. In this, on a more sedate and deferential stage, Lloyd George was his faithful lieutenant and Theodore Roosevelt his avatar. Wilson, on this account, effects a Presidency which will contain and express the violent contradictions in American political practice as popular commitment to individualist egalitarianism grates harshly upon the corresponding facts of bullying self-assertion, the absolute power of money, and the sudden advent of American military imperialism. That grating noise is what we hear in the politics of news. Pulitzer gets the credit. William Randolph Hearst gets the blame.

Pulitzer deserves well enough all the same. Max Weber's little tribute to contemporary journalists in 1918 might have sounded odd in America without Pulitzer's proposed founding in 1903 of the first ever graduate school of journalism at Columbia University.

No doubt Pulitzer himself was in it only for the prestige. There was so much quarrelling over the terms of the foundation, that the school didn't open until 1913. But universities are constituted by the appeal to the best of their society, and the Columbia School's formal profession of such ideals as moral courage, pursuit of the facts undeterred by whether the journalists offended the powerful or whether the newspaper would lose circulation by publishing uncomfortable or unpopular truths, did much to give institutive reality to such virtues.

So, too, did Pulitzer's famous prizes. Never mind that their awards have been so often disfigured by venality and favouritism. They were assigned for the reward of serious journalism, especially of a kind which helped social reform, which reported on and therefore helped alleviate misery and oppression. There is nothing else like them and they do honour to the profession as well as to the old man.

In this foreshortened history, Pulitzer runs away with the liberal prizes, while Northcliffe's effigy can be dandled from a pole. There is enough truth in this to hold the distinction between British and American journalism. It would, I think, be possible to do the same thing as between British and mainland European newspaper owners and their products. Northcliffe, Rothermere and Beaverbrook were essential agents in the special brew of hysteria, chauvinism, anxiety-mongering and issue stupefaction which characterises so much of British twentieth-century journalism and the news reporting at the centre of its industry. No doubt as individual men, Northcliffe may deserve some praise for his part in devising a coherent policy for ending the First World War and Beaverbrook similarly won Churchill's admiration sufficiently to be awarded a government post in charge of aircraft manufacture for the Battle of Britain. As press lords, however, they ventriloquised their newspapers' voices.

By the same token no doubt, Pulitzer, benefactions and prizes on behalf of truth-telling journalism notwithstanding, shared the same revolting egoism and arrogance as any cartoon illustration of the millionaire mogul. He insisted on his subordinates doing exactly as he instructed with the cold passion and heated obduracy of a Renaissance tyrant. He too fired employees on a caprice, bent to toadies, gloried in fame, gloated over wealth, was abject in his quest for power over others.

The position of such men is unique in history. Small wonder they turned into such monsters. Their characters fitted them for the position; their position distended and bloated exactly those characteristics which carried them upwards. They became grotesques, none more so than William Randolph Hearst.

In common with the other three (though Pulitzer left Budapest without much money), in common with most newspaper bosses whatever the folklore, Hearst came from a well-off, indeed in his case extremely wealthy, family. His father George had left Missouri and driven a team of oxen 1,500 miles across the plains, the desert and the Rockies to join the Californian gold rush which opened in 1849. By 1857 he owned a sixth of the fabulous Oplin mine, he had shares in the eponym of the gold rush, the Comstock Lode, he married the daughter of a grand Missouri family and built a house beside the Golden Gate.

It was one hell of an inheritance for William, who turned into a clever, rather stiff practical joker, thrown out of Harvard, as mythology has it, for delivering chamber pots to professors with their own portraits engraved upon them. He went straight for the thrilling, squalid, exuberant life of newspapers.

Father bought him the *San Francisco Examiner*. Like all of them, the young man had a keen unfulfilled feeling, part sympathy part prurience, for the life of the city poor, its noise and garish lights, its unprivate intimacies and candid sex, its street drunkenness and the terrific roar of the factories where they worked and sweated and learned their enviable knowledgeability. His newspapers would catch the dirty allure and the reeking familiarity of this world and reflect them back to its inhabitants. So the *Examiner* put its circulation up steeply, and Hearst went east to spend his father's legacy on New York's *Morning Journal*, declaring himself for the Democrats and as Pulitzer's first rival.[42]

He made the news all right, conspiring to spring a beautiful Cuban from jail where she was locked up for political plotting, and going down to Cuba himself during the brief American hostilities with Spain, being photographed for his own front page taking a clutch of unarmed Spanish sailors prisoner on the beach. That morning, and subsequent mornings too, the *Morning Journal* sold 1.6 million copies.

Hearst made the decisive shift in the content of a daily paper from news to time-killing, from some version of informing the public to mild entertainment and warding off the insufferable blankness of boredom. He introduced the agony column (Annie Laurie, Dorothy Dix, Beatrice

Fairfax), the pin-up picture (drawings only), and the comic strip page (*Krazy Kat, Buster Brown*). He ran for Congress in a ten-gallon hat, married a girl from the chorus line, renamed his paper *The American*, tried for mayor of the capital, invented (like the Harmsworths) his own political party, backed movies with millions to get his mistress in the lead, opposed the war, abused the Wobblies (International Workers of the World), backed the navy and built as his refuge the insane folly of San Simeon in California, an overwhelming brew of Alhambran, Renaissance and Gatsbyan grotesquerie, where he died a solitary death, resurrected for ever by Orson Welles as Citizen Kane.

These men and the many like them stand at the main gate of modernity. In their curious way they understand it well. Intuitively, we shall say by way of explanation, they felt strange currents pass through them, and found a way, a partial and extravagant way, of harnessing those energies.

They felt the stirrings of vast masses of people who had never known how to speak in public about anything at all, and certainly hadn't been asked. They sensed that the moment of the demagogue, armed with God knows what ideological rant, had come, and thrilled at the thought. They saw that this weird new confection, the newspaper, made a headlong world briefly intelligible to the unprecedentedly great expectation of poor, free people determined to hand prosperity to their children; their imaginations seethed at the sight and they found they could speak strange tongues. They saw that they could cause wars or peace, and they loved it. So they fired and hired, bullied and hustled, drank and fornicated, becoming legends in their own minds and for the space of brief times.

CHAPTER THREE

Public Opinion and Mass Politics:
Gentlemen of the Press

The history of the press, as told by Jürgen Habermas[1] for the then German Federal Republic but generalised to the leading economies, is a tale told about the establishment of a necessary fiction, 'the public sphere'. In the public sphere, public opinion forms itself out of the experience of those who gain access to it and from the information for which the space itself was designated as site of collection and locale of debate.

The public sphere, by Habermas's account, is a category special to bourgeois society. That is to say, as the new class became conscious of itself in the eighteenth century, first in Britain and then in Europe, and as the absolutism of the *anciens régimes* broke up under the impact of new mercantile capitalism, so it required for its own assertion and for the sake of competition within itself a social space marked out for the free exchange of the knowledge and organisation necessary to its coming to power.

In this new kind of political economy, news was itself a tradable commodity. The rise of a dependable market calculus turned on sufficiently frequent and exact intelligence. Private postal services could become properly public with the coming of print. Publication inaugurated the public sphere. Print publication had long broken the monopoly of the sacred classical tongues. Certainly print was public, but in the new freedom of vernacular publication, each print was intelligible only to those who could read the language. So the claim can forcefully be made[2] that print and the new capitalism to which it gave such impetus together gave shape and energy to the nation-state. By 1700, the British state could provide the security, the bureaucracy and the taxation levels to succour capital.

The authority of the impersonal state generated the civic realm whose counterposed authority derived from the corresponding significance given to the individual. Private life becomes defined as the realm of personal meaning, sanctioned by the administrative efficiency of the state. The father of each family was appointed intermediary between privacy and publicity. Economics snapped off from the household and began its metamorphosis into a science. The private conversations of merchants in market or *souk* were filtered, compressed and simplified into publishable and public news, the merchants themselves styled by the times *custodes novellarum*, 'keepers of the newest things'. The things they kept included the movement of the mighty (court news), of market prices (today's quotations of stock) and police advice about threats to property or commerce (law reports and political dangers).

Thus London's *Daily Intelligencer of Court, City and County* which started in 1643 presaged exactly the layout and contents of the city's *Times* two and three centuries later. The new press was the debating space of the new bourgeoisie, which had shed and ruthlessly demoted its original leaders, the burghers and their craft and shopkeeping membership.[3] The new class comprised the state officers – lawyers, doctors, scholars, administrators – as well as the mighty merchants and bankers who at once focused and repelled the interest and attention of the state.

The class held in sometimes bitter tension the opposition between the princes of capitalism and the scriveners of power; at one and the same time, the new class components must contain private freedoms (of consumption and expression) and public regulation (of the same quantities). The press became the site of struggle between private opinion and public authority. Opinion would compel authority to justify itself in public. Its bar was and remains the press. The press was called as adversary to, and plaintiff before, the state.

As we have already seen, the abrupt incarnation of the press barons after 1890 permitted them to appeal to the ancient rights of free speech, uncoerced belief and sectional criticism so strenuously won first for the bourgeoisie and then for working classes by two centuries of press struggle. They not only made the appeal, they presumed their entitlement. So it was that the public force of privately accumulated opinion was captured and bridled not on behalf of the commonwealth but for personal power and colossal profit.

The capture was only ever partial, the bridling thrown off time and again. The monster egos of three generations of these men has not yet broken in what became known as public opinion. All the same, it is not as strong as it was. Public opinion is a central concept in the constitutions, written and unwritten, of modern more-or-less democracies. It is a necessary fiction in law.[4] As such, public opinion impels or delays legislation according to an imaginary balancing of its judicious self-formulation and the legal enactment of its preferences. Emancipation is the outcome of public opinion so making itself felt that the law must change accordingly and for the better. In the teeth of the twentieth century's abominable record of cruel and unnatural legislation, the ideal of a benign and enlightened public opinion bringing justice to justice remains an irresistible necessity and the place of its free play the forum of the polity.

The press is the forum of public opinion. But the period of its greatest successes and prominence has also been the period in which public opinion has lost so much of its normative command. With the coming of the post-Northcliffe press and then the gradually universal diffusion of radio and television, the gathering and discussion of the news of the world came more and more to resemble any other manufacturing industry. No doubt the practice of news evaluation has indeed retained some of its historical force in the making of the great fiction, public opinion. At the same time, as manufacturing industry in general learned at least partly to systematise and control the rhythms of mass consumption, public opinion became viewed as a mere medley of preferences. More or less articulate, it was simply *there*, an actuality to be sounded and manipulated by the helots of market research not in the name of critical reason (the *idea!*) but as the mysterious current driving forward the blind hordes of the consumers.

The news industry did not simply follow this trend, it led it. Because it was the predominant site for mass advertising, it could do, according to its conventional wisdom and proprietors, little else. We may pass over the contemporary fact that the best daily paper in Europe, *Le Monde*, carries comparatively small amounts of advertising and costs much the same as British broadsheets or the *New York Times*. For the purposes of a history of this kind, the mutual embeddedness of advertising revenue, consumer behaviour and writing political journalism is as fixed as geography.

The trouble is then that nobody can agree on what is meant by public opinion, with the dismaying result that, as is now the case, it is hard to find a journalist whose views, reflecting a considered and intelligent section of a well-informed public, would count for anything much among the political élite. In the key biography of Walter Lippmann which follows in the next chapter, there came the late turning point in his career when Lippmann decided, against all the high-principled trimming of his fifty-year career, to speak out in open criticism of the President and his conduct of the war in Vietnam. No one can doubt that Lippmann's criticism weighed significantly with Johnson in his decision not to run for a second term.

It wouldn't happen now. Only thirty-odd years later, the grand opinion-ators count for much less. There are lots more of them for one thing, and opinionation itself has dissolved into opinion polling. If, at a solemn moment, one were to look for the sovereignty of the people, it would be hard to know where to find it. The polls report a murk of attitude, belief, argument, prejudice and intuition, in which one cannot tell the difference between careful judgement and petulant caprice.

All this is not to say that modern democracies can no longer identify the source of their own authority or that civilisation expresses itself by checks on a five-point scale. But at a time when governments themselves have become sensitive to the vagaries of public moodiness by way of opinion polling, it is hard to discover any binding relation between public author-ity, the daily press and the lived allegiances of popular politics.

The eighty-year history of political journalism up to the turn of the millennium is therefore a story of the slow dissolution of authority and the diffusion of the idea of an interlocking series of educated publics. It is also of course a corresponding and contradictory tale of how the political jour-nalists came to celebrity as they shed authority; how he and she kept up the old adventuring even in their passages around a smaller world; how each held on to self-respect and respectability by telling the truth as they could find it and by keeping themselves in a condition of tense, unsympathetic incredulity whenever they came near the powerful.

In his controversial study of what the power elite does with its power, C. Wright Mills tried to describe the ideal public which would hold power in check.

In a *public*, as we may understand the term, (1) virtually as many people express opinions as receive them. (2) Public communications are so organized that there is a chance immediately and effectively to answer back any opinion expressed in public. Opinion formed by such discus-sion (3) readily finds an outlet in effective action, even against – if necessary – the prevailing system of authority. And (4) authoritative institutions do not penetrate the public, which is thus more or less autonomous in its operations. When these conditions prevail, we have the working model of a community of publics, and this model fits closely the several assumptions of classic democratic theory.

The public and the mass may be most readily distinguished by their dominant modes of communication: in a community of publics, discussion is the ascendant means of communication, and the mass media, if they exist, simply enlarge and animate discussion, linking one *primary public* with the discussions of another. In a mass society, the dominant type of communication is the formal media, and the publics become mere *media markets*: all those exposed to the contents of given mass media.[5]

Wright Mills's 'public' and its opinion remains the necessary fiction at the heart of our mostly unexpressed theory of a democracy; his 'mass' is an adequate picture of what actually happens. But the practice of our public education is justified by the fiction and in terms of an informed citizenry, and the conduct of everyday citizenship may be understood as a struggle to make our particular corner of the mass conform, on this issue or that, to the theory of publics, bending the will of princes, heartening the heartlessness of money.

Once upon a time, in the nineteenth century, the public art of literature taught its readership how to live gallantly and self-reliantly within the frames of politics. The art of the novel was to find a balance between the truthfully recorded facts of life and the passionate demands of a personal subjectivity for which the novelists forged a quite new language. A thoughtful reader from any social class would find out how to square public duties with private passions by reading *Great Expectations*, *Anna Karenina*, *Jane Eyre* and *The Bostonians*.

Then films came along and transposed storytelling to a realm of such high, objectless yearning that ordinary passion could not breathe the same air, and politics became such a shadow-play of agonised extremities, dark wickedness and shining virtue that everyday opposition to power elites was too trivial to dramatise.

In its turn, television returned passion to the close-up actuality of domestic friction but had no means to silhouette the drama of politics. The screen was too small, the faces too near.

The old, minatory connection between private lives and public places is then held together by political journalism. Since the end of the First World War, the political journalists have written the art of the possible and, at their best, have taught how to live a decent private life on behalf of your bit of the public one.

Listening to the cacophony of the press, whether then or now, it may prove hard to discern the still, sad music of any humanity at all. But it is not so very much harder than it was to hear Dickens or Tolstoy above the tumult of published words in the London of 1848 or the Moscow of 1869, and by something of the same process of argumentation, familiarisation, contingency, patronage and judgement, a canon of good or great journalism emerged from the bitter warfare of circulations and machine-guns.

Just like the older canon of poets, playwrights and novelists, the new tradition of journalists, their lives and works, was painted into both popular and professional memories as a long sequence of frescoes with multiple narratives, glowing imagery, heroic figures and audacious action, all stamped with a variety of styles and signatures, a collective work of art stretching forward into the future, teaching other artists how to live that sort of a life, commemorating itself to all those who only read and cannot write as the only life, glamorous, public, brave and so on.

That is how traditions sustain themselves and from that ground the innovations grow. Memory, and the experience of reading the words, fixes several versions of history. The making of journalism as it seemed to Max Weber in 1918 was a not ignoble thing, its best practitioners more upright and faithful to their calling than many scholars, more scrupulous by far than many politicians.

This is not how it seems to journalism's first historian, Phillip Knightley.[6] The simple moral of his fine book is that, in the famous truism, the first casualty of war is the truth, but that the only duty of the journalist is to that truth. The power of his tragi-comic history is, however, rather diminished by the importance he ascribes to the earnestness and uncontested objectivity which every journalist should bring to the task of telling the truth.

In truth, no doubt, the truth of the First World War was made damnably hard to find, certainly at first. It was during those years that the construction of propaganda machinery by governments was completed. Knightley tells us that Britain's Defence of the Realm Act, which handed over to the British government for the rest of the century powers of injunction (which became the infamous D-notices), of censorship and examination of *all* messages, marks the moment at which modern propaganda was born and also, he claims, began the deep 'undermin[ing] of public faith in the press'. He goes on, with great severity, to say that:

A large share of the blame ... must rest with the British war correspondents. They were in a position to know more than most men of the nature of the war of attrition on the Western Front, yet they identified themselves absolutely with the armies in the field, they protected the high command from criticism, wrote jauntily about life in the trenches, kept an inspired silence about the slaughter, and allowed themselves to be absorbed by the propaganda machine.[7]

It is hard not to applaud. But to do so is to allow us to use the historical record only as material for self-congratulation in the present. There can be no doubt that much of the daily press behaved as Knightley says, and the press owners were unbending in their support of government lying. At the same time, however, the journalists wrote and reported out of a frame of feeling they shared with the civilians and, come to that, with plenty of those at the front.

After the twentieth century's death-toll in battle, after the passing of patriotism as a shared value in most of the rich nations, it is usual for people to express if not outright pacifism then at least marked misgivings about the necessity of war. In the case of the First World War the position is hard to assail, and Knightley is openly contemptuous not just about the conduct but about the justification offered by their government to the British people at any time between 1914 and 1918.

He underestimates, I think, the force of emotional circumstance. This is not a way of saying that, unfortunately, in time of war passion gets a bigger say than reason. Truth in that, no doubt, but the point is rather that nobody can think, let alone narrate, without the language in use carrying its emotional evaluations in the very choices of words and in every involuntary or intentional inflection.

Of course one may write prose as evacuated of authorship as possible: the instruction brochure or the teach-yourself-chemistry textbook; or one may write in as author-audible a way as one finds in an autobiography or an apologia. When one is writing of matters of the life and death of nations including one's own, then the writing, good or bad, will carry with it the sincerities, dreadful or dignified, of the day, and be inseparable from the feelings which flow through social life as indispensably as blood.

So the *Morning Post* was a byword among the soldiers for ranting patriotism and ignorantly militaristic cant. 'Little Mother' published her 'Answer to a common soldier' who had written a short time after the July 1916 Battle of the Somme to doubt the value of its legendary slaughter. Her repellent sentimentality even, it seems, after the death of her only son, gives us some kind of measure of widespread feeling about the war among civilian British.

'There is only one temperature for the women of the British race and that is white heat. With those who disgrace their sacred trust of motherhood we have nothing in common. Our ears are not deaf to the cry that is ever ascending from the battlefield from men of flesh and blood whose indomitable courage ...'[8]

etc. etc. No one can write like that now. But the *Morning Post* was, it said, flooded with tearful letters of approbation and had to reprint the appalling thing in a special leaflet of 75,000 copies.

Reporting from the front to an audience capable of living in this stiff uniform of rapturous duty could only mean sharing something of the same hysteria. It was how the war sustained itself. Even young officers full of detestation for such stuff, as intelligent and caustic as Robert Graves and Siegfried Sassoon, were forced to concede that the only likelihood was that the war would be fought to a finish.

These were the feelings, common and overwhelming, of a highly self-conscious, self-defining and powerful nation. The journalists, lied to by the staff and by official communiqués, caught in the cross-currents of a vast tide of events of which no one could tell the direction, victims like the battle generals themselves of crude, constantly disrupted telephone technology and human runners with handwritten missives, had few principles and little tradition to guide them.

They acquired both, to the best of very varying abilities. But it is a distortion to say, as Knightley does, that all journalists were shamefully complicit in a 'sordid conspiracy to keep the truth from the people'.[9] There is, on the other hand, no doubting the rightness of his account[10] of the military mendacity and excursion, its absolute determination to tell only its own story and suppress all others, including the by now well-known stories of military incompetence.

The people, after all, could learn pretty well what was going on from the men in the family who were fighting in France. Most of the killing was done seventy or eighty miles from Dover. The Channel is only twenty-three miles wide. Every day *The Times* published a list of officers killed in action (this is class-bound Britain in mourning but there again, the ratio of junior officers to combat soldiers killed on the Somme was three to one[11]). If you turn up a handful of strictly local papers and their reporting of the war, you find trite and conventional language enough, and an attitude of more or less patriotic support. You don't find any questioning of the war aims but you do find bleak, adequately precise accounts of the engagements of the local regiments, the pitiful quantities of ground won or lost, and the still agonising expressions of sympathy in that clipped, bare, enduring manner. It is as though, in their smaller compass, even the journalists of the

Northern Echo, the *Abergavenny Chronicle*, the *Sheffield Star*, the *Oundle, Raunds and Thrapston Times*,[12] had anticipated the lesson taught by Ernest Hemingway in *A Farewell to Arms*.

> I was always embarrassed by the words sacred, glorious and sacrifice and the expression in vain... There were so many words that you could not stand to hear and finally only the names of places had dignity. Certain numbers were the same way and certain dates and those with the names of the places were all you could say and have them mean anything.[13]

It is the lesson well learned by Hemingway's fellow American journalists in the Second World War: Martha Gellhorn, Ed Murrow, Ernie Pyle, A. J. Liebling, John Hersey, but it lives in the extraordinary mute anguish, the taciturn endurance, the implied resolution to see the thing through these local English and Welsh reports embody. They are qualities to offset the ghastly sportsman's heartiness which so roused the hatred of Robert Graves: 'We could not understand the war-madness that ran everywhere, looking for a pseudo-military contest. The civilians talked a foreign language; and it was newspaper language.'[14]

As one would expect at a moment of acute national emergency when violent action in another place threatened men in every family, and when national government and military leadership were known to be at odds and even more certainly known not to be in control of events, the press attained its first peak of influence.[15] It was sufficiently united in the view that the war must be won, but there were several serious editors, supremely C. P. Scott at the *Manchester Guardian* and C. E. Montague reporting for him, who were very far from the credulous and supine militarists despised by Siegfried Sassoon. The weekly (London) *Nation*, voice of the Fabian Society Left, was fiercely critical of the inept Asquith government and strongly advocated peace treatying in 1917. The Liberal *Daily News* had a grand old stager called H. Perry Robinson whose reports pretty truthfully mirrored the darkening stoicism with which, rightly or wrongly, most people lived through the war after the mindless elation of its first year had dissipated. (This took time; it was not until after the terrible opening of the Battle of the Somme that Robinson's careful, militarily exact reports assumed their ultimate grimness.) Something of the cultural turn is caught by an anecdote told in a letter to the *Darlington and Stockton Times* by the stout, middle-aged leader of the local Special Constabulary, one Fred Nattrass.

I saw a tommy walking up Brunswick Street carrying full kit, still muddy, very tired. A neighbour came to the door. 'Hey, Jack, where've you been?' The soldier scarcely looked up. 'On t'Sommie.' 'Seen owt of our Stanley, he's on t'Sommie.' The soldier trudged on. 'Nay; Sommie's 'ell of a big place,' he said.[16]

No one, after the hosts of books and films, the deep, ineradicable embedding of the Great War in modern memory,[17] can doubt the facts of shocking waste, incompetence and the arrogant, terrified concealment of these failings by the high command and politicians. British journalists (like German ones, as Max Weber remarked), as patriotic as the next man at the time, lacking a strong tradition of journalism, put down by heavy bosses, made the sense they could of what they were told. Doing so, they found a few famous men to praise after the event. This is the story of one of them.

Arthur Ransome is by common consent among the greatest half-dozen or so English writers for children. As anyone who has loved the books knows, the pleasure they give lasts a lifetime and is no doubt intensified by its origins in childhood when, if one were lucky, the terrific freedoms and happiness so plainly and tellingly recounted in *Swallows and Amazons* and the other twelve novels about children coincided with and confirmed in one's own experience that life, like literature, held out a promise of happiness that would be kept.[18]

Obviously this is not the place to concentrate on them beyond saying that here is another journalist-novelist, and that the plain, expository manner of the prose as well as the open easiness of the bond with the author[19] which Ransome engenders comes straight from his excellent reporting.

It is less well known that Ransome only began publishing for children in 1930 at the age of forty-six and that *Swallows and Amazons* was his twenty-first book. His father was the professor of history at the University of Leeds and, though himself much bowed down by weary debts bequeathed by an over-speculative parent, posthumously sent young Arthur to what was then, with all the usual reservations, the most vigorous and cultivated of English public schools, Rugby. There the boy fostered a great delight in folklore, was routinely bullied for short-sightedness, but had acquired his most abiding passion from a very early age when his family had taken every university vacation in the hills of the Lake District. His father taught him an absolute devotion to fishing, which lasted a lifetime, and he joined the great dynasty of sailors who entered their mystery on Coniston Water and

Lake Windermere, and became a Wordsworthian lover of his wonderful home hills:

> No matter where I was, wandering about the world, I used at night to look for the North Star and, in my mind's eye, could see the beloved skyline of great hills beneath it. *Swallows and Amazons* grew out of those old memories. I could not help writing it. It almost wrote itself.[20]

The passion for the Cumbrian hills and the passion for fairy stories did not converge for very many years but he spent those years making himself into a disorderly but copious writer. He quit science at University College Leeds after a year, joined a publishing company, was inspired by the life of William Morris and by the time he was twenty was turning his hand to scraps of occasional journalism. His dearest and kindliest family friends had been the Collingwoods near Coniston, W. G. his honorary uncle a well-known painter, palaeontologist and Ruskin's personal secretary, his pianist wife, Dorrie, Ransome's fond and honorary aunt, the son Robin, five years his junior, his close friend and sailing companion and later, alongside Bertrand Russell, one of the two unmistakably great English philosophers of the twentieth century. In London he became friends with two poets, Edward Thomas and Lascelles Abercrombie, met W. B. Yeats and Ellen Terry, listened to his new friend and literary hostess Pamela Colman Smith tell Jamaican fairy stories in the dialect, published his first book at twenty, was taken on by Martin Secker, and seemed set fair for success.

It is hard, with contemporary publishing in mind, to recover the happy teemingness of literary London and New York in 1910. The whole little world of it was poured into Bloomsbury and lower Manhattan and, as P. G. Wodehouse put it soon afterwards, any suicidal novelist jumping out of a window would certainly land on the shoulders of a passing publisher. But Ransome doubly postponed success by his first marriage, to a madwoman, and by contracting himself to an embezzling and bigamist publisher.

He took to his heels, found a new contract to work on translations of fairy tales in Russian (subsequently learning 'the easiest of the languages'[21]) and set off across the Baltic to St Petersburg at the moment war broke out. Ransome promptly wired his agent to find him work as a war correspondent (the agent wired back, 'What war?'). Never having been a daily journalist but by now able, when he needed to, to turn out 6,000 words in a day, and in addition having the singular qualification for an Englishman of understanding Russian, he came home to tout for journalistic work. He was far too myopic to be conscripted and the Foreign Office showed interest in his espionage potential, so he set off back by steamer and sledge to the Finland border and on to Petrograd.

Ransome was an involuntary but entirely composed adventurer, the more remarkable for suffering from severe digestive haemorrhages and blinding headaches all his life, enduring a dozen operations without complaint (in one of them coming round while under too light a Russian anaesthetic) and fainting fits without serious injury. Gentlemanly but boisterous, he delighted in the noisy company of Russian writers to and from the war, and launched happily into the dependable work of dispatching news telegrams to the *Daily News* under tuition from Hamilton Fyfe, Northcliffe's star political reporter, and Guy Berenger from Reuters.

They taught him the crazy telegram jargon immortalised by Evelyn Waugh in *Scoop* ('never write DID NOT GO instead of UNWENT'[22]) and as Ransome always did, he made fast friends in the most mobile and transient of circumstances. But he says nothing much about being muzzled or deceived about the dismal progress of the war on the Russian front, and indeed did his bit to launch a British war news agency, the main business of which became, as Ransome cheerfully admits, that of 'a more and more expensive and obvious propaganda bureau'.

His reports, uncensored and unhindered, tell the stories of what he did and where he went. He went to the front and nearly fell into a trench full of Germans; he talked to every class of Russian about the war; he saw the phantoms of hatred, civil war and the coming emptiness beginning to gather and float above the Russia he had come, loving man as he was, to love well.

He sent off his two or three telegrams a day and in 1916 dispatched home in the diplomatic bag his translation of *Old Peter's Russian Tales*, still in print eighty-odd years later. Reporting above Russian lines and in Russian support he was almost shot down in the little aircraft in which he was a passenger, and became a reluctant hero in the *Daily News*. Working for a progressive paper gave him freer access than if he had been in the pay of the grandly official and imperial *Times*. He went to Romania when it joined the war, jumping an ammunition train, cucumber-cool under his first taste of bombing; back in London he told the government that Russia would be out of the war and into social breakdown within a year; then he went back to Riga and Petrograd. Looking at Russia was, he wrote:

> Like watching a frozen Russian river … listening for the first cracks in the ice that would become a chorus, until suddenly, under the spring sun, the motionless river would break up with a continuous grinding roar, when

the still calm of winter would change to violent motion, with huge blocks of ice thrown high in the air and swept irresistibly away to the sea.[23]

In 1917, Ransome was invited by J. L. Garvin, grandee editor of the *Observer*, to become its correspondent (as well as that of the *Daily News*) in Russia which, in spite of his own 'pinkish' (his word) credentials, opened to him the doors of the oligarchy. But it was on the street that he found his most vivid parable of the state of the nation. He had watched a general in a sledge step out of it on the Nevsky Prospekt to address two soldiers carrying a heavy box who had, cumbered with their load, failed to salute him smartly enough. The general, beside himself with rage, knocked them both down. He ordered them to their feet. He struck them down again. A little time later the revolution of the century broke into motion like Ransome's great melting river.

He reported a country in great good humour gleefully burning the archives of the secret police. On 14 March he wired the *Daily News* directly from the Duma (anyone could get in; people slept in it) as the members struggled to appoint a government legitimate enough to ward off civil war.

Ransome counted as an advantage his own ignorance of formal politics. He hadn't had 'to acquire ... the political colonising of a newspaper' like his colleagues and was strongly of the heretical view that 'the holding of views (any views) made it harder ... to see the facts.'[24] Ransome's viewlessness made him the most visionary of prophets. He was right to predict that Russian soldiers would stop fighting and begin to go home; he was right in being first to report directly from the Workers' and Soldiers' Soviet; he was right to tell his *Daily News* readers that the ubiquitous red flags – over the Winter Palace, in the hand of the statue of Catherine the Great, on the front of the buses – were the flags of victory.

When Alexander Kerenksy, the leader of the government, fell, Ransome was back in England – what inordinate and exhausting travels those old correspondents undertook so blithely! – but on 21 December 1917 he returned to Petrograd carrying the trust of the Foreign Office in his judgement and reports. He befriended Karl Radek, leader of the Foreign Commisariat, who had rifled a parcel of Ransome's and been much taken by its contents: a complete Shakespeare (whom Radek knew by heart), a chess set, books on fishing and folklore. Radek introduced Ransome to the leading Bolsheviks, including Lenin and Trotsky, and to Evgenia, 'a tall jolly girl' who was Trotsky's secretary. 'The telegrams to the *Daily News* were in flat contradiction to those of almost every other correspondent,' including all the Americans except John Reed. Living beside these resolute, cheerful people Ransome refused to believe 'the rubbishy propaganda' poured out by their enemies; he thought the Soviets would win and that it was right that they should. He wasn't rich and he travelled light; he was quite untainted by the hysterical fear of Bolshevism which stoked the engines of hate in *The Times*, the *Morning Post*, and William Randolph Hearst.

He saw Trotsky most days and Evgenia every day (after a year or two he married her). He was there at the moment Lenin persuaded the National Executive of the Soviets to sign a desperate peace with Germany, and when the Soviet government moved east to Moscow, Ransome went with it. When in March 1918 the Social Revolutionaries assassinated the German ambassador in an effort to incriminate the Bolsheviks and seize power from them, Ransome was on hand to tell Radek and Lenin himself (truthfully) not only that his own commitment was always to Anglo-Russian friendship but that he would travel by train with Radek to the pleasant little market town where the assorted ambassadors (most importantly the very dim American ambassador) were holed up waiting to see who was winning.

Once there the task was to persuade the diplomatic corps to move to Moscow and acknowledge the new government. Ransome was Radek's not-always-heeded counsellor in this. Their efforts at persuasion failed. The Tsar was executed in July. The diplomats decamped. Ransome, part journalist, part Soviet adviser, part secret service agent, wholly Englishman and adventurer, got Evgenia out of Russia and in as Secretary to the Legation in Berlin and, as Germany collapsed, began to send in telegrams to the *Daily News* about the hardly credible plotting of the Allies against Soviet rule in Moscow ('though I should by then have realised that any idiocy was possible to our Foreign Office so long as our officials welcomed the entirely unscrupulous persons who needed no credentials other than hostility to the Bolsheviks'[25]). When the Germans surrendered, their army was used to shell Russian factories. As Ransome began to gather material for an intended history of the revolution he also prepared a report 'for very unwilling ears at the Foreign Office', some of which found its way to the *Manchester Guardian* and all of which was published as his book *Six Weeks in Russia.*[26]

The six weeks lasted from the end of January to the middle of March 1919 and during that time Britain, France and the United States had launched their armed intervention in Russia. More young men were dying pointlessly, this time in an effort to prevent the Red Terror from disturbing an already disturbed and mutinous ex-soldiery and unemployed proletariat right across Western Europe, let alone in the restless industrial cities of Detroit, Pittsburgh, Cincinatti and Chicago.

The Foreign Office wanted nothing from Ransome which might disappoint interventionists so they arranged to arrest him at the Finnish border and keep him quiet in jail. As one would happily expect, they were reckoning with the wrong man; Ransome entered Russia as a friend of Lincoln Steffens and brought back, in his unpolitical way, the irrefutable case against intervention.

It is hard now to imagine the life of journalists when their everyday reporting was so intertwined with the business of always duplicitous, generally lethal, dependably stupid diplomacy. Ransome took pains to avoid politics in England, writing for a living and fishing for fun. He spoke Russian, he was English, he was an obvious recruit at a time when the great game was as badly played as it always is, and he was reprehensibly honest. Being so, he makes his striking contribution to the shaping of the narrative of journalism and does so in virtue of being so like and unlike most colleagues: like them in courage, dedication, composure, nonchalance; unlike them in his understanding of other peoples (including their language), in unpolitical quickness of sympathy, in his sailor-traveller's tolerance of other mores, in the blessed simplicity of his conception of right conduct and duty.

When C. P. Scott read *Six Weeks in Russia in 1919* (it was, to the credit of the British, a bestseller) he invited Ransome to Manchester and offered him a free hand as the *Manchester Guardian*'s correspondent in Russia. In a characteristic twist of class privilege and its deceits in old England, the head of Scotland Yard, who liked him, wangled for Ransome the visas withheld by the Foreign Office and Ransome chugged back across the North Sea in the world's filthiest old steamer to Bergen and on to Estonia.

With astonishing calm he walked to and through the Soviet lines, talking his way politely out of being shot as a spy, found and talked to Lenin, whom he knew already and who had come round to feeling grateful for the way *Six Weeks in Russia* had given a human face to revolution. Ransome moved with his amazing ease of disposition between Red and White lines, while he compiled his dispatches for the *Manchester Guardian*, recovered Evgenia from the wrong side of the lines, spoke up with timely good cause on behalf of the Estonian peace treaty with the Russians and for the umpteenth time passed out with appalling stomach trouble.

Evgenia nursed him back to health in the quiet cold of the Baltic shores. Unhampered by censors, he wrote his plain, fair, domestic and exemplary articles, one of which, to general acclaim from the *Manchester Guardian*'s readership, told the story of Mira,[27] Karl Radek's sometime typist, an active socialist, who had become a cavalry brigadier, riding with the Cossacks from

Poland to the Crimea, her troops all the time armed, reinforced and clothed in British equipment sent for the use of the White army. And in another such article,[28] Ransome simply described the funeral of the great anarchist philosopher and leader, Prince Kropotkin, and the devastating authority, visible even in the cortège, of his proud, anarchic and aristocratic nose.

He wrote home about the famine and the typhus; he wrote a little masterpiece about a sailing trip with his new 8-ton yacht he took with 'the First Mate' (Evgenia) in the Baltic,[29] and played a little part in calming down Anglo-Russian relations when, rightly infuriated by the insolent militarism of the dreadful Lord Curzon, Bukharin and Litvinov were about to respond in kind. Ransome fixed up a walk in the woods, and the British head of mission, forbidden by the murderous Curzon to speak to the murderous Reds, bravely and on the quiet settled a compromise.

Then in late January 1924 Lenin died and the anchor of the Revolution was broken off. Trotsky was out of town, convalescing, and kept out of town. Zinoviev was shot. Stalin was poised for his terrible office. Ransome went home. He had done with reporting Russia after eight years of it[30] and its happiest legacy was his long, second marriage to Evgenia.

Scott at the *Manchester Guardian* sent him to Egypt and printed Ransome's articles with a note of his own to say: 'that they contradicted the policy of the paper but if these were the facts, the policy would have to change, and change it did'.[31] He went to China and his articles became *The Chinese Puzzle* which Unwin published in 1927 and the hiatus in Ransome's writing career started with a series of little essays on fishing,[32] which came far closer to his heart than did ever the awesome names and numbers of Russian war and civil war and revolutionary peace. C. P. Scott saw that the next capital to be in trouble was going to be Berlin. He asked Ransome to go as correspondent. Ransome declined and began to write *Swallows and Amazons*. It almost wrote itself.

We learn to live a life by finding a part in a story. A new form of productive labour – which is to say, a new kind of job – makes its historical debut. People do the job and live the life. It becomes a social role, maybe, with good fortune, a profession. When work becomes professional, it takes on respectability.

As we saw, across the years of deathly warfare, newspapers rose to their unprecedented prominence in the life of their times and stayed there. Ordinary people wanted to learn the news urgently; governing classes wanted to make the news in their own image. Both felt a duty to truth, at least intermittently; both craved the consolations of news fantasy.

These contradictions threw up the press lords, Northcliffe, Rothermere, Beaverbrook; Hearst, Pulitzer, Luce. They came in at the great portals of power – Congress, parliament – but they reeked, a little gamily, of demagoguery, jingoism, megalomania, worse. Lloyd George and Woodrow Wilson must needs shake hands with them, but as one palliating Lucifer.

The moral and social ambiguity of these men was and is reflected in their editors and reporters. Sought out and ostracised, mobbed and outlawed, awarded celebrity status by and debarred as hacks from the company of the *haut ton*, they have floated uncertainly between the honourable status of writer and the shameful one of a hired mouth with a nose above it trained only to sniff out bad smells. Political correspondents have had to learn to live a life as split and striated as that of their subject-matter, the politicians. Their best examples have found a particular kind of integrity; living so, they lent colour, drama, fulfilment to the collective life of the profession; their worst have served time, mere power, old corruption, and have been well paid on both sides for doing so.

Every early story helped, for better and worse, build the life of the political journalist into a career another generation could follow. Arthur Ransome, unpolitical man, nonetheless came from a social class and a personal experience which left him pretty well at ease with the famous and the powerful, and with ready access to both in London. As a writer in the New Grub Street of his day, practising a bit of journalism for casual earnings came naturally; dropping into the Foreign Office did so as well. When he got to Russia he made the same calm and courageous assumptions about his own inviolability and the common availability of other human beings, even if the other person was Lenin, and acted accordingly. He never betrayed his duty to tell the truth but he never compromised his natural patriotism either. Thus and thus his history becomes part of the story of political journalism.

It is instructive to see the similarities in a parallel biography. Konstantin Paustovsky was born in Kiev in 1893, nine years after Ransome, went to university in Moscow and, unable to join the Army (like Ransome) because of acute myopia, became a medical orderly on a hospital train, thus confirming the Russian metaphor, silhouetted by Tolstoy and Pasternak, that the mighty steam train captures the motherland's vast, slow destiny.

More to the point, after being sacked from the medical service for writing a satirical letter about the Tsar and after working in a munitions factory and then as a fisherman, he got a job as a journalist in Moscow. He puts one in mind of James Thurber's self-deprecating introduction that 'he has not worked as a cow-puncher, ranch-hand, stevedore, short-order cook, lumberjack or preliminary prizefighter';[33] the point about Paustovsky is that he mostly had, and this too is part of the political journalist's career. A little episode with an epileptic officer behind the lines, during which Paustovsky has to shoot the officer's dog when it nearly throttles him, reads in translation like Thurber in one of his most clenched understatements.

> 'You've got blood on your back,' said the innkeeper.
> 'It was the dog. He went for me. I shot him.'
> 'Oh the things that happen,' the innkeeper cried. 'What the world is coming to!'
> The officer had gone limp and quiet.[34]

Paustovsky's two brothers were killed in action on the same day. He had always read omnivorously the Russians, Scandinavians, French, Chekhov above all. He began to write, two forces compelling him. The first was that same wonderful simplicity and directness of perception he shared with all the great Russian writers such that to see the almond trees in blossom 'like brides' is as solidly set down as the second, his clear vision of his people, the workers and 'their intolerant, sober sense of right and wrong, as concrete as the burdens on their backs'.[35] By way of his living and his writing, as the Revolution approaches, he becomes convinced that no one can be at peace in Russia without 'defining his attitude to the working class'.

Never such innocence again, we might say with the poet. But all the worse for us if so. Paustovsky still keeps that purity of seeing and that straight allegiance before us as ideals of journalism when in 1917 he gets a job on a Moscow newspaper and is dispatched to send reports from a scruffy little town called Yefremov near Tula; his task is to find out 'what Turgenev's Russia is thinking about'.[36] He goes. He dreams repeatedly of a row of telegraph poles stretching across a snow-covered plain, meets the best-known agony aunt in the country, a man of 'pathological conceit, affectation and vanity', recites Blok and Lermontov passionately in a café to young working-class women who know the same poems by heart themselves, and is there writing in Yefremov on the amazing day when the Tsar is arrested in his train, the church bells crash out, a band is playing and people sing the 'Marseillaise'.

Paustovsky returns to Moscow and spends his days as reporter for the new, very short-lived paper, *Government by the People*, arguing the future with the Populist Socialists who were his colleagues and passed their spare time in the Journalists' Café. The café was, inevitably, smoke-filled, crowded, noisy; its coffee was bitter as quinine, its quarrels violent, its celebrities included Andrei Bely, author of *Petersburg*, Voloshin the poet, and 'king of the reporters', coughing, boisterous, brilliant and (of course) lovable Gilyarovsky. 'Time you switched from six to ten point type, young man, and from that to bold. Journalism is six-point, poetry ten-point, prose bold. Strap yourself to your chair and work.'[37]

Paustovsky is sent early in 1918 to cover Lenin's address to the demobilised, mutinous soldiers in the vast Lefortovo Barracks, waiting to go home after the bad peace has been patched up with Germany at Brest-Litovsk. 'Gradually, through the noise, I was beginning to make out the quiet, simple words. Lenin wasn't urging anyone to do anything. He was merely giving these embittered, inarticulate men the answers to their unspoken questions.'[38]

He reports regularly the meetings of the Central Executive in the Bolshoi Theatre, admiring Lenin, his gaiety, his ease, his certainty, reporting the attempted *coup d'état* by the faction called the Left Social Revolutionaries, dodging their bullets, until he is captured doing his reporting duty, first by anarchists then by Soviet soldiers, almost executed by both. He quits to succour his ailing mother and makes another Russian epic of a railroad journey to Kiev. The city is crazy, civil war at the gates, weddings and a job for him as literary editor within. His editor believes that literature is a form of teaching, a sermon, but 'it seemed to me a gift from the future. It reflected man's perpetual longing for perfect harmony and undying love, cherished in spite of love's daily birth and death ... draw[ing] us to the golden age of our desires.'[39]

Not often that journalists, even the greatest writers among them, write like that.

Paustovsky is press-ganged into a fatigue company of the Red Army with a drunken, murderous, abusive lunatic in command, finally and satisfyingly shot by one of his own soldiers. He writes when he can, finds his mother and sister, gets a new job in Odessa proof-reading the local paper and in December 1919 watches the appalling evacuation of terrified White-sympathising townsfolk barely in advance of the Red Army, clinging to gangplanks thrown across to the rescue ships, until the gangways themselves bend and give way and their 'terrible human load' falls into the sea to be drowned.

Revolution and civil war took their time spreading over the colossal geography of Russia. Paustovsky sees them come and go three times: in Moscow, in Kiev, in Odessa; and in Odessa he returns with indomitable hopefulness to his trade of journalism as well as the art of writing. He joins the staff of the *Seaman*, a newspaper written for that precise audience, translated the same day into French, English, German, always selling out in minutes.

The editor, Ivanov, appointed by the Sailors' Union, is a charmer, ex-reporter on the revolutionary byword *Russian Word*, generous-hearted, knew instinctively, deductively where to 'find copy'. The *Seaman* published news of the whereabouts of ships, the details of cruel and neglectful injustices on the part of shipping lines and individual captains, the names of dishonest boarding houses worldwide and those where lodgers were cornered by the Salvation Army. When the savage cold of the main office of the paper became so severe that the journalists couldn't write, Ivanov disobeyed strict local orders and ordered the chopping up of an enormous oak sideboard, big as a church, down in the basement. The house versifier commemorated him:

The press is vital to our land.
I'll guard it with my dying breath.
My pen will never leave my hand
Nor shall my colleagues freeze to death.

The staff loved the paper. The journalists themselves set the type and rolled off the sheets of differently coloured paper (originally intended to make the packets for tea-leaves), and all the while they talked the blood-stained, unknowable, literary, scarcely reported politics of the Revolution. Their one terrific newspaper scoop was to steal from the city's provincial committee the forme on which Lenin's famous 1921 speech on the New Economic Policy had been set up for official release in Odessa. 'The tea-wrappers rustled and the machine hummed, printing the historic speech.'[40] The whole staff – by then Paustovsky was assistant editor – was intensely excited and perhaps in danger. The issue sold out in minutes, the city buzzed, 'the sense of being citizens ... filled us with joy.' The only thing to match it in the redoubtable history of the *Seaman* was their publishing (for the first time) work by Isaac Babel.

The centrifuge of the Revolution, now disparaged among *bien pensant* historians but still the most stirring example of a people trying to grasp power of their own accord, whirled both Paustovsky and Ransome now closer to the centre, now to the very edge of events, dropping them now cold, now hungry, under fire but always observant, always hopeful. The huge upheaval of the society served the principles of their kind of journalism well. Steady, brave, untainted by any desire for power or even fame, they kept faith with the craft of writing and produced an artless personal record which took on the volume of history and the grandeur of art. Their achievement was as different as it is possible to be from that of a third worthy of the press, bigger by far than the Russian-speaking Englishman and English-speaking Russian, a colossus of the world to come and, as he rather assumed, the chorus of its conscience.

CHAPTER FOUR

Walter Lippmann: The Real Voice of America

No quantity in political and intellectual analysis is more casually invoked or less intelligently deployed than power. Power is the name of a conceptual blank. In a shrewd, all-too-brief analysis, Steven Lukes[1] marks out the obvious attributes of power: its necessarily coercive force (and therefore the distinction from assented-to authority); its key appearance at times of conflict; its *un*intentional manifestations as well as its being the blatant instrument of will. On its less visible side, he draws attention to its capacity not merely to coerce behaviour but to shape and therefore to exclude certain thoughts (a point dazzlingly made by the May 1968 graffito in Paris, 'ils pensent, donc je suis'). He classifies one-, two- and three-dimensional views of power. In the first, attention focuses on the relations between decision-making (order-issuing), subjective interests and conflict. The subject-matter in hand is the clash of groups and individuals. In the second, analysis takes in not only coercion but such dimmer, ubiquitous presences as influences, manipulation and exclusion. Covert behaviour is part of the field. In the third, analysis extends the field to include latent, even unacknowledged conflict, for example as between 'real and subjective interests' (a group may want what harms it). It includes not only 'power to ...' but also 'power over ...' The exercise of power is not a zero-sum game in which what one loses the other gains. Power may be generated in the creation of new social movements; the power of a crowd, for example, varies in efficacy according to its size and scope, its topographical theatre, its collective purposes.[2] Moreover, this more pervasive view of power commits the analyst to consider the inactivity of instruments, the force of circumstance, particularly the weight, continuity, factuality of social and political institutions.

Power by this token includes the sheer mass of cities and thrones and power, the only way to study which, it is suggested, is to see its conduct and its spectacles as an unbroken sequence of self-dramatisations. States, Clifford Geertz remarks, are as various as literatures. To understand them is to read the texts of their embodiment. He goes on:

> Investigations into the symbolics of power and into its nature are very similar endeavors. The easy distinction between the trappings of rule and its substance becomes less sharp, even less real; what counts is the manner in which, a bit like mass and energy, they are transformed into each other.[3]

To practise political journalism would be to take in (without being taken in by) Lukes's three dimensions *and* Geertz's symbolics. Let us see if it is the case that we find a sufficiently gifted individual taking the good luck of propinquity and the advantage of detachment in such a way as to be crowned king of the political journalists. The case in hand is Walter Lippmann.

Lippmann is a towering figure in the history of journalism and a significant one in the history of politics in the twentieth century. His unremittingly successful and eminent career lasted from the moment he left Harvard in 1910 to the months between 1965 and 1967 in which he used his regular column 'Today and Tomorrow', a thirty-six year feature first of the *Herald Tribune* and then (after 1962) of the *Washington Post*, to oppose Lyndon Johnson's war in Vietnam. He was an eager insider of the Woodrow Wilson administration during the First World War, and in a trice a lofty commentator in the pages of *New Republic*. He wrote resonant philippics against government policy; he was himself an active conspirator as well as proposer-columnist in the so publicly secretive gambits of Presidential nominations (once finding his own name tossed into the ballot); he was personal friend and particular enemy of half a dozen presidents; for fifty years, they asked him for advice, took it, ignored it and one of them at least set his staff to put Lippmann down and see him off.

Almost single-handedly and quite unreflectingly, Lippmann recast the whole scope of the feasible life of the journalist. Up to the moment of his entry on stage Britain's newspapers had editors, French and Italian ones had insurrectionists, American newspapers had reporters. Lincoln Steffens, Josiah Flynt (another early user of the word 'graft'[4]), H. L. Mencken, Ida Tarbell, Robert Park were a mixed bag of writers but they had in common a certain method which in turn implied, as methods do, a certain morality. They sought the facts which at that stage of their trade seemed uncomplicated, hard little particles which would settle into a straightforward narrative of their own accord.

Such facts were made to gleam in the muck through which the Olympian heroes of journalism were raking by the light they cast on corporate power. The muck the journalists raked was money, and they turned Theodore Roosevelt's pejorative into a badge of honour. Such a conception of reporting committed those who held it to a certain populism, even to socialist sympathy (although Mencken at least came to scorn democracy), but their avocation was, so to say, sociological rather than philosophical. The facts would speak for themselves and the Constitution would do the rest.

Lippmann changed all that. As a symptom, he can stand for the entry of the intelligentsia into everyday journalism; or for the opportunist advent of a wealthy cultural elite at the very intersection of politics and the press and at the exact moment of their mutual implosion; or for the anachronistic heroism with which Lippmann himself appealed to the Federalists' ideal of a polity given human shape and moral purpose by an interlocking network of intelligent publics; or for the hand-over-fist social climb of a clever, slightly petulant, hero-worshipping and sanctimonious young man with a great deal of charm and any number of personal virtues, capable in good faith of arranging to advance himself at the expense of less adroit colleagues by any means other than violence.[5] Signifying so much, Lippmann is his own best story. Its sound is soothing; there is no fury in it.

He was born in 1889 of wealthy Jewish immigrants on Lexington Avenue, Manhattan; he never afterwards referred to his Jewishness nor did it in any way impede his progress. He was an only child, enjoyed expensively educative vacations in Paris, Vienna, Florence, Venice, Ruskin in hand, and went in the natural course of things to Harvard in the fall of 1906. Among the *jeunesse dorée* he shone with a gilded radiance. The extraordinary intellectual freedoms of the place were patrolled by its legendary president Charles W. Eliot, and Lippmann was instructed in their content by such stars of old galaxies as Irving Babbitt, George Santayana (who compiled the lineage of 'the genteel tradition') and the doyen of American pragmatism, William James, who, impressed by one of Lippmann's essays in a student magazine, asked him, in the Cambridge way, to tea.

He had learned French and the classical languages at school and on the tour; he acquired Italian, German and enough Spanish from Santayana. Lippmann was a burly, strikingly handsome young man of a warm, impulsive nature. He made friends easily and his lifelong tendency to seek out and venerate certain men as heroes came in part from his disposition and in part from that micro-climate in the Victorian weather which nurtured hero-worship and the idea of great men as the twin energies of history. Lippmann may be offered to us as a pragmatist theoretician of the tensions between power and authority,[6] but his veering judgements on the putative presidents of his time, made and in the making, bear witness to his Diogenic search for high-minded and visionary leaders such as would have thrived in either Cambridge. Lippmann finally found his ideal incarnation of the born leader in the substantial frame of Teddy Roosevelt.

He also met and became close friends with the English socialist Graham Wallas, since 1886, member with Shaw, H. G. Wells and Beatrice Webb of the Fabian Society, which was dedicated to the rational understanding and reform of Great Britain in the name of social justice. The society eventually became the intellectual arm of the Labour Party and although Wallas himself got fed up with it, his kind of high-minded, radically earnest policy-and-political analysis which Lippmann found in such of his books as *Human Nature in Politics* and (in 1914) his ironically titled *The Great Society* spoke straight to the big heart of the young American.

He became (briefly) a socialist, indignant for social justice along with his friend and classmate John Reed but quick to use his charm and his idealism to win the friendship and patronage of the already celebrated Oliver Wendell Holmes and the about-to-be-mighty Judge Learned Hand. The same attributes led him to quit graduate study under Santayana and brought him to the door of Lincoln Steffens. While Steffens was lecturing at Harvard, Lippmann had promptly, shyly, remorselessly made his acquaintance, and now, in a winning turn of phrase he used more than once, wrote to Steffens to say 'what I have dreamed of doing is work under you.'[7] Steffens took him on as assistant at *Everybody's*. He did some rough trade journalism. He completed his basic training. He wrote for left-wing magazines like *International* and *The Masses*, he rode the crest of the rather low, brief wave of socialism in America, but (like Wallas) he too became bored by the messiness, the noise and sheer incompetence of the comrades, and took his enthusiasm, what George Eliot elsewhere called a 'high objectless yearning', as well as an impatient, even splenetic, temper elsewhere.

In 1913 he brought out his first book, *A Preface to Politics*, the sort of thing amazingly well-read, optimistic young men at either Cambridge tend to write, but singular in being the first book to Freudianise its subject. On the strength of it he got a job on the neonate political-critical-cultural-progressive-respectable weekly *New Republic*. It made quite a splash. He could say what he liked. He began a new book. He went to London and met the literary leftists of the *New Statesman*, signing them up for contributions back home. He came home as war broke out, polished off the new book, a pompous effusion inexcusably titled *Drift and Mastery*, fell out with John Reed (who went off to join Ransome in Russia and a little later to write *Ten Days that Shook the World*) and thereafter became the absolutely punctual and reliable clock-puncher and copywriter he remained all his life, never missing a deadline, never doing anything less than a workmanlike job.

He also became, although gradually, an influential advocate of his country's going to war. He brought back his well-chosen haul of contacts with London's leftish intelligentsia; he was as deeply Anglophile as Harvard mostly made its progeny; he had a juicy job and free hand on the *New Republic*; he had met, been patronised by and hero-worshipped Teddy Roosevelt; he was held in universal esteem for his charm, his good looks, his gift for high-principled political trimming, his enviable ease with big words and capital letters, his unfailing veracity, his tact with the great. He couldn't fail, and he didn't.

His appointment to the *New Republic* restored Lippmann to the little bit of social topography where he most flourished. He did so because such a circle reproduced, at only a few years' remove, the ardent, high-souled intellectualising of Harvard as well as its thick insulation from some of the harsher facts of life.

It is always easy to scoff at such exclusiveness, and even easier to live within it and ignore the scoffers. Insomuch as political elites are hardly likely to relinquish their mystery along with their privileges, it is probably better that there are such journalists as Lippmann (and there have been very few) who move easily in the same circles. But the cost is high. Once his distaste for radicalism, every bit as much a social as it was an intellectual thing, turned Lippmann fastidiously away from his classmate John Reed and the socialist congregation, he had no alternative way of grounding his experience in the life of that elusive historical entity, ordinary Americans. Presidents and other such celebrities are, no doubt, ordinary enough – they bleed when cut, they tremble at last things – but the twentieth century teaches that fame and power combine to make those who win them decidedly peculiar.

At such a moment of recognition Lippmann comes into his own. He thought all his life about the bearers of power whom he had known closer up than any other journalist. The problem for him, one which he scanted and which the cloud of portentous approval through which he moved all his life kept obscured, was how to connect these men to the abstract periods he rolled over their deeds. Lippmann took to high-mindedness young and one can't regret it. Too few journalists can even spell the best names of human aspiration and nobility. But using words, as he did, with dignity bestowed a manner on the man. Dignity soon expands to a big belly. Lippmann's quickness and charm, his pleasure in the company of the mighty, his quest for the philosopher-king, his sensitivity to slights, his commonplace snobbery compounded niceness with pomposity. If he is the greatest journalist of his time, we had best follow the making of his character in his story pretty faithfully. Achievement and mission can only be understood as the moral product of character.

So it was no surprise that Lippmann left the Socialist Party in 1915 rightly breathing scorn on the 'dilettante rebel [still with us] who so often mistakes a discussion in a café for an artistic movement or a committee meeting for a social revolution'.[8]

To give him his due, from the start he wanted to write in a new political language, just as his Harvard classmate T. S. Eliot wanted to write in a new poetic one that would 'purify the language of the tribe'. The First World War demanded such a language; it looked to Lippmann as if it would be the occasion to combine his own love of European culture, America's constitutional ideals and the new kind of political pragmatism his teachers at Harvard had contrived.

Gradually he moved away from his boyish enthusiasm for Teddy Roosevelt's Bull Moose gunslinging towards Woodrow Wilson's Princetonian moralism. Always in search of a great leader and repelled by the raucous *mêlées* in which American democracy sweated out its decisions, Lippmann gave Wilson *New Republic*'s editorial support and at twenty-seven was rewarded by dinner at the White House. He sat next to Edward House, Anglophile Texan colonel, turned himself into a fervent advocate of America's going to war in 'the cause of liberalism and the hope of an enduring peace', sent fulsome messages of support to the President, in May 1917 married a gorgeous young socialite called Faye Albertson, and then went off to wage war from Colonel House's covert policy and propaganda unit at the New York Public Library.

Lippmann was nearer the centre of power politics than he ever chose to be again. Across the New Year of 1918 he worked all the hours that came on Wilson's famous 'Fourteen Points' for a peace agreement and postwar settlement. The fourteen points were intended to catch and hold the attention of the people of Europe in spite of their governments. But governments then and now will not be ignored or bypassed, and the people, wherever they may be found, are never self-conscious enough, let alone knowledgeable enough, to find ways of bending governments to their will.

So the fourteen points were blunted and Germany made hostage to reparation and revenge. But Lippmann kept up on behalf of his masters the attempt to present the war and the peace which would come out of it as a moral crusade. Newly gazetted Captain Lippmann went off to a conference of the Allied powers on propagandising this view – a view, one had better add, which by July 1918 could only be held by those who had remained a long way from the battlefront, and there found Northcliffe,[9] well qualified in fervour, uncertainty and ignorance.

By October the German army was spent and the nation on the brink of famine and of revolution. The Germans appealed for peace on the basis of the fourteen points. The Allies cut up rough as they saw their territorial gains challenged and their cupidity towards reparations the Germans couldn't afford anyway thwarted. Armistice came on 11 November, the Allies began their deadly planning of the Versailles settlement and set off on the short road back to war in 1939. Lippmann's endearing enthusiasm and unamiable sycophancy overflowed in a gushing letter to Edward House:

> I must write you this morning because I couldn't possibly tell you to your face how great a thing you have achieved … This is the climax of a course that has been as wise as it was brilliant, and as shrewd as it was prophetic. The President and you have more than justified the faith of those who insisted that your leadership was a turning point in modern history …[10]

Admittedly Lippmann wrote this effusion on Armistice Day. But it is a token of his journalism: utterly uncynical; impulsively attracted to moralising power; sincerely enthusiastic; innocently open-handed with hostages to posterity. It is an unexpected list of qualities for the doyen of the century's political journalists and, on a cheerful day, a heartening historical career to admire.

From Paris Lippmann returned home to the *New Republic* and acknowledged John Maynard Keynes's utterly bleak judgement on the final peace treaty as clinching. Most of Keynes's long essay was published in the journal and Lippmann, ditching his allegiance to Wilson, sat back and applauded.[11] Journalist of the day, he was bought up for a regular column in *Vanity Fair*, then as now a monthly split between a glittering show of intellectual seriousness and the showy glitter of fashion accessories, whether clothes, jewels, perfumes or ideas. Then in 1922 he settled with old Joe Pulitzer's son and heir, Ralph, to become the famous Frank Cobb's deputy editor at the grand New York daily the *World*.

Lippmann was clapped into his new chair by the éclat which accompanied publication of his book *Public Opinion*. It *is* a classic, surely, in the analysis of that commodity form of media, the audience. In his own version of the grand manner – a good deal of Plato, a glimpse of Madison – he busily sawed away at the branch he was sitting on, no doubt aware that the success and stability of the American daily newspaper was as assured as the dominance of his nation over the world. His argument was that the common people simply could not assimilate, let alone decide upon, the complexities of world politics. A new class in a new kind of policy institution would have to do the work assigned to public opinion. Journalist-intellectuals could only do their bit by processing information for the benefit of the power elite. Democracy is reduced, without relish or regret, to the pious ratification of decisions taken by a technical staff entirely removed from daily experience.

You can't say Lippmann was wrong; you can only say things might have been done better. At the *World*, he certainly didn't behave as though he believed his own argument. There Lippmann joined some of the best journalists alive. Herbert Swope, Ring Lardner, E. B. White before he went off to start the *New Yorker*, were all on the books and when Cobb died of cancer in 1923 Lippmann took over as editor, hired James Cain, stood up hard for his staff, wrote a daily editorial and was much in demand at the grand Council on Foreign Relations, an informal group of public opinionators nominating themselves from the universities, the classy newspapers, the well-connected banks and businesses.

He was a prodigious worker. In the summer he used to quit Manhattan for an upstate house on the Hudson, write his daily editorial and then anything up to 4,000 words a day for his next book. Lippmann and his wife Faye had no children but adopted a ward, Jane Mather, who came to live with them; for all his devotion to her, nothing broke into his stern schedule or his busy travelling between the power elite of his country and the world.

Those journeys brought little solace, whatever they might do for vanity. The force of circumstance for a journalist as serious about his world-historical trade as Lippmann was enough in the 1920s and 1930s to break anybody's spirit, especially somebody who had gone so hopefully to Paris in 1918. In Europe tides of social revolution came in across Russia and went out over Germany; Mussolini declared the advent of a new kind of *Duce* who hardly fitted the company of the Federalists. At home, even before the 1929 Wall Street crash, the spectre of revolution flitted through people's dreams, and the state of the nation under supine Presidents did nothing for the peace of mind of more faithful democrats than Lippmann. He had concluded in *Public Opinion* that that democrat was mistaken who believed 'that if political power could be derived in the right way, it would be beneficent'[12] and found that the mere instrumentality of power is the crux of politics, not its legitimacy nor its origin.

This was heresy at the *World*; it is heretical still. It is also not self-evidently true, however much a piety believed in by all latterday makers of US foreign policy. Lippmann can't be held responsible for their more irresponsible sallies, but he was a formative influence of the view that foreign policy was best kept well away from the democratic process except as a ratification of elite wisdom well after the event.

The history of Lippmann's intellectual career is not so much the familiar American fable about the former egalitarian leftist moving over the years out of radical extremism into the dependable upholstery of conservatism. Rather, Lippmann was a unique figure in American politics, the statuesque thinker-moralist, direct heir to Hamilton, Adams and Madison, who came to repudiate the people and to commend power to the hands of a very different but no less unprecedented figure in twentieth-century politics, the highly educated, systems-confident, authoritarian-rationalist, planner-manager.

We shall see a lot of this figure later, when the United States goes to war in Vietnam, but he proves an odd protégé for the Harvard class of 1910. To understand how Lippmann contributed to the formation of such a leading character in the cast of modernity, it is necessary to follow more of his efforts to write American politicians into the role of hero of the times.

He tried Al Smith for the part. In 1928 Smith was a runner for the Democratic nomination, well equipped with Irish Catholic immigrant forbears, boyhood scullery work at Fulton Fish Market, Tammany Hall training, state governorship, social reform legislation and big crowd, big city, big noise charm and popular appeal. Herbert Hoover was his stolid and solid opponent and, although the Democratic partiality of the *World* required Lippmann to treat Hoover to a little vitriolic abuse, he thought both men equally 'men of destiny' (his phrase). He (unlike Evelyn Waugh) saw through Mussolini with no trouble when he met him in 1929 and summarised the decade with what, at this distance, one can only see as a quite unearned loftiness in his new book *A Preface to Morals*.[13] The great man who is its leading character is fearless and unacquisitive, moving 'easily through life' without 'doubt or ambition' since 'nothing gnawed at his vitals' (Lippmann could turn a stately period but he was unsparing of a stout cliché) and whether finding life comedy, tragedy or farce 'would affirm that it is what it is, and that the wise man can enjoy it'.

No doubt such an attitude made up a little for the unaccommodating nature of contemporary events. Lippmann found democracy in incurable bad health, and dismal politics were made worse when, in October 1929, the Wall Street crash rolled round the world and the *World*. The Pulitzers, who had left it undercapitalised for years, pulled the plug and Lippmann, shamelessly quoting Bunyan's Mr Valiant-for-Truth in his last editorial, lost his job.

Not for long. He was already, at forty-one, the biggest name in political journalism and his wealth was hardly touched by the crash. The *New York Times* tried to capture him, the *Herald Tribune* did so. They would pay his globe-trotting expenses (essential to the job, but including restorative weeks at Bernard Berenson's big little place on the Via Bolognese), 25,000 dollars a year and a big haul from syndication. His first column, signed under the head 'Today and Tomorrow', appeared in September 1931; the last one in 1967.

The *Herald Tribune* was a Republican businessman's newspaper but for all Lippmann's departure from his early and short-lived radicalism, he was no stooge of the business lobby; keenly read as he was (every morning in those days), his readership often thought him a dangerous leftist and far-too-freethinker.

He remained his own man but that man was pretty well in thrall to and enthralled by the way things were. He was, in any case, the first journalist to play his part, having written it himself.

This was, we might say now, his biggest accomplishment, greater by far than his worthy additions to the literature of pragmatism. He gathered up his remarkable education, his social privilege, his precocious success and the extraordinary collection of his powerful acquaintance and turned it all to the good account of his plump, stately and periodic prose. The result was his own unmistakable idiom, an intellectual signature as legible and famous as any great American writer of the century.

It wasn't that his judgement was infallible or that he had the traditional nose for news or even for the readiest topic to hand. He scarcely wrote about the 1929 disaster and while Martha Gellhorn was writing her letters to Harry Hopkins on the condition of the working class in America, Lippmann was fretting about a balanced budget and the bad example which wholesale government borrowing would set the poor. He learned nothing about the new economics from his friendship with Keynes and, having come to know Franklin Roosevelt personally, in November 1931 dismissed him in a long-notorious miscall as 'a kind of amiable boy scout'.[14]

The boy scout became America's greatest president of the century, beloved by a whole country other than its nastiest, richest members, and opposed by Lippmann all the way to the White House as a slippery charmer with few principles and no grasp of public matters. Lippmann jollied himself along in his column by saying that while things may be tough for the young, 'For them there remains, come what may, their own energy and the richness of the earth, the heritage of human invention and skill and the corpus of human wisdom. They need no more ...'[15] In the end, Lippmann came out for Roosevelt, the readership was scandalised and human invention did its bit for the young by inventing the New Deal.

Not for the first or the last time Lippmann turned his judgement back to front. He backed the Deal, backed deficit financing, abandoned the gold standard and signed on for Keynes's economics.

His readers saw him and his President as outright leftists and the new wealth tax as well down the road to communism. Hearst's newspapers were flecked with foam, the right was on the march up one side of the hill and the left up the other. Governor Huey Long presaged an American version of National Socialism, abruptly left headless by his assassination, and Lippmann's nerve, never strong, began to give. Seized of a fear of dictatorship in spite of his taste for Platonic philosopher-kings, when Roosevelt swept back to power in 1936 and set out to pack the Supreme Court with New Deal supporters, Lippmann accused him of power-drunkenness, a taste for dictatorship, enacting a *coup d'état*.

Lippmann doesn't come too well out of his observations of Hitler and fascism. He had nothing to say about the pogroms or about Mussolini's invasion of Abyssinia, nothing about Spain; he wrung his hands over French and British passivity and cowardice, but thought, even so, that Chamberlain was making the best of a bad job. He didn't foresee the humiliation and disgrace of the 1938 Munich settlement; thereafter the outbreak of war was only a matter of time.

Lippmann was in London in July 1939, keeping company with a group of the English elite (including Churchill, who wanted to meet him), who opposed appeasement of Hitler. Joe Kennedy, by contrast, Jack's father and American ambassador in London on the strength of his millions, was all for giving Hitler anything he wanted and got out quick when the bombing began. By the time Lippmann was home, war had been declared and he became the forceful and dignified advocate of giving help in kind to Britain without committing troops as America had done in 1917.

Give Lippmann his due, nothing broke his fixed routines. When the time for his fact-and-interview-gathering European vacation came up in early 1940, off he blithely went to gaze eastwards from the Maginot line only four months before the French surrender shook him into a determination to do all he could to rejoin America's destiny to the England (his word) for which he felt so strongly. 'Destiny' was a sound enough word to use in 1940 and Lippmann used it. He paid no attention to Japan and precious little (then or subsequently) to the plight of his fellow Jews, but the then hideous alliance of the Reich and Soviet Russia was justification enough for him, if not for all Americans, a monstrous and unprecedented threat to the great American freedoms.

So he helped the national hero of the First World War, General John Pershing, write an influential and powerful plea to help the British with armaments (antique destroyers, in fact); and he chided Roosevelt with irresolution until the President was back in power in November 1940, when Lippmann promptly sent him a congratulatory telegram and threw all his weight into preparing his partly hostile, partly indifferent readership for military production and the draft.

His high style matched up to such an occasion. There was a proper weight and volume to his phrases which on another typewriter might have sounded pretentious:

Almost all of us grew up in an environment of such easy optimism that we can scarcely know what is meant ... by the satanic will. We shall have to recover this forgotten but essential truth – along with so many others that we lost when, thinking we were enlightened and advanced, we were merely shallow and blind.[16]

Five weeks later the Japanese struck at Pearl Harbour and the argument about whether or not to join the Allies was over. The economy, tided over the worst of days by the New Deal, would now expand colossally to fill to overflowing the nation's bank accounts and, in 1945, open a forty-odd year era during which, Americans would conclude, Cold War kept the great consumer peace.

The United States had been in uniform only a few months when Lippmann, dauntless as ever, flew to London and, in a swift sporting tour, captured conversations with Churchill and Eisenhower, was briefed by Keynes on the Bretton Woods settlement he would single-handedly contrive in 1945, and fulfilled his quest for a man of destiny by meeting de Gaulle once again, befriending him for life. In de Gaulle, he discerned that ideal leader who walked with history, faced down evil, kept up the liberty France itself invented, and spoke the kind of prose whose rhythms moved in Lippmann's bloodstream. Democracy had elected too few such men, and indeed de Gaulle came up to scratch. He redeemed Vichy and he later did for the rebellious parachute colonels.

Lippmann had a quiet war. He gazed at the battle view from the same eminence as the commander-in-chief, and when in 1943 he published *US Foreign Policy: Shield of the Republic*[17] he sold half a million copies because it set out, plainly and masterfully, a postwar world of interlocking alliances and realms of influence which would, the idea was, neutralise communism without requiring of the United States the office of a world policeman on duty no matter where trouble flared up. Woodrow Wilson's puritan righteousness, still deep in Lippmann's character, would find expression much more in terms of fellow-feeling between a world fellowship of constitutional liberals than in the impossible idealism of a global federation.

Roosevelt, mortally ill, was again acclaimed by his country as President for his legendary fourth term, Lippmann by then the only one of his electorate with any misgivings, and went off to Yalta to divide up the world with Stalin and Churchill. Churchill produced his infamous back-of-an-envelope distribution of the zones of influence.

Rumania	Russia 90%
Greece	Great Britain 90%
Yugoslavia	50–50
Hungary	50–50
Bulgaria	Russia 75%, the others 25%

Stalin studied the sheet for a moment, and then silently pencilled a large check by the figures.[18]

Plenty of people died on that check, but so they would have done on any other. Roosevelt, you might say, was one of them: the colossal strain of the years in office upon his crippled body broke his capacious heart, and Lippmann greeted the peace with pretty well his first completely unqualified eulogy of the dead hero whose name was by now, at least at home, hardly better known than his own.

Lippmann gets the credit for the phrase 'Cold War' as Churchill does for 'Iron Curtain'[19] and he also gets the credit – a very great deal of it – for seeing the shape of its menace before anyone else in Washington, as well as for his principled opposition to it (allowing for occasional retrenchments) over the first twenty-odd years of its waging. The two disgraceful omissions from Lippmann's wartime writing and his extended, necessary meditations upon the moral conduct of the world at war were the death camps and the atomic bombs. His sharp criticism of the readiness with which America and Britain filled the political and emotional hole left by the disappearance of the Nazis from the world stage with the old bogey of communist egalitarianism was punctual and punctilious, and all the better for coming from such a pillar of the Constitution.

The fight to deter the United States from defining its foreign policy in terms of hatred for and obstruction of anything the Soviets might be up to was the biggest of Lippmann's career, and he couldn't possibly win it. No journalist could, and it provides us with a measure of a journalist's mighty work that at best it bears its witness not only to how the world is but how it ought to be and might have been. It is, in the philosopher's algebra, a counterfactual business. Good journalism can only criticise what actually happened by pointing to what might have happened instead.

Lippmann saw that the United States would seek to line up its subordinates, whether European or its twenty stooge nations in Latin America, in order to put down anyway and if possible humiliate the USSR. Faithful to his ethical pragmatism, he commended a recognition of the wants, assumptions and needs of others, in this case the Soviet view that eastern Europe was its backyard, that Germany had twice devastated the motherland in twenty-five years, and that balancing power and not exerting it more than one needs to in order to keep that balance was the better part of valour. Churchill was also on the anti-leftist rampage and as Lippmann told Secretary of State James Byrnes, the Right had been too disgraced by fascism to give any kind of moral lead into postwar life.

The British people were sufficiently of the same view to rout Churchill and his genteelly right-wing party in the general election of 1945. Byrnes, persuaded by Lippmann's heterodox politics, invited him to become head of a new State Department propaganda office. It was a very powerful position. The best thing Lippmann did for journalism was refuse the offer. He had things to say in public.

The short, secret and intense conflict at the centre of American power in the summer of 1945 fixed the position of nuclear weaponry in the Cold War. It confirmed the weapons, on each side of the iron curtain, as the responsibility of politicians and the military, refusing to submit the question to public judgement. The power conflict denied science itself any role in deciding mass destruction as a deliberate policy in human life.

Having refused office, Lippmann knew nothing of this debate. He was not an imaginative man in the sense that he intuitively grasped the import of other people's experience. Hiroshima meant nothing to him as an awful ineliminable presence in human memory and imaginings. He dealt in abstractions and was attired in their full habit. Nonetheless he knew and said that American power was overwhelming, would puff itself up further yet, and fatally lacked not only the practical wisdom which teaches humility 'but also the good manners and courtesy of the soul which alone can make great power acceptable to others'.[20]

Nearly sixty years after this was written, after Baroness Thatcher and President Reagan and Dr Kissinger, it may seem merely risible to ask even for good manners, let alone humility. But in the drama of world forces as Lippmann daily wrote it, he was above all magnanimous in writing parts for such forgotten Bostonian maidens as modesty, charity and grace. These creatures, slight but steely, were at their best at the limits of social and political power.

So Lippmann warned against unthinking hostility towards the Soviets at the same time as he criticised Stalin's assorted shows of bellicosity and was abused on all sides for his pains. Then on 5 March 1946 at Fulton, Missouri, Churchill, out of office but in his highest style, drew on the full armoury of his rhetoric to align America and Britain side-by-side against the merest hint of military obduracy by his sometime allies, on the other side of the iron curtain.

Cold War was declared and Lippmann spoke out so candidly against it he estranged any number of All-American readers and acquaintances. When he went on one of his grand tours around the European capitals in April 1946 he came back convinced and horrified that the British were using the defeated German Army in readiness to hold a frontier against the Soviets and pulling the United States with them into the manufacture of their very own, vastly heavier and more absolutely cast and riveted iron curtain. Lippmann was fifty-seven and he spent most of the next twenty years set against his government.

After Churchill's Fulton speech one more document clicked and turned the lock of American foreign policy on any door through to mediation with the undoubtably horrible Molotov, Soviet Foreign Minister, and his hideous master, Stalin, who tied with Hitler and Mao Zedong as top killer of the century. The document that best encapsulates the many dimensions of the Americans' anti-communism, their suspicion of the Soviets and their unreflective certainty of their own admirableness, is George Kennan's famous Long Telegram of 1946. There could hardly have been a single more cited, more influential, more completely expressive statement in the epoch.

The paper was subsequently published in *Foreign Affairs* in 1947 as 'The sources of soviet conduct' and circulated simply everywhere. It appeared under the cypher 'X', although the authorship was unmistakable to anyone in the trade, and, under his alias, Kennan announced in magniloquent prose that the advent of the Cold War was America's historic and unrefusable opportunity to assume leadership of what would shortly be described as the free world.

It was a simple, stirring tale whose occlusions, caricatures and comic-strip plot all appealed nicely to political executives on each side of the Atlantic. The plot was boldly unsupported by facts in any form, most notably lacking the terrible statistic of the Soviet death-toll of more than 20 million between 1941 and 1945. Indeed, the Second World War is mentioned only as the occasion for the dislodgement of the British from the throne of power and the assumption of its heritage by the United States.[21]

By contrast, though without acknowledging the casualties, Lippmann saw the Russians as engaged in a massive and suspicious exercise of self-defence so complete nothing could breach it, especially Germans. He wanted a foreign policy which would treat all difficulties, points of tension and consequences of inattention not as every one the moment of international inflammability but as separate units of misunderstanding. Keeping an eye on pragmatism's injunction to avoid mistaking stupidity for evil,[22] he enjoined avoiding crisis by *not seeing the world in such a frame*.

It couldn't be done. In 1947 the President enunciated the Truman Doctrine. The British were almost bankrupt and could no longer help fight on behalf of the nasty Right in the Greek civil war; Greece and Turkey appealed for help to the USA and characteristically the supernal new power made this, to Lippmann's distaste, into the opportunity to declare support for any 'free peoples … resisting attempted subjugation by armed minorities or by outside pressures'. Thus Truman and Dean Acheson, the haughty new Secretary of State, took the first steps on the road to Vietnam.

But the biggest European question of the day was the solvency of the continent itself, the other side of a steadily narrowing Atlantic and the biggest, most booming economy that warfare along with its consequent energies, effort and money, had ever created. The Left was strong all over Europe. It had justly thrived in the struggle against the abominable Right; it had its long connections with the Comintern; even Britain had a Labour government armed with a landslide majority. The collapse of national economies – France, Italy, Britain, the Lowlands, let alone Germany – was an immediate possibility. In a gesture of enormous simplicity, innocence and generosity – however much one must add to those ingredients the old smell of self-interested *imperium* – General George Marshall, Secretary of State and most honest of Americans, invited all European nations to take part in a continent-wide programme of reconstruction paid for out of the vast American budget surplus.

He launched the plan, commemorated in his name till the end of history, on behalf of the Administration at the Harvard commencement on 5 June 1947. The programme had not yet cleared Congress, brimming with Republican anti-communist hate as well as the usual snarls about there being 'no grasp of any business principles'[23] in the Plan. Stalin and Molotov were badly rattled; they desperately needed the capital; they knew the scheme meant they would never see the cash from Germany which they craved as some kind of reparation for all the Nazis had done to Russia; they dared not open the hoarded darknesses of twenty-five years of their post-revolutionary rule. They knew, as the State Department knew, that if they and their satraps took the money they would have to forswear the ideological extravagance of their economic policy. Molotov cut out any Soviet participation with a histrionic huff in the conference chamber and made sure that the so-far-democratically-elected governments of Poland and Czechoslovakia swept out as well.

The United States and Britain hated the admittedly hateful Soviet leaders. They began to plan for a merging of their sectors of portioned-out Germany. The Soviets went home to their blasted and impoverished land, the remaining Europeans applied for 20 billion dollars over the next four years, and the dollar divided Europe and ruled the waves of the world trade cycle for the rest of the century.

The American centres of power – Washington and its never-very-critical press – seethed with an ineradicable hatred of communism. At this distance one can say that Lippmann kept his nerve and his balance when all about him important people lost both. He had no truck with the hysterics who wanted to drop atomic bombs on the enemy and he always viewed the construction of the Federal German Republic as a quite unjustifiable perpetuation of the consequences of war, let alone an imposition of American power.

He was right, all right. American troops in Germany would see in the new millennium and Lippmann had been dead for nearly two decades before Germany became once more its own, single nation.

It struggled to be so even in 1948. The Soviets closed the roads into four-nation Berlin. They wanted urgently to block a West German state and to force the Allies out of the capital which was at once a powerful symbol and a rich trophy. Blockade seemed insuperable. Amazingly, in one of the most inventive and effortful collaborations of the Cold War, it was overcome. Between 24 June 1948, when all the ground routes were closed, and mid-September 1949, 2.4 million tons of flour, meat, vegetables, chocolate, coal, blankets, fuel – no bombs nor bullets – were flown into Tempelhof airport and another half-dozen improvised airstrips by devoted aircrews, plenty of whom had been flying bombers in the same sky four years before.

The Berliners themselves were quite clear where they stood: a quarter of a million of them outside the Reichstag building to hear the young and old warhorses of the Left – Neumann, Reuter, Willy Brandt – pledge not to capitulate to the Russians. The blockade was cracked and Lippmann, who spoke German, knew Berlin, had met political leaders in Poland and Czechoslovakia as well as in both Germanies, celebrated its end as a victory, for sure, but also as a faint sign that steely resourcefulness as well as resolute peaceability might also win the day, one day.

He didn't give Truman any credit, however. He even urged him to resign before the 1948 election and was as dumbfounded as everybody else when Truman defeated Thomas Dewey and was comfortably returned to the White House. Startled but grand as ever, in November 1948 Lippmann left for Europe and dinner first with Franco, then the Pope.

By early 1950 the arctic cold of this new kind of war had settled into permafrost. The Russians had successfully exploded a trial atom bomb; the Chinese had completed an appalling civil war and Mao Zedong had assumed power on behalf of the party; the President had mobilised the 1940 Smith Act to put in train the deportation of 300 subversives and to ensure the round-the-clock surveillance of a great many more, and Senator Joseph McCarthy reared up monstrously holding 'a piece of paper with the names of two hundred and five communists presently employed in the State Department'.[24]

Lippmann, compelled as much by aesthetics and snobbery as by a moral politics, viewed McCarthy with complete distaste. The man was a coarse, florid, sweaty bully who spoke vulgar prose and traded in melodrama. Lippmann himself, his reputation making him untouchable, had little to say about the hothouse neuroses which poisoned the air and the judgement of both Congress and Administration for so long, destroying careers, executing the Rosenbergs ('Mr President, those people have to fry,' said the Attorney General), defiling the country's good name. As usual, Lippmann conducted himself as one who couldn't be touched by the spattering kind of dirt thrown up by the crowds of conspirators and sycophants jostling commonplace men as they exercised their absolute power. He wrote only of the great abstracts which were called down to fill out rumour and justify war.

So he addressed McCarthy merely in passing and was caustic (in print) about Dean Acheson's paying such *canaille* any attention at all. The great affairs of state not the petty ones were the business of the pair of them, and they were pretty great just then, as the most mighty battle of Cold War broke out in Korea and nobody knew quite what to do or whom to blame.

The blame is unclear even now. Things had been at their darkest when, on 16 December 1949, Mao had concluded a difficult and ambiguous alliance with Stalin, and it then seemed to the Washingtonians as if the iron curtain stretched first from Stettin to Trieste, and then from Sofia to Shanghai. Korea had been casually split along the usual power lines in 1945 and the Americans had run a puppet state in the south until 1948 when Dr Syngman Rhee with his Ph.D. from Princeton had been assigned the powers of a dictatorship only death would manage to take back from him. In the north, land reform by Kim Il Sung and the same robust methods with those who disagreed with him as Dr Rhee used in the south had exiled class enemies and concentrated hostility on either side of the 38th parallel. As the American general who was effectually governor until 1948, John Hodge, wrote, 'We are dealing with poorly educated Orientals … who stubbornly and fanatically hold to what they like and dislike'. The not-so-very-well-educated Occidentals in Washington had written a little before fighting started in Korea:

> The Kremlin is inescapably militant. It is inescapably militant because it possesses and is possessed by a worldwide revolutionary movement, because it is the inventor of Russian imperialism, and because it is a totalitarian dictatorship … It is quite clear, from Soviet theory and practice that the Kremlin seeks to bring the free world under its dominion by the methods of Cold War.

This was the policy statement of the National Security Council's memorandum 68, written in 1950 by Paul Nitze, toughest of cold warriors. Lippmann's phrase now characterised an era and the world's attitude towards it.

The Korean War began after a couple of years' skirmishing along the 38th parallel, the equipping of a hundred thousand young Koreans with the very latest death-dealing toys, and the momentary defeat of Dr Rhee in an election he had been careless enough to permit.

Truman and the new American will-to-power turned Korea into a test of American resolutions. American forces were committed, the United Nations was summoned to stand up for the Free World, and after General MacArthur had been forced to retreat further than was compatible with his manliness, he gathered up the colossal firepower of his nation in the Pacific and surged up across the frontier until he was ready, as he once put it in a lively little interview, 'to have dropped between thirty and forty atomic bombs ... strung across the neck of Manchuria ... [to] spread behind us a belt of radioactive cobalt, from the Sea of Japan to the Yellow Sea'.[25]

Fifty years later the historian shivers at such dementia. MacArthur's arrogant vanity got him the sack from Truman for insubordination, and a tickertape welcome from his adoring New Yorkers. *Lèse-majesté* and Far Eastern incineration were the tropes of his tactics. Lippmann learned from his old friend James Reston of the *New York Times*[26] that the Chinese would square a settlement in Korea in return for a pay-off in Taiwan (then Formosa). Acheson, roaring cold warrior, dismissed the idea. Lippmann was angry. The fighting with the Chinese, like so much of his nation's policy, had far less to do, he judged, with keeping the world safe and American power well placed than it had to do with quieting half-crazy and wholly ignorant anti-communist senators. At every turn he found his cautious, traditional precepts flouted. To balance world power, to treat every political-geographic conflict locally and on its merits, to recognise the power of others, to resist the globalisation of politics and the identification of American interests with the globe – all these were being violated daily and would be traduced and destroyed in the penultimate station of Cold War in Vietnam.

So it was that the whole world was, in the phrase, gradually aligned on the notorious East–West axis, with its faultlines juddering every time the tectonic plates moved in Berlin, Prague, Budapest; in Tehran, Tel Aviv, Kabul; in Saigon, Phnom Penh, Manila. First NATO was devised and attested with West Germany enrolled. Then Korea was fought over and devastated at the cost of 33,629 American lives, 686 British ones, 750,000 Chinese soldiers and, they say (for no one knows), 4 million anonymous Koreans once neither Northerners nor Southerners, a seventh or so of the whole population. By 1956 the first US advisers were in Vietnam. Five years later the first slabs of the Berlin Wall were laid and in 1962 the concrete foundations for nuclear missiles in Cuba were poured and the hands of the mighty hovered over towards the button which assured mutual destruction.

For much of this time Lippmann was the voice of critical deliberation over what he saw as injudicious and arrogant hostility, even provocation, in the perilous staring-out and bottom-baring which was the behaviour of the primates in cold warfare. He took something of the God-view, no doubt, as well as the biggest salary ever known until then for a regular political columnist, but in doing so he devised an idiom, a structure of concepts and a critical habit with regard to government which kept alive a style of democratic debate turning less on personalities, and crucially on an idea of political issues and human nature as the proper subject-matter of reason and public welfare.

Nobody had done the job like that before. Journalism would be less of a force for good if Lippmann hadn't shown people how. Not many journalists came up to his mark subsequently, but that matters less than that some of them tried.

These things being so, Lippmann may be excused his intermittent windiness, the ghostly capital letters which stand in front of every abstraction, the utter lack of commonplace human sentiment up on the heights of his world-viewing. He may also be forgiven his errors of judgement on individuals and the constant disappointment he found in the way they so consistently failed his impossible standards.

He was wrong about Wilson, Hoover, above all Roosevelt; he couldn't see the wooden obduracy and self-righteousness which made John Foster Dulles so dangerous a Secretary of State; he was, like all of us, much too charmed by John Kennedy. In his own little domestic drama in 1937, when he fell tempestuously in love with Helen Armstrong, wife of a close friend, he found himself, like many men before and since, trapped between passion and the rigidity of his own code of conduct. Committed to candour and honesty, he acted secretively and mendaciously. Sworn to decisiveness and resolution, he vacillated and equivocated. Finally he and Helen – quick, hot-tempered, sharp-tongued, wholly loyal, extremely pretty – made out, but he never showed any sign in his writing of the knowledge of protracted crisis and its irresolutions, its arbitrary rules and sudden declensions, which the experience of his divorce surely brought him.

With regard to Dwight Eisenhower, all the same, it wasn't hard in 1952 for Lippmann to be right about the amiable soldier–simpleton who could embody for his people an impossible dream of easy-going, uncontentious and likeable authority. Much the same was to go for Ronald Reagan in 1980 and it was such a childish longing of the people which made Lippmann dismayed with democracy. Yet Lippmann was himself far from proof against the reassurances of flank-rubbing. When his country was accused of experimenting with the release of deadly bacteria during the Korean war[27] he indignantly repudiated what he thought a straight slur. It is not unendearing: 'the two highest responsible men in the United States government ... have said on their word of honor that there is no truth of any kind in the charges. Both of these men happen to be old personal friends, and I believe them ...'[28] The history of journalism since Lippmann's ingenuous declaration may be written as the replacement of credulity by a bitter kind of scepticism. The same is true, perhaps, of the frame of common feeling about politics across the epoch. Mistrust supplants endorsement. This change takes a generation.

Lippmann himself changed only very gradually; by the end of the Korean War he was sixty-four and settled even in certain kinds of willed ignorance: the economic lessons Keynes had given him didn't really stick; he continued to believe in America's high moral purport and to see any falling short on the parts of, say, Lyndon Johnson or Richard Nixon as defects in the moral characters concerned and not as expressing something true and fundamental about the American imperium.

In 1953 he had fourteen years of public commentary still to go. He fell in, more or less, with George Kennan's notion of the 'containment' of communist ambition, but unlike Kennan[29] he allowed himself gradually to acquiesce in the division of Germany as a fact of Cold War only to be put right far into some unlooked-for future. He dealt in grand issues as conducted by powerful forces, large abstractions and great men. His everyday experience, moving unhampered from the typewriter in his library to the offices of the mighty, gave him little contact with the sudden meanings of dissent, vengefulness, catastrophe; and when accidentally he brushed up against either vileness or chaos, he just looked away. Helen, quarrelsome and devoted, kept him clear of the hardnesses, the induration and colossal tedium of politics. The pair took their vacations punctually, walked their poodles daily and lived in many mansions of extreme comfort.

To note these advantages is not to jeer. Lippmann dominated his form of public writing; he gave it authority and kept it clean. It was, in its way, as grand an achievement in assessing the moral worth of the first superpower across a century as was, let us say, Kipling's or Gore Vidal's comparable work in their different intellectual forms. Given the way he lived his life, it is no surprise that he came to prefer highly intellectualised elites led by irreproachably upright heroes of history to the raucous messiness of Congress. He had, however, the honesty needed to disavow this preference when, first in Vietnam and then, more comically, in the Watergate apartment block, it all went wrong.

Even then he took his time. He showed no particular urgency about anything. When in 1954 John Foster Dulles wanted to rescue the French at Dien Bien Phu by dropping a few atomic bombs, he was mildly reproachful. When the British and French lied themselves into the disgraceful Suez escapade of 1956, his reflex Anglophilia led him to support the idea of bringing down Gamal Abdel Nasser as the usual kind of Arab dictator, quite failing to see either Nasser's decent, liberal and modernising propensities, or Anthony Eden's trivial petulance.

Much in his commentary on the day was *bien pensant*. He wouldn't have had the access he did if he had been otherwise. But (by God) it meant he could tell his readers the way of the world from right up close to the figures who made the history. He didn't *live* events (like Martha Gellhorn or William Shirer) but he *knew* them. When he went to Moscow in October 1958 Khrushchev himself gave him and Helen an extended audience, and the four articles on their meeting fairly tumbled out of their joint notes in the room at the National Hotel, bringing their multitudinous readers worldwide nearer to this particular historical helmsman than anything before or since.

These articles represented the biggest coup of his career and put him at the summit of the ambiguous profession of which Max Weber had announced the advent forty years before. Lippmann was maestro of the old generation of grandee friend-of-the-President commentators, first of the new generation of vastly rich and assiduously toadied-to celebrity analysts, themselves subject and object of interview. The Lippmanns's Washington party lists read like a Homeric version of the Great Gatsby's. When he turned seventy, the excellent American way with generosity brought him the acclaim of both politicians and press. At a vast dinner for the occasion at the National Press Club he described the calling of his life and that of his audience. His slight haltingness makes the effect the more moving.

> If the country is to be governed with the consent of the governed, then the governed must arrive at opinions about what their governors want them to consent to. How do they do this?

> Here, we correspondents perform an essential service... We make it our business to find out what is going on ... to infer, to deduce, to imagine, and to guess what is going on *inside*, what this meant yesterday, and what it could mean tomorrow ...

> It is no mean calling. We have a right to be proud of it.[30]

It could stand as epigraph to this book and it gives the lie to the old bromide about truth and its casualty status. Lippmann's point is not so much that journalists such as he tell the truth – more than a mere record of the facts – but that they dwell in the interpreters' houses, which are to be found with the names of good enough newspapers hung on the outside.

He wasn't through yet. But the truth about *his* life was out. It was not to be found in this or that article, or on the shelf full of books in his name. The truth of his life was the shape it gave to one public narrative of the day, the story told about How to Be a Journalist. Living the latter part of that big story, Lippmann became, of course, a television star. The hardly less famous Fred Friendly, journalist turned TV news producer, invited him to CBS and for 2,000 bucks screened Lippmann at his best, talking about the news of the world, on 11 August 1960.

It was intellectual television at its most popular and won extraordinary ratings. Lippmann did one a year for the next six years and for not 2,000 but 15,000 dollars a time. Still handsome, almost venerable, genial and warm, he conquered the airwaves at once and, as it were, ushered in the first television President, John F Kennedy.

As usual, he was uncertain about the contender, and as usual became his advocate. This time the President didn't last long enough to reveal his inadequacy for Lippmann's heroic statuary. Lippmann fell in happily with all that tarradiddle about the new style in Kennedy's Washington. Never reticent with professional rhetoric about great intangibles like 'the moral climate of the nation', Lippmann gave Camelot personal advice and sufficient public endorsement. The test of a President at the time could only be, for Lippmann, his handling of the Cold War. Kennedy was beaten up by Khrushchev at their first meeting in Vienna in June 1961. Khrushchev was his dreadful predecessor's pupil. Like almost all those who wield vast power, he saw no irony in that fact; also like most leaders he lacked imagination. He was not short, however, on either irony or subtlety. He gambled a lot but never his shirt.

Kennedy took his own comparably enormous egoism with greater solemnity. After winning the minor diplomatic passage in Vienna, Khrushchev ordered that the flood of refugees from the Soviet to the Western section of Berlin be stopped by the simple brutality of a high, floodlit wall with barbed wire on top and machine-guns trained on it twenty-four hours a day. In April 1961, after the farcical debacle of Cochinos Bay – the Bay of Pigs – in Cuba when right-wing militants exiled to Miami tried with American money and guns to overthrow the hugely popular Fidel Castro, Khrushchev had had his eye on the island as a place from which to irritate the United States into easing the tightening noose of nuclear weapons surrounding every border of the Soviet's western front. With Castro's complicity, he began to put his own missiles on the island, pointing at Miami.

The thirteen-day story[31] is the most frightening little nightmare in the annals of the Cold War and everybody has heard it. When the minutes of Kennedy's secret committee ExComm were finally published in 1999 there was once again an extraordinary chorus of approbation for the President's conduct of the affair by oldish men who were at the time young and adulatory and making it. It puts one in mind of his admirer and lieutenant Arthur Schlesinger, himself an occasional journalist, and his embarrassingly pop-eyed adulation thirty-five years earlier: 'It was this combination of toughness and restraint, of will, nerve and wisdom, so brilliantly controlled, so matchlessly calibrated, that dazzled the world.'[32] Kennedy, it will be remembered, had received news of the nuclear installations from high-altitude surveillance. After secret exchanges with Khrushchev, he announced their whereabouts in a television broadcast to the nation, together with his ultimatum to the USSR that the ships bringing the installation equipment must not cross an imaginary quarantine line in the Atlantic, 500 miles out from the Cuban coast in the free waters of the international Atlantic. It seemed certain that the American Navy would open fire. On 24 October 1962, at 10 a.m. EST, the Soviet cargo carriers touched the invisible line, shut down main engines, rolled a little in heavy seas and turned round.

Lippmann, almost alone among the big commentators of the day – Joseph Alsop, James Reston and company – had advocated negotiation when the news first broke, proposing a plan (later promulgated on the quiet) to trade the Cuban missiles for obsolete American equivalents in Turkey. Kennedy, of course, thought such a move would make him look spineless and dismissed it. When Kennedy came out looking like the hero of an old American folk-tale in which the victorious poker player gazes down the barrel of the bad man's gun and doesn't blink, Lippmann clapped as loudly as the rest and spoke with every bit as much wind as Schlesinger of 'not only the courage of a warrior, which is to take the risks that are necessary, but also the wisdom of the statesman, which is to use power with restraint'.[33]

The restraint was less apparent to the allies in Europe, where Soviet bombs would first have gone off. I. F. Stone claimed that the key issue for

Kennedy was his own standing, convicted of dithering at Cochinos Bay and after a poor year in Congress. Humiliation at Khrushchev's hands would have had him pilloried by the opposition. Yet a temporary setback to the Democrats does not now, and did not then, seem much of a pretext for hemispheric incineration.

All the same, Lippmann blessed the end of the day and its famous victory and was rewarded by Philip Graham, publisher of the *Washington Post*.

Graham had long had the ambition to turn the *Post* into the second national newspaper, beside the *New York Times*. No doubt it was really Katherine Graham, first lady of the press, who fulfilled this ambition some years after her husband's suicide,[34] his always volatile disposition finally broken up by drink, an ardent and desperate love affair, and his manic energy. But such was Lippmann's standing that the first key move in building such a status for the paper was securing his name on a byline.

The deal, first and probably last of its kind in print journalism at least, made the stuff of American fables. It was as big as the Ritz. For two columns a week and a further sixteen articles a year in *Newsweek*, Lippmann would pile up a million dollars in ten years, with a Manhattan apartment, full research and secretarial help and ocean or airliner tickets wherever he and Helen wanted or needed to go. Lippmann was well over seventy, the *Herald Tribune* had taken him for granted as part of the institution for years; yet he started at the *Post* and in *Newsweek* in January 1963.

That year 1963 took some facing up to for a man his age. The military advisers in Vietnam numbered 15,000 and they lost a key little battle in the hamlet of Ap Bac;[35] Lippmann's friend and man of destiny Charles de Gaulle led his country out of NATO; the civil rights movement was on the boil in the South; Ngo Dinh Diem, the US creature–president in the Republic of Vietnam (the strictly American designation), was found dead in a white suit and a bloody little alley.

The White House, it is by now certain, had sanctioned the murder. The Administration was on its way to assume full control of the war. On 22 November 1963 their own President was murdered in full view of the nation as he was driven in an open car through Healey Plaza in Dallas.

In the astonishing atmosphere of anguish and the determination to maintain continuity with which the United States impressed the world during the last weeks of 1963, Lippmann also stood for steadiness. He had been charmed but, he said, not bewitched by Kennedy; he had high hopes of Lyndon Johnson as well as feeling – dutiful and excellent patriot that he was – that he *owed* the new President his American allegiance.

As never so largely before, Lippmann became the object of sedulous Presidential solicitations. He was invited to stay at Johnson's Texas ranch and while Lippmann for his part treated Johnson's lavishly personal cordiality with commendable dryness, nonetheless he defended the President against all those Washingtonians bereft of Kennedy's damned and beautiful people. At the same time, as he put it in an icy dictum:[36] 'There are certain rules of hygiene in the relationship between a newspaper correspondent and ... people in authority ... which are very important ... Newspapermen cannot be the cronies of great men.[37]

Lippmann stuck to his precept. Johnson attended his seventy-fifth birth-day party and Lippmann (a bit late in his career) backed the 1964 civil rights legislation when the President, angered to the limit by the triple murder of the activist boys in Mississippi, drove the law through even before the bodies were found in the concrete embankment of a new freeway. But it was on the whole rare for Lippmann really to go deep into home as opposed to foreign policy and particularly so for the frozen era of Cold War, when that was always the biggest story in town.

So Johnson's noble vision of 'the Great Society' of which the President spoke at his own inauguration in January 1965 received Lippmann's endorsement. But the test of Johnson's mettle was for him the cold warfare turned so very hot in South East Asia.

Lippmann had long followed the lead of de Gaulle (who had reason to know) in recommending a negotiated end to the war. As Daniel Ellsburg once put it, no American in Washington or Saigon could have passed a term paper on Vietnamese history at that time. But the President, always fiercely sensitive to criticism and fearful of his own ignorance, was follow-ing his advisers deeper into full-blown warfare. All the other big colum-nists, carefully scrutinised by the White House staff – Alsop and Reston especially – were supporting hawkishness, and heavy bombing of the North had been intensified. Lippmann, all the while agonising over possi-ble damage to America's standing as guardian of that well-known entity the Free World, wrote steadily on behalf of 'a peace offensive'. He was old, he once said, and he was damned if he was going to be one of the century's many old men sending much younger men out to get needlessly killed.

Looked at from this distance, Lippmann was saying no more than many of the younger generation of journalists were to say, often with a much more biting inflexion. But not only was he among the first to say it, he could speak with his unrivalled authority, without any taint of the newly modish leftishness now casually worn about town, and speak also in the President's ear.

With Johnson our history arrives at the moment at which journalism matters intensely, even to those at the summits of power. Lippmann knew very well the most senior foreign policy officials in the White House – McGeorge Bundy and Dean Rusk, both academics from Harvard. They heeded him as at once the people's spokesman, custodian of public opinion and policy consultant. So Johnson hauled Lippmann into the White House one April evening in 1965, and Lippmann, having heard out a long, uneasy, blustering monologue from the President, advised McGeorge Bundy to offer Hanoi an unconditional ceasefire, and went home.

Instead, the government intensified its bombing campaign, and lied like mad about the consequent civilian casualties. Lippmann kept up his hostile but judicious criticism. Johnson tried to suborn him by granting personal and flattering access, but he spoke crookedly on the issue. Once he saw he had failed to seduce the journalist he turned on him savagely and Lippmann struck back.

The two men never met face to face again. Throughout 1966 Lippmann kept up his minatory admonitions. His objections were less moral than strategic: the USA did not have to wage a war which entangled none of its interests and threatened none of its people. Everything Johnson was doing, and doing 'wilfully, personally, arbitrarily, self-opinionatedly'[38] was in danger of ruining his country. When Lippmann bent an ear to listen not to the voices in the corridors and state-rooms of power, but to the rising hum of dissent from his juniors, it came to him in a rush of feeling that public opinion, the quiet ghost, possessed presence both of mind and of conscience.

Feeling the breath of that presence upon him, Lippmann denounced both President and policy for arrogance, vaingloriousness, duplicity. In a quite unparalleled exchange, Johnson replied in vilifying, personal accents and white tie and tails at a diplomatic dinner. He had set his henchman to going through Lippmann's career looking for gaffes, and put the vengeful results together himself.

Not because of Johnson's attacks but in any case soon afterwards, Lippmann took his bow. His last personal column appeared in the *Washinton Post* on 25 May 1967 when he was four months short of his seventy-eighth birthday. His profession bade him reverent farewell. In the autumn, a substantial fraction of the American people gathered as near to the steps of the Pentagon as they could get in order to press home their arguments against the war to the men inside who had helped destroy the career of the President and tarnish for a generation their country's good name. Those arguments were Walter Lippmann's.

CHAPTER FIVE

Ardour and Detachment:
Fascism, Communism and Journalism

Nothing was the same again for journalism after Walter Lippmann. He changed the terms of reference while he lived them. Undoubtedly he had great gifts and was gifted with golden luck as well as brass neck. He made it, most conspicuously by making friends. He kept up a terrific high-mindedness which even at this date is capable of inspiring journalist or human being, while nonetheless sounding kind of dated by the time he signed off in 1967. Refusing to discuss politics – by which he pretty exclusively meant the clash of great powers and the rumours of wars – in moral terms, he yet remoralised and purified the whole diction of political journalism and, it may be, the language in which his readership talked about the world and its affairs.

He was a journalist in an unusually full sense, but not as the word is normally understood. That is, he wasn't a reporter and didn't bring home the news, for all that he talked first, at length and face to face, with the men whose decisions made news and history. He rewrote the role and narrative of the job, but nobody has come near to doing the job in the same way. It will take half-a-dozen further short stories to bring out the variousness of the journalist's tale as it came to be formed in the years between the two great world wars and into the second.

If culture at large may be temporarily defined as the ensemble of narratives we tell ourselves about ourselves,[1] then journalism is the everyday domestic conversation of a society as it first devises, disputes and circulates those stories – as it tries out their *grip*. The useful heuristic 'journalism as the first draft of history' canonises History itself in rather too capitalised a way. History, no doubt, gets retold according to the shifting demands of generations, classes, nations, let alone the bullying requirements of power and rule. But one reason for the uncertain status of journalism in the conversation of humankind is its preliminary and provisional air, its inevitably hasty contrivance out of the unsatisfactory bits of information which are its origin. It won't do to call journalism the official gossip of a society because such a formula ignores the authority which sits easily and queasily beside the routine deprecation with which people speak of it. 'You can't believe all you read in the newspapers' is no more piously intoned than 'I heard it on the television.'

Such a thought does a little more to unsettle the square simplicity of Phillip Knightley's approach to journalistic ethics in his classic work.[2] Journalism must be written, everyone agrees, out of the immediacy and bewilderment of lived experience. That is what it is to report on life. This being so, the value allegiances and human sympathies of the journalist can only be excluded at the price of making him or her stupid. David Halberstam, hero of a later moment in this history, remarked of the common predicament of American journalists in Vietnam that only

> Objectivity was prized and if objectivity in no way conformed to reality then all the worse for reality … In truth, despite all the fine talk of objectivity, the only thing that mildly approached objectivity was the form in which the reporter wrote the news, a technical style which required the journalist to be much dumber and more innocent than in fact he was. So he wrote in a bland, uncritical way which gave greater credence to the utterances of public officials, no matter how mindless those utterances.[3]

Halberstam's remarks do not take out a licence for lying or even for partiality. Any report will be partial to the corner of the world in which the reporter stood. The faith the good reporter keeps is with *truthfulness*, for sure, and also with a handful of such optimistic universals as decency, moral respect, freedom from sycophancy, insubordination towards hateful oppression, hatred of cruelty and greed. The character of the good journalist is made up of the good examples that have gone before. Antonio Gramsci was another such example, the more so for our present purposes because so famously partisan.

Gramsci was born in 1891 in Ales, Sardinia, one of the handful of tiny little market towns in the foothills above the one main road which, running from Sassari in the north to Cagliari in the south, links up the island. When Gramsci was only six, his father, a minor local official of a little social standing, was sent to jail for six years for some kind of financial dishonesty, and could as a consequence barely get sufficient work when he came out.

Gramsci was brought up in desperate poverty as one of seven children whose mother, working under the grim duress of the only labour she could sell as an honest woman, the drudgery of seamstressing, conducted herself with the courageous stoicism which served as a key emblem in the imagery of the revolutionary socialism at the heart of her son's life and writing.

He had to learn the terrible lesson of stoicism for himself. He was a delicate infant, suffering then and all his life from digestive failure, and after the age of four showing the signs of compacted torso growth and spinal atrophy, better known as hunchback.[4] His mother endlessly massaged the 'sort of hump on his back'[5] and the doctor recommended the family to suspend the little boy from the ceiling beams in a kind of sling.

Gramsci went to a dismal local school (of the kind portrayed in that wonderful movie about the Sardinian peasants, *Padre Padrone*), was a formidably good pupil even so, heard about the Sardinian miners' strikes brutally broken up by the military in two successive years, loved history and philology, left the local school early to add his mite to the family income, but at eighteen went back to study at the lycée in Cagliari. His elder brother Gennaro taught him socialism and his young poet-teacher Garzia, who also edited the local newspaper, taught him Dante and gave him space to write in *L'Unione Sarda*. At the end of 1911 he won a very small scholarship to the University of Turin and went to live the classically impoverished life of a revolutionary student, cold, ill, underfed, lonely, dutiful.

His health was dreadful; he could barely keep up with his work; he befriended his fellow student and Sard, Palmino Togliatti, later Italian Socialist leader, and joined the Partito Socialista Italiano with him. He wrote for the left-wing *Avanti!* – edited by the then socialist Benito Mussolini – and for another leftist weekly, *Il Guido del Popolo*. When the First World War started he left university and dedicated himself to political journalism, which he turned into a very inclusive term of art. His regular columns in *Avanti!* and *Il Guido* were conceived and written as school texts for an only recently literate proletariat. They were forceful, teacherly, careful, elementary.

They also sought always to interpret and understand culture as the means of political change. Gramsci felt all through his damaged body the saturating power of the Church in the life of the Italian poor. Indeed, his famous conceptual coinage 'hegemony' named this phenomenon – thereby adding the whole business of culture to economic control – as part of what Marxist revolution must grasp and change.

His journalism was intended as a pedagogy to this end. He was the first to identify the importance of the theatre for revolutionary theory, and when at twenty-five he began to write theatre criticism it was Pirandello he was quick to count as a member of the socialist vanguard, and Ibsen's leading character in *A Doll's House*, Nora, as a heroine of the new Italian feminism.

In 1917 his position as a leading journalist and commentator of the Left led to an invitation to write a short pamphlet for the Young Socialists. Gramsci called it *City of the Future* and in it he spoke with blazing confidence of the coming socialist order and its promise 'of the integral fulfilment of the whole human personality ... Wealth would no longer be an instrument for maintaining slavery ... Schools would educate intelligence ... This is not Utopian.'[6] A little later in the pamphlet he writes of his hatred of indifference and pronounces himself a partisan. 'Living means taking sides.'

Gramsci stands here for the inevitability of judgement and its entailment, however rough and ready, of an ethics. His framing of events in the story of class struggle reveals the truths of class partiality in – the story of the year – the reports published about the 1917 Russian Revolution. The First World War became for him and his comrades a war fought on behalf of capital by workers whose interests it could not serve and whose young men it destroyed without mercy.

No one could say such an interpretation was false, and Gramsci ran *Il Guido* and wrote most of it single-handed according to the bright enlightenment Marxism brought to the moment. When the journal folded in 1918 he wrote full-time for *Avanti!* until a group of four young socialists, Gramsci and Palmino Togliatti, Angelo Tasca and Umberto Terracini, joined together to found *L'Ordine Nuovo*, 'the New Order'. The weekly lasted as such only twenty months, but it has since become one of the key reference points in any assessment of the century's intelligentsia and the efforts of intellectuals to teach the people to seize the day.

The journal had a programme.[7] It was, as I said of Gramsci's earlier work, teacherly, but not pedantically so. It taught how to set up workers' councils in the factories along the lines of the Russian Soviets. Before *L'Ordine Nuovo* wound up, there were such councils in all the main factories of Turin.

Turin was capital of the Left. Since 1914 the Fiat workforce had quintupled, Piedmont was the domain of the Italian steelworkers, the wool and cotton factories remained predominant. Gramsci and his comrades reported on the making of the Italian working class as it happened and warned as the shadow of Fascism began to gather and darken over the north.

> Bonomi's arrival in power, after the entry of the fascists into Parliament, has the following significance: Italian reaction to communism will become legal rather than illegal. To be a communist, to fight for the coming to power of the working class, will not be a crime merely in the judgement of a Lanfranconi or a Farinacci, it will be a crime 'legally'; it will be systematically persecuted in the name of the law, and no longer merely in the name of the local Fascist squad. The same process will take place in Italy as has taken place in the other capitalist countries. The advance of the working class will be met by a coalition of all reactionary elements, from the fascists to the *popolari* and socialists: the socialists will indeed become the vanguard of anti-proletarian reaction, because they best know the weaknesses of the working class and because they have personal vendettas to pursue.[8]

This is political journalism as class education. Gramsci spots the political train truthfully, and announces its direction. The whole country was braced for revolution. Lenin and the Bolsheviks were victorious in Russia. Germany had experienced a year of insurrection in 1918–19 and there, for a season, the Social Democrats had won out. Italy would be next. Gramsci, barely thirty, moved gradually from political journalism to political leadership. His brother took over the business-editing of *L'Ordine Nuovo* and Gramsci and his comrades attracted the direct attention of Lenin, who criticised them for a trifle of over-optimism.

Lenin, nonetheless, was an indispensable ally, and when in August 1920 the workers in Turin occupied the Fiat factories it looked as if the Italian revolution had begun. In the event, as so often on the journey of hope, quarrelsome comrades bred factions and factiousness bred splitters, until both the Socialist and Communist parties had missed their chance, such as it was, and Gramsci continued to write in the newspaper as though steadiness and calm reason would see the party through.

Communists are and should continue to be cool, level-headed reasoners; 'if everything in the PSI has fallen to pieces, then it is necessary to reconstruct everything, to reconstruct the Party.'[9] The enemies within would prove a lot less trouble than those without. Before the end of the year, Fascist insurrectionists had opened fire on a Bolognese rally of the Left and killed ten people.

From the beginning of 1921 *L'Ordine Nuovo* became a daily, with Gramsci, now a member of the central committee of the Italian Communist Party, its editor on 1,100 lire a month (as a student he had lived on seventy). The paper was now the party daily and as such suffered a certain stiffening of mind and manner. Such a position, however, gave Gramsci the chance to grapple with and be the first person to theorise the coming of the new monster of Fascism now undergoing its first, horrible parturition in Italy.

Gramsci told his readers without rhetoric that the choice was between 'battle or death; struggle or annihilation',[10] and with great acuity saw the divisions in Fascism between petite bourgeoisie and landowning capitalism, pleading with southern Catholic peasants and northern socialist proletarians to perceive and unite under their common interests. In his classic essay,[11] Perry Anderson credits the journalist Gramsci with understanding for the first time on the Left how utterly different the Western European case was from the Russian, how settled and stable civil society was in these countries, how contained the state, and how protracted the struggle would be even to contend with the massiveness of 'the hegemony'. Only by forging coalition with groups or parties still uneducated in and alien to the doctrines of socialism could a revolutionary *culture* be grown capable of overcoming the permanence of Church and capital in a nation otherwise dispersed across its several nationalities.

These topics sit quite at odds with what is thought of as the journalist's subject-matter, hence Gramsci's classification as a political theorist. But a theory is a narrative arranged in such a way as to provide an explanation of mere events. The daily opinionation of a Walter Lippmann, the severely objective report of an Ed Murrow are alike stories with which to enclose (and therefore explain) other stories, in particular histories. Gramsci took this activity further, of course, because his theoretic story had to get much more in. His thought was an effort to win Archimedean leverage on the whole class show from the *outside*. If art is the dream of the good life as lived without the battle for survival waged against both nature and social class,[12] then journalism when it is well done is the artless artfulness of a society talking to itself of such needful hopes and expectations.

By this token Gramsci was an ideal, idealising journalist, muffled up, no doubt, by the dreadful jargon of party communism, but daring ('a trade union leader becomes *a banker of men*' [Gramsci's emphasis]), bold ('the socialists will become the vanguard of anti-proletarian reaction'), vivid ('fascism … is the attempt to solve problems of production … with

machine-guns'), humane ('how [can] one enable [a trade union member-
ship] to express its will and exercise its sovereign right of deliberation?').

This language became exhausted into cliché by repetition over the short
twentieth century, was poisoned by treacherous use, and at last was enfee-
bled by its lack of grip upon actuality. In Gramsci's hands it remains strong
and stirring; it serves as a reminder that journalism is a protean form and
as capable of expressing noble aspirations as any other kind of writing.

In May 1922 Gramsci left Turin, gave up his editorship and quits this
history. He had been sent by the party to Moscow, met his half-Italian wife
Julia Schucht there, and returned to Italy by way of a sojourn in Vienna in
1924. The Fascists had won a gerrymandered election, and a leader of the
Socialist opposition, Giacomo Matteoli, had been beaten to death by
Fascist thugs. Gramsci became a deputy for Sardinia in Mussolini's Italian
Parliament. In 1926, as Russia rigidified into Stalinism and the dazzling
visions of revolution began to disintegrate, Il Duce arrested him, rigged a
trial and put him away until he died eleven years later. Iron-willed to the
end in spite of desperately bad health, he wrote copiously for the whole
time but in the exigent, traditional form of the prison notebook.

Over the border a fifteen-year-old Austrian girl was waiting unwittingly for
the arrival in Vienna of an eager young American journalist sent to run the
Vienna desk single-handedly for the *Chicago Tribune.*

William Lawrence Shirer was born in Chicago in 1904 to first-generation
German immigrants. His father exchanged farming for the laborious
professional self-education of a lawyer. Shirer senior was of admirably
liberal views and strong human sympathy for the striking railwaymen it
was his federal duty to prosecute. Friend of Clarence Darrow, admirer of
John Dewey, Shirer's father taught his son a passion for the tumultuous city
and, before his son was ten, died of a burst appendix. His mother took the
family to her home town in Iowa, where young William read with bright
eyes the local dailies for reports about the war and became high-school
correspondent for one of them. He went on to the local college, edited the
college newspaper and worked his way on the Cedar Rapids *Republican* for
the summer vacations. He was fired up by the courage of the people he met
in the left-wing working-class movement, the Wobblies; he hummed Joe
Hill's songs, and heard the avocation of journalism call to him imperiously.
He scooped an interview for the *Republican* with Jack Dempsey by waking
up the great man in his sleeper. When he left college with his degree, he
made, for the first time, the slow, deliriously exciting journey beyond
Chicago, first to New York and then, by good luck and a determined

pushiness which didn't come naturally, to a job in 1925 on the Paris desk of the *Chicago Tribune*, passion and plaything of Colonel Robert Rutherford McCormick, autocrat of pious republicanism and American patriotism, self-righteous enemy of Europe and its corruptions, and a wholly capricious boss.

Shirer met the Lost Generation one by one in Paris, made friends with a gangling, myopic colleague called Jim Thurber, and joined a cheerful, gregarious work-all-night and drink-all-day bunch of happy-go-lucky journalists as ripe and flavoursome as could be for blending in the rich vineyard of journalism folklore. The *Tribune*'s rickety open office at the back of number 5 rue Lamartine was, glimpsed from the start of the following millennium, as American as Paustovsky's office at the *Seaman* was Russian.

Colonel McCormick notwithstanding, the *Tribune* as Shirer remembers it[13] was the local daily of the American Bohemians, such American news as they reported being either expanded or simply fabricated by Thurber from a dozen words pasted on a cablegram while in other corners of the garret the house poet and the house novelist got on with writing the new American literature.

Shirer lived the perfect Parisian life of young American writers in the 1920s, met the stars, drank with Fitzgerald, bought books from Sylvia Beach at Shakespeare and Company, sat outside at the Closerie des Lilas, read in the Luxembourg Gardens, talked timorously to dazzling courtesans, and fell for Isadora Duncan. Between times (for, as Hemingway said, 'in the newspaper business … it is such an important part of the ethics that you should never seem to be working'[14]) he got a decent rise to 50 bucks a week, became a full-dress foreign correspondent, was later sworn at by McCormick for 'communistic' (because anti-dictatorial) views, and did a spell in London which taught him to detest the English upper classes but to admire the BBC.

He roved Europe for the *Tribune*, in 1928 recognised at once for what it was the turgid theatricality of the horrible menace of Mussolini's public rhetoric, and reported from the League of Nations in Geneva in ways which caused his fiery boss to describe his reports as 'heavy as bride's cake' and relegate him back to Paris.

It wasn't the sack. That was to come. He parted from a (married) lover in France and collected another working in Vienna; open, innocent, ingenuous, talkative – Henry James's American abroad in person – he loved every minute of the job and every great European capital he was sent to. He befriended the great Dorothy Thompson, the wife of the Nobel Laureate novelist and drunk, Sinclair Lewis, but, more importantly, up to

that time her country's best, most voluble and combative foreign correspondent with much to teach the young Shirer, generally in a shouting
match. And back in London he quickly became on close terms with
Aneurin Bevan and his wife Jenny Lee, youngest MP in the House of
Commons. Shirer made friends happily, easily and for life. Some of them
were extremely famous but what comes through about him is that friendship counted first, however interesting in itself fame might be. It makes
him easier to like than Lippmann.

No doubt he hadn't Lippmann's mind. But he had his own percipience,
his probity, his strong human sympathy; and his good luck. In 1929 he went
home for the first time in four years, was summoned to the Colonel's presence and in an apocryphal scene – 'Don't fall for all those socialists and
communists there. Don't let all the counts and countesses take you in'[15] –
was ordered back to Vienna to take charge of the *Tribune* office. He
returned and duly fell in love with his wife to be.

Like all his contemporaries in the trade, he was an intrepid traveller,
though some of the others travelled a damn sight more luxuriously. Shirer
himself, like the London *Times* man, Peter Fleming, had his imagination
quickened by tales of explorers and old empire, so lit out for remoter terri-
tories, starting with Afghanistan. He dropped in just after Emir Amanullah
Khan – who had tried to modernise the country a trifle, had brought his
wife out of purdah,[16] renounced the *droit de seigneur*, befriended the neighbouring Soviets – had been chucked out for his pains. Shirer heard bullets
crack over his head for the first time and had his 1,500-word dispatches
tapped out in Morse in hot little tin huts, just as the folklore dictated. He
threaded the Khyber Pass in an ancient Hillman while brigands fired at
him from the ridge above, then was, of course, welcomed to safety by a
cheerful British lieutenant at the North-West Frontier.

He did a report from the archaeological dig that found the Sumerian site
of the original Flood; he interviewed King Faisal of Iraq and was captivated
by Gandhi; he married Tess and nursed her through an almost mortal illness
in India; he was blinded in one eye by a ski pole on the slopes; and in October
1932 he was sacked without warning and by telegram with a promise of a
month's severance pay the honest Colonel McCormick never sent.

Economic depression at home and home isolationism rendered the
Vienna office redundant just as an ambitious Austrian prepared to provide
all the news fit and unfit for print for the next thirteen years.

The Shirers took out their modest savings and spent a thousand dollars
on a very cheap year on the Costa Brava. Just as they left they were

bemused to receive a cable from McCormick, who had forgotten that Shirer had been fired. However, he remembered in the nick of time and Shirer went off to his sunny Catalonian room to write his great, unpublishable novel, the rhythms of his composition punctuated by the rhythms of guitar practice by his fellow tenant, Andrés Segovia.

They were down to their last hundred dollars when he got a junior job on the Paris edition of the *New York Herald*. As street riots and insurrection brought down one French government after another, and the local fascists and royalists poured into the Place de la Concorde to beat up the inefficacious political class they so detested, Shirer was sent out on the streets with them, while gunshots cracked overhead once again, only this time outside the Hotel Crillon. He was back on the job as a straight reporter. On 9 August 1934 an old friend offered him a first-class press agency job with Universal Service in Berlin. A fortnight later he was at the centre of world history.

After Hindenberg's death, Hitler solved the problem of the vacant presidency by appointing himself head of state as well as head of government. Warily – much more so than Dorothy Thompson, who was ejected from the country for some plain speaking about Hitler – Shirer began to report on Hitler's progress, his oratory, the astonishing raptures at the Nuremberg rallies, the Wagnerian magnificence of the military displays, all couched in the censored prose permitted by the new, all-surveilling authorities commanded by Dr Goebbels.

He walked the wavering line between courage and foolhardiness, delicacy and outrage, with honest carefulness. When the great conductor Wilhelm Furtwängler kept Jews playing in the Berlin Philharmonic, kept German and Austrian culture going by playing Mozart and Beethoven, Shirer reported Furtwängler's publicly asked question, 'What should we come to if political denunciation is to be turned without check against art?'[17] Long after 1938 when the Shirers answered the question in the only domestic way such good people could answer it, political journalists would work up a little moral temperature by demanding of themselves how to reconcile the duty to report on what they saw frightful regimes doing to people with their own natural sympathy for suffering humanity. The moral convention seemed to turn into a convenient precept not to 'interfere'. William and Tess Shirer risked certain expulsion, probable imprisonment, possible death by hiding and healing wounded Jews, helping them when they could out of the country. 'A drop in the bucket,' Shirer observes in passing. He goes on to report, with a tremor, the beheading for 'treason' (a ceremony in Nazi justice not now much remembered) of two young

German women he knew personally 'from aristocratic families – they both had silken dark hair and lovely, refined faces.'[18]

As the pogroms intensified and the hideousness of the regime became daily more apparent, Shirer learned to mistrust his informants, Goebbels's plants, and to stitch together a line of people who concealed their treason to their country and their faithfulness to a universal humanism by an abject and ostentatious display of patriotism. Steadily he sent back to Universal Service accounts of Hitler's attacks on degenerate art, the transmutation of pure into 'German' science, the lunatic rejection of Einstein's theory of relativity as part of the Jewish bid for cosmic domination, the 'Strength through Joy' holiday camps for Hitler Youth; equally steadily the US papers who bought the service cut back the reports (except when Shirer landed Goering as intermittent columnist) and tucked them away on the inside pages.

Shirer watched Hitler move, step by enormous step – conscripting a huge army, founding the Luftwaffe, occupying the Rhinelands – towards a European war while always protesting, in rhetorical performances by which Shirer admitted himself always impressed, how sincerely he wanted only peace for his country. Caution clashed with principle when Shirer was syndicated across the USA with a report on a brief suspension of Jew-baiting during the 1936 Olympic Games. He was singled out by Goebbels as an enemy of the people, and was abused by name on the German radio and in the press. He tried to have the thing out with Goebbels's deputy and failed. The authorities believing him to be scared off, Shirer wasn't expelled. In any case, the colossal showcase of the Games made the world believe that the German people, young, blond, athletic, had hit upon the good society.

The rules of Universal Service were, moreover, strict; Shirer could not be 'editorial' in his reporting. He may have angered the propaganda ministry, but it wasn't his place to identify for what it was Hitler's humbug about peace and the cynicism with which he openly advanced his military plans. Shirer saw it but could not say it. By some criteria for journalism this would count as a due observation of objectivity.

Friction with the authorities was a permanent state of affairs, picking up the propaganda leads but then checking, revising, countering them by mere implication and turning them into something telephonable to Paris or London meant that bedtime lay well into the small hours and after a compulsory drink and gossip in the newsmen's inn. When his wife suffered fearful complications at the birth of their child, Shirer was torn between hectic attempts to check and cover the sensational news of Hitler's notorious Anschluss with Austria and desperate dashes to the bedside of his dangerously ill wife. It still makes for a vivid, anguished tale, especially as dramatised, a touch heavily, in the film made for CBS of the second volume of Shirer's autobiography, *The Nightmare Years*, in 1995.

Shirer had to live his own story. The human interest in question was his own. He compounded the density of domestic life by changing jobs. He was eager to be taken on by the *New York Times*; Universal Service was folding up; Shirer would be kept on as deputy in Berlin to the senior man in the second agency owned by Hearst. The man in question, an Alsatian American, was pro-Nazi. Shirer was suddenly fired. The same evening he received a cable signed with a name he barely knew inviting him to dinner at the Adlon Hotel in Berlin.

On 27 August 1937 Shirer met Ed Murrow of CBS, for dinner. Murrow offered Shirer the job of CBS news editor on mainland Europe. Murrow was based in London; Shirer did a trial broadcast and voice test standing on a packing case in order to address a microphone immovably stuck on top of its seven-foot stand. After keeping him on tenterhooks for four days, CBS confirmed the job.

Radio journalism was at this time barely ten years old. Broadcasting depended on written scripts read aloud, with their content more a matter of front-page immediacy than analysis. CBS was in any case competing with NBC, though more for sources of news than audiences. (Their HQ recoiled incredulously when Shirer, first with one piece of papal news, arranged 'the usual bribes' for Vatican officials in Rome.)

Shirer set up shop in Vienna but all the news, as 1938 opened, was in Berlin. Hitler had sacked the true-blue soldiers at the head of his armed forces, made himself commander-in-chief and replaced the career foreign minister with the dim, vain and obedient von Ribbentrop. The action moved abruptly to Austria. Hitler coerced the already fascist government of Austria to appoint straight Nazis to the key posts in Cabinet, and when Shirer brought CBS a genuine scoop about the incipient annexation of the country by Hitler, the company responded by despatching him, in a spasm of old American royalism, to meet the King of Bulgaria.

This ludicrous expedition coincided with the birth of the Shirer baby, delivered by caesarean in the nick of time as the Catholic nuns devoutly brought Tess – thrombotic and treated only with leeches – to death's door in the name of natural rhythms. The Austrian government tottered towards capitulation to Hitler. The Austrian Chancellor broadcast to his nation on 11 March, called off a national plebiscite on the union with Germany at Hitler's command, and as delirious crowds milled in the streets of Vienna, Shirer struggled to get some kind of report broadcast from the radio headquarters already guarded by stormtroopers. Failing, he trudged home at three in the morning.

As he got in Ed Murrow rang. The line was likely to be tapped. Shirer said, 'The other side has just crossed the goal line';[19] 'Fly to London,' Murrow replied. The Luftwaffe had taken control of the airport. Shirer flew to Berlin, scraped a flight to London by way of Amsterdam and at 6.30 that evening made his first and *the* first live broadcast to the USA as the CBS correspondent on the spot. Until that moment, Bill Shirer and Ed Murrow alike had simply lined up their spokespeople in front of the microphone. The autocratic William Paley, no less arbitrary and authoritarian than the good Colonel McCormick, didn't allow employees to speak impromptu on air.

That night they did. With all flights fully booked, Murrow had chartered a plane to Vienna on his own initiative and a CBS cheque, and ran the Austrian end of things. The next night he and Shirer, still in London, changed news broadcasting for ever. By luck and nerve and on the phone, they orchestrated a European news round-up, circling the capitals on the ether from Paris to London to Berlin to Vienna to Rome, each with a suitable spokesman, each introduced by the two friends and newscasters. They had to improvise at every step, book precisely timed telephone calls through jammed exchanges, learn at first hand the vagaries of short-wave transmission, line up their tame correspondents and parliamentarians, keep on good terms with the Nazi bullies blocking the switchboard. In London, Ellen Wilkinson, future Labour minister, was ineffable. 'The British people are annoyed at Hitler … but no one wants to go to war'.

It was a coup. No news broadcasting service had done such a thing before. It set the form for the future broadcasting of politics. So they did it again the next night. Shirer and Murrow became a double act known, whatever the national temper in the USA favouring isolationism, from sea to shining sea. CBS and William Paley, having forbidden them the air, couldn't give them enough of it.

In London Shirer reported Chamberlain's acquiescence in the Anschluss and admired the eloquence and accuracy of Churchill's criticisms of the Prime Minister. 'If we go on waiting upon events … how many friends will be alienated, how many potential allies shall we see go one by one down the grisly gulf?' Shirer was determined to commission Churchill to speak for CBS; fine, said Paley, offer him 50 dollars. The great man, short as usual of ready cash, asked, modestly enough, for 500,[20] but Paley, mindful of his millions, wouldn't pay.

By the time Shirer returned to Tess's bedside, anti-semitism had launched its first brutalities in the Viennese streets and Hitler had appeared on the balcony of the Hofburg Palace to announce with the usual magniloquence the annexation of his native Austria, all deliriously applauded from below.

This was the epoch of crowd politics and crowds have as many different characters and lineaments as individuals.[21] Hitler's crowds throbbed with propinquity and with an ecstasy of yearning. Even as Hitler gathered and focused this intensity into himself, the quiet voice of a broadcaster talking to a whole nation not in a crowd but dispersed in millions of homes announced his supersession. Goebbels tried to enforce collective listening in works canteens and on street corners. The facts of domestic life defeated him.

It was Hitler's moment, no doubt; more lastingly if in a diminuendo, it was Shirer's and Murrow's as well. They broadcast their account of the news daily and from the centre of world history-in-the-making. Shirer's work schedules were tolerable only for a man practising his avocation and at a time when bearing witness was an absolute necessity. His wife was barely out of danger but he was bracing himself, in mid-April 1938, for the dictator's next enlargement of the nation's 'living space'. Shirer had local troubles as well with Mr Paley. His boss, out of a mixture of parsimony and an even by that date antiquated dedication to live broadcasting, refused to buy the recording equipment that would have enormously expanded CBS coverage as well as – despite what Paley believed – augmenting their authority and immediacy at once. As Shirer remarks with terrible calm, 'to let audiences *hear* a bombing we could start recording when the bombs began to drop' (his emphasis).[22]

Shirer decided to move his office to Geneva and the family left after a horrible little nightmare at the airport when Gestapo women officials tore the bloodstained bandages from Tess's still open and unhealing wounds in order to satisfy God knows what savage libido in search of concealed currency. The Shirers caught the flight as the propellers turned and some airport stooge snapped at them for holding up the departure.

When his wife had recovered, Shirer sent her and baby Eileen to the United States. He had seen little enough of them; now, until he quit Europe at Christmas 1940, he would see nothing of them but a weekend in Paris. His next stop was Prague and even CBS gave him a daily five-minute slot (only, they emphasised, if the news of the day really were to warrant it. It did).

The journalists wait, as journalists will, drinking. The Czech government has Hitler's ultimatum to confine its army to barracks and, effectually, hand over the northern territory – Germany's Sudetenland – to the Reich. Colonel McCormick sends Shirer's replacement on the *Tribune* a cable: 'Wars always start at dawn. Be there at dawn.' The German Czechs in the Sudetenland rise in insurrection. The Czech army puts it down. Shirer is forbidden to broadcast. Chamberlain flies three times to see Hitler. The German papers brim with dutiful lies. Shirer watches both men at length from only a few yards away, attends another couple of gigantic rallies at which Hitler raves and bellows quite out of control. Shirer isn't convinced that Hitler's military threats really go to the heart of his German audiences, ardently as they admire their leader.

The same was true enough in Britain. The disgraceful settlement in Munich (which a few lip-pursing revisionists sixty-odd years later now find it to their taste to defend) was greeted with widespread, even hysterical, relief by a majority of the country. Czechoslovakia had no voice in its own fate; it was disposed of by an Englishman and a German. Shirer watched Chamberlain from the hotel lobby as the British Prime Minister trod upstairs, yawning convulsively, to tell the Czech ministers what was going to happen to their country. Then Chamberlain turned in and slept like a top.

This was news even for CBS. But Shirer was, he says, 'badly scooped'[23] by the NBC man who had posed as a German official and obtained the full text of the agreement direct from the Führer's headquarters.

It didn't matter much. Between them Shirer and Murrow had themselves written and spoken or arranged for 500 broadcasts during the three weeks of the Czech crisis. They had inaugurated transcontinental round-ups. They were masters, as nobody else was, of immediate, truthful and vivid news-broadcasting. Unlike the BBC, still stifled and immobilised by its respectability, by its cumbersome system of 'reference up' from one executive level to the next, by the translation of news into the passivity of reported speech, Shirer and Murrow taught by example the sheer excitement of actuality, the thrill of contact over thousands of miles, the daring of defining events just as they became visible in the turbulence of life-in-earnest. No sooner had newspapers learned to do these things, to turn story into history and accident into eventuality, than radio upstaged them and did so with a living voice.

Radio news was a huge success. Shirer and Murrow may not have had the access to the mighty that Lippmann commanded. They certainly matched him for fame. Not until war was being globally waged did the BBC catch up with the method. The newspapers, on the other hand, never flinched, as we shall see; broadcasting and the press became so absolutely intertwined that it became impossible to tell which was host and which parasite. Together they constituted an industry for the manufacture of news. By the late twentieth century that industry had turned to manufacturing politics itself.

Steady to his duties Shirer continued his reporting of the German lies with which every next territorial annexation was adorned, until at last, to Shirer's weary relief, the British government finally braced itself to some kind of principle and pledged solidarity with Poland when its turn came. Shirer went to report the Führer's response to Chamberlain's statement, made on 1 April 1939, and had the live broadcast abruptly cut off in Hitler's mid-foam. The Polish invasion was already booked for early September.

Shirer loved it all: loved the rush and jumble, the last-minute phoning of commentators, the improvised studios, the flying everywhere in bitterly cold aircraft, loved even the gravity of the moment and the terrible danger of it. He reported that too, tried to tell Americans what he believed the Nazis were up to, but to tell them both truthfully and gingerly for fear he'd be thrown out of Germany and no longer even be able to warn of the phantoms of hatred and the coming emptiness.

> Neither Germans nor foreigners in Berlin believe for one second that Hitler will stop now … The goal is the domination of Eastern Europe down to the Black Sea. If it reaches it, Germany will not only be the most powerful country in Europe, but it will be invulnerable to the blockade which lost it the last war. The raw materials and food so necessary for its existence will be available in its own backyard … Because Germany must hurry to complete its tasks while it can still bear the tremendous economic, financial and psychological strains. The Nazi economic machine is now at its peak. So is the military machine.[24]

It was a brave piece of work, and no one in the United States gave it either credence or attention. Not that it mattered much. Credence was forced on Americans first by the notorious Molotov–Ribbentrop pact in midsummer, when the Kremlin, so often violated and betrayed by France and Britain ever since 1917, and rebuffed for one last time in their attempts to make common cause against Hitler, signed the treaty which left them innocently unprepared against Operation Barbarossa two years later.

Shirer made a brief visit home (five days out from Liverpool) for a family reunion, and to meet the boss of the Columbia Broadcasting System for the first time. Paley had given a stern, utterly serious, newsman, Ed Klauber,[25] the responsibility for ordering CBS news and, with Murrow, he had made it the quickest, most alive and imaginative such programme then to be found anywhere in the world – even though Klauber continued Paley's policy of, with unimaginative rigidity, forbidding the broadcasting of recorded material.

Like everybody else Shirer veered in his hopes and, having been sent to Berlin, made his news reports out of his apprehension. He never quite prepared a guard against the Nazis' effrontery and lying. Hitler, with his usual swiftness and recklessness, prepared his invasion of Poland, while the British, with the complicity of the press, concealed cowardice behind diplomatic procrastination. Once the deal with Moscow was fixed and the Baltic states had been carved up by the great dictators, Roosevelt sent off pointless telegrams to heads of state asking them all not to do anything bloodthirsty, and Hitler mobilised first the obedient liars in the German press, then his tanks. While the British ambassador, Neville Henderson, still supposed himself to be in negotiation with Ribbentrop, the Wehrmacht crossed the frontier. It was 1 September 1939.

Shirer, like everyone else in Germany, was cut off from Paris and London. He reported street scenes in Berlin and tried, as journalists will, to take the nation's temperature by watching it go to work. At this stage no one knew of the murderous deceptions with which the Nazis had simulated border transgressions by Poland. He waited in suspense for two days until the British and French fulfilled their promises to the Poles.

Shirer knew his own allegiances. He 'felt lousy' reporting official German lies on CBS, trying to devise little verbal signals to indicate the mistrust due to German propaganda. God knows what the so-called precept of objectivity in news reporting prescribes at such a moment. So he did what a brave and decent man would do. And he did it alone. NBC suspended broadcasts from Europe for fear they might violate the principle of neutrality. Still the prohibition on recording held – recording the screams of tank tracks on the roads, of dive bombers in the air, of human beings in disintegration. Shirer's complicated duty was to report as news the only news he had to hand, given him by Goebbels's Propaganda Ministry, but not to report all that news as truth, to sift between the routine accusations of warmongering by the British and French and the hideous certainties that when the Nazis announced official beheadings of treasonous citizens who had been listening to the BBC, these would be the facts.

There is an affecting faithfulness about Shirer's late years in Berlin. He wrestles with himself and his obligations to objectivity, truthfulness and natural justice and decency in the pages of his diary[26] but never loses his feel for a good story even when it favours the wrong side. A reporter's passions pull him apart. There is the thrill of breaking the news of the amazing daring with which Germany's U-boat 47 stole into Britain's naval base at Scapa Flow in the Orkney Islands and sank a battleship at anchor. There is an honest man's fury at the cynicism and hypocrisy with which Russia invaded Finland. 'I have raged for thirty hours; could not sleep though little chance anyway.'[27]

Natural humanity is his guide to action. He does a live Christmas Day broadcast from Kiel, the first foreign correspondent to be allowed to visit the German fleet. He sees almost the full might of the national navy docked peacefully under a full moon. He likes the men. They sing, inevitably, *Stille Nacht, Heilige Nacht* for him. He broadcasts from on board a U-boat, tempted in a crazy fantasy to declare the position of the fleet to the open airwaves, knowing he'd be executed and knowing also that, at this early moment of warfare, the international brotherhood of sailors would forbid a Christmas Day attack.

After five months during which Hitler accrued only the modest additions to his empire of Denmark and Norway, the Blitzkrieg opened at the beginning of May and the German army swept past the outflanked and irresolute French, occupied Belgium and the Netherlands, and began to roll up the British Expeditionary Force and incarcerate the routed French.

Shirer followed the retreating armies through Belgium and picked over the forlorn and putrid debris of retreat. He was coming up, of course, with the German vanguard and, in the vast incomprehensibility of battle, reached, as every educated battle journalist of the twentieth century must, for Tolstoy's immortal remarks in *War and Peace* that 'the individual who plays a part in historical events never understands their significance. If he attempts to understand them, he is struck with sterility.'[28] The trouble was that in spite of the novelist's admonition it was Shirer's job to attempt non-sterile understanding, and his plain duty to acclaim the morale, fitness and discipline of the German army for what it all too apparently was. When one reads the dispatch in which he reported the fall of Paris, the best-loved city in Europe for any American, and learns that at the same time he heard of bombs falling on the suburb of Geneva in which his wife and child were again living, then one is pleased to pay tribute to his plain truth-telling, his steadiness before the victory of a national leadership he detested and his certainty of a devastated Europe.

When the French surrender on 21 June, he and his old friend Walter Keir of the *Herald Tribune* are the only Americans to be in Paris rather than to follow the government to its temporary exile in Bordeaux. Marshall Pétain announces the nation's disgrace by radio loudspeaker in the Place de la

Concorde. There are German staff officers in the Hotel Crillon. De Gaulle broadcasts from London his historic message of resistance on behalf of the Free French. The next day Hitler humiliates the French High Command utterly by arranging for the surrender to be signed in the very railway coach, a national monument, in which the Germans surrendered at Compiègne in 1918.

Shirer is present. The terms of armistice are brutal, mendacious, dishonourable. Then, as a friend says to him, Shirer scoops the world. Broadcasting live to the USA without knowing if his country can hear him, being recorded at the same time for Goebbels in Berlin, speaking impromptu from shorthand notes for thirty minutes, he finds he has brought off a dazzling coup – for some time it was all America had to go by about this momentous day – because a German technician had failed to cut off the live line and confine Shirer to a recording. Shirer has jumped Hitler's embargo by several hours. The Führer is furious.

France surrendered its huge forces with scarcely a fight. Shirer was bemused. He was also, as a known Francophile and Anglophile, under watch. He heard Hitler in the Reichstag threaten the people of Britain with impending and certain defeat, and was braced by that country's blunt broadcast rejection of any peace deal. After so much pusillanimity, he thought, the old country for all its snobbery, its gross inequities, its fadedness and stolidity was at last coming up to scratch.

Shirer watched it do so from the other side. His own information from the American Embassy was that the Germans simply didn't have the small landing craft, the barges and tugs capable of crossing the Channel. Shirer went looking for the signs that things would go wrong. How could any decent journalist have done otherwise?

He saw the waves of bombers flying overhead to attack RAF airfields but he could find none of the stockpiling of weapons and equipment one would expect in advance of an invasion. He toured the coastline for twenty-four hours, stopping only to toast with the French *patron* at the hotel the sound of the Allied bombs falling around them on the town of Calais despite bland German insistence that nothing of the kind was going on.

Shirer proved a shrewd military judge. Although the tours were intended to persuade all the neutral correspondents that the Germans were preparing for invasion on a broad front from Ramsgate to Lyme Regis, he hadn't seen enough evidence to persuade him. Plainly he couldn't say so in his broadcasts, and in any case the censor cut out any critical vocabulary (he wasn't allowed to call Germany 'aggressive'[29]). Not for the first time, Shirer wondered if it was time to go home. He was forbidden to mention British bombing raids, even as the microphone picked up and broadcast the thud of explosions as they happened (the Germans changed the mike to cut out the sound). Censorship became more and more obdurate and CBS at home were none too understanding. He fiercely resisted becoming a mere mouthpiece for the propaganda of the Reich. The ravings of its press and the constrictions of his work were taking the heart and mind out of journalism.

Shirer had a straight and admirable way with his interpretation of his duty to his avocation. He knew his political allegiances to democracy and his personal affections for Britain and France. He acknowledged spontaneously the exuberance, the physical radiance and glowing health of German youth, especially in uniform. He was quick and accurate in his liking for people. He recognised the historic necessity and moral force of a due impartiality in reporting, of fidelity to the facts as he could determine them, and of a proper awareness of his own and other people's ignorance. In such journalism, the reporter aspires to see from two impossible sanctuaries: the view from nowhere[30] and the shock of art. In the first, he or she sees as God sees every component of a human action. In the second, the journalist becomes artist and turns immediate particularity into the universal experience of humankind. Shirer's directness of observation and purity of diction, his honesty and innocence (this is no ironist of history), his dogged perseverance and shrewd eye for detail match him up well to Henry James's famous adjuration to the novelist, 'try to be one of those on whom nothing is lost.' Shirer and Ed Murrow, fast and unalike friends, likely Americans, join the third Mrs Hemingway as showing to their profession, and their readers too, how best to live the journalistic life-history as undemonstrative heroes. At this distance and with such an enemy in front of them, it doesn't look so difficult. But, as the later tales of journalism abundantly show, courage, honesty, truthfulness, stamina cost a lot of living. They are the price of experience. As William Blake told us, they take 'all that a man hath'.[31] Nor were his moral conclusions obvious to everyone. Three American correspondents at the time broadcast Nazi propaganda willingly, and one of them was a great poet, Ezra Pound.

By November 1940 Shirer had displeased the Nazi authorities once too often. As the war deepened not even people from neutral America were safe. He dispatched his wife and child from Geneva, via a long hard bus journey to Portugal and on across the Atlantic. After fifteen years' news reporting in Europe, the first household name in American newscasting, he prised himself and his secret diaries out from under the suspicious noses of the Gestapo at Tempelhof Airport and on 13 December said goodbye in Lisbon to Murrow, who was returning to London, and sailed for Manhattan for the tumultuous welcome awaiting him on the dockside.

William Shirer and Walter Lippmann lived the twin versions of the classical journalist. Those huge American distances gave them sufficient detachment to meet journalism's precept about objectivity. Shirer came to see for himself, of course; he was there all right when Hitler's tanks rolled into Vienna and Paris. Lippmann had a look as well, but not for him the immediacies of news. He saw himself indeed as taking the view from nowhere, even if nowhere stood noticeably close to the White House. He answered the phone as History speaking, while Shirer spoke for that good guy and representative American, Shirer himself.

By 1930, Europeans, by contrast, could not escape engagement. Least of all if they were French and had, as was the case with André Malraux, pretty well coined the concept 'd'être engagé' as meaning politically committed; and where could a good man commit himself except to the Left?

Malraux is less a figure in this big fresco of journalistic careers than he is a subject in popular journalistic mythology. But like those other mainland European predecessors, like Paustovsky and Gramsci, he found that writing the history of the present was also making history and that, in the circumstances of the Europe of the age of ideology, making history was damned close to making it up. There were in any case such compelling *récits* to listen to: the glories of fascism as so abruptly assembled out of antique iconography, modern mass militarism and the movie camera all summoned the youth of France to heaven or to hell. At the same time the old street cries of the Revolution had been uttered, heard and had triumphed at the continent's eastern edge. Someone who was truly French could doubtless heed only the latter call. The intense melodrama implied by the simple historic slogans of the Parisian street – 'vive la liberté', 'ni Dieu, ni maître', 'justice simple', 'j'accuse' – exacted the allegiance of every political native.

A more antique drum was also being beaten; the one that led to the French socialism of 1848. An intellectual like Malraux didn't have much choice. He had been called. He was called as much by nation as by socialism. Either way the synonyms were justice and art.

Four decades or so ago Malraux's features carried, in France, the same iconic charge as Che Guevara's elsewhere. The haggard, handsome, heroic face, lined by having weathered unthinkable horrors and shouldered fearful responsibilities, bore the battle honours of the century as visibly as his several uniforms, the featureless drab of the 1925 Kuomintang volunteers, the similarly workmanlike but unmistakable kit of the aviator in Spain in 1936, the fully military well-cut uniform of the Maquis commander in 1942. In each agon of the century Malraux was there in action and there in writing also, the gallant soldier-airman indistinguishable from the intellectual-propagandist. His journalism, if that's the word, arose directly from his political engagement. The titanic struggle of the European epoch was between fascism and socialism. Both would eventually collapse. But at Malraux's moment, as at Goebbels's, there was nowhere else to move and the instruments of victory were the tank, the bomber, the machine-gun and, of equal power, the radio broadcast, the broadsheet newspaper, the factory noticeboard and the poster.

Malraux was born to an *haut-bourgeois* family in Paris in 1901. He was a dazzling student of art and archaeology who never took his degree, publishing his first book before he was twenty and working for a rare books dealer while specialising in Indo-Chinese and Buddhist sculpture.

He lived his specialism on the spot. At twenty-two he was first cataloguing and then appropriating the ancient and beautiful relics of Khmer temples along the 'royal way' of Cambodia's kingly progresses. A year later he led a caravan of massive ox-carts laden with his spoils out of the rainforest and into Phnom Penh. He was intending to supervise their carriage back to France, presumably to add them to a national collection. But he never got the chance to explain; the French arrested him forthwith and he was sentenced by a colonial court to three years. A quicksilver defence then established, in a *coup de théâtre*, that there was no legal title to the statuary. So Malraux came home. As he did all his life (it was the journalist in him), he divided up the experience and turned it into fiction, his second novel *La Voie royale*.

The relevance of fiction, for him as for so many of the characters in this book, is acute. It wasn't just that the journalist was a writer (or the other way round). It was also the case that the fiction served the purposes of journalism for both writer and reader. It was written and read *to find out what was going on*. When he published *Les Conquérants* in 1928, it appeared first as a serial in three numbers of *Nouvelle Revue Française*. As Edmund Wilson, himself a political journalist and literary critic, later wrote, 'We are dazzled by an unhoped-for searchlight into a region of the world previously dim and distant.'[32]

The hero of the novel is an adventurer-intellectual with strong and reckless preferences for insurrectionary politics. In 1925 Malraux had returned to Indo-China. His first novel had been written in a spirit of outrage at 'the vast graveyard'[33] of Europe, and of revulsion at the stifling mediocrity of French bourgeois life (a move conventional for French intellectuals since Baudelaire, whom Malraux so much resembled in features). As many commentators have noted, its hero's life is so close to Malraux's own that, 'it is impossible to say which [is] remembered and which imagined.'[34]

During his second sojourn in Cambodia Malraux committed himself to an anti-colonial and nationalist movement and for eight months worked as one of its keenest activists, founding, editing and writing its insurrectionary and fiercely anti-French newspaper, *L'Indochine*.[35] Among his astonishing gifts was a precocious certainty about the new political art of propaganda, which he also turned with such success to the promotion of his own career. Several of our heroes have shown this talent – Lippmann, Gramsci, Hemingway – but none with Malraux's dash and flair, let alone his inventiveness with the facts.

These qualities had already caught the imagination of the French press and Malraux was an early version of the adventurer-journalist whose shadowy glamour lends his story an attractiveness directly related to the very little of it which is visible. It is hard not to conclude that Malraux cultivated this elusive gleam on his now-seen-now-lost career, just as he cultivated in his writing an understated knowingness about unmentionable horrors casually encountered, courageously dealt with. He was an early proponent of the doctrine of life's absurdity which serves a certain elegance of posture, a self-deprecating but redoubtable vanity.

At the same time, such a stance has to be hard earned and Malraux's was. He went north from Saigon into Canton and there joined the Chinese revolutionary movement, the Kuomintang, then tussling violently with itself as to whether it would lead a communist or a nationalist campaign against colonialism. In the event Chiang Kai-shek broke with the communists and turned his forces on his sometime allies, but for a couple of years after his arrival from Saigon and before the split Malraux was in charge of Kuomintang propaganda. It is part of the hazy glamour surrounding his life that not even his friend and biographer Jean Lacouture is certain whether Malraux was really, as the tale goes, a member of the Central Committee of the Kuomintang. But as the strong, handsome, marvellously cultivated archaeologist, art historian and already world-weary but always committed novelist-reporter of the further reaches of the mysterious Orient, he does much to thicken the narrative plot of journalism.

Malraux's calling as adventurer, revolutionary, combatant and propagandist adds a lot to our thick, rough storyline. Before the communists were defeated in the Kuomintang, the movement seized power in Canton. When he came home to write *Les Conquérants*, he told the story, turning a *coup d'état* into a *coup de théâtre.* After the book came out it was taken so straightforwardly as political commentary-with-dramatisation that, in a famous and caustic intervention, Trotsky himself, by then exiled from Soviet Russia, wrote a critical response to its political diagnosis. Malraux, he says, lacks the science of revolution, Marxism, and fails to see that Borodin, the actual Bolshevist bureaucrat who appears as a key character in the novel, was a creature of the bourgeoisie who ultimately provided the cash for Chiang Kai-shek's victory. Trotsky says, with the austere finality that comes from having been People's Commissar for War presiding over the Red Army while at the same time writing his propaganda classic *Literature and Revolution,* that Malraux should have 'approached the masses with more freedom and daring'. He vitiates his novel, Trotsky claims stingingly, by his 'little note of snobbish superiority, seeming to make excuses for his passing alliance with the insurrection of the Chinese people, perhaps as much for himself as to the academic mandarins in France and to the peddlers of intellectual opium'.[36] But the author of the novel was the man to whom, when the French authorities closed down his insurgent newspaper *L'Indochine* by confiscating the type, the local Annamese workers brought bundles of replacement type carried in their knotted handkerchiefs. He is also the man who went immediately to Spain the moment civil war broke out. Malraux organised the international section of the Loyalist airforce, flew sixty-odd missions in combat, designed and printed posters in encouragement of his comrades, and wrote the second great novel to come out of the war, *L'Espoir.*[37]

During the action an American journalist, Slade, dictates a report from the centre of Madrid where the loyal population is being bombed by Spanish fascists flying German dive-bombers. He hears a young man ask a woman beside him whether she thinks that, Juanita's arm having been torn off in an explosion, her fiancé will still marry her. Slade then addresses his own people in his report much as Malraux himself addressed the Americans in an essay for *The Nation.*[38]

We, the democratic people of the world, believe in everything except ourselves. If a fascist state or a communist state disposed of the combined strength of the United States, the British Empire and France, we should be struck with terror. But since it is *our* strength, we don't believe in it.

Let us find out what it is we want. Either let us say to the fascists – or to the communists if need be –'get out of here! If not, you will have to deal with us!'

Or let us say, once for all: 'Down with Europe.'

L'Espoir is a panorama of a novel. Or a newsreel. It glimpses innumerable representative lives, a score in detail: a fireman, an airman, a journalist, a crowd of peasants watching for the first time an enemy aircraft squadron being routed, a prisoner waiting with fifty others for execution by firing squad – 'The most appalling thing about the prisoners was their courage. Obedient they were, but not passive victims.'[39] Malraux filmed his own novel in Spain a year before the civil war ended.

Throughout the 1930s he lived a riven life. In all his writing he cursed Europe and the bourgeoisie for all he was worth, and spoke a bitter elegy over the end of the continent. His most famous novel, *La Condition humaine*, is as much a slice of reportage as it is a fiction. Its subject is the attempted coup of the Communists in Shanghai in 1927, at a moment when ruthlessness and optimism about communist revolution in the Far East could still be worn as badge of honour. The unforgettable opening pages in which Tchen steels himself to murder a man asleep behind mosquito nets in front of him fuse history and immediacy together with the artistry of great journalism.

Malraux was not, however, done with bourgeois France or with the passions of commitment. When France declared war he was thirty-eight. He at once volunteered for service in a tank regiment, was wounded, captured by the Germans after France's disgraceful surrender and, after four months as a prisoner of war, escaped. He began a new novel while spending a couple of years on the run, at which time he joined the Resistance movement, in particular that section of it which took its name from the *maquis*, the thick growth of brush which straggles over the white limestone *causses* of southern France. Between 1942 and 1944 he was Colonel Berger of the Maquis and writing underground pamphlets and leaflets, largely summarising the prohibited and absolutely dependable BBC news broadcasts and calls to arms for circulation to the people of occupied France.

Propaganda leaflets on behalf of the French Resistance constituted an exceptionally pure kind of news reporting in the narrative mythology of journalism. Unlike propaganda from rulers, these had to be accurate. They had to win trust. Distributed by hand and under pain of beatings, prison or worse, their factuality and a few liturgical slogans about freedom and the struggle were their marks of fidelity and trustworthiness. Deep in the contexts of lies and bullying they bore their witness to the small truths of neighbourhood place names, numbers of the dead (theirs and ours), the reports of distant victories which might one day be close.

On 22 July 1944, after a short engagement on Route Nationale 677, Malraux was captured, bleeding heavily and in uniform.[40] He was interrogated, quite gently ('curiously' is Malraux's own word), his wounds treated. He was a cool customer: 'Even that night, dying seemed to me banal. What interested me was death.'[41] (It's a bit of a flourish.) Then the Gestapo called him in and questioned him, surrounded by others undergoing torture, naked men being beaten, a soldier solemnly bashing on a large piece of tin to drown the screams. They had, for the Gestapo's purposes, picked out the wrong Malraux. He wasn't their wanted man. A day or two later, back in a room locked up with dozens of others, he heard women singing the 'Marseillaise' at the full pitch of their lungs. The Germans had left Toulouse abruptly, falling back northwards. The Allied break-out from Normandy had begun. The Allies were in sight of Paris. The prisoners battered down the door by ramming it with a huge old table standing in the middle of the room.

Like so much in Malraux's life, his release from German hands is another moment of unforgettable theatre. An autobiography, whether written down or not, may be a fiction, but to make a good yarn it has to be lucky with its facts. It is, no doubt, stretching things to use Malraux as I am doing. But the bright, explosive flashes of his life lend themselves, as Lacouture says, to the journalists' mythomania precisely because Malraux was himself one of them *and* an exotic; a scholar-intellectual and a man of action; a reporter of history and a maker of it. He had the irresistible attributes of celebrity; he was suffused with the glamour of enviable heroism and he was the archetype of *un honnête homme, gauchiste*, man of the people, democrat.

Malraux finished his combat in an inevitable, dazzling blaze of glory, leading his tanks into Alsace-Lorraine, the very grounds of war for seventy-five years, chasing after the retreating Germans. He was forty-four and with plenty still to give the mythomanes. For our purposes, however, he has only one more appearance. Then we wave him farewell from a very respectful distance as he mounts the ramp of honour to be welcomed at the top by his friend and comrade, by then President de Gaulle, in order to become his country's first Minister of Culture at just the moment when its imperial archaeology – Indo-China, Central America, the northern littoral of Africa – passed out of its hands.

In these brief news flashes from 1945 Malraux was summoned by de Gaulle, whom he then hardly knew. 'General de Gaulle asks you in the name of France if you will help him.'[42] De Gaulle had started his own new party in an attempt to transcend parties, Mouvement de Libération Nationale, but the armies of fascism and communism were still fighting bitterly, and European communists confidently expected to inherit the earth. In late October 1945 Malraux became de Gaulle's Minister of Information in a brief coalition government. He wrote the government's communiqués, he initiated wall and canteen newspapers all over Paris, and he also wrote for *Combat* and *Action*, revolutionary newspapers of the factious Left.

He told their readership plain truths: 'The government of General de Gaulle is not only the government of France but the government of Liberation and of the Resistance. It is not for us to put it in question. It's just that the government says war and revolution are antinomous terms.'[43]

He wrote ringingly of nationalising the currency and destroying the system of capitalist credit in the process, but all this only in the legitimate name of the government of France. Well over half a century later it is easy to forget that between 1945 and de Gaulle's dramatic return to the presidency and his rewriting of the Constitution in 1958, French governments came and went at the rate of three a year, that a military coup, with paratroopers primed to drop on Paris, impended in 1958, and that neo-fascists, many of them survivors of active collaboration with the Nazis, hovered on the edge of regional power for the whole period. Malraux's example reminds us of the stalwart honour of the European Left over the years of fascist ascendancy. The Americans' horror of communism, everybody's horror at its monstrous Soviet distortion, conceals the acknowledgement still owed to Leftists for their defence of democracy, let alone liberty and fraternity.

Malraux, like Gramsci, betokens a life lived in the argument of politics and in an era in which passionate partisanship in the name of the greater good was at the heart of political conversation and therefore of the journalism which conducted it. His function here is to dramatise the single identity of writing history and making it. Writing in action.

CHAPTER SIX

Fascism and the English

The tale of press complicity with fascism was once told as an everyday story of ruling class folk (Lord Rothermere, Mosley and the Mitfords) snuggling up to Mussolini and admiring (as Lloyd George did) Ribbentrop's manners, Hitler's strength of will. Lord Rothermere, for sure, himself as pretty well crazy an autocrat as his dead brother Northcliffe, strongly favoured Hitler's brand of fascism and officially supported Mosley's Blackshirts. Old Rothermere told his editors exactly what to do and say and as a consequence five of them came and went at the *Mail* in the 1930s; he used the subeditors to find chorus girls prepared, for enough money and champagne, to go to bed with him, the fat old monster.

The *Daily Mail* with all due mindlessness supported fascism and rearmament at the same time. Beaverbrook's *Daily Express*, now supplanting the *Mail* as circulation leader, consistently opposed rearmament and happily predicted the certainty of peace until war itself was certain, and even then postponed its outbreak ('No war this year' 18 July 1939; 'Experience shows that a battle postponed never takes place') and at the last, on 11 August 1939, it said 'Britain will not be involved in a European war.'

Leader-writers in the *Express*, like leader-writers in any mass circulation paper owned by one of the grand viziers, did as they were told. They were men of not much intellectual distinction or stiffness of spine in moral matters, and certainly Rothermere and Beaverbrook were far too heavy for them. But neither editors nor owners were as awake as they might have been to the little lying ways of government and, even if they had been, government itself was, on the whole, credited with doing the best it could for the country (if not for other countries to whom it had obligations) and with being, for the time being, repository of political wisdom, judgement, artistry of the possible, commonsense and so forth.

Owners and editors alike were wholly dependent on government. Richard Cockett bluntly describes the then state of play:

> The 'free' and 'independent' press of Britain is at best merely a partisan political weapon controlled by politicians for their own purposes, and at worst a mere arena at the disposal of Whitehall to play out a game of interdepartmental warfare. The reasons for this have to do with those 'informal' contacts that are such a hallmark of the English way of life and the peculiar and uniquely English relationship that exists between the government and the press in the dissemination of government news.[1]

Cockett goes on to assert that such a relationship 'always to the advantage of government' exists to this day. One way of reading the more-or-less British half of this history is as a chronicle of change in this relationship until one can say that such advantage is perhaps less fixed, but no greater a force than it was on behalf of reason or happiness, truth or importance.

However that may be, Cockett proves the case to the hilt for Britain in the 1930s. Neville Chamberlain came to the prime ministership in 1937, inheriting a press officer in 10 Downing Street and a news department at the Foreign Office. No files on the birth of the office survive. But it was apparent that one motive on the part of the brief Labour government of 1929 was to balance the vociferous prejudices of Conservative ownership by arranging political correspondents in three groups meeting in the lobby (the vaulted rendezvous for parliamentarians and their constituents in the House of Commons). Group one, the editors, would be allocated ministers for briefing; group two, political and strategic specialists, would be received by senior civil servants from state departments; group three, mere reporters, would collect the paperwork.

Thus the birth of the lobby, from which stronger-minded broadsheets did not secede until the late 1980s and rejoined with severed noses a decade later. It was flagrantly manipulative but the information from which any checking could begin was barely obtainable elsewhere. Or not at least until that watery political device known as leaking became part of the political climate about the time the *Guardian* left the lobby. The ludicrous conditions for lobby briefings were that sources were anonymous, policies without originating responsibility ('unattributable'), arguments, opinions and predictions caught from thin air, 'off the record'.

This is language – 'sources', 'off the record' and all the rest – a whole society has long since learned to mistrust. Chamberlain made a bosom friend of one Sir Joseph Ball, former spy chief and utterly unscrupulous political investigator, bound only by loyalty to Chamberlain. He was tapping Anthony Eden's phones when Eden finally broke with the appeasement policy towards Hitler. He persuaded the Tory Party secretly to buy an antique radical journal called, unendearingly, *Truth*,[2] with which to voice a coarser version of Chamberlain's policies than could be accommodated by Rothermere and Beaverbrook. It ended, like Chamberlain, on the anti-Semitic, anti-American, anti-Churchill and pacifist Right, as well as, by happy consequence, of no account whatever.

Truth is now forgotten, though it is worth quoting a delicious review in respect of the title of this chapter, unearthed by Cockett and written by one Anthony Gibbs, of a volume of Hitler's watercolours published by the German Ministry of Propaganda:

> They are perfectly charming ... If you look at these pictures and forget for a moment that they were painted by a man named Hitler you will see at once, I think, that here is a man with an appreciation of little things. Here is rather a shy man, afraid to venture into great perspectives, who prefers to look for a less ambitious and more intimate beauty and to find it in forgotten corners ... We know that Hitler can make a face like a dictator. Is it possible that the real Hitler, the genuine little Adolph, is a gentle sensitive child, intensely occupied with his own shy moods ...?

It is dated 17 August 1938.

There was little criticism of the lobby system, or of the parallel but rival news department at the Foreign Office. The two agencies clashed; the Foreign Office came to doubt the Prime Minister's judgement, but the two were alike in wanting to make a perfect match between the statements they issued and the reports the press published. The lone voice of Robert Dell, old hand on the Geneva or League of Nations desk at the *Manchester Guardian*, spoke out against the system. 'We ought to know what the FO says, we ought never to believe it without verification.'[3]

It was a timely, inaudible reminder. When Chamberlain became Prime Minister, the owners and editors (and therefore the makers of editorial policy and prose) of the *Daily Mail*, *Daily Express*, *Observer*, *The Times* and even the anti-fascist *News Chronicle* were all on his side. They looked forward to forgetting the dire settlement of 1919 at Versailles, to restoring Germany's lost properties, and in J. L. Garvin's words in the *Observer*, to 'obdur[ing] all entanglements direct or indirect in Eastern Europe and keeping out of every conflict into which we are not inevitably drawn.'[4] The old bromide 'the public interest' was new in those days and much deployed among editors by Ball and company to suppress unwanted views, to such good effect that even Sir Walter Layton, editor of the always respected *News Chronicle*, did just that with copy from one of his senior men reporting well-deserved criticism of the notoriously pro-Nazi and wholly inadequate ambassador to Berlin and his handling of the Spanish crisis in waiting.

Most editors except Crozier at the *Manchester Guardian* come out badly from the period. It is worth remarking how many gratefully received the English upper-class bribe of a knighthood. They depended, however, on their favoured status with favoured sources and, since these were only two – 10 Downing Street and the Foreign Office – when reports collided violently, as they did, rivalry was settled by the chief executive keeping the news of the day well away from the Foreign Office.

Chamberlain was jumpy about the press. Lord Halifax, a close ally holding the archaic office of Lord Privy Seal, had been told, in one of several deferential visits to Hitler, that the German Chancellor thought 'democracy paralysed the capacity to face facts by its love of talk' and that such talk and love of it was engendered 'by a licentious press'.[5] Goebbels leaned on him to the same effect: 'nothing caused Hitler more bitter resentment than personal criticism in the British press' and Halifax came duly and contritely home to get the editors and their owners into a row. He saw them and told them – Dawson, editor of *The Times*, Beaverbrook at the *Daily Express* (where they couldn't quite subdue the house cartoonist David Low), Southwood (*Daily Herald*), Harmsworth (son of Rothermere) at the *Daily Mail* – and they fell into line.

With the two exceptions, brave and I suppose predictable, of the *Manchester Guardian* and, intermittently, the *News Chronicle*, the English press was now at the service of a doomed policy and a craven government. Beaverbrook, of course, loved being on the secret inside of things and was clear in any case that war was bad for profits, as anybody, especially a German businessman, must know. So he led the way with this leader, bylined to the unknown and not-quite-believable Selkirk Panton:[6]

> We have listened so much to tales of strife and confusion in distant lands of Central Europe … We do not wish to be disturbed with the threat of it at breakfast in the morning. We want to sit down to our midday meal in contemplation of plenty. And when night comes we desire to sleep … without the dream of evil.

The other editors and their bosses were hardly so complacent or inane, but almost to a man they shared the view that a newspaper's national allegiance at a time of acute crisis was to its government and not to informing its public. It cannot simply be said that this choice was wrong, although it was certainly the case that those who held it were also guilty of toadying and cowardice before political power. But it marked a historical split in the history of journalism, when the press lost touch with public opinion by keeping in with the political elite.

Public opinion is no doubt a blurred concept and may go several ways at once. The *Express* held its high circulation by keeping up its style of cheerful somnambulation. But the *Daily Mirror* painted a much grimmer future to a rising readership, while outside the political frame of the breakfast table two famous by-elections were fought, in one of which (at Bridgwater) a journalist from the *News Chronicle*, Vernon Bartlett, won on a straightforward anti-Munich ticket, and in the other, at Oxford, the Master of Balliol, A. D. Lindsay, radically disturbed the heir presumptive. The historical judgement, however, can only be that government mendacity, moral indifference and routine cowardice were all actively connived at by editors and owners of the main titles even while, as people will, good enough men persuaded themselves that such was, for such a time, the best thing to do.

An exemplary tale will show how this could happen. Robin Barrington-Ward was Geoffrey Dawson's deputy at *The Times* through these years, later his successor, and was not only unfaltering in his loyalty to Dawson and the paper's support of Chamberlain but sincerely committed to the success of the policy of appeasement. Nor was this the result of any cowardly spasm as routinely charged by class warriors. Barrington-Ward had been for nearly three years an infantry subaltern in the First World War, subsequently a brigade major. Five years after that war ended he had written to his mother:

> Can one ever get people to know what WAR is and, by consequence, to rise up for peace? Have our sons (if we ever have any) got to be killed in the way I (for one) have seen hundreds killed and in even fouler ways than that ... I don't know what to wish – whether that a few more people had *seen* a man blown in half, or a man gassed, or had lain several hours in a shell-hole with the half-buried and long-dead dead.[7]

These were feelings he never changed, and may serve as a reminder that *The Times* acted not wholly without principle during the years of support for Chamberlain's utter inadequacy, right up to the moment when Chamberlain, to his incredulity and outrage, was ejected from office and replaced by Churchill whom he rather despised than feared.

These days revisionist historians of a piously Rightish disposition at work are attempting a little rehabilitation of Chamberlain. It can hardly wash. Not only do we have to hand such clear evidence of that habitual authoritarianism exemplified in his leading the press like a cut bull, but Hitler's very own dictatorial assumptions struck, it seemed even to Lord Halifax (himself of that view), a strong chord in Chamberlain.[8] As to the policy itself, its moral poverty and practical failure were plainly in view to plenty of journalists below the level of the editorial board at the time and turned into the terrible finality of events within a year.

Indeed, some political correspondents were so baffled and angry at their editors' obedience to Chamberlain that a little flurry of semi-official, single-author, pamphleteering publications floated out, long since led by Claud Cockburn's *The Week*, joined in its turn by the well-known *King-Hall News Letter* (which lived on into 1960), the *Whitehall News-Letter* and others. There were dissenting but junior voices in the press. But the most powerful and most unanswerable judgement on the conduct of the press and its supine complicity with the Prime Minister came from the great philosopher of his day, himself an intellectual who had, he admitted, kept too far away from everyday politics until its conduct forced itself upon him, now stricken with mortal illness at the age of only forty-nine, and 'broke up my pose of intellectual detachment'. In his *Autobiography*, written at top speed during 1938 when he knew he had little time left to set out his ideas for 'a science of human affairs' in the name of human better-ment, Robin George Collingwood wrote:

> The newspapers of the Victorian age made it their first business to give their readers full and accurate information about matters of public concern. Then came the *Daily Mail*, the first English newspaper for which the word 'news' lost its old meaning of facts which a reader ought to know if he was to vote intelligently, and acquired the new meaning of facts, or fictions, which it might amuse him to read. By reading such a paper, he was no longer teaching himself to vote. He was teaching himself not to vote; for he was teaching himself to think of the news not as the situation in which he was to act, but as a mere spectacle for idle moments ...

> ... the forces which have been at work for nearly half a century corrupting the public mind, producing in it by degrees a willingness to forego that

full, prompt and accurate information on matters of public importance which is the indispensable nourishment of a democratic society ... have trained up a generation of Englishmen and Englishwomen to be the dupes of a politician who has so successfully appealed to their emotions by promises of private gain (the gain of personal safety from the horrors of war) that they have allowed him to sacrifice their country's interests, throw away its prestige and blacken its name in the face of the world ...[9]

That is, I believe, the judgement of history on that short era. But the combination of a proper horror at the thought of a new war where the old had been so frightful and a commitment to Chamberlain's autocratic and secretive but all-English method shaped at least intelligible motives in one distinguished journalist.

Robin Barrington-Ward was that all-Englishman. Son of one of His Majesty's Inspectors of Schools, educated at Westminster School, founded with William Camden himself as its head in the sixteenth century, then at Balliol College, Oxford, centre of the university's intellectually gilded youth, he was awarded the MC and DSO during his exemplary years in the trenches and at staff headquarters. In 1919, at the age of thirty, he became, without prior experience of journalism, assistant to the famous editor of the *Observer*, J. L. Garvin. Barrington-Ward was cultivated, ascetically handsome, devout; a fluent classicist, music-lover; a furiously high-minded democrat from that most upright and self-examining segment of England's public-spirited bourgeoisie which came out of world war determined never to go back in, and at the same time watchful at all costs of the class above it in the English social hierarchy which had so pointlessly killed those who put their trust in it.

Barrington-Ward stands for a lot of British social history, *The Times* for even more. At this distance, after so many years during which *The Times* has been just one more broadsheet but with an owner unlike his predecessors interested only in circulation and in the imposition of his absolute will at all costs over corrupt trade unions but not at all in his mighty newspaper's name, it is pretty well impossible to recapture a sense of the original's dignified importance. For over a century the paper was scrutinised by all foreign heads of government and by the European chancelleries for what it revealed about the British government's plans. It guided their responses and, by implication, shaped opinion among the most influential of its own readership alongside that of the home Cabinet.

As we have seen, it is very difficult to disentangle policy and commentary in this process. Geoffrey Dawson told Chamberlain what he thought, and thereby confirmed the Prime Minister in his convictions. Dawson, appointed by Northcliffe in 1912, was himself autocratic *and* (as a matter of patriotic duty) subservient to the elected head of government. Barrington-Ward followed him in perfect fidelity. Dawson's allegiance was to empire and, as it was duly put, 'his commitment to statecraft was too great for that journalistic compulsion ... to seek out the truth in all things ... to hold his fidelity.'[10] His most infamous and well-known admission was made in a letter to his Geneva correspondent, then in Berlin:

> I did my utmost, night after night, to keep out of the paper anything that might hurt their [the Germans'] susceptibilities. I can really think of nothing that has been printed now for many months past to which they could possibly take exception as unfair comment.[11]

Barrington-Ward was adjutant to this doughty commander from 1927 to 1941. He wrote a large proportion of those global editorials; he issued directives (to the chagrin, at times, of the celebrated military correspondent Basil Liddell Hart) to the newspaper's specialists; he chose the letters for the letters page and, in a grand progress, toured the offices of his senior correspondents each morning. He dined out at the club with the mighty, and was back at his desk after dinner until midnight. He corrected the paper and then went home to bed.[12]

Over the three years between 1936 and the outbreak of war, he maintained not without self-righteousness that attitude of rather icy and insolent self-confidence which was until recently the best-known face of English ruling class authority. In a letter to Churchill, at the time out of office and all favour, Barrington-Ward wrote in 1936:

> *The Times* attaches great importance both to effective readiness in the defence of democratic civilisation and to the maintaining of close relations with like-minded powers. At the same time we have always taken the view that it is the negative, if indispensable, side of national duty. On the positive side, *The Times* has always held that this country should most firmly decline to take part in the formation of 'fronts' until or unless the choice of a 'front' is positively forced on us.[13]

There sounds the authentic voice of the English ruling class of the twentieth century up to, say, 1963. If it puts me happily in mind of the immortal scene in the comic novel *England, Their England*,[14] in which English diplomats, Old Etonians to a man, hitch up their sharply pressed trousers in perfect unison and say nothing, it has its coldly formidable side. When, however, Barrington-Ward later expressed with his habitual firmness the view that the time gained by the procrastination and duplicity of the Munich policy for the rousing up of public feeling was essential to bring the nation in common purpose to war, he might have been right.

Even if Barrington-Ward *was* right, Chamberlain remains as squarely in the wrong as public opinion (on this matter pretty easy to determine) put him in the following decades. For not only had he offered toadying support to Mussolini, and been inexcusably gratified by the staged applause of hired *Fascisti*, but no sooner had the rebel Franco, with lethal help from Germany and Italy, won power from the elected government of the Left in Spain than he was off to ensure that the General's nineteenth-century army be kept in neutral during the coming unpleasantness.

As Collingwood said, nothing could excuse newspaper irresponsibility towards the victims of the rebel military in Spain, and the same applied to the even less prominent victims of Italy in the first expedition of new imperialism in 1935.

The exemplary journalistic narrative which illuminates these topics was compiled well away from Barrington-Ward's high offices and long horizons, even if its leading characters dined at the same clubs and were on nodding acquaintance. Evelyn Waugh, in a way always surprising in someone who filled so stoutly the later role of stout clubman, was at once languid and ardent in the pursuit of *being there* wherever *there* was. He went either for the purposes of making enough of a living to dine out and drink up while he wrote the novels to bear witness to the harsh truths he served, or he went in a spirit of delighted incredulity and expressionless disdain at the vanity of human wishes wherever one found humankind.

The most important consequence for his nation's literature was no doubt the novels, and perhaps especially those recklessly candid, merely truthful novels which dealt with the subjects for which he was hired as journalist. But Waugh himself introduces a different act into the drama. For sure he is one of those journalists whose report is guaranteed by his presence. Lippmann or Barrington-Ward, the great opinionators, do harm or good according to their propinquity to power; *there* is where power is, and authenticity and (therefore) authority flow from addressing its occupant. Waugh, Ernest Hemingway and George Orwell share a common zeal for *presence* in remote, dangerous or difficult places where news is new because so little is known about them. These men belong to the class of adventurers for whom, very often, journalism is secondary either to writing novels (or poetry) or just a way of paying for the lark.

In the case of Evelyn Waugh's first sally into a journalism which paid sufficiently and wasn't a bit of pocket money earned from the *Daily Graphic*, he made his long journey into remote destinations for that most painful as well as melodramatic of reasons, to forget an unhappy marriage. His first wife (also, confusingly, called Evelyn) had risen from a valetudinarian bed to join a lover in a healthy one, and left home with all her effects. Waugh, anguished and censorious, makes not a reference to the rupture in his *Diaries*,[15] but by December he had, according to the usual English class methods of judicious introduction, acquired the job of reporting from Addis Ababa on the coronation of Ras Tafari, Haile Selassie to be, Lion of Judah and temporarily ally of both Italy and Great Britain.

Heartbroken he may have been, but Waugh was in cracking form. He sailed from Marseilles in October 1930 by way of Port Said and Djibouti and, once in Addis Ababa, is for the first time 'able to watch the machinery of journalism working in a simplified form'.

> A London office is too full and complicated to enable one to form opinions on any brief acquaintance. Here I knew most of the facts and people involved, and in the light of this knowledge I found the Press reports shocking and depressing. After all, there really was something there to report that was quite new to the European public; a succession of events of startling spectacular character, and a system of life, in a tangle of modernism and barbarity, European, African and American, of definite, individual character. It seemed to me that here, at least, the truth was stranger than the newspaper reports.[16]

Waugh was careful to take out unwarranted exoticism, pointing out that the Emperor's marble and malachite entrance halls were no different from those in one-night cheap hotels, that the emperor's coach had belonged to the Kaiser, that the ceremony itself was absolutely interminable and the food – tinned pineapple and three varieties of salt beef – inedible. 'I become', he wrote in his diary, 'slightly hypocritical as soon as I am away from my own background, adopting an unfamiliar manner of speech and code of judgements.'[17] It is a remark which would add a lot to some theory of journalistic production.

But he didn't miss much. 'Chained people disappeared from the streets as soon as distinguished visitors arrived.'[18] He lunched with the Emperor, as one of our later worthies would, forty years later. He ventured, with an amiable American professor, into the uncharted interior and Waugh's description, beyond doubt truthful, became indistinguishable from the level calm with which the crazy farce plays itself out in his novel *Black Mischief.*

> In the corner lay our hamper packed with Irene's European delicacies. We clearly could not approach them until our host left us. Gradually the frightful truth became evident that he was proposing to dine with us. I tore off a little rag of bread and attempted to eat it. 'This is a very difficult situation,' said the professor; 'I think, perhaps, it would be well to simulate ill-health' and, holding his hands to his forehead, he began to rock gently from side to side, emitting painfully subdued moans. It was admirably done; the abuna watched him with the greatest concern; presently the professor held his stomach and retched a little; then he lay on his back, breathing heavily with closed eyes; then he sat up on his elbow and explained in eloquent dumb-show that he wished to rest. The abuna understood perfectly and, with every gesture of sympathy, rose to his feet and left us.
>
> In five minutes, when I had opened a tinned grouse and a bottle of lager and the professor was happily mumbling a handful of ripe olives, the Armenian returned. With a comprehensive wink, he picked up the jug of native beer, threw back his head and, without pausing to breathe, drank a quart or two.[19]

It proved, for Lord Rothermere's purposes, ample preparation for war in Ethiopia. Waugh's agent was instrumental in getting him the assignment but by now he was a well-known enough name, he had already visited the country, he was in the eyes of the *Daily Mail* sufficiently in the same political camp to ratify the noble Lord's ignorant and energetic taste for boots, flags, uniforms and a neat little war.

Such phrases imitate in monochrome the vivid, brutal kindliness of Waugh's novel *Scoop*. In practice, as a war correspondent, what he most powerfully recorded was the ragged and incompetent nature of all such correspondence. He was one of the first journalists to arrive, in mid-August 1935, an old Ethiopia hand. Everyone had his book, one of the most recent about a region with the shortest bibliography in the world. It was a place which, as he said, 'Few editors could find … on the map or of which they had the faintest conception of the character.'[20] But with a mixture of glee and apprehension that this little war might be the presager of the so-much-mentioned larger one, the newspapers of the world sent their most august, military and well-travelled men, including (it is a pleasure to note) H. R. Knickerbocker from the Hearst empire, to be variously immortalised in *Scoop*.

The conflict was about nothing very much and both sides had worked themselves into a fine state of self-righteousness about it, the Abyssinians because of all that national pride in being a warrior nation with a centuries-long tradition of courage under arms, the Italians because they were full of a fine new fascist frenzy and knew, as Waugh knew, that they possessed the unanswerably better armaments and couldn't lose.

All stories then (and, even in the days of email, still) were sent in a highly concentrated form (by telegram) and expanded into the house style by the addition of editorial moisture and kitchen compounds (hence the splendid and faithful telegraphese of *Scoop*). Waugh, recently admitted to the Church and disgusted by both the venality and barbarism of the Abyssinian state, was on the Italian side and confided in by the Italian chargé d'affaires.[21] The Italian, inevitably a count, told Waugh that all his officials would be leaving the country by the end of September. Waugh realised that he had indeed bagged his scoop, but also knew that the Post Office officials in Addis Ababa, selling telegram space at the then rate of half a dollar per word, also had the habit of selling at the same time the juicier fragments of news to interested rivals. Waugh therefore sent his exclusive out in Latin which, not surprisingly, the desk clerk at the *Daily Mail* couldn't read. Waugh lost his scoop, was officially rebuked and resumed his indifference to the fake commodity of news as defined by the editorial desk.

He knew well, for example, the legendary Francis Rickett who appears in the novel with only minor hyperbole as the super-calm, beringed, perfumed and impeccable English adventurer who has purchased Ishmaelia as a little speculation. Rickett was in real life acting for American oil investors, and the Emperor, in an effort to thwart the Italians and deprive them of the only spoils he might have, sold the oil concessions to Rickett.

For the grandee correspondent of the *Daily Telegraph*, yet another knight-at-arms Sir Percival Phillips, this was exactly news as news desks conceive it. Waugh must have known what was up, and paid no attention. So he was fired, and went to visit Bethlehem for Christmas.

He took the trouble to go back to Abyssinia (pretty considerable trouble: train to Marseilles, boat the length of the Mediterranean and down to Djibouti, terrible old train again to Addis). After the country's inevitable defeat, the bombing and, it seems, the poison gassing of tribespeople,[22]

Waugh returned for a month to check, in his words, 'the end of the story' for his 'war book' before going home in January 1936. He had won an interview, with rare dash, with Mussolini; now he wanted to add a little more weight to his account of the new Roman empire in Africa. In spite of all his instinctive resistance to high political effect and his sardonic eye for the preposterousness of office, Waugh had been impressed by Il Duce. In an article-length letter to *The Times*, he summarised the Abyssinian upheaval with caustic certainty as now over, as being of no great issue for world peace, as an imperial settlement no different from many British settlements of a much more lucrative kind and themselves not much older than the century.

Waugh thus misses out the war, although his reporting is no less certainly true and accurate for that. What he typically misses may be found in the writing of a fellow-reporter in the Abyssinian war, Herbert Matthews of the *New York Times*. Matthews, who went on to Spain, was a likely enough young man, pleased with his job and himself, enjoying the adventure, a political naïf and a hardy sort of body. Knowing nothing of European politics and less about Africa, he took to the fascists because they took him in, were courteous, smart, modern-looking and well-equipped, Americophile, and victorious. Henry Luce's *Time* and the *New York Times* were alike, innocently pro-Italian.

The result was journalism of the tritest kind. He tells us, in a burst of candour, that 'all is fair in love and war', that 'gas is a dirty weapon', that 'the war of the guns was a sound that never stopped for five days except during the nights', that 'the Ethiopians had fought with ferocity and disdain of danger' and, with an unhesitatingly sacerdotal inflection, 'we who lived and who shall perhaps die far less well another day, could at least pity them.'[23]

If truth is a casualty, truism and cliché are not, and Matthews's banal reportage, written in dead prose, seen with a dull eye, is the occasion for reminding ourselves that journalism is a branch of literature as history is, and will only be truthful in so far as it is well written. For sure, lies may also be well written. But a report about the living experience, the shaped event, the warm and breathing person or, come to that, the meaning of the broken corpse is good and true in virtue of the excellence of the writing. The novelist–philosopher Iris Murdoch once said that great art is goodness in action; it is a selfless gazing at and recording of *what is there*.[24] Only a little journalism comes up to such a standard, but that is no reason not to hope for it.

The standard is the more relevant in considering a journalist who on one controversial occasion at least departed conspicuously and on his own admission from the more deontic and heavy-footed accounts of what it is to tell reporter's truth.

Claud Cockburn was the very devil of a reporter and, casting himself for this mephistophelean role by way of a mischievousness deep in his disposition, seems now the more irresistibly devilish for the sea-green incorruptibility he kept up all his impoverished life. He never ratted on his commitment to a low-key communism, sometimes with a party card, sometimes without, but learned, as he remarked, as much from the Magnificat ('He hath put down the mighty from their seats') as from Marx or Morris.

> And, paradoxical as it may seem, communism has – or at least very often has – a particular appeal to people brought up in English public schools and universities, especially people with a classical and Christian education. The Greek dramatists and both the Testaments smoulder with passages which, at any rate to a young man, are incitements to revolt against orthodox society, to throw in his lot with 'have-nots' against the 'haves'.[25]

We shall meet several more of his kidney in these pages, some much put upon by the state and some themselves too devilishly unpatriotic for other stomachs. Few, however, turned away the opportunity for safety, reputation, wealth, great office so consistently as Cockburn and, having done so, he sired a little lineage of junior devils without which journalism would tell less truth.

One arresting aspect of his writing is how instantly he puts one in mind of Evelyn Waugh. The same dryness of understatement, the same delight in calling rude names from the back of the classroom, the same pleasure in human comicality, the same terseness of narrative all remind us that these men were friends at Oxford, and that truths in literature may be near whatever the ideological differences of their authors.

Claud Cockburn was born in 1904 (a year after Waugh) to a family of titled lineage, one of whom was one of the great thinkers of the Scottish Enlightenment, but to a scion of it never out of luck but mostly out of pocket. His father joined the Far Eastern Diplomatic Service and raised his children in Beijing (known of course to Cockburn as Peking) and in Seoul, before returning at forty-nine to Hertfordshire in which he pined cheerfully for the Chinese hills. He filled the young Claud's life with incorrigibly picturesque uncles, dispatched him to a second-order public (private) school, and quickly removed him when he was dispatched soon after the end of the First World War to be of help to the collapsing Austro-Hungarian empire. So Claud lived in Budapest, which he loved dearly, and learned German, and went to Oxford to work and play, and won a travelling fellowship from *The Times* in the nick of time to keep his creditors at bay. 'In those days,' Cockburn writes, 'it was nearly impossible to be sacked by *The Times*. You just got a less interesting and important job at the same pay. This civilised policy worked excellently and removed the root cause of many journalistic crises. This cause is fear of the sack.'[26]

He was sent to Berlin and liked that, too. *The Times* decided it would like to 'train' him which meant, as he knew, preventing anything too 'viewy' in his reporting ('viewiness' being for *The Times* quite the worst thing in journalism), but he hunted views with striking aplomb, only being hauled back by penury and disgracing himself in Printing House Square by '*playing a joke on the Times*',[27] feeding into the always nonchalant machinery a blandly correct report on a revolutionary agitator and an incident at Calvary.

It was, you might say, a bit of an injury to truth. *The Times* didn't mind at all, and sent him promptly to New York and Chicago, where he interviewed Al Capone, wrote reports home of watching the New York Stock Exchange go over the tumultuous waterfall of October 1929, desperately tried to respond to little tidal waves of telegrams from London – 'must have tomorrow latest' – and found an inevitably impassive, laconic, polite mentor called Wilmott Lewis who advised him, 'Best to maintain a certain distance. Better to decide for oneself what to send.'

The Times wanted to keep him, pressed him to stay, but Cockburn had been reading Lenin and found that his mad certainty and astringency sorted well with the lessons of Wall Street and the Magnificat. He had, this cheerful wanderer, always travelled light but with a pure heart; his heart was set on bending what gifts he had not to some such vague abstract as fomenting the revolution, which never seemed to him likely to cure society's ills, but to providing a different source of information about the causes of those ills and those responsible both for the illness and the cure.

On his return to London in 1930, he noticed, rather as Russian radicals did of the photocopier in the 1980s, that the mimeograph machine made the circulation of print unprecedentedly cheap and easy. One patient person, inured to the clatter of the Gestetner, smudged typescript and mucky hands, could publish anything. Sage voices, ignoring the mimeograph, pronounced £10,000 as the minimum to start a new weekly. Cockburn thought he could do it on 40 quid in under a month. The result was *The Week*.

It was his alone, plus a friend who loaned him the money and tidied the office ('I was constantly frustrated by the habit people have got into of considering that nothing important can be done without going through the ritual of a conference').[28]

They rented an attic in Victoria Street, a copying machine, a secretary. They reckoned they needed 800 subscribers. They began with seven.

And yet little less than two years later this small monstrosity, *The Week*, was one of the half-dozen British publications most often quoted in the Press of the entire world. It included among its subscribers the Foreign Ministers of eleven nations, all the Embassies and Legations in London, all diplomatic correspondents of the principal newspapers in three continents, the Foreign Correspondents of all the leading newspapers stationed in London, the leading banking and brokerage houses in London, Paris, Amsterdam and New York, a dozen members of the United States Senate, twenty or thirty members of the House of Representatives, about fifty members of the House of Commons and a hundred or so in the House of Lords, King Edward VIII, the secretaries of most of the leading trades unions, Charlie Chaplin and the Nizam of Hyderabad.

Blum read it and Goebbels read it, and a mysterious war-lord in China read it. Senator Borah quoted it repeatedly in the American Senate and Herr von Ribbentrop, Hitler's Ambassador in London, on two separate occasions demanded its suppression on the ground that it was the source of all anti-Nazi evil.[29]

It was a triumph of genius in a journalist, certainly, of amazing stamina and capacity for work, and it was a lucky break. Somehow the old Scottish impostor Ramsay MacDonald, then Prime Minister, wagged a copy of *The Week* in the air when talking to journalists at some world-changing economic conference, and said that it was this kind of negativism and doom-crying which poisoned the climate of cooperation he among many was so concerned to foster. Thereafter the phone in the attic never stopped. Every European paper wanted a sub. *The Week* was off.

But it was a perilous life, perched always on the edge of an incipient lawsuit. They were too poor to pay up and too smart to ignore. Cockburn circulated rumours, which are part of the facts for one thing and rarely disproved for another (this is Cockburn's Heresy). He was followed by stout blondes set after him by von Ribbentrop. Lord Louis Mountbatten passed his copy of *The Week* to the King. Finally, Harry Pollitt, First

Secretary of the Communist Party in Britain and a bluff old bruiser, offered Cockburn a job as political correspondent-editor-and-everything-else on the party's daily, the *Daily Worker*. The salary was to be roughly a seventh of what he was by then earning from *The Week*.

Cockburn took it, and went to Spain. Once there, he found, as he always did, another case of huge characters with which to people the novel of his life, this time including Mikhail Koltzov, foreign editor of the Soviet Union's daily, *Pravda* (the translation of which is, of course, Truth), and Otto Katz, head of the Republican News Agency, both of whom would be later executed by Stalin for honesty and independence.

'These were', Cockburn writes, 'indeed in Clarendon's bitter phrase, "reproached and condemned times"', however little he lost his natural merriment. In a controversial episode, Cockburn arrived in Paris direct from the Spanish front. Weapons were desperately needed by the Left, to be shipped as contraband across the Franco-Spanish border. The French Prime Minister, socialist Leon Blum, needed to be jolted into inaction, and to allow the passage of the weapons by tipping the wink to his customs men. Would Cockburn write up an entirely fictitious story of anti-France rebellion among the Moroccan soldiery at home to encourage Blum in judicious inactivity? Cockburn would and did. The story was run in the French nationals. The weapons got through and the Republicans won the battle. Cockburn was delighted.

There has always been a lot of huffing and puffing about the ethics of this. Richard Crossman, a journalist and later Labour Party minister, agonised about it in the *News Chronicle* – 'necessary but distasteful'. The admirable Knightley won't have it at any price; Cockburn's justification of his action 'rendered Cockburn unfit to report the Spanish civil war'.[30]

This is impossibly wooden. Political correspondents feel and bleed, they have convictions and allegiances. In any job, the events of history may break and insist with their weight and urgency on a reordering of any human being's deepest values. You could not remain an honest journalist, or an honest person, and do such things at will; you would lose all trust. But on this occasion, trust was trusted in by comrades themselves at the end of their tether. What could a comrade do but turn his craft to help? And having done it turn a cheeky smile at all those people who had always hated his values in any case?

Besides, he was and remained the man he was: working for *The Week*, the *Worker*, liminal man, mocking (Irish rather than Scottish), insider-outsider, indiscretion raised to moral precept, devilish sly, funny too. Such a figure is indispensable to the history in hand. He is like Milan Kundera's devil laughing helplessly at the angel who rejoices 'in how rationally organised, well conceived, beautiful, good and sensible everything on earth was',[31] and laughing on behalf of a messier scheme of values.

That was Cockburn's vocation, hellish or heavenly according to your eschatology. He followed it through wartime, through the closing down by the government of the *Daily Worker* (as being likely to encourage social dissent) and, rather genially, *The Week* itself, when a careful police inspector helpfully gave Cockburn a lift back to Victoria Street from the Café Royal in order to shut up shop for the duration. He was then continuously and pointlessly tailed until the political darkness lifted and *The Week* returned to the street (the *Worker* never really left it, being published in a pirate edition but left unprosecuted).

He resumed his duties at *Week* and *Worker* but, as victory brightened in the sky, felt his passions subtly alter. He met General Charles de Gaulle at some length while on a mission poised between diplomacy and journalism in Algiers. The Communists and the Free French were united against fascism and, on the whole, against the dark suspicions nurtured in London towards littler parties. The same suspicion was eventually shared by President Roosevelt, no less, when he described Cockburn and the General's press attaché (happily named Laguerre) as 'two small-time connivers'.[32] They promptly founded the Small-Time Connivers' Club and carried on as before. At a time when the Americans were just beginning to show signs of that xenophobia and anti-communist fever which finally boiled up in McCarthyism, General de Gaulle, grand, amused, visionary, democratic, unconquerable, really did look like a world leader.

As the war subsided and Cockburn resumed daily political journalism, the world he had to study for his living began to get him and his wife Patricia down unbearably. He had to support the British Labour Party, now in government, for one thing, and that meant listening to the appalling kitsch with which Ernest Bevin conducted a foreign policy of crude effectiveness. The Americans were paying for the reconstruction of Europe, but turning the world into their empire as they did so and demanding as rent such an ecstasy of anti-communism that the Cockburns quit daily journalism, moving to the west coast of Ireland where they found, as they would, a dilapidated eighteenth-century house with a sixteenth-century watchtower abutting it, and a great many historic holes in its roof.

As they arrived there in 1947, Cockburn was listed by the US House Un-American Activities Committee as being one of the 200 (or perhaps 300) most dangerous Reds in the Western world. Cockburn bore this appointment with a mixture of gratification and embarrassment and the Irish of County Cork watched with excitement as unidentified documents were placed discreetly in his hand by a local official. This mystery endured for as long as Cockburn's earnings failed to match the increasingly desperate repairs needed by the house. Then the great John Huston came to Cork, bought the film rights to Cockburn's eponymous novel *Beat the Devil*. The writs ceased coming and the watchers outside the house were called off by the debtor's office which sent them.

So Cockburn and family remained in and loved Ireland as the south of that great country set about becoming, in its own rum way, a haven from Cold War (no nuclear weapons, no hounding of the Left, plenty of municipal housing, adequate pensions), such that Cockburn could make enough of a living by writing for a revivified *Punch* under the editorship of another princeling of misrule, Malcolm Muggeridge. And then in 1961, in Greek Street, London, *Private Eye* was started, the spirit of *The Week* walked again, and Cockburn resumed his place as the unignorable source of acute government embarrassment. The era of the young *Private Eye*, hottest moment of Cold War, marks the moment at which British journalism began to shift from deference to mistrust in its view of political power. Cockburn relished ambiguity. He was also to be paid for his labours as embarrasser-in-chief by that sedately Conservative organ, the *Sunday Telegraph*. To fly such multicolours at a masthead was only possible in the strange world of the 1960s.

George Orwell's is a name, from sufficiently far off, to bracket with Cockburn's in the category of dissenting journalism. Raymond Williams, a natural sympathiser with Orwell and his most exigent critic, once said 'in the fifties, along every road that you moved, the figure of Orwell seemed to be waiting'[33] and because Orwell's last great classic novels *Animal Farm* and *1984* were so appropriated as anti-Soviet propaganda, Williams set himself to diminish his stature for the purpose of restating a fuller-hearted socialism.

That particular engagement is set in the heart of Cold War. But when Orwell first came to some sort of fame it was as much more of an awkward cove than Williams will allow. Born in 1903 into a respectable but not wealthy family, he was a solitary, rather withdrawn child who read avidly (Shakespeare and Kipling) and won a scholarship to Eton, which gave him a posh accent and far-from-expected class attitudes by way of 'its tolerant and civilised atmosphere' (Orwell's own words). In a not-very-Etonian way, he joined the Colonial Police and served five years in Burma, during which time he conceived his well-founded, fully experienced and lifelong hatred of all empires and all imperialism.

Finally he quit and, in what one might call a resolute frenzy, committed himself to live as close as he could to degradation, disgustingly deprived and casual labour, mortal illness, cold, misery. Always a writer, he was at extreme pains to stock up his experience of his chosen subject-matter, not only so that he would never lack living examples upon which to draw but so that he could hold together his absolute moral allegiances and the content of his prose in an unusual and self-conscious unity. This is not normal training for a journalist. But I would suggest that it is what happens, in part deliberately and in part unconsciously, to any one of them who aspires to human and not machine-turned reporting.

Out of his submersion in the destructive elements of poverty, squalor and untreated illness came a classic sequence of books and essays – 'How the poor die', 'A hanging', 'The spike', 'Common lodging houses', 'Down the mine' and, of course, *Down and Out in Paris and London* followed by *The Road to Wigan Pier*.[34] These, it seems to me, can all be straightforwardly treated as journalism. The articles appeared in respectable weeklies – *Adelphi, Time and Tide, New Statesman and Nation*; *Wigan Pier* was published by Victor Gollancz as part of the Left Book Club list; all were used by their readership as one uses and needs the latest news. Orwell brought the news about what is now called the underclass to people with conscientious beliefs about social justice and mutuality in the hope that they would do something about it. He did so in a prose of unexampled plainness and immediacy, with metaphors of the simplicity and suddenness of a smell and with a moral directness called blunt but actually piercing.

> It was a disgusting sight, that bathroom. All the indecent secrets of our underwear were exposed; the grime, the rents and patches, the bits of string doing duty for buttons, the layers upon layers of fragmentary garments, some of them mere collections of holes, held together by dirt. The room became a press of steaming nudity, the sweaty odours of the tramps competing with the sickly, sub-faecal stench native to the spike. Some of the men refused the bath, and washed only their 'toe-rags', the horrid, greasy little clouts which tramps bind round their feet. Each of us had three minutes in which to bathe himself. Six greasy, slippery roller towels had to serve for the lot of us.[35]

The style is the man all right; no other journalist, no other writer of his century so directly declares himself to us while simultaneously retaining a deep reserve. Perhaps you devise such a manner from the forced, repellent intimacy of such experience. 'Here are the loathsome physical facts, mine too; but don't touch *me*.' (You see something of the manner in certain photographs of concentration camp inmates.) Perhaps he learned that bareness of style from the famous reports on poverty written by Mayhew and Rowntree at the start of his century, perhaps he took the crudeness of display ('here, smell this') from Kipling, although it was there at the same time in the best American prose of his day.

Whatever its provenance this is unmistakably journalism of the highest order, bringing to us the actualities of that human condition, dying thus about us every day. Ezra Pound once defined great literature as 'news which stays news', and that will do as a test of Orwell's journalism.

The Road to Wigan Pier is a great classic. I can only forbear to quote from the wonderful essay 'Down the mine' because it, too, is as well known, as much discussed as *Wigan Pier* and as morally and politically simple. Each takes for granted the necessity of socialism as proved by the vivid objectivity of the facts. *Homage to Catalonia*[36] is a bit more complex in what it votes for. It is nonetheless a work of journalism in the sense that people read it to get news they could believe, about what was not only a site of cowardly betrayal by their country but also a snakepit from which every previous legible utterance (even, as he saw when he chose, Claud Cockburn's) was a lie. Spain, as Martha Gellhorn told us, was *the* defining issue of the years before and, for many, those during the Second World War. Orwell couldn't help but go. He went, he said, with the idea of writing newspaper articles but 'I had joined the militia almost immediately ... in that atmosphere it seemed the only conceivable thing to do.'[37]

There then follows one of the most remarkable reports of remote politics ever written. What Orwell had found was the actualisation of his desires. He was faced with the vision of the good socialist society become reality: real no doubt in the terms of 1937 – dress, deference, distribution and brought about by the presence of war and of an enemy for whom such a way of life was an obscenity – but real for all that.

It was the first time that I had ever been in a town where the working class was in the saddle. Practically every building of any size had been seized by the workers and was draped with red flags or with the red and black flag of the Anarchists; every wall was scrawled with the hammer and sickle and with the initials of the revolutionary parties; almost every church had been gutted and its images burnt ... Servile and even ceremonial forms of speech had temporarily disappeared. Nobody said '*Señor*' or '*Don*' or even '*Usted*'; everyone called everyone else 'Comrade' and 'Thou'; and said '*Salud!*' instead of '*Buenos días*'. Tipping was forbidden by law; almost my first experience was receiving a lecture from a hotel manager for trying to tip a lift-boy. There were no private motor-cars, they had all been commandeered, and all the trams and taxis and much of the other transport were painted red and black. The revolutionary posters were everywhere, flaming from the walls in clean reds and blues that made the few remaining advertisements look like daubs of mud ... And it was the aspect of the crowds that was the queerest thing of all. In outward appearance it was a town in which the wealthy classes had practically ceased to exist... Practically everyone wore rough working-class clothes, or blue overalls, or some variant of the militia uniform. All this was queer and moving. There was much in it that I did not understand, in some ways I did not even like it, but I recognised it immediately as a state of affairs worth fighting for.[38]

The vision clouded and broke up. Although Orwell found the same solidarity, the rousing combination of courage and good humour in the trenches, he also found indiscipline, worn-out weaponry, planlessness, and the sort of filthy conditions (there were no latrines dug) he had trained himself sternly and unavailingly to tolerate. He had joined, as being the nearest to his own beliefs, the POUM militia, where this acronym translates as Party of the United Marxist Workers.

But there were other parties at bitter odds with POUM and almost as many betrayals as accusations of betrayals. The Russians had arrived to provide weapons, to take charge as having experience of their own civil war, and to meddle murderously in the hope of ensuring that if the Republicans won there wouldn't be anyone inconvenient left in charge.

Orwell learned all this as a section commander. He discovered the truth in the old joke about 'mañana', the bitter cold of nights west of Barcelona in the Aragon mountains, the shortage of water, the ragged but not irrelevant attempt to run a democracy in an army (NCOs were elected). And in Catalonia he saw, as he thought, the stirrings of a different and more radical revolution which had been obscured by the fixing of the Spanish fight in the Anglophone press as 'Democracy or Fascism'. What he hoped was ultimately on its way, after the enemy was defeated, was the final disappearance of the genteel bourgeoisie, as well as of Church and old landowners. The anarcho-syndicalists were in charge in the north-east, and they not only believed in but had even implemented a society of the common ownership of property and production in the hands of a democracy without a state.

As Orwell carefully explains, that was not what communists either from the Republic or from Moscow wanted. He thought the communists were, in the immortal phrase, right but repulsive. There was a war to win before the revolution could be inaugurated. He also remarked that Franco was less fascist than pre-fascist and feudal. Much like the colonels in Greece in a much later *coup d'état*, what Franco wanted was 'noblemen with Van Dyck faces',[39] inscrutable old peasants, colourful bandits, sage old priests, delicious townsgirls in taffeta and mantillas.

When he went back on leave to Barcelona, after 115 days in the trenches, the communists had declared the POUM (because it admired Trotsky) a traitorous body, and anarchists 'objectively fascist'; all the horrible blood-thirsty hoo-ha of left sectarianism had cut loose. Orwell records it all, his bitterness, his anger. He returned to the front with his comrades, leaving erstwhile comrades killing each other, and was, promptly and cleanly, shot through the throat without damage to caryotid or windpipe by an unquestionably fascist bullet. He went home and wrote his generous, modest, accurate report.

His view of what it all meant left him, however, without a rational or upright view of what his own country could and should do in 1938. He had reported the riven nature of the movement for which he had risked his life, and reported also the ruthlessness with which Soviet Russia, leaders of the European Left, exploited and intensified these credulous quarrellers. He wrote some helplessly gesturing pieces of journalism about the imminence of a British variant of fascism, with the only salvation being a new mass party 'whose first pledges are to refuse war and to right imperial justice'.[40] To say that in July 1939 is and was an inanity. Even though the best journalists write stupid things on a bad day, as we have seen, their habits of thought – that compound of character and method[41] – ought to protect them against lapses like Orwell's. His case is a warning against too ardent a membership of any political movement if one is to be able to think straight. The heavy jargon of correct thinking in this or that segment of the then Left weighed down his brain. The trouble was that the bankrupt nullity of everyday political values in Britain at the time was even worse than passionate intensity.

Few people now would doubt the rightness of Collingwood's sentence on his leaders and his daily press; so when war came, both men welcomed it. It turned the blur of day-to-day inconsequence into an event with a clear outline. Terror and its attendant helplessness is largely a result of not knowing what is going on. From 1940 this Second World War firmly defined action and its significance, whatever the outcome was going to be. This, it transpired, was a help to everybody, but particularly to the journalist.

CHAPTER SEVEN

The Important Fact of Fictions about Journalism

The first casualty of war is truth, we all say, and it is the duty of journalists, as of intellectuals,[1] to tell the truth and expose lies. At the present moment any such precept is apt to cause a tremor in the bosom of the pious liberal so much a target for vilification by self-confident neighbours further to left or right on the one-line axis of political allegiance. What, after all, is truth? they seem to remember that not-very-funny jester Pontius Pilate asking;[2] and who is to say?

The plain fact, as the plain blunt man or woman is apt to say so patly, is that once one has the facts clear it's not difficult to decide upon the truth. This is important in a back-to-front kind of way. The truth may elude the reporter, but not the lies. And indeed to nail down by naming in public their lies for what they are is one powerful way to hold the powerful to account. Such is the self-justification of journalists since their coming to birth in the late nineteenth century. The weight and political significance of such a claim on behalf of modern democracy is what gives the journalists their always veering status and occasional fame; they represent themselves as representing us in the always bitter and protracted struggle to keep power down and truthfulness up; to bring us the news of the world in the name of finding rational and admirable ways to run that world; to purify the language of the people and not merely to maintain but to embody the best conversation of the society, best because plain, affirmative, honest, calling its members to high ideals, bringing out the best in them.

These are the noble lies of journalism, Plato's famous oxymoron in *The Republic* coined to describe the tale told to the people that they might comport themselves according to standards of truthfulness and virtue as a consequence of believing 'opportune falsehoods'.[3] The crux is belief. The lie is noble because although false it makes people act better than they would without it.

The regular way to take all this is to say that conduct is guided not by lies but by ideals. One listens to the tale told of truth-seeking, power-defying, democracy-upholding journalists and, after letting the cat have its laugh, attends to the handful of instances in the history of journalism in which its heroes and heroines have turned opportune falsehood into lived actuality.

The myths of journalism, like those of any other trade, live in the historical biographies which, taken together, compose the ensemble of narratives constituting a culture. That is the subject-matter of this book. But those same myths gain force from fictions intended to concentrate history into something more intensely imagined, something more passionate and compelling than yesterday's news, something fiercer than may be allowed in this man's vain column or that woman's embarrassing headline.

This is the bell of art, which calls us sometimes to Bacchic worship, sometimes to icy contemplation. Plenty of art in journalism, as we saw and will see: Gellhorn's matter-of-fact reporting, Cockburn's playing the Fool, Gramsci's sermons. But the art of journalism stands close to the canons of scientific observation as they have become moralised into method by three centuries of experimental recording and faithful counting in and out of laboratories. These things being so, we might even claim for journalism the position of prime shaper of the way everybody sees the world. Journalism on the page and on the screen teaches in spite of itself the trade sanctions of truthfulness, authority for the evidence, the finality of the facts so far as they are determinable, the openness of consequences, the remoteness of closure.

These brave standards are carried aloft by the heroes we see, listen to and read. The coincidence of hero-journalist, news event and ethics method is the joint form of trade myth. It is where fact meets fiction, and they intertwine.

These perambulations surround a clutch of fictions – novels and movies – which on the account I have just given are as much part of the history of journalism as the biographies here interwoven with the short twentieth century. The fictions help constitute that structure of feeling within which news is invented, written and spoken. This first selection is brief enough – three novels, four movies from the first half of our chronicle. Each story is chosen as identifying a particular narrative strand in that corner of the world tapestry which depicts journalistic manners and morals, parables and puzzles. A strand gleams a little as you look at the picture, and you follow it through its story. This is what it is to follow a profession and its examples.

Somebody once asked the great French poet Mallarmé whom he judged to be the greatest of all French poets. 'Victor Hugo,' he replied, 'so much the worse for us.' I feel the same about *Citizen Kane*. It is the greatest movie ever made about journalism for sure, about wealth, about America. Plenty of people say that it is the greatest movie ever made, *tout court*. But its clichés, dazzling as they are, are still clichés even though they were the first that ever burst in such a pyrotechnic cloud over the future of Hollywood melodrama. *Citizen Kane* causes one to have the heretical thought that the cinema is inescapably a kitsch form.

As all movie-lovers know, Orson Welles at twenty-six and in 1941 made this version of the career of the mightiest of all time of newspaper barons and political careerists, William Randolph Hearst. In the movie Hearst, played up of course for all he was worth by Welles himself, is turned into a colossal, simplified magnification of an already epic figure. That moment of America, its unearthly combination of its money, its freebooting semi-democracy, its massive geography and the lurid craziness of its cities, produced some monster worthies. The actual Hearst is of a piece with Teddy Roosevelt, Henry Clay Frick, the original Rockefeller, let alone the class enemy Eugene Debs and the crowds of new writers thronging into the country's still empty Pantheon.

All generations remember like this: 'We shall not look upon his like again.' But corporate power and managerial subjection order more subdued identities in the new millennium. Hearst both was and had a colossal character; scandal, disgrace, failure never put him down. When the resplendently cynical Gore Vidal (who had, after all, met the man) cast him as King Lear in one of his Narratives of Empire novels, Hearst is dry and witty, 'the eagle-like face with the clear close-set eyes … ravaged by his misadventures upon the heath of bankruptcy', a 'genius who had discovered that the only truly credible – not to mention profitable – news was what one invented'.[4] His conversation was punctuated by 'curiously high-pitched nervous laughs' and leapt from one global crisis centre (it is 1940 in the novel) to another, spotting, while he talked, the Gobelin tapestry, the priceless Han dynasty chessmen in the room where he is chatting.

Even Welles allows him to say in the movie:

You're right, Mr Thatcher, I did lose a million dollars last year. I expect to lose a million dollars this year. I expect to lose a million dollars next year. You know, Mr Thatcher, at the rate of a million dollars a year, I'll have to close this place in sixty years.

But even this grandiose joke is turned by implication against the speaker. Stupefying wealth goes on for ever, its possessors are untouched by loss. Or, loss of money at least.

For Kane loses everything, his standing, his conviviality, his power (though the Hearst empire still stands today, as Vidal reminds us). This is Welles's All-American moral. We watch open-mouthed with admiration as, with dazzling compression and audacious image-making, Welles takes us along Kane's precipitous rise to fame, power, wealth. The young hero has dash, charm, looks. He is entrancingly reckless. For the first time, front pages spin towards us out of the screen, announcing the scoops, the coups, the bold predictions and almost-truths which drove the circulations up and up, and his own political career with them. The glitter, the dazzle of the style, the swiftly cut and foreshortened storytelling, the documentary newsreel quotations bring Kane-Hearst to his peak only halfway through the movie.

As everybody has said with Penelope Houston, at the time 'one got the conviction that if the cinema could do *that*, it could do anything', but the brilliance of both direction and acting on Welles's part enriches and endorses what were already commonplaces in 1941: that newspaper owners are the most ruthless but also the most irresistible among the grand viziers of capital; that dash and charm go well with egomania; that all hands on board the ship of politics are dirty; that all power corrupts, etc. and that a good man will, when he must, tell the truth to his old friend who has gone to the bad, but only after he has resigned his job and got drunk.

Joseph Cotten plays the good man and, as the house theatre critic, owes it to his artistic duty to cut to tatters the wretched performance of Kane's mistress in the opera company Kane has bought to provide her with a star-ring role. When he has done what a good man must do on behalf of art, and Kane has read the copy still wound into the typewriter, the one true friendship of Kane's life is broken, he is rudely ridiculed, his political career, poisoned by venality, disintegrates. His mistress-become-wife ('forty-nine acres of nothing but scenery and statues. I'm lonesome') lapses into alcoholism. Kane loses all the wit and intelligence Hearst retained in life and, played by Welles as though solidified from the neck down in a stiff, corseted three-piece suit and with a ghastly, staring plaster mask of a face, falls to patrolling alone the echoing cloisters of Xanadu, the script's brilliant synonym for the sumptuous pastiche, San Simeon, in California. Then his most famous of all last fictional words, 'Rosebud' is revealed to us as his lifelong longing for the lost happiness of his poor rich childhood when he rode 'Rosebud' his toboggan across the snow and had not been marked down for greatness by his inevitably tyrannical father.

A journalist comes to find the key to 'Rosebud'. He thinks aloud at the end:

> Mr Kane was a man who got everything he wanted and then lost it. Maybe Rosebud was something he couldn't get, or something he lost. Anyway I don't think it would have explained everything. I don't think any word can explain a man's life. No, I guess Rosebud is just a piece in a jigsaw puzzle ... a missing piece.

Jigsaw is invariably a cliché-metaphor and the sleigh chucked casually into the incinerator at the end of the movie, a neat enough commonplace. But the immitigable force of this low-art piece of sorcery lives on less in its oracular banalities about the American dream, the corruption of power and the disappointments of wealth, than in the terrific endorsement it gives to the place of the press in twentieth-century life.

There had been newspaper movies before, and dozens of novels, but *Citizen Kane* was the first to bring the energies of the new media themselves to re-enchant the world they created. The year 1941 was the heyday of propaganda. Welles mastered its orchestration first time round and did what all political propaganda is intended to do: mystify power, not by darkness but by dazzle (it is an agreeable paradox that a film which does this should be shot in so many subtle shades of *noir*). In this case the politics in question is not its executive heart but made up of the aura of sacredness and profanity around it, largely in the hands of the press. *Citizen Kane*, we could say, inaugurates the epoch in which politics and media are mutually embedded.

It is not, however, until the last twenty years of the century that the press and television take the lead, and news-making becomes the news itself.

In the meantime, *Citizen Kane* puts the black art of propaganda to the service of what press power and the press barons who incarnate it believe about themselves and their services to humankind. It is a film without irony, a work (no doubt) of genius which worships exactly where it intended to subvert.

The seven texts of this chapter comprise a diagram of leading myths of the trade; *Citizen Kane* stands at the head. It sanctions the myth of press power as the blood flowing in the veins of politics; of crazily competitive vainglory and ambition as the driving force of public life; of the solitude of success and of the inevitability of failure; of the good man who opposes mere virtue to megalomania, and wins.

At the other end of the diagram is a comic novel, the work of a comic genius and Englishman who spent almost all his writing life in America. P. G. Wodehouse published *Psmith Journalist*[5] in 1915, a year or two after he first arrived there at the age of thirty-four having made a bit of a name for himself as a journalist and school storywriter. It was one of the first half-dozen of the list of his novels and musical comedies, which topped ninety. It stands here for that mythopoiea of journalism which advocates the telling of truths on behalf of the poor and powerless, and in doing so offends the mighty who are presently oppressing wretchedness as they always have.

Of course it also approves and embellishes a larger myth in which a mannered, apparently effete but actually steely Englishman and Old Etonian befriends a plain, blunt, honest American from Wyoming, the pair of them joined in the spontaneous amity proper to Anglo-American relations and grounded in a common, liberal-minded decency. Because this is a comic novel but also because Wodehouse earnestly believed it (and why shouldn't he?), both young men are also gallant, generous, quick in sympathy and wholly unsnobbish. Psmith affects a speech of elaborate and unstoppable periphrasis such as Wodehouse himself concocted (with great affection) for the melodious counterpoint of Jeeves and Wooster.

In this novel the idea of such an Englishman joining the ranks of the muckrakers is agreeably comic, but no more unlikely than, say, the actual and attractive careers of Messrs Harold Evans and Christopher Hitchens as we shall discover them much later in the century. But Wodehouse had been much struck by all that Lincoln Steffens had done for human emancipation with his 'The shame of the cities' series about St Louis, Cleveland, Chicago, Pittsburgh, Philadelphia and New York for *McLure's*. He had been delighted that so genteelly entitled a periodical as the *Ladies' Home Journal* could carry journalism and serious writing in the way it did.

So Wodehouse invented *Cosy Moments*, a domestic weekly with a dependable diet of bread-and-milky articles and stories for American households of uninquiring respectability, sent its editor off on three months' sick leave and encouraged his English and American heroes to turn it into a muckraking crusader of the new school.

The old contributors are summarily fired and withdraw clucking in outrage to Bridgeport and Poughkeepsie. The paper takes up a promising lightweight boxer who contributes a column ('I swats him one in the lower ribs. He hollers foul but nix on that'), and it runs a campaign against some dreadful slums and their extortionate rents which fairly sends the circulation rocketing up. The two boys discover the name of the big-time grafter who profits from the slums and is running for mayor. Psmith (the 'P' his affectation to dignify the most anonymous of names) and Billy Windsor win the protection of a felixophile gang leader whose cat they rescue, and ward off the gangsters sent to close down the paper. As Wodehouse himself says drily in a preface,

> The conditions of life in New York are so different from those of London that a story of this kind calls for a little explanation. There are several million inhabitants of New York. Not all of them eke out a precarious livelihood by murdering one another, but there is a definite section of the population which murders – not casually, on the spur of the moment, but on definite commercial lines at so many dollars a murder. The 'gangs' of New York exist in fact. I have not invented them.[6]

The whole thing is done, as always with Wodehouse, at the peak of cheerfulness and brimming over with good will. Psmith himself proposes the editorial policy in a memorable speech. (Another of his amiable mannerisms is to use, with excessive courtesy, the old socialist appellation 'comrade' when speaking to anybody else including the plug-uglies.)

> 'You, of course, are the editor, and my suggestions are merely suggestions, subject to your approval. But, briefly, my idea is that *Cosy Moments* should become red-hot stuff. I could wish its tone to be such that the public will wonder why we do not print it on asbestos. We must chronicle all the live events of the day, murders, fires, and the like in a manner which will make our readers' spines thrill. Above all, we must be the guardians of the People's rights. We must be a searchlight, showing up the dark spot in the souls of those who would endeavour in any way to do the PEOPLE in the eye. We must detect the wrong-doer, and deliver him such a series of resentful biffs that he will abandon his little games and become a model citizen. The details of the campaign we must think out after, but I fancy that, if we follow those main lines, we shall produce a bright, readable little sheet which will in a measure make this city sit up and take notice. Are you with me, Comrade Windsor?'
> 'Surest thing you know,' said Billy with fervour.[7]

I can hardly resist quoting the luscious orthography devised by Wodehouse to render the Bronx accent, or some of the splendid scenes of knockabout in which Spider Reilly's gang attempt to put it across the dauntless duo and their unquenchably faithful office-boy Pugsy Maloney. It is a pleasure to hear in this very early Wodehouse a graver note struck which he rarely played in the later stylisations: 'Psmith's lot had been cast in pleasant places and the sight of actual raw misery had come home to him with an added force from that circumstance.'[8] It is also indispensable to hear Psmith's euphemistic diction in full play, partly for the joy of it, partly because something in American journalistic and intellectual life still partakes of the myth that the right sort of Englishman combines the rhetorical tropes of meiosis and periphrasis in a style which is the man: composed, courteous; courageous, high-minded. (Maybe we shall find one such.) His life and his co-editor's having been threatened, Psmith responds:

> Psmith, gazing sadly at Mr Parker through his monocle, spoke quietly, with the restrained dignity of some old Roman senator dealing with the enemies of the Republic.
>
> 'Comrade Parker,' he said, 'I fear that you have allowed constant communication with the conscienceless commercialism of this worldly city to undermine your moral sense. It is useless to dangle rich bribes before your eyes. *Cosy Moments* cannot be muzzled. You doubtless mean well, according to your – if I may say so – somewhat murky lights, but we are not for sale, except at ten cents weekly.'[9]

The paper wins, naturally. The crook pays up to repair the tenements but loses the election anyway. Billy Windsor gets the prime journalist's job he longs for. Psmith goes home to England. *Cosy Moments* returns to 'catering for children with water on the brain, and men and women with solid ivory skulls'. But this sparkling yarn does as much for our purposes here as heavier dishes with solid moral purposes served up by such as Upton Sinclair, with impeccable political lessons to teach about the horribleness of property-owning bosses, the corruption of big city politics in the USA, and the necessary bravery of journalists in defence of truth and on behalf of the exploited classes.

Gaiety and merriment of disposition such as P. G. Wodehouse's are no more rarely American than they are rarely British. They are rare either side of the water. The movie *His Girl Friday* (1937) has both qualities famously, and fits this collection of mythopoeic fictions-about-journalism rather better than the predecessor it adapts from stage and screen, *The Front Page*.[10]

His Girl Friday is, first of all, written and directed (by Howard Hawks) at a headlong pace. In a way long since vanished from the cinema screen, it is unremittingly verbal, wisecracking in a specifically American way no doubt, but so fast and (especially for Rosalind Russell, never defeated but always one pace behind, which at this pace leaves her gasping) so filled with fury that the jokes and their swiftness themselves conduce to the glamour myth about being a journalist. Being a journalist, the old old story says and said first in *His Girl Friday*, is a job for life lived at breakneck speed with devoted friends who are also rivals pursuing stories which are also fictions in cities which are theatres of glamour for the sake of trifling victories and forgettable defeats.

Cary Grant, at his brilliant best, plays opposite Rosalind Russell in what Stanley Cavell treats in his essays with hardly less brilliance than his subject as a 'comedy of remarriage'.[11] With great daring Cavell claims Cary Grant is right when he phones his editor to tell him to tear up the front page because he and his ex-wife have the big story and to 'stick Hitler in the funnies' (this is 1940 and Roosevelt is manoeuvring for support for Britain in the Senate) and to 'leave the rooster story alone. That's human interest.' Cavell goes on:

> 'What is news is determined by what human beings are humanly interested in, and you cannot know this apart from consulting that experience. Maybe it is in a rooster; and maybe Hitler is not news but just a problem about which we know what must be done.'[12]

Cary Grant is of course journalist and news editor (or at any rate senior and celebrated enough to tell the city editor what to do) with a crazy, unstoppable drive to chase and find good stories, and an utterly cheerful, charming indifference to and ruthlessness about what happens to other people, including wives and comrades, as he does so.

The moral point, however, is not aimed at the amoral journalist. It is that some people simply are like that, and there is quite enough of a moral kind to say in approval of such people. In any case, without them there simply wouldn't be any news journalism around, and we need journalism not because modernity makes us want news but rather because in modern society we have got to have enough information to stop things getting even more out of hand, to hang on to something frameable as sanity.

Rosalind Russell understands enough of all that, and has been herself a very successful journalist and wife beside Cary Grant, doing the same work, called to the same vocation. Something in her, timid and wrong *or* sound and sensible, has made her mad at Cary Grant's madness. She has divorced him before the beginning of the film. At its start, she arrives at the office with her new affianced, a pleasant, incurable rube played to perfection by Ralph Bellamy. From the start Cary Grant simply won't countenance either that she will give up being a journalist or that she will marry Ralph Bellamy. What she will do is come back to him, without his having to be any less mad than the madness which drove her off in the first place. His needs and wants are inseparable: he needs her intimately; he needs her as a journalist. His, Stanley Cavell says,

> are the plans and traps of what is called a newspaper man – they are expressions of his nose for news, which is to say, for a pair of convictions first that the world at all times presents a false face to its inhabitants, second that under the opportune eruptions of a big story there is a truth behind that face that the right nose can track down.[13]

The big story on hand is found in the Criminal Courts Building where most of the action takes place. In a jammed press office, the city newspapermen wait for the execution of a self-confessed murderer, a pitiful defective creature hardly responsible, barely guilty, desperately poor, a figure from the darkest alley of Martha Gellhorn's letters to Harry Hopkins of a few years before. The wretch, however, is victim (and agent) in *comédie noire*, never darker than at the moment when he escapes, having retrieved his gun, and is hidden by Rosalind Russell with Cary Grant's delighted complicity in a roll-top desk in the press room.

Her purpose, naturally, is to protect her story. The awful politician, mayor-running-for-Congress, is to have the murderer electrocuted to boost his giddy popularity. A pardon arrives. He tries, with the sheriff's help, to conceal it.

By then Rosalind Russell is, in spite of her other self, utterly caught up in the job once more. Many of the relentless twists of the tale turn, like the Goon Show, on crowds of people (newspapermen) tumbling into the empty press room, seizing a telephone from the black forest of them on a huge central table, and tumbling out again leaving the room eerily empty once more – except, at a later stage, for the hapless and incompetent killer sealed in the roll-top desk. Russell and Grant have their most vital conversations – their true *connections* – on the telephone, and at the marvellous moment when, to one's quick thrill of sympathy, she chucks off her hat and coat, grabs a phone and asks for Walter (Cary Grant) we know that Bellamy's poor rube has had it.

He, unhappy chap, hasn't a chance against Cary Grant's brutality (mistaking him for a much older man, framing him, in a vicious jape, with a coat full of dud dollar notes). He reminds us, however, of that old stand-by, the real world. He stands for the readership. Russell quits the readership when, even more thrillingly, she calls up Grant at the paper, can't reach him (as is the way of telephones) and shouts down the line, 'Tell Walter I need him.' So she completes the journey at the start of which she said, to the ex-husband she wants as much to be back beside as he himself wants her, 'You wouldn't know a half-way normal life if you saw one.'

The clinching moment, the one at which her own callings come true to her, called alike by the man and the job, is when she interviews the killer, locked in the grill of a free-standing cage within a larger cage of iron bars, every move under surveillance. The murderer tells his pitiful story, an abject creature. She leaves him with her exclusive; she murmurs 'Good luck.' She needs luck herself, and she has plenty. She loves the work for one thing and, as Cavell puts it of the love story, 'They simply appreciate one another more than either of them appreciates anyone else, and they would rather be appreciated by one another than by anyone else ... whether or not they can live together under the same roof.'[14]

For the pair of them, life is journalism but only life if they are together. We take from the film the obviously mythic surface (but not shallow) details about news and newspaper people: clamour, cynicism, telephones, rivalry, trust-in-truth and sticking-with-the-story, sentimentality, violence. 'Finding and publishing the truth is a source of pleasure even if you cannot make the truth prevail, and it is itself described and depicted as an adventure,' says Cavell.[15] So we find in the film also new depths to the myth. Finding out truth is an adventure. Writing the news (real news, not robotic reporting to camera) makes for aliveness in those who do it. News itself has consequences, but you had better remain indifferent to them (one character in *His Girl Friday* throws herself through a window in order to show the journalists *what they have made her do*). The keenest (that is, sharpest, most alive) journalists improvise news (would that mean it couldn't be art?).

His Girl Friday is radically optimistic. It is also intelligently self-critical. As it silhouettes the myth of journalism and lends it such power, it climbs above it, showing us the cost of news-fiction in ruined lives (the young woman throwing herself from the window) and rotten souls (the candidate for mayor). There are dozens of lesser films and novels commemorating that delicious mixture of seediness and sweetness. Even as good a movie as *Front Page Woman*,[16] which Howard Hawks must have had in mind for *His*

Girl Friday, rests solidly on the uncriticised necessity to do *anything* to beat your rival to the story. Here, too, local graft is the nub and the rival journalists will violate any common decency to win. In a gleeful joke, the male journalist (George Brent) leaves a false trail to the jury's voting papers for Bette Davis to find and lead with in her story. Her scoop is scooped, justice takes the hindmost. All the progressive watcher can do is find some little encouragement that here, in 1935, a woman plays newspaperman.

By the time we reach a great press movie like *The Sweet Smell of Success* in 1957, however, a quite new frame of feeling is being built in order to contain and inform the myths of journalism.[17] The sublime optimism of *His Girl Friday* is replaced by a bitter distaste for and cold-eyed analysis of, as Pauline Kael put it, 'dollar and power worship'.

The writing is its best feature, as well it might be since the words belong to Clifford Odets. But the direction is well up to scratch, as darkly lit and dramatically highlighted as *Citizen Kane*. The tone, however, has inside it an unusually hard edge: a certain settled bitterness; what one might think of, indeed, as an older kind of bitterness.[18]

Burt Lancaster plays the leading gossip columnist of political life, a sort of Walter Winchell figure but with an arrogance and sanctimony allied to insolent candour even with the powerful. His demeanour is justified by the attention everyone pays to his column. Tony Curtis puts his Martian and masklike good looks to wonderful purpose as a snapper-up of unconsidered malice and salesman of gossip, trading his trifles to Burt Lancaster and others under the professional vacuity of the title of press agent. His repellent little household gods are money and success. He is horrible in this, and in the lying and callousness he effortlessly displays in the worship of these idols.

In this he is quite unlike Cary Grant's Walter-character in *His Girl Friday*. Walter's interest is in that pure impurity, news. He isn't really self-interested at all except in so far as his is the only life he's got. Tony Curtis, on the other hand, is that familiar figure, an abject social climber, and Burt Lancaster an ice-cold, hotly egotistical product of the rigid deceptions of celebrity.

He has a sister, his only family. He adores her. She is piteously in love with a solid and worthy jazz musician, overwhelmed by her brother, unstably vulnerable. Burt Lancaster orders his hireling Tony Curtis to frame the musician and break off the relationship. It looks as though Curtis is coming into his own, as several pots of political scandal he has been cooking come to the boil.

The musician turns out to be too principled to frame (as a communist, incidentally, and a marihuana smoker: these were the deeps of Cold War).

The sister first tries to kill herself, then rejects her brother; she goes to her sweetheart. Those who have been fearful of scandal tell the blackmailer to publish and be damned. Burt Lancaster is broken and Tony Curtis finished.

It is a less audacious film than *His Girl Friday* but it declares a different mood, one in which journalistic excesses in the name of fame and fortune must needs be put down by everyday principle and decency. Journalism itself emerges irrepressible. Its Mephistopheles waves away the twin darknesses prefigured by Burt Lancaster and Tony Curtis, one granite-featured and expressionless, the other fawning and petulant. They personify journalism-gone-to-the-bad, the devil tells us, but that other part of journalistic myth, honest public opinion and inextinguishable personal integrity, will always put it back to rights. America's political homeopathy never fails.

A couple of novels remain to complete the landmarks on this first map of myths. *All the King's Men*[19] was the best known of a clutch of more-or-less political novels written by Robert Penn Warren during the 1940s, alongside his worthy poetry written in the style of what were called 'the Southern Agrarian' poets. Warren wrote out of his experience of the South – Louisiana, Tennessee, Arkansas, Kentucky – their architecture and agriculture; their racial inheritance, necessarily; their thick, hot, violent texture, the stuff of William Faulkner's mighty novels.

In *All the King's Men* Warren picks up aspects of the life of Huey Long, the extraordinary demagogue who was elected Democratic governor of Louisiana at the age of thirty-five in 1928. He defied the oil and real estate barons to exempt the poor from property and poll taxes, built 2,500 miles of paved road in a state which had only thirty such miles when he began, gave schoolchildren free books and buses, treated blacks as equals, ran the law courts as his courtiers, never touched the Ku-Klux-Klan. When he became a Senator in 1930 he pitted himself against Roosevelt and threatened to scupper the 1936 Presidential election by running on his own ticket. The polls put him at 4 million votes. Poor Southerners, black and white alike, adored him.

Warren saw in Huey Long's story at once an American and a world emblem. He gives his hero-politician an overwhelming public rhetoric which took in the best bits of fascism and communism – National Socialism if you like – but above all was spoken directly to his audience and constituency of the rural and city poor. In one remarkable page in the novel, Willie Stark (the Huey Long character) offers himself to his people to be confirmed by them as they roar his name – 'Willie, Willie, we want

Willie' – and then, in a huge, slow, mounting growl vote with their throats for his promises.

He promises them a hospital.

'The biggest and the finest money can buy. [It is his money that will buy it.] It will belong to you. Any man or woman or child who is sick or in pain can go in those doors and know that all will be done that man can do. To heal sickness. To ease pain. Free. Not as a charity. But as a right. It is your right. Do you hear? It is your right.'

The roar came …[20]

Willie Stark plays to and for the crowd's roar, his popular vote. But he means what he says. This is mass politics and the time is the time of such effects and causes.

The hero of the novel alongside the 'king' of the title is Jack Burden, sometime doctoral student, then journalist with a gift for persistent and uncomfortable revelation, now the Governor's press secretary, lifelong friend of the Governor's enemy, in both moral and class terms, Adam Stanton, son and heir of the old order and the Governor's nominee for director of the new hospital.

There is old money and old power in Stark's way: the Stantons and Judge Irwin, a traditional figure from every Southern novel, standing on the long verandah of his grand colonial house, implacable, upright, handsome, creaking-voiced and lantern-jawed; aged and ageless. He must be defeated. Stark sets Jack Burden to dish the dirt on him. 'There will be something. There's always something … And make it stick.'[21]

Jack Burden is, I think, one of the very first investigative reporters to bring down a public figure. We follow Burden through the legal documents and by way of a mad old medium until he has the deadly evidence of the Judge's one financial crookedness, and of the way the upright old Southern gentleman Stanton, his closest friend, covered up for him.

Jack loves Anne Stanton but marries a succulent cheesecake called Lois. (The novel is strong on clichés but, like *Citizen Kane*, confident of them.) After almost twenty years, while he returns close to the beautiful, cool, blue-linen-dressed Anne, and sees her often, she becomes Willie Stark's mistress.

Warren grasped what Welles had also grasped: that the darkness and violence of American politics were stained all through by sex but that, what with the lack of illumination and the noise and the elbowing crowd, the evidence was always damned hard to find. There is a scandal. Stark is forever 'tomcatting about', his son has a girl pregnant, the other party is on to it.

The Judge can call them off. Jack Burden shows him the documentary results of his journalistic investigations. It is a good scene, the Judge is austere, angry, admits the truth, softens. He didn't know the then Governor had protected him … 'his failing', Irwin hands down, 'was a defect of his virtue. The virtue of affection for a friend.' Cheerful and confident, the Judge bids Burden farewell. Burden is moved but unmoved. When he is gone the Judge shoots himself accurately through the heart. He was Jack Burden's father. Private passions break out and flood over public action.

It is a world we have lost, one in which the death of a judge spreads slowly like a tiny drop of blood in a clear glass of water. These were communities in which such things were true, and for all the overuse of the word today, communities are not the same thing at all. In a splendid *coup de roman*, Penn Warren makes Jack Burden the Judge's sole heir to a fortune launched with a crime.

He stays on as the Boss's press secretary, but he refuses to do the dirty work any longer. The good journalist knows what he knows, but stands up at last to old corruption. The novel, however, doesn't stop there (nobody ever wished it longer). Tom Stark, the Boss's son, is a handsome hunk of a footballer. He is mortally injured in a big match. Adam Stanton, who cannot live with the facts of dishonour or duplicity, lives as close as he can to the facts of poverty, filth, degradation. He learns of his father the some-time Governor's concealment of the Judge's single wrongdoing. He learns, from the clumsy termagent who is Willie Stark's secretary, of his sister's affair. He shoots the Governor in the stomach, and then himself.

Stark dies slowly, as does his son. Jack Burden the truth-teller gathers the story into its agreeable closure by at last marrying Anne Stanton. There wasn't, after all, much money left by the Judge. They leave his fine colonial mansion.

It is no doubt a tale of the passing of an order, the order of the capital of a post-bellum state and the men who ran its politics, lived in its city, spoke to its masses, were greeted in the street by its citizens. It is also the early version of the investigative journalist who, at that date, is himself tied to the same families and has the blood of the same power elite and its inevitable corruptions running through his veins. The book is set in the 1930s, when Huey Long was a national celebrity from a local theatre of power. But it came out in 1946, by which date journalistic truth-telling was largely uprooted from its neighbourhood and found its estate not in geography but played out on the huge screen of national front pages and their brand-new distributor and magnifier, the television screen.

The last great fiction of the tales of journalism in this first collection is the most famous of all. Evelyn Waugh's *Scoop* was published in 1938[22] and was, as we have seen, as close to his own journalistic experience of the Abyssinian war as was possible within the conventions of his kind of novel-writing, let alone his tearing high spirits, his genially unpredictable racism, his zest for human weirdness and his utter freedom from hypocrisy. *Scoop*, you might say, is objective journalism with its Tartuffian sanctimony struck out. Editors naturally mean what they say. All that foam-flecked, histrionic outrage is a big act.

Acts are performed by actors, and no one can doubt that an action driven and shaped by phoney feelings, and worked up into a public melodrama, carries whole peoples and their politics along. Something of the kind is one definition of fascism. Waugh writes from his heart, right enough, but his heart is a mixed creature, now caustic and contemptuous, now unexpectedly tender and diffident, but in either case pretty accurate as to moral judgement, above all in his judgement that the world is a comic place and that most of the people in it who exercise temporal power are fatuous and stupid.

Nobody of course dare tell them so, least of all tell Lord Copper, Waugh's press baron modelled on the brothers Harmsworth, owner of the daily *Beast*, modelled, to one's pleasure, on the *Daily Mail*. The only two replies to any dictum of the stout Lord which his timorous foreign editor, Mr Salter, will venture have long since become the oldest joke in the newsroom: 'Definitely, Lord Copper' (when right) and 'Up to a point, Lord Copper' (when wrong).

The novel's hero, William Boot, who contributes a weekly column on rural-natural history to the *Beast* (still alive, I'm glad to say, in today's *Guardian*), is mistaken for a more celebrated namesake, and despatched with a rich train of accoutrements to Ishmaelia to report on its satisfying little war. This turns out to be an early incendiary version of the later, larger more arctic affair. Waugh saw first the emptiness of the slogans of Marxism even when levelled against so anachronistic but resourceful a sacred pirate as Ras Tafari, later the very same Haile Selassie brought low by simple journalistic reporting of the legendary kind.

Waugh in the novel as in life is even-handedly delighted and disdainful at what Boot sees in Ishmaelia. Boot learns his trade with always startled nonchalance, beginning with the extraordinary jargon-code of the telegrams despatched by the *Beast* and devised, in an early version of Orwell's Newspeak, to save words and therefore pennies. Thus:

OPPOSITION SPLASHING FRONTWARD SPEEDILIEST STOP ADEN REPORTED PREPARED WARWISE FLASH FACTS BEAST.[23]

He is helped to translate by another of the horde of journalists who pile into the country and pile out again. This bravo, first a competitor then a collaborator, delivers himself of this definition of journalism, heartfelt by Waugh.

> Corker looked at him sadly. 'You know, you've got a lot to learn about journalism. Look at it this way. News is what a chap who doesn't care much about anything wants to read. And it's only news until he's read it. After that it's dead. We're paid to supply news. If someone else has sent a story before us, our story isn't news. Of course there's colour. Colour is just a lot of bull's-eyes about nothing. It's easy to write and easy to read, but it costs too much in cabling, so we have to go slow on that. See?'
> 'I think so.'[24]

The politics which is to be turned into news is powerfully summarised by Mr Salter for Boot's benefit in yet another instance of the author's savage prescience, this time of the late twentieth-century gentility known as political correctness.

> 'You see, they are all Negroes. And the Fascists won't be called black because of their racial pride, so they are called White after the White Russians. And the Bolshevists *want* to be called black because of *their* racial pride. So when you *say* black you mean red, and when you *mean* red you say white and when the party who call themselves blacks say traitors they mean what *we* call blacks, but what *we* mean when *we* say traitors I really couldn't tell you. But from your point of view it will be quite simple. Lord Copper only wants Patriot victories and both sides call themselves patriots, and of course both sides will claim all the victories. But, of course, it's really a war between Russia and Germany and Italy and Japan who are all against one another on the patriotic side. I hope I make myself plain?'
> 'Up to a point,' said William, falling easily into the habit.[25]

The joke is from life. In the 1960s the British journalist Keith Kyle was told in Addis Ababa by a Kenyan official for United Nations that 'there is racial discrimination in Ethiopia. The Ethiopians are white: everyone else is black, except that a few Europeans and Americans are honorary whites.'[26]

A few fragments must serve to place Waugh on our diagram. He wasn't writing farce. Any journalist who retains a sufficient taste for rue and takes a dose of the detachment officially as part of his equipment will recognise the unaffected truthfulness of Waugh's account of the desperate invention of stories to keep the newsdesk happy, of the headlong scatter to be first with such facts as could be put together, the rivalry, the jealousy, and the drink. Boot the perfect innocent sails through it all undefiled, missing (as Waugh did) the spurious action, catching as a consequence (as Waugh didn't) the big story-that-there-was-no-story, but befriending the pleasant, outrageous English dandy who makes a fortune to add to his fortune out of it all anyway.

It's easy to point the moral and admire the adornments of Waugh's short novel. Boot tells the truth in telegrams composed not in jargon but in the language of postcards ('ALL ROT ABOUT BOLSHEVIK'). Exploited without pity by the German girl who picks him up, uncomplaining of awful food and seedy living, Boot makes good, enters history and, as Waugh's hero, is gathered into the bosom of trade mythology.

There he stands, in spite of himself, and still standing after sixty-odd years, for simplicity of heart, colloquialism of diction, honesty of purpose, and in immunity to corruption. He meets the whole mad world, Lord Copper, Dr Benito, the giant Swede, Kätchen, the frenzied mob of fellow-journalists and the dim, bemused Ishmaelians with courteous acceptance and mild determination. He returns home to celebrity and rejects it. 'I've been treated like an ass.' 'Yes,' said Mr Salter sadly, 'that's what we are paid for.' For Lord Copper, a future beckoned 'full to surfeit of things which no sane man seriously coveted', above all, 'the incommunicable contentment of monolocution'.[27]

No sane journalist or indeed any other kind of human being could dissent from either judgement. But happily for myth-makers, nobody is happy being sane all the time.

CHAPTER EIGHT

The Blessed Simplicity of Action

Soon after the declaration of war finally arrived, and Britain kept its promise to Poland, Orwell reflected, during a review of a book by Malcolm Muggeridge in which Muggeridge took the temperature of his patriotic gore, that he found by that date surprising kinship with patriotism.

> I know very well what underlies these closing chapters. It is the emotion of the middle-class man, brought up in the military tradition, who finds in the moment of crisis that he is a patriot after all. It is all very well to be 'advanced' and 'enlightened', to snigger at Colonel Blimp and proclaim your emancipation from all traditional loyalties, but a time comes when the sand of the desert is sodden red and what have I done for thee, England, my England? As I was brought up in this tradition myself I can recognise it under strange disguises, and also sympathise with it, for even at its stupidest and most sentimental it is a comelier thing than the shallow self-righteousness of the left-wing intelligentsia.[1]

To anybody knowing only a little of Orwell's reputation, that closing expression of contempt will in turn surprise them. Its vehemence comes, in part, from a dislike of himself and things he had written about his hopes for socialist victories across Europe, his detestation of so much that was (that still is) awful about stuffy, snobbish old England. Like Muggeridge, like many Englishmen especially of the literature-loving fraction in his class, for a lot of the 1930s he hadn't *known what to feel*. So much was hateful about his country but it was his country in a way that wasn't quite the same for a pledged wanderer like Cockburn. The declaration of war cleared his vision. In that splendid short novel *The Shadow Line* Joseph Conrad speaks of the relief and reassurance felt by the young captain as, on assuming his first command, he enters 'a dynasty ... continuous in experience ... and in the blessed simplicity of its traditional point of view on life'.[2] Something of the same kind of thing was felt by Orwell and then, one would guess, by all journalists on all sides as they set themselves to balance truth-telling with the duties brought by membership of dynasty or just family.

Not that Orwell was ever one to write cheering-yourself-up journalism. By disposition he remained a solitary man, his marriage to Eileen O'Shaughnessy affectionate but a bit at arm's length, his moral reflexes always leading him to a slightly coarse insistence on the bad, especially the dirty and smelly side of things. He was, it must be said, always a little of an old misery and so, when he writes affirmatively, it is all the more moving. In the single most memorable opening of any piece of journalism during the Second World War, he begins, 'As I write, highly civilised human beings are flying overhead, trying to kill me.'

It is the first sentence of his great pamphlet-essay *The Lion and the Unicorn* (who were, in the nursery rhyme, it will be remembered, 'fighting for the crown'). The pamphlet, about 25,000 words long, was one of a series dreamed up by three Anglo-German-Jewish intellectuals, one of them Orwell's publisher Fred Warburg, and Orwell himself. The other pamphlets included Bill Connor's ('Cassandra' of the *Daily Mirror*) *The English at War*, T. C. Worsley's *The End of 'The Old School Tie'*, Ritchie Calder's *The Lesson of London*. All the writers were from the left-intelligentsia Orwell intermittently despised, in whose constituency he was counted, whose limits he battled in his journalism to transcend, never with greater success than in *The Lion and the Unicorn*.

His is a studiedly selective vision and a justly famous paragraph in it has been many times pillaged.

When you come back to England from any foreign country, you have immediately the sensation of breathing a different air. Even in the first few minutes dozens of small things conspire to give you this feeling. The beer is bitterer, the coins are heavier, the grass is greener, the advertisements are more blatant. The crowds in the big towns, with their mild knobby faces, their bad teeth and gentle manners, are different from a European crowd. Then the vastness of England swallows you up, and you lose for a while your feeling that the whole nation has a single identifiable character.[3]

The details he then picks out are like those of a newsreel or a news-paper's front page. They fix in one image one corner of the society, unlike the rest; they are then set in arbitrary juxtaposition; they are each singular, but immediately recognisable; you look at each and suddenly the focus spins and elongates; you can see a picture of the nation.

This was the part of Orwell's argument that most got under Raymond Williams's skin a generation later and caused him to write a short book putting down Orwell.[4] In the 1941 pamphlet Orwell wrote exasperatedly that the country 'was like a family with the wrong members in control',

> a rather stuffy Victorian family with not many black sheep in it but with all the cupboards bursting with skeletons. It has rich relations who have to be kow-towed to and poor relations who are horribly sat upon, and there is a deep conspiracy of silence about the source of the family income.[5]

Williams burst out in reply: 'If I had to say which of Orwell's writings have done the most damage, it would be ... the dreadful stuff from the begin-ning of the war about England as a family with the wrong members in charge.'[6] What Orwell saw and Williams couldn't stand was the massive continuity of English (and therefore British) life, naturally including much that was and is detestable, which included the stolid philistinism and gentle decency of a Labour Party remaining mostly and recognisably the same, as well as radically altered, ravaged by time, incompetent and optimistic, its lineaments discernible as such to Orwell, Williams, and to millennial Britain.

It took a kindly Jewish-American to rebut Williams in the right accents,[7] and it is indicative of the force of his argument as well as of the original one that Orwell is still so obviously worth our regard. It sounds rum to stress that gentleness of British life, which Orwell identified as so crucial in 1941, and to claim that it still abides when all about us the papers work them-selves into a phoney rage about scrounging asylum-seekers and report the pointless street murders of black children. There is however an always fluc-tuating gap between press passion and private feeling, closed only at rare moments by journalism of exceptional rightness and good fortune. The point of this account of *The Lion and the Unicorn* is that Orwell found one such moment; his good fortune was the presence of war.[8] He made of that coincidence between his feelings, his prose and his geography a statement going well beyond the surprisingly large sales of his two-shilling pamphlet (10,000) and in doing so he caught more than a moment (enough for most poets). He imagined and communicated a way to picture the long revolution of a society's historical wheel. Nobody would write an essay quite like *The Lion and the Unicorn* now. But in order to write intelligently about that society on the move, one would have to use Orwell's methods.

Once it was written, he found himself less shy about writing regularly in that vein. Orwell adopted a column in the Left-Labour weekly newspaper *Tribune.* The easiest way to characterise his three years of weekly articles in *Tribune* is to say that he wrote them while *happier* than he was before or since. At times he still wrote sourly and still harboured fantasies of a social revolution in which, incredibly, the wartime Home Guard, one of whose most punctilious sergeants he was, would serve as the people's militia in the van of unprecedented change. The change came, all right, but the successful nationalisation of all the utilities, heavy industry, the railways and the establishment of the first national health service in the world didn't need the Home Guard to enforce them, only an electorate. Indeed, Orwell never really saw how revolutionary, say, the health service would prove, casually disparaging it in a journalistic 'Letter from England' to the then Marxist journal in New York, *Partisan Review.*[9]

His tone to the Americans is unusually sour. His *Tribune* column 'As I Please' is dependably domestic, politically sunny, expressively pungent. His biographer chooses a few plums from the series,[10] and I shall similarly thumb out some fruit of my own. It won't do to dismiss these few touchstones of his wartime journalism either as decontextualised or as written for the tiny minority of readers who saw a copy of *Tribune.* What was read by larger numbers in daily papers has vanished from memory, whereas what Orwell wrote has stuck – unevenly, in the folk memory; caught up for commemoration right here.

Think of the Heralds' Office solemnly faking pedigrees and inventing coats of arms with mermaids and unicorns couchant, regardant and what not, for company directors in bowler hats and striped trousers! What I like best is the careful grading by which honours are always dished out in direct proportion to the amount of mischief done – baronies for big business, baronetcies for fashionable surgeons, knighthoods for tame professors.

With no power to put my decrees into operation, but with as much authority as most of the exile 'governments' now sheltering in various parts of the world, I pronounce sentence of death on the following words and expressions:

Achilles' heel, jackboot, hydra-headed, ride roughshod over, stab in the back, petty-bourgeois, stinking corpse, liquidate, iron heel, blood-stained oppressor, cynical betrayal, lackey, flunkey, mad dog, jackal, hyena, blood-bath.

No doubt this list will have to be added to from time to time, but it will do to go on with. It contains a fair selection of the dead metaphors and ill-translated foreign phrases which have been current in Marxist literature for years past.

I have never understood why the *News Chronicle*, whose politics are certainly a very pale pink – about the colour of shrimp paste, I should say, but still pink – allows the professional Roman Catholic 'Timothy Sly' (D. B. Wyndham Lewis) to do daily sabotage in his comic column. In Lord Beaverbrook's *Express* his fellow-Catholic 'Beachcomber' (J. B. Morton) is, of course, more at home.

Looking back over the twenty years or so that these two have been on the job, it would be difficult to find a reactionary cause that they have not championed – Pilsudski, Mussolini, appeasement, flogging, Franco, literary censorship; between them they have found good words for everything that any decent person instinctively objects to. They have conducted endless propaganda against Socialism, the League of Nations and scientific research. They have kept up a campaign of abuse against every writer worth reading, from Joyce onwards. They were viciously anti-German until Hitler appeared, when their anti-Germanism cooled off in a remarkable manner. At this moment, needless to say, the especial target of their hatred is Beveridge.[11]

There were others writing something like this at the same time. J. B. Priestley, a much better known novelist then, joined Orwell in broadcasting for the BBC, with the approval of the Ministry of Information – Orwell to India, his vehement anti-imperialism notwithstanding; Priestley to the nation and the USA. In the latter programmes, Priestley was blunt to a fault: his journalistic and broadcasting persona as 'Jolly Jack', a stout, honest, pipe-smoking, beer-drinking Yorkshireman with a good, strong north-country accent became well known, well loved too it seemed, and was in any case true to character. He reminded his listeners of the decadence as well as the grossness of class inequality in a people's war. He wrote and spoke the script for a rather good propaganda news movie *Britain at Bay*;[12] he was outspoken to Americans about isolationism and their indifference to Hitler's overarching global ambitions; 'the American frontier is the English Channel.'

THE BLESSED SIMPLICITY OF ACTION 171

The outbreak of war marked the BBC's opportunity. But it was of course an arm of propaganda. Its charter, its governors, above all its founder director-general, the Scots dominie with the beetle brows (Sir, then Lord) John Reith, had endowed the corporation with a name for massive rectitude not necessarily separable from saying what it was told to say by government.

Nonetheless, its political-cultural commentators were far from being hired mouths. They included, as well as Orwell and Priestley, T. S. Eliot, William Empson, Venu Chitale (an Indian woman writer speaking to her divided people in an effort to hold the secessionist Congress Party and the pro-British in the common endeavour of anti-fascism). They in turn called in Louis MacNeice, E. M. Forster, Dylan Thomas.[13] But the true authority of BBC news reporting reposed in the nine o'clock bulletin, read by one of a team of announcers with perfect BBC names – Alvar Liddell, Cedric Belfrage, Stuart Hibberd – in a distinctive, indistinguishably correct voice and poised, simple, direct prose. The voices were placed exactly at the centre of that register known to phoneticians as 'received pronunciation', but they were so popularly taken to heart that when the Germans hired the Irish quisling William Joyce to broadcast his pro-Nazi propaganda (quite a lot of it accurate) his voice and exaggerated elocution earned him the dismissive nickname of 'Lord Haw-Haw' and he was as much listened to for laughs as for fear he might be right.

The BBC was undoubtedly the voice of Britain, both official and informal. It was generally believed to be telling the truth, and Churchill had taken to heart the point of his Ministry of Information adviser who told him that the best aid to morale would be to tell the whole truth;[14] he after all had become Prime Minister because he grasped, even relished, the fact that wars must sometimes be fought, that this was one such occasion, and that the only wages he could offer were those of 'blood, toil, tears and sweat'. It is therefore difficult to analyse the BBC's journalism of the wartime period precisely because English class loyalties and formations together with the extremity of the nation's predicament made it possible to create a style of exceptional impassivity, cohesion, and formality in which no break was really discernible as between government, propaganda, and the utterances of the Corporation.[15]

By the end of the war things would be different, and this was due largely to the invention by one man of a quite different way of doing things – no less oracular, no less judicious, but resting for its calm authority and precision of judgement upon that man's own integrity, the remarkable extent to which he embraced his country's best political ideals and principles without being any the less the quick, unpriggish, likeable and always over-working man he was.

No doubt Edward Murrow had his weaknesses. But in him formation and opportunity combined to make an almost ideal broadcaster-journalist. His origins were pure American, building a decent life from not very much, handing it on to more prosperous children by way of plain making-do at home, Quakers in the tradition, and modest success in an excellent local college. He and Shirer were of a type, Murrow quicker, more stylish and daring, having more natural command, Shirer more cultivated, better read, his mind more commonplace.

Murrow's father gave up on a small farm in North Carolina and went west, in 1913 when Ed was only five, to become a hired logger in the pay of the Lumber Trust in Washington State overlooking Puget Sound. The boy listened with his two brothers to his (maternal) grandfather's tales of the Civil War, shot ducks and trapped rabbits, earned his tuition fees by stack-ing lumber and emerged from Washington State College, appropriately, with a B.A. in Speech. The First World War didn't touch him, but the Wobblies did. They were fired on during a peaceful protest on a steamer in the Sound, five killed, thirty-two wounded. They fired back and killed two deputies and were all arraigned for sedition and murder. Strikes by the loggers followed against pitiful wartime wages, and the loggers were put away for treason. In almost the only evasion of his life, Murrow later denied, in his long, bitter and victorious duel with Joe McCarthy, that he had carried an International Workers of the World card when he was fourteen or fifteen.[16]

His college ran a first-class drama society, a good debating team, and the first college course in radio broadcasting anywhere in the world. It also led Murrow to the presidency of the National Student Federation and to meet Janet Brewster, Mount Holyoke College rep, every bit his equal in good looks and good wits. He left college with a paid post on the books of the Student Federation. By September 1930 he was arranging broadcasts for CBS and pulling in as contributors Ramsay MacDonald and Albert Einstein. He won a desegregation fight when the Federation convention was held in Atlanta, and in 1932 his flair, initiative, his sheer visibility won him the post of deputy director of the Institute of International Education.

The point of the institute was to encourage international understanding and at twenty-four Murrow was already a little of a national figure. He was elected to an emergency committee helping to find situations for academics exiled or in flight from Hitler: for (among others) Paul Tillich, Kurt Lewin, Martin Buber, Hans Morgenthau, Herbert Marcuse.[17] In 1934 and 1935 Murrow also arranged, as a minor task for the deputy director of his institute, for two large summer schools to be conducted for American exchange students at the University of Moscow. By the time McCarthy got hold of *that* it was 1953 and the self-evident desirability of the exchange and criticism of ideas by university students had been replaced by an indurate and terrified refusal to think about anything.

At twenty-seven Murrow was appointed 'director of talks' in the new department of educational broadcasting at CBS, legally required of them by the Federal Communications Commission. William Paley marked him down for the European desk. There was everything to play for in political broadcasting. At the beginning of the decade there were only three daily national news programmes: one at noon for five minutes, one at four-thirty also for five minutes, and a quarter of an hour at eleven o'clock at night. Nobody listened to any of them.

So Murrow and his new wife Janet went to London and, in due course, in Berlin at the Adlon hotel, he hired Bill Shirer to join him. Murrow's enormous gifts, his reputation and his force of personality made it impossible for the NBC still to ignore the competition and masquerade as the American equivalent of the BBC. Murrow cut clean through stuffy old English rules, phoning the people he wanted directly, including Churchill, who was delighted.

Vigorous, serious, unstoppable he may have been, but he still had to accommodate CBS and New York suppositions that nothing much happened in Europe, that nobody should use a tape recorder, and that if there's nothing much to broadcast, fill the airwaves with school choirs singing *Volkschmaltz*. Between them, Murrow and Shirer matched up New York's demands for German choir children performing Ovalteeny folksong *and* for eye-witness accounts of Hitler's arrival in Vienna. Over the three years of their collaboration up to the Battle of Britain, Murrow and Shirer devised the forms of modern political news broadcasting: on-the-spot live commentary ('being there'); interviews with the leading actors in the drama if you can get them, with their lieutenants if not; lastly, round-the-continent reporting, a voice in every capital or key location, so that the listener could build in his or her imagination a simple little map corresponding to the geographic pattern of the voices and in doing so take bearings as a citizen of the world. Then the voices led back to London and to Murrow's crisp, incisive, personal summary, closing always with his farewell signature, 'good night and good luck.'

When the fighting began he became almost an Englishman, but always a journalist. For the Americans the BBC was both impossible and admirable. It couldn't be parodied. Murrow used to tell a story with gleeful wonder about one of the bombs that fell on Broadcasting House. Cedric Belfrage was reading the nine o'clock news when a loud explosion sounded over the air. Involuntarily he paused. Somewhere a voice said, 'It's all right.' 'I beg your pardon,' Belfrage said to the listening nation, and went on with the news.

That sort of thing, the buttoned-up, unquestionably courageous, always correct kind of conduct became the American synecdoche for wartime Britain, true and too good to be true. Murrow behaved just as well; as much an American as Belfrage was English.

For one thing he worked so damned hard. The two main news broadcasts went out live to the States at 12.15 a.m. and 3.45 a.m., while the bombs were falling. In daylight there was much to be done by way of reconnaissance, driving the streets in his open car, patrolling the Underground, soliciting Churchill, Attlee, Morrison, Beaverbrook for interviews, acting between-times as an air-raid warden (for which he was issued an official uniform) and coming back to the studio, exhausted, haggard, driven, good-humoured, cheerful, his hands shaking on the cigarette he always wore like a badge, to write and speak what he had found.

He followed the lessons of the plain American style being written at the same time wherever fatigues were worn by Martha Gellhorn, Ernie Pyle, A. J. Liebling. Its touchstone was its first-handedness, the tokens of that the small details of landscape, weather and human quiddity which gave such actuality to his account of being there. The CBS house rules forbade, in a little frenzy of detachment, 'emotionalism in reporting', but no rules could stop Murrow's determination to bring out the extraordinary power of the historic drama he felt himself privileged to act in. On New Year's Day 1941 he openly reminded his audience in the USA – 15 million of his people – that the future of world freedom was in their hands: America could no longer isolate herself from an omnivorous fascism.

On Saturday 7 September 1940, the peak of the Luftwaffe's day-and-night raids on London, Murrow drove down beside the Thames to Tilbury, crossed by ferry to Gravesend, saw the thick black clouds rising from the miles of docks, the roaring orange flames from the oil tanks. He and his companions watched from a ditch the Hurricanes wheeling above the big slow Dornier bombers, and when the air combat cleared they went to a pub.

Before eight the sirens sounded again … We went back to a haystack near the airdrome. The fires up the river had turned the moon blood-red. The smoke had drifted down till it formed a canopy over the Thames. The guns were working all around us, the bursts looking like fireflies in a Southern summer night.

The Germans were sending in two or three planes at a time, some-times only one, in relays. They would pass overhead. The guns and lights would follow them, and in about five minutes we could hear the hollow grunt of the bombs. Huge pear-shaped bursts of flame would rise up into the smoke and disappear. The world was upside down. Vincent Sheean lay on one side of me and cursed in five languages; he'd talk about the war in Spain. Ben Robertson lay on the other side and kept saying over and over in that slow South Carolina drawl, 'London is burning, London is burning …'

It was like a shuttle service, the way the German planes came up the Thames, the fires acting as a flare path. Often they were above the smoke. The searchlights bored into the black roof but couldn't penetrate it. They looked like long pillars supporting a black canopy. Suddenly all the lights dashed off and a blackness fell right to the ground. It grew cold. We covered ourselves with hay. The shrapnel clicked as it hit the concrete road nearby. And still the German bombers came.[18]

It's the click of the shrapnel which counts. He spoke quietly enough, but with an edge to his voice which belied its evenness, 'metallic poetry' someone said. Driven to exhaustion but still determined to bear his witness to what he saw, to the human importance he believed it to have, to his ardent wish that his own people at last make the difficult commitment which was, he was certain, their political duty, he filled his throat to over-flowing with the depth of his feeling and, during more than one broadcast, his voice broke.

Often he would have to follow 'air-raid precaution' rules and throw himself to the ground, 'mouth open, hands over ears', often he would have to dodge under the night cover of rubble or doorways to avoid the concus-sive blasts; always he was out in the ruined city or along the river, pledged to live out with its people, most of them poor, the whole hideous and thrilling action.

His seriousness and urgency matched the moment; many people felt the same, such that everything afterwards smacked of anti-climax. There was a long way to go before that was true of Murrow; it became true, eventually.

For he was already at the peak of his fame, and only descended from it when fatal illness gripped him in 1963. Churchill would invite him round to Number 10 for a nightcap (there were no railings barring off Downing Street then, and a single policeman at the door), and Murrow would tell him of the way the wind was blowing in Washington, or describe his own adventures in London. He went out to report the fighting in the western desert of North Africa in the spring of 1943 – and there delivered one of his most affecting passages.

He passes a little cleft in the stony ground 'knee deep with morning glories'; but there is 'a cold cutting wind ... It is a cold country with a hot sun.' He notices – this man's observations are so much more than observations, they are significances, that's what makes him a great and a lucky journalist – he notices the way the ambulance drivers nurse their loads over the smashed roads: 'You can see them lift on the wheel, trying to ease the shock for the wounded back behind.'

> Where the road cuts down to meet the stream there is a knocked-out tank, two men beside it and two men digging a grave. A little farther along a German soldier sits smiling against a bank. He is covered with dust and he is dead. On the rising ground beyond a young British lieutenant lies with his head on his arms, as though shielding himself from the wind. He is dead, too.[19]

Listening to this, or reading it, abruptly closes the distance between the events out there and our hearts within us. There is nothing much to do with such a moment except give a little gasp and feel the pity of war, the pity war distils. But you can't doubt that this is one of the things you have journalism *for*.

He did a live broadcast from a Lancaster bomber during the huge raids on Germany (later made into an unforgettable 78 r.p.m. gramophone recording), remarking, as they wheeled above Berlin caught in a searchlight beam, that human beings were roasting in the hellishness below as well as in the heavens above. Then they came home and a cool English girl invited them over the intercom to 'pancake now'. William Paley, now colonel, had forbidden Murrow to go to Berlin but he went all the same. On D-Day he despatched colleagues with the Airborne and went out himself across the Channel on 7 June. By now Murrow spoke not only to but for both sides of the Atlantic.

> Early this morning we heard the bombers going out. It was the sound of a giant factory in the sky. It seemed to shake the old grey buildings in this

bruised and battered city beside the Thames. The sound was heavier, more triumphant than ever before. Those who knew what was coming could imagine they heard great guns and strains of 'the Battle Hymn of the Republic' well above the roar of the motors ...'[20]

He watched the British 1st Airborne Division drop at Arnhem, he followed Patton across the German border early in 1945, and he was first through the gates of Buchenwald with the liberating American soldiers. On 15 April he gave one of his most famous broadcasts; it is as bare as Gellhorn's, as agonised as Richard Dimbleby's; how could it be otherwise? Yet he repeatedly objects 'for most of it I have no words'[21] and ends by imploring his listeners simply to believe what he reported in his 'mild account'.

British newspapers had long indicated that the concentration camps would open up with dreadful revelations. It took some time and a famous cartoon by David Low in the *Evening Standard* of tied bundles of Jews being loaded on to a goods train, but by 1942 reports were plentiful if inevitably patchy. The *News Chronicle*, the *Manchester Guardian*, the *Daily Herald* (Labour's official daily) all provided regular reports and in December 1942 Anthony Eden, Foreign Secretary, made a statement in the House of Commons about mass arrests, deportation and wholesale shootings across occupied Europe. The *News Review*, a British weekly modelled on *Time* magazine, carried an accurate description of the gas chambers.[22] The entire readership of the British press (only *Truth* remained unspeakable) knew that something appalling was in store. But no one was prepared for what they found.

At thirty-seven, after nine years in Europe, Murrow came home with his wife and child. He was enormously famous, the first journalist ever to be recognised by just everybody in the street. He bore the fame impatiently; he couldn't live in its white space. He came home with passionate beliefs about the importance of the work of the broadcast reporter, and the political debate such a figure should initiate. He found CBS entering the new, fierce competition of the airwaves and much less convinced than he was of the commercial encouragement that might be given to democratic argument. So they tried to sideline Murrow as vice-president of CBS and he hated it. He watched Shirer lose his job as anchorman on a news-and-discussion programme, partly because Shirer had lost something of his vim and acumen, partly because such programmes didn't catch the ratings. But Murrow's would and did, so he went back to the microphone in 1947 with a ten-year contract and 20,000 dollars a year travel expenses to hunt out his news. He picked the topics and voiced what he thought;

William Paley winced a bit but swallowed it. Murrow was unremittingly self-critical. Himself incomparably popular, he was dismissive of ratings wars, opinion polls and market research.

As the arctic of Cold War began to deepen and tighten, Murrow never wavered in his classical American liberalism. For a journalist the keystone of the doctrine is freedom of speech, but although Murrow was far from counting himself an intellectual, he was well aware of the inadequacy of such freedom on its own. The key freedom was set in an arch of connected values each holding up the other. Freedom, you might say, was for a man like Murrow (as for every good Constitutionalist) the practice of virtue itself. The freely speaking man not only treats ideas as the grammar of his motives to act well,[23] but in so practising his freedom of speech and therefore of action, treats the exchange of ideas as the innately democratic and necessarily courteous business of public life, without which the arena of the polity is abandoned to the care of the gun and the rat.

These convictions were most completely displayed and vindicated in Murrow's nationally conducted engagement with Senator Joe McCarthy.

In 1948 he had taken up with an eager young news broadcaster and Columbia graduate of twenty-two called Fred Friendly. They together edited a three-part series of long-playing recordings of the twentieth century's historic moments, featuring Murrow himself at times, which sold enormously well and was called *I Can Hear it Now*. Murrow began, with Friendly's help, a new radio series first called *Sunday with Murrow*, then *Hear It Now*. Murrow broadcast the new programme from Korea, replaying the assumptions of good and evil which served him well on the Western front of Europe but which were to be so radically questioned a year or two later below the 38th Parallel by James Cameron and René Cutforth.

When he came back he began to see that the Second World War and the Cold War were fought by very different weapons, some of which were wielded by his own countrymen. *Hear It Now* had had one of its greatest successes when it traced the journey of a pint of blood from the donor in the USA to the Korean battlefield; it brought in an extra half million pints in response from the audience.

Senator McCarthy was after different blood, had drawn it from State Department, Hollywood, the education service; he could smell it now among the liberals and lefties of CBS. In November 1951, in spite of Murrow's to-be-expected scepticism about television and himself on television, *Hear It Now* became *See It Now*. Murrow's serious gaze and calm mouth became as well known, as popular-because-trustworthy as his clear, calm American voice.

The programme had been going well, and so had McCarthy for a further couple of years when in 1952 Fred Friendly came to Murrow with the story of Air Force Lieutenant Milo Radulovich. In Murrow's and Friendly's conception of the programme, *See It Now*, like all good journalism, didn't just report news, it made it. It uncovered stories which threw into particular and dramatic relief the danger to or the health of the constitutive values of the society and its mighty Constitution.

Radulovich's case indicated an unpleasant rise in national blood pressure. He was like to lose his commission in the USAF not, as his inquisitors were careful to say, because of any kind of disloyalty on his part but because his father read communist newspapers and his sister had communist sympathies. They engaged withal in 'highly suspicious activities'.[24] A *See It Now* crew went to talk to Radulovich and two senior Air Force officers came to talk to Murrow and Friendly.

CBS bosses refused to advertise their own programme, so Friendly and Murrow wrote out cheques to the value of 1,500 dollars to the *New York Times* for a single advertisement. It read:

The Case Against Milo Radulovich A 0589893.

Produced by Edward R. Murrow and Fred W. Friendly.

They edited five hours of interview down to a thirty-minute programme. It spoke for itself except for a brief summary by Murrow at the end. Neither father nor sister was a communist. Father read Serbian-Yugoslav newspapers from his home-town. Murrow said 'We believe that "the son shall not bear the iniquity of the father" even though that iniquity be proved, as in this case it was not', and he pointed out that the function of the armed forces was to protect individual rights.

There was enormous mail in support of the programme. But that, though it heartened Murrow and Friendly, misses the point. Television debate is the context not the text of politics, and Murrow was calling the Air Force not to televisual account but to its political oath. Radulovich was reinstated. McCarthy's thugs produced photographs of the Moscow summer school run by Murrow in 1935. Murrow left behind him, as he flew to Korea at the end of 1953, instructions to prepare a film on the life and times of Senator Joseph R. McCarthy.

It went out on 9 March, advertised and paid for once again by Friendly and Murrow without the benefit of the CBS logo. It was lethal. Pretty well without commentary, it juxtaposed shots of McCarthy's contradictory statements, unevidenced allegations, sweaty and raucous bullying of witnesses, insolence to high office, false attribution, wanton innuendo and shameless mendacity. Murrow, in his habitually quiet and serious tones, pointed out the staple in McCarthy's methods of Senate investigation of whomsoever he chose. McCarthy was protected by House immunity from any redress, armed always with the immitigable power of subpoena, and with 'the half-truth' up his sleeve. Murrow ended:

> We must not confuse dissent with disloyalty. We must remember always that accusation is not proof and that conviction depends upon evidence and due process of law. We will not walk in fear, one of another. We will not be driven by fear into an age of unreason if we dig deep in our history and our doctrine, and remember that we are not descended from fearful men, nor from men who feared to write, to speak, to associate, and to defend causes that were for the moment unpopular.[25]

McCarthy bellowed and foamed and accepted time from *See It Now* to answer the case. It went out on 6 April. He put up his usual performance, and in an answer broadcast later, Murrow rebutted each allegation one by one with a care, accuracy and patience disallowed in the disgraceful procedures of the Senator's investigations. But by now McCarthy's gobbling vanity had led him to provoke the Army by calling George C. Marshall a traitor, and by the end of the year he was done for. Egregious as ever, a year or so later McCarthy came up to Murrow at a Washington party, placed his arm around Murrow's shoulders and, grinning, said 'No hard feelings, Ed?' Murrow threw off the oafish arm, and broke away.

See It Now stayed in the headlines it helped write for another four years. Its boldness, its judicious choice of subject, above all the integrity, the fame and the indifference of its great anchorman, as well as the intelligence of Fred Friendly, had inaugurated the era of news and political commentary on television. That era was itself, however, short-lived. However much the grand liberal democracies continued to play their politics with a theatrical flourish, television and all the news media proved to be far more preoccupied with profit than with politics, with audience size than with the state of the polity or the health of the nation. They cut their politics in the cloth of circulation figures, and turned substance into spectacle.

To say so is not, at this stage at least, to sing a song of deturpation over the destruction of mind brought by chat-show television. It is to say that, gradually, television and politics became, in the Anglophone and NATO-dependent nations, mutually embedded. One might notice as the first sign of this tendency CBS's taking *See It Now* off the air in July 1958.

Murrow thought so. He kept going, perhaps half-heartedly, with *Person-to-Person* and *Small World*, chat shows, by today's standards, of severe intellectualism. But in a famous indictment made before the grandees of the trade and their commercial directors, he spoke out for outspoken, controversial and politically fearless television debate, for the explicit collusion of ideas, for these things as the respiration of a democratic polity.

He stayed in the public eye and, for all the adulation I have described here, was as much the victim of abuse from America's crackpots, bigots and hoodlums as any good man will be. But by 1960, although he was only fifty-two, his killing work schedules as well as some other, mysterious and finally sinister affliction drove him into a year's leave of absence. When he returned, alienated from CBS, the new President invited him to become head of the United States Information Agency, the public and cultural relations office of the world's biggest superpower.

He took it, and his salary dropped from $200,000 per annum to $21,000. Not long before it was scrapped, *See It Now* had, controversial as ever, run a programme on the just-broached and still uncertain link between cancer and smoking. Murrow, in his twelve-, sixteen-, sometimes twenty-hour days had always smoked unfiltered Camels – sixty, seventy a day. After thirty-odd years the total must have neared a million. He suffered his own cancer for three more years within the offices of the USIA and did, of course, a powerful job. Then, moving stiffly and slowly, in great pain from shocking doses of cobalt radiation, he resigned. Laden with honours (including an honorary British knighthood which his Anglophilia required him to accept) but grim in spirit, he died in 1965.

Murrow's central place in the Pantheon of American, indeed of world journalism, is partly due to his good fortune in being the very first of his species. It is also, as is not always the case, naturally due to his enormous personal attributes – his stamina and all-American dedication to his work, his steely character and its fitting happily with those fine American principles seeking public expression during the Second World War. It is also due to his fame.

Fame, or celebrity as we'd now more usually say, has become one of the most powerful engines in society. That society maintains and perpetuates itself as a sequence of images of which ordinary people are mostly spectators but from whom a small minority are selected for personal appearance in the spectacle. One can argue that this has always been the state of affairs:

all states have their theatre; only the dramaturgy alters with history.[26] Either way, whether as novelty or custom, the spectacular society of the present has a more changeable cast than in previous dramatisations: access to centre-stage is less controlled by inheritance and lineage than it was, its appointments more sudden and less intelligible.

In these circumstances, it is no accident that the leading figures of the spectacle-making industry themselves become stars of society. They offer to mirror us to ourselves; we accept the offer and appoint them to celebrity. This is plainly apparent from the earliest days of Hollywood.[27] But Hollywood (in its self-image) was 'non-political'; it has never understood that its non-politicality is a fraud.

The politics of the present is charged with envy, cast by publicity, and impelled by attribution. This does not mean that its principal actors are all frauds and its audience all gulls. People watch the action more or less sardonically, more or less complicitly, because that is what there is. To be chosen by publicity is acknowledged to be a random business, hope feeds envy, one may be chosen oneself. No one can be indifferent to celebrity. The energies which impel the show are ours; we attribute importance to the leading actors. Without us the show cannot go on.

There are signs in the day-to-day conduct of Ed Murrow's journalism that he understood these things but saw it as his avocation to transcend his own celebrity by turning people's gaze away from himself towards the content of political action. My brief account of his working life is intended to point that moral. Perhaps it will make it clearer if I take a contrary biography, one of pyrotechnic self-display as well as undoubted spirit and singularity, in order to show not something trite about fame being the spur but something about journalistic celebrity as the vehicle of mass desire.

Dorothy Thompson's is the exemplary tale, and in making it so I must start from the ebullience and headlong garrulity of a woman always vehemently her own, even as she became a pennant blown by the gales of passion sweeping across America at the end of the war.

An outline of her earlier years reads like a manual in discovery of the free artistic spirit of libertarian American women. Child of an English north-countryman converted to the Methodist ministry who, filling in for a fellow-minister during a short church trip in New York State, met and married a working-class girl and so stayed put. Their first child, Dorothy, was born in 1893, sped through Syracuse with a blazing passion for poetry, became one of the brightest lights in the company of Gertrude Stein's lost generation beside the River Seine, and sold some articles to the Paris desk of the *Philadelphia Public Ledger*.

She was big, sexy, handsomely square-featured; power suit, starched blouse, long stride; she courted fame, and fame was duly bewitched. She won a full-time post effortlessly from the *Public Ledger*, settled in Vienna, learned fluent German, and after a romance that can only be called whirlwind, married Sinclair 'Red' Lewis, muckraker and socialist novelist of America, Nobel prize-winner and an irredeemable drunk.

She fell in love with a beautiful German actress; she and her whole kitchen were beaten up by Lewis when he was drunk, and bore up adoringly under the endless hours of self-recrimination when he came round; she wrote consistently fierce attacks on Hitler from the moment of his coming to power and while everybody else suspended judgement; she interviewed 'the little man', 'formless, faceless ... ill-poised, insecure ... the eyes alone notable, they have the peculiar shine which often distinguishes geniuses, alcoholics, and hysterics.'[28] She assured the readers of the *Public Ledger* that Hitler would never be Chancellor, but when he assumed that office, she so vigorously assailed him in 1934 that she won her supreme triumph by being thrown out of the Reich by order of Dr Goebbels.

Her whole personality sorted happily with this distinction. Even at home in America, where there were still large pockets of Hitler support and much larger ones of Hitler indifference, this recognition lit her name in lights. As well she might, she loved it. Her popular strength was the way her thought issued in vivid spurts of abstract passion; it was this which gave such simple readability and colour to her columns. A lifelong Republican, she was appointed on exile from Germany to the Republican *New York Herald Tribune*, and her column 'Off the Record' appeared opposite the space left for Lippmann's 'Today and Tomorrow'.

She was an enemy of federal government and so anti-Roosevelt. But all through the 1930s she splashed the vivid hues of anti-Nazism over her two 1,000 word contributions per week. In 1940 she concluded that, Democrat or no, Roosevelt must stay in office to steer his country through the war she had so confidently predicted for seven years already. The *Herald Tribune* couldn't stomach her apostasy and so, after taking Wendell Wilkie out to lunch to justify her defection (he took it amiably), she moved 'Off the Record' wholesale to the *New York Post*.

She was a great tank of overwhelming, often overwhelmed feeling, firing off her passionate certainties like a cloud of incandescent gasoline. To put things so is not, I should add, a male diminution of ardent womanliness (she was always at odds with Gellhorn, who scorned her rhetoric). She anticipated the ingenuous reflexes, the flaming jets of certainty in which tabloid political argument would all be illumined by the 1980s. This was the ground of her celebrity. There was no doubting what she felt, or the direct, appealing vulgarity with which she expressed it.

She was thus buoyed up on a vast, gassy cushion of both support and hostility. Her own intense ardour was blown hotter and huger as the correspondence in support and denigration rolled in. She had to blow this gale of feeling into the public's face, demanding of her people that they go to war against the monster of Nazism, welcoming the German-Soviet pact of 1939 as the bringing together of the two halves of Antichrist, affirming in response the great Anglo-American (and, for her, Christian) alliance 'to stop the destroyers of civilisation in their tracks'; to the English, as much her applauding admirers as the Americans, she wrote, 'The Abbey stands, the Museum lives, the Commons meet. Because the human will cannot be broken.'[29]

There is a lot of that in Dorothy Thompson, less embarrassing then than now, no doubt (she never doubted its sincerity herself). It was gallant of her as well to broadcast for CBS a series of talks 'On the Record' addressed to a 'good German', nominally 'Hans', an enlightened Junker of the Prussian upper class, publishing it as a short book (in English), called *Listen Hans*. In doing so, she was beginning her end-of-war campaign, which was to bring her mass obloquy and vilification, to treat the Germans, even in defeat, as first of all human and only contingently Nazi.

This was probably the best of her, both in terms of political expediency and idealism. In one of her countless, often tedious public addresses, this time in the New York town hall late in 1945, she predicted famine and the death of millions in central Europe, and she drew shocked gasps from her audience when, in a savage trope, she suggested it would be more humane to reopen the gas chambers for German children.

She kept going in this vein, now much more unpopular but still famous, known in any street in New York and most in London, praised by other columnists as the 'American Valkyrie', 'our Boadicea',[30] standing up and therefore standing for an American purity of heart, for the will to do (because one can do) *something* about human misery, for dauntlessness, sleepless energy, torrential verbosity, for the self-justifying virtue of campaigning itself.

As the suspiciousness of the epoch darkened and took hold it tainted her name, as it would anybody's with a will to find a way to treat enemies better. She threw herself behind WOMAN, the World Organisation of Mothers of All Nations, begging the President who might still listen to her because she was Dorothy Thompson to end the Korean War, berating the readers of the excellent *Ladies' Home Journal* to support world disarmament. But in 1951 even Eleanor Roosevelt accused WOMAN of being in the control of the Communists and although Thompson answered her fiercely and personally, she decided to quit.

Her fame had shrunk a little from the days in 1940 when her column, her 200 syndications, her public addresses made her probably the best-paid woman journalist there has ever been. She was, with Lippmann, one of the first of the columnists, and it is the whole point of a column to be seen and heard, to blaze like a torch, to quicken the feeling and the pulse of the breakfast table and the subway, to sound echoes from the vaults of history and to make, on behalf of smaller scenery, a big thing of today's life and yesterday's death.

It was a harder task to address, as Thompson did, the coming actuality of domestic inaction in wartime, and at a moment when all those at home were preoccupied by what was happening at great, invisible distances. She tried to fill those distances with feeling, and thereby to close the gap between passivity and action. Easier by far to write and speak, as Murrow had to, from the centre of that action and allow the plain telling of the facts to settle into its own order.

That became the national style in wartime. The best of American culture (for once the right word) speaks through it. Out of a crowd of contenders, the two best writers, Abbott Joseph Liebling and Ernie Pyle, must serve to suggest the throng behind them.

Liebling indeed wasn't really one of the same crowd as Pyle, for he had joined Ross's *New Yorker* in 1935. But the *New Yorker* was in khaki like everyone else, and he was its house French specialist, having gone from Dartmouth and the Columbia School of Journalism to the Sorbonne as a medievalist. When war broke out he was in Paris until the fall of France, took his French to Tunis,[31] and then to the Normandy landings. During his wanderings he wrote a striking review of the underground press in occupied France, 'Notes from the kidnap house'.

He groups them under three headings – communist, socialist, and the more or less Gaulliste remainder. He notes what moral credit the Left has accumulated by its bravery in leading the popular resistance, with the non-Gaulliste Right abominably compromised by Vichy. Some of the quotations are now painful to read.[32] Alongside the lists of those killed in expeditions for the Resistance, and allowing for the expression of vengefulness to be fulfilled, are the still shining declarations of what 'a free

Europe of free citizens' would be like, after 'our common experience of slavery' (this from *Libération*). Time and again, the underground presses express misgiving that after victory the 'same old striped pants' as had been soiled by collaboration would be restored to power by the Americans. They report brave gestures of contempt flung at their captors by imprisoned heroes of the Popular Front, and they offer tips on how to thwart stool-pigeons, informers and suchlike. *Combat du Languedoc* ended one report by publishing a list of traitors and saying, 'On the day of liberation, patriots will sweep away the obscure rabble of informers for the Gestapo.' Liebling ends with a story of a communist informed upon and shot while escaping by the gendarmerie. 'We know them', said *La Voix du Nord*, but Liebling adds bleakly, 'Until some assurance to the contrary is received, many writers in the resistance papers seem to fear that the Allies are coming to rescue the gendarmes.'

Liebling did his bit by crossing the English Channel in a landing craft and duly writing about it, but it was Ernie Pyle who became the US troops' own favourite and most-read correspondent and who was, in their judgement, the most vivid and accurate of correspondents at the front. Hemingway (who hardly knew him) introduced him to some military companions in Paris in 1944 by saying (there are many versions), 'This is the Pyle who writes the truth for doughboys from the asshole of the war; I'm just the haemorrhoid who writes for officers.'

Pyle lends himself to as memorable a cartoon version of the US journalist at war as Dorothy Thompson at the town hall in New York. Like her, however, he was quite spontaneous in this. He didn't complete his journalism degree at Indiana; he wrote an aviation column for one of the chains and then a sort of Wandering American column, telling quirky, perky, sad little tales of human endeavour and failure[33] from Alaska to Central America. He flew to England in 1942 to cover the training of the GIs, and from then on was the GIs' own newspaperman, refusing grand strategic narratives or explanations, concentrating on what he could see and how he felt the soldiers feel.

He writes in terse sentences set in short paragraphs. He comes to a tactical point – that's as general as he gets – looks up and imagines he sees puzzlement on his readers' faces. He pauses, explains the point very barely, and goes on. He arrives in a little French village, smashed and empty. The ditches are full of dead men, one without head or arms or legs. There is a brick-red American tank, its turret blown off, smoke still drifting up from it. A British aircraft lies upside down. He finds a solitary American in a field. It turns out there is a pilot still trapped alone in the upside-down aircraft. He has been there a week.

A man lay on his back in the small space of the upside-down cockpit. His feet disappeared somewhere in the jumble of dials and rubber pedals above him. His shirt was open and his chest was bare to the waist. He was smoking a cigaret.

He turned his eyes toward me when I peeked in, and he said in a typical British manner of offhand friendliness, 'Oh, hello.'

'Are you all right,' I asked, stupidly.

He answered, 'Yes, quite. Now that you chaps are here.' ...

His left leg was broken and punctured by an ack-ack burst. His back was terribly burned by raw gasoline that had spilled. The foot of his injured leg was pinned rigidly under the rudder bar ... Yet when we found him his physical condition was strong, and his mind was as calm and rational as though he were sitting in a London club. He was in agony, yet in his correct Oxford accent he even apologised for taking up our time to get him out.

The American soldiers of our rescue party cussed as they worked, cussed with open admiration for this British flier's greatness of heart which had kept him alive and sane through his lonely and gradually hope-dimming ordeal.

One of them said, 'God, but these Limies have got guts' ...

We don't know whether he will live or not, but he has a chance.[34]

This is how he does it. He fastens on a small tale and tells it tersely, tells it about rifle repairmen and heavy ordnance mechanics. One colonel told his officers 'Ernie Pyle is with the regiment' and they 'looked at me and I felt embarrassed'. He sees a man baling out of an aircraft 10,000 feet up catch his parachute on the tail of his aircraft, sees the parachute tear away, 'then a tiny black dot fell through space, all alone.' He is bombed by his own side: 'Anybody makes mistakes.'

In the end he became a sort of talisman, overprotected by the staff so that he could no longer see his subject. He fought clear of that, and then, when he had had enough – he was forty-five, his wife was intermittently in an asylum – the generals begged him to take himself and his gifts to join the troops in MacArthur's awful, brilliant, island-hopping campaign across the Philippines towards Japan. He went, grizzled, aching, twice the age of the infantrymen he accompanied, and was shot clean through his steel helmet by a machine gunner who had lain silent all day as the troops moved past him.

The last report from the war was published in the *New Yorker* a year and three weeks after the leading events which it described. John Hersey's *Hiroshima*, I cannot doubt, is the finest piece of war reporting I know and one of the greatest examples of journalism as literature we have.

In part, of course, this is because the event itself was so utterly frightful and momentous. We approach it, quite rightly, with a mixture of horror and reverence. The most commonplace account of the barest facts is shocking and almost always touching, as witness our response to the kind of children's writing with which Hersey closes and where the light mixture of cheerful recollection and fleeting sadness is hardly to be borne.

Hersey is aware of all this. Outrage would be useless, satisfaction of course contemptible. He was well equipped, had coincidentally been personal secretary for a while to Sinclair Lewis long after the latter's separation from Dorothy Thompson. He later became a respectable novelist; he had been a reporter in Italy and the Philippines for *Time* and *Life*. But he never wrote so well again, for he never had such a subject.

In the tone of his telling he somehow manages to absorb something of Japanese correctness, less a matter of understatement than (as it were) fastidiousness. Where one is not allowed to mention what is disgusting but where the most ordinary domestic scene turns into something that disgusts, then small gentilities will mitigate plain horror. So Hersey describes Mr Tanimoto, a slight, thin, devout Methodist minister of quite amazing stamina, laboriously poling a heavy boat across the Ota river, going to rescue injured people stuck on a sandbank after taking refuge from the fires in the water. They were too weak to climb into his boat. 'He reached down and took a woman by the hands, but her skin slipped off in huge, glove-like pieces. He was so sickened by this he had to sit down for a moment. Then he got into the water and, though a small man, lifted several of the men and women, who were naked, into the boat.'[35] With a superhuman effort, he moves them to a higher bank, but the water rises during the night and they all drowned anyway.

Time and again Hersey pierces us with such details, described with his mild, almost Japanese quietness. Perhaps most terrible are the twenty soldiers a German pilot finds, sitting quite still and quiet under some low trees. 'Their faces were wholly burned, their eye-sockets were hollow, the fluid from their melted eyes had run down their cheeks. (They must have had their faces upturned when the bomb went off; perhaps they were anti-aircraft personnel.)'[36]

Hersey tells his story by finding six survivors when he arrives in the summer of 1946, following them through the days after the explosion. He happens upon, or else he chooses, survivors who mixed selfless heroism with endurance. In any case, he finds a kind of numb will-for-life (often disappointed by death) and a general recourse, in an extremity which could not bear much thought or any search for explanation at all, to bedrock Japanese values such as formal courtesy, self-containment, muteness in suffering, attentiveness to the needs of others. Maybe one would find in all peoples in such circumstances such attempts to keep (as it were) perfectly still, to thank others for small help, to return inside oneself, and each according to local custom. Hersey found these things in Hiroshima and, in spite of the devastation, turned his tale of a visit to inferno into one of the chance of restoration.

He denies himself irony, except twice, once at the expense of Almighty God, once at the expense of almighty science. The German priest visits a crippled victim, desperately ill with radiation sickness, one of Hersey's characters. She asks why God permits such suffering. "'My child,' says Father Kleinsorge, "man is not now in the condition God intended. He has fallen from grace through sin." And he went on to explain the reasons for everything."'[37] On the second occasion, he notes that nobody at all in Hiroshima heard the American short-wave broadcast by the new President telling world listeners in a shout that no other country in the world could possibly have developed such an amazing bomb. Hersey remarks that Japanese scientists were amused by the American determination to keep all the research details about the results of the explosion secret. The key research about effects was done at the point of explosion and for twenty years afterwards by tens of thousands of the dying inhabitants of Hiroshima.

The moral of Phillip Knightley's pioneering history of war correspondents is that the authorities always try, largely successfully, to wrap things up well away from the newspapers, and that the reporters oblige them. He ends his section on the Second World War with a man from Reuters looking back and saying, 'It wasn't good journalism. It wasn't journalism at all.' It is too clunking a conclusion that Knightley so insists on poking into us. The journalists chase after the fact. They turn it into a tale, tall for preference. Good man, good woman, and good journalist are not exclusive terms however. The tale of the Second World War as told by Orwell, Murrow, Pyle and Hersey plays down the sound and fury. But it still signifies plenty, to the credit of journalism as well as of humankind.

Chapter Nine

Cold War and Cruel Peace

The Second World War was good for the British press and for the standing of British journalists. Even with the newsprint and paper shortage in 1947, 87 per cent of all British adults read a daily newspaper, one in four of them the *Daily Mirror* or the *Daily Express*.[1] A dozen daily papers shared a circulation of well over twenty million daily readers;[2] by 1957, when rationing was ended and the abundance of the amazing, long, postwar boom which lasted until 1973 had begun to flow, daily sales touched 30 million. That people read their papers did not necessarily mean that they believed them or always did as they were told by them. They disobeyed the *Daily Express* and its little demon of an owner with his unqualified support for Churchill; they ignored his flat refusal to countenance anything other than the way he wanted the world to be.

Beaverbrook was Lord Privy Seal in the interim government before the general election of 1945 was held, but he was Churchill's creature now and his whole heart was given to winning the old man's country for him. So the *Express* ran potty headlines about an imaginary Labour Party caucus, headed by Harold Laski and staffed by fellow-travellers, which would run the country; one *Express* headline announced that 'Socialists Decide They Have Lost' and another found in the nick of time a 'Late Swing to Tories'. But all was lost, the Labour majority was 146, and in a mixture of rage and effrontery the *Express* ran the headline, when the result, long delayed by counting the overseas service vote, was finally known, 'National Socialists'.[3] The circulation of the *Express* went on serenely upwards, however, unaffected by its aggressive idiocies, while the only evidence that the press was in tune with the people was the *Daily Mirror*'s circulation, which went even higher than the *Express*'s and in 1964 touched five million, a figure never reached again by anybody.

The leading journalist at the *Daily Mirror* was William Connor. He wrote under the pen-name Cassandra, assigned him by one of the directors; he was, as he said, a bit startled to find himself a woman ostracised by fellow-women for telling uncomfortable truths and finally put to a disagreeable death. But he took up the burden of his byline gamely, and when he returned from uniform after four years and resumed his column at the paper, he opened it immortally by writing 'As I was saying when I was interrupted, it is a powerful hard thing to please all the people all the time.'[4]

He had joined the *Mirror* from the advertising agency J. Walter Thompson in 1935. His father was a clerk in the pension department of the Admiralty, and Bill Connor went to the local school in Wood Green and was a Londoner all through. He joined the paper the same day as Hugh Cudlipp, who as editor was to see the circulation top 5 million; he became close friends with Philip Zec, one of the trio (with Low and Vicky) of great British cartoonists of the era. Connor, to his delight, found work on the paper congenially larky, a tendency which matched his own deplorable taste in practical jokes.[5]

On the *Mirror* in those days journalists picked up any writing chore that needed doing, and Connor turned his hand to military and aviation reports until the director appointed him to the name and the column, an innovation in tabloid London in 1935. The manner and style of the column developed, as one would expect, over time but from the start it was couched in the short, punchy, no-nonsense-from-you-mate style which was the *Mirror*'s answer to the *Express*'s patriotic drumbeating. Manner and topics were inveterately jocose, as often as not strictly domestic ('Herrings for breakfast', 'The clock at St Pancras') but unaffectedly, bluntly political when that was the preoccupation of the working class and male readership with whose heart Connor's own heart beat as one. He went to Germany, spoke the language, loved the landscape, detested the Nazis and was arrested by them just before war broke out. Dr Goebbels didn't miss much in the papers; after the war Connor's name was found on a Nazi death list, something of which he was naturally proud. He set out the essentials of the enemy in a sketch of Hitler immediately after he became the paramount public enemy: 'Suffers from acute monomania, with periodic fits of melancholia. Frequently bursts into tears when crossed.'[6]

In March 1942 his friend and ally Zec drew an unusually powerful cartoon. It showed a ragged and exhausted sailor clinging to a few timbers lashed together, alone on a big sea and beneath a darkening sky. Connor suggested the caption, 'The price of petrol has been raised by one penny (Official).' The obvious point was the human costs of gas at the pump, but Herbert Morrison, Home Secretary, took a huge huff, accused the *Mirror* of blaming merchant navy casualties on profiteering and warned the editor that with any more trouble he would close the newspaper down as he had the *Worker* and *This Week*.

The *Mirror* had been at once strongly patriotic and independently critical of government. It was all too much for Connor. He wrote a valedictory column and enlisted.

In the House of Commons you will have heard how criticism is received. The Government is extraordinarily sensitive.

They are far too glib with the shameful rejoinder that those who do not agree with them are subversive – and even traitors … I cannot and will not change my policy. In the past I have applauded politicians who have got out rather than knuckle under. Today I applaud my own funeral. I believe, like Edmund Burke, that the Government should understand that it holds good in this country that 'He that wrestles with us strengthens our nerves and sharpens our skill. Our antagonist is our helper!' … Mr Morrison can have my pen – but not my conscience.

Mr Morrison can have my silence – but not my self-respect.[7]

Just before he went into the army his pamphlet *The English at War*,[8] one of those commissioned by Martin Secker along with Orwell's *The Lion and the Unicorn*, came out. It had been a shrewd judgement on Secker's part; the essay showed Cassandra at his most forthright and faithful-hearted; it is full of sentiment, slightly idealised and melodramatic, like a first-rate cartoon, all the more moving for that. Cassandra in this form joins, shall we say, the best songs of Vera Lynn, the best jokes of the Crazy Gang, the best movies of the Army Kinema Unit as the great monuments of British popular culture. What he writes is much more than evocative, though he begins with evocation and invocation: a fine Zec drawing of a small boy kneeling in the packing case which is his safe bed on the platform at Aldgate underground station. He sprinkles a series of anecdotes from the press of the day across his pages, each juxtaposed to contrast the endeavours and endurance of war with the continuities of English class snobbery and the disparities of wealth, self-indulgence and display which Connor abominated. When the war was over and won, these, he prayed, would be swept away by the newly self-confident and wholly indispensable Common People whom he apostrophised on his last page:

Fighting for democracy loses some of its point if it is going to lead us back to where we were on September 3, 1939. The English can and will endure anything, provided they are able to believe in their cause. That cause would be immeasurably fortified if the people knew that they were fighting to hold the better things that belong to the past and the far finer things that can be wrested from the future. VICTORY WITHOUT A NAME is a laurel wreath laid in desolation and sorrow. To struggle for life alone may be to lose everything that makes life worth while. But to fight for a way of living that is more kindly and that is more merciful and more tender is the only reason why this war can be justified.[9]

He went back to the *Mirror* after spending some of his military time in the British Army newspaper unit, resumed his column, patrolled the dying British Empire in Malaya, Palestine during the British mandates, Pakistan, Australia. His columns[10] retained their never-formulaic mixture of unshakeable loyalty to the class which read him, whimsy (he wrote copiously of his love of cats), food and wine (shepherd's pie, a mammoth Spanish chicken soup), and his plain, trenchant, egalitarian and generous recommendations to his readers on how to judge and live their politics. He bade Stalin farewell by allowing his courage and naming 'his shiftiness, his cruelty ... his evil purpose and unspeakable methods' and ends bluntly, 'Few men by their death can have given such deep satisfaction to so many.'[11]

In one astonishing expedition, he interviewed Senator McCarthy while the Senator was having dental treatment. Perhaps this quotation best commemorates Cassandra, as he gave McCarthy some of the treatment McCarthy had himself doled out during his inquiries. It is not exactly gentlemanly but it is marvellous journalism.

Cassandra tells McCarthy how Mussolini was lynched in a Milan street and how, in the photo of him hanging there upside down, the corpse reminded Connor of the living McCarthy, so much so that he wondered (aloud) if dictators dead would look like would-be dictators alive.

Joe shut his mouth, and I think what could be called a shadow of pain clouded his face. The dentist looked as if a blockbuster had hit him ... I said that there should be no cause for distress anywhere as it was clearly understood between Mr McCarthy and myself that this was going to be a frank conversation of the type that formidable and powerful politicians could handle in their stride.

Would the Senator therefore calm the dentist and put the nurse at her ease? Mr McCarthy growled 'Relax' ... From the dentist's with all its corrosive jollification, we moved back to the Senate Office Buildings where the Senator indulged in a little verbal mayhem himself, denouncing the British for killing American soldiers for the sake of commercial gain. The few odd calculations that I was able to make about blood spilt in two World Wars and treasure piled up in the second which made the United States easily the richest and most powerful nation on earth, made no impression on McCarthy ... I was now in the role of a violent extraordinary trophy that the Senator had brought home for his friends to see. He remarked that he had never seen anybody like me before and I replied that in his case neither had I, and I hoped that it would never occur again.

A rancorous time was had by all, and after remarking that I hoped his teeth hurt for ever more the fragrant encounter came to an end.[12]

It's all there. The bad jokes, the brutality, the self-confidence, the refusal to do anything but name moral and political bullies and rogues for what they are, the absence of deference to the celebrated, the slightly boastful but unshakeable stand on principle. Cassandra and his moment made things like this possible in English tabloid journalism. They aren't possible now.

Connor's brief was to write about England, his concerns were local, his way was pawky. He didn't ignore world politics, nobody in such a job could. He once observed that since the United States had taken over the world they were welcome to it. He, for his part, was going to write for and about his own blessed people.

The *Daily Mirror* saw things that way. Its collective voice in the 1940s and 1950s implied a group of vociferous, comfortably opinionated English working men. That is to say they had come to a settled and confident view about the indispensability of their place in society, their deserts and their comparatively modest expectations.[13] Their politics were those of their powerful trade unions and the new government which even they nevertheless believed to be 'too bureaucratic', 'too interfering by half' and so on. One favourite style of opposition was spoken by the 'cheeky chappie' kind of stand-up comic, and another – Bill Connor's – was bluntly outspoken, critical, tolerant, far-sighted but near-concerned. These men in a man's world, deeply respectful of Mother but only in Mother's place, were not consumers of the kind everyone in all social classes has now become. Easy to idealise them, and take quite out of sight the grudgingness, the sudden blazingly hot show of temper, the untenderness, the absence from family. But they belonged to no one but themselves, just as their country, in an important way and in spite of its preposterous ruling class, belonged to them.

The journalism of the *Mirror* matched their way of life, which is to say that the newspaper's excesses were a source of grunted, passing amusement to men of deep political stability for whom all large political events were filtered through the texture of a close group of fellow working men at factory and club. The mass production methods which Henry Ford put in train in 1910 or thereabouts and which were perfected in America, Britain and Germany made possible the mass political movements of between the wars, and the mass propaganda and newspapers as well, as Northcliffe was first to realise. But they also ensured that men (the working population being largely male) laboured in groups of comrades, bound often by common danger, by common tasks and common enemies. Most of the heavy labour – docks, iron and steel, coal mines, shipyards, car assembly – was just that: heavily laborious drudgery. They had their everyday politics, and they had their newspaper ones. As I said before, members of the social class which depends for its labour and rewards upon reading naturally over-estimate the significance of reading. Newspapers matter less than they think.

That being so, working-class men sought a particular, fairly easy-going experience when they picked up the *Mirror* and folded it in a coat pocket to be read in a break with a tin of cold, sweet, milky tea. They used it as a source of corroboration of what they knew they felt and as a prompt to piquancy when they didn't know what they felt. In Aneurin Bevan's titanic struggle with the British Medical Association to inaugurate the National Health Service, the excellently socialist house cartoonist at the *Mirror*, Philip Zec, drew in one picture a gigantic pile of votes in favour of the service flanked by Charles Hill, BBC's 'Radio Doctor' and himself a poor creature of anti-democratic prejudices, counting a tiny heap of BMA votes against.[14]

Elderly doctors called the NHS a Nazi proposal – 'something very like that regime which is coming to its sorry end at Nuremberg'[15] – but the *Mirror* knew where it stood, and said in a moderating voice:

Older doctors have money to make. They want to be able to sell their practices. But a nation's health is not to be bought and sold. The young doctors, those who were in uniform, know that the new service will be their service in the patients' service. That is the future.[16]

Mirror readers, when they read this, nodded approvingly. For the rest, the *Mirror* itself told them,

We shall go on being sensational to the best of our ability. Sensationalism does not mean distorting the truth, it means the vivid and dramatic presentation of events ... It means big headlines, vigorous writing ... everyday language ... Every great problem facing us – the world economic crisis, diminishing food supplies, the Iron Curtain – will only be understood by the ordinary man, busy with his daily tasks, if he is hit hard and hit often with the facts. Sensational treatment is the answer whatever the sober and 'superior' readers of some other journals may prefer. No doubt we shall make mistakes, but we are at least alive.[17]

Matthew Engel observes, 'it has probably never been put better.' Sobriety and superiority were attended to in other quarters, ones very much more in thrall to how the United States required that the world should be understood. The *Mirror* had put away recollections of Zec's magnificent cartoon honouring the sword of Stalingrad, the jewelled original of which had been on display for so many weeks in Westminster Abbey. Cold War was reduced to the 'iron curtain'.

Even out of office, it seemed, the old man Churchill could bind his country by his rhetoric to the United States in its crusade against the Soviets. The American chariot careered towards the iron curtain as designed by both sides in an alloy compounded of four elements: Stalin's peculiar dreadfulness; the nuclear bomb; the Marshall Plan; and the Truman Doctrine. Stalin was what he was: we know enough about that now. Nuclear weaponry is pretty familiar after sixty or so years as well; it has however been forgotten,[18] as the biographer of the atomic bomb so compellingly put it in 1988, that Niels Bohr, father of nuclear physics, 'saw ... all the way to the present, when menacing standoff has been achieved and maintained for decades without formal agreement but at the price of smaller client wars and holocaustal nightmare and a good share of the wealth of nations – and stepped back'.[19]

The Soviets exploded their trial atomic bomb in 1949 and by then enough was known from all the inquiries at Hiroshima to hold the world for half a century on the crazy fulcrum known as the balance of terror, acronymised by a wag of a strategist as Mutual Assured Destruction.

The Marshall Plan was the boldest action ever taken on behalf of a postwar wasteland. It rescued European capitalism when capitalism was the only saviour in sight in 1945. The vast parties of communism in Western Europe had no programme in hand of transnational rehabilitation. Within individual countries, many torn by class strife, which lay also along the splits between Left and Right, resisters and collaborators, there was only agreement that after two wars in thirty years, the continent had better find another way to resolve its differences and aim at an inclusive rather than a competitive kind of prosperity. The cure for starvation, subversion and underproduction was doubtless effective planning and the restoration of markets. But the basics of such survival, let alone revival, simply weren't there: water, food, energy, capital – and the greatest deficiency was capital. Until the dollars came, Britain was bracing itself to halve its food rationing allocation, to expect one and a half million unemployed, to shut down portions of the electricity grid at a time when the Siberian winter of 1946–7 was freezing the breadth of Europe.

General George C. Marshall, best of Americans, had taken over at the State Department and had concluded that Stalin reckoned that all he had to do to dominate Europe was wait. Sixty years later, we might think instead that all the tyrant wanted was to rebuild his shattered land, within whose much-invaded frontiers even paranoids might reasonably want to feel safe. But in 1947 a new wooden-faced totalitarianism was offering to fill a large enemy-shaped hole in Western sensibilities, vacated by the Nazis after their defeat. So Marshall offered the vast American surplus created by war production to most European economies, including the Soviet ones. The USA was making far more goods than it could sell to itself. The Europeans were to be given the dollars to buy them. The Republican press, brimming with anti-communist hatreds after recent Republican victories in Congressional elections, thought it was all some kind of dole. The *Herald Tribune* said solemnly that 'there seems to be no grasp of any business principles in connection with this situation',[20] and the *Wall Street Journal* rightly detected the hand and theories of John Maynard Keynes in the deal and dismissed it accordingly. In the end Marshall had to hustle it through Congress by setting the drums of *grande peur* to throb with anti-communism, and the leader-writers – the brothers Alsop at the *Herald Tribune*, James Reston at the *New York Times* – danced for decades to its atavistic rhythms.

It's still hard to tell whether these men truly believed in the possibility, even the likelihood, of the nuclear war to which they referred with such insouciance. The variably corpulent, bibulous and agreeable Joseph Alsop was not an imaginative or subtle man and, like many journalists on the inside of politics, was quite unable to modify his glee at being there with any touch of irony which might have given him a distance from which to see the whole charivari more judiciously. He exuded judiciousness, of course, as a badge of office, but it was of the kind which claims so knowingly to know that the 'Korean war was a direct consequence of the Truman-Louis Johnson disarmament program plus one other event ... the Communist victory in China.'[21] Johnson was Secretary for Defense and his failure to prepare for a European nuclear war was a bee which buzzed in the Alsops' bonnet for a decade.

> It is impossible to find any informed official in Washington, in uniform or out, who sincerely shares this Johnsonian view, or who believes that the current level of expenditures will provide in time even a skeleton defense for Western Europe. Yet partly because of Johnson's undeniably effective bullying, and partly because of the tradition of paramount civilian responsibility, the Joint Chiefs of Staff now seem prepared to go along with Johnson. If they do, this will render Acheson almost powerless ...[22]

This is perfect-pitch Washington music. Its terms of analysis are strictly confined to the chambers of power. There is no rational argument, only 'bullying'; readiness to incinerate a continent (not the one Alsops live in) is taken for granted; status accretion or reduction is at the origin of all motives ('Acheson ... powerless'); judgement is ratified not by substance but by whom you know ('informed official').

This is however the all-muffling, heavily atmospheric climate in which the Truman Doctrine was promulgated. Truman knew no foreign policy but he liked being President, was jaunty, cocksure, wide open to persuasion. The Soviets wanted control over the warm-water straits and therefore the ports of the Black Sea. The alarm bells rang at the Pentagon, and Navy Secretary Forrestal sent the fleet to the eastern end of the Mediterranean (Britain controlled the western end from Gibraltar). Hand in hand with Arthur Vandenberg, his Senate foreign policy chair, Truman distinguished for everybody between the two ways of life in the contemporary world (the Senate rumbling in assent). One was 'based upon the will of the majority' with 'free institutions, representative government ... guarantees of personal liberty' and so on. The other, alas, was 'based upon the will of a minority forcibly imposed ... rel[ying] upon terror and oppression, a controlled press ... fixed elections'.[23] Once the Truman Doctrine was spoken, the process whereby the monolithic institutions of Cold War were bedded down and cemented in, first across Europe, then across the globe, can be traced through headlines.

The brothers Alsop, especially Joe, will serve to indicate what solid cold warriors of immovable rigidity thought of developments which emerged, as much as anything, from Britain's near-bankruptcy and the virulence of Ernie Bevin's anti-communism. Bevin had come to detest the communists when he was a trade union leader in Taunton and Bridgwater, and he wasn't going to stop. He knew that he could draw upon great reservoirs of such feeling in the USA, and he did so.

He wasn't left to get away with this completely by the British press.[24] Nor was it only the progressive dailies which opposed turning Soviet Russia into the new enemy. There was a strong sediment of pro-Russian feeling among most of those who had been in uniform as well as among the millions who had taken in the epic tales of the Barbarossa campaign and the thousand-day siege of Stalingrad, who knew something of the inconceivable casualty list of Soviet soldiers and civilians and on whom it had dawned that these were working people not so very unlike themselves. The *Daily Herald* and the *News Chronicle* had to remind Churchill that he was only party leader and not prime minister, and warned Bevin that a principle of human solidarity could not just be waved away by playing power politics with Washington.

Beaverbrook's newspapers also took, politely but firmly, a critical stance. Since 1919 Beaverbrook himself had been of the view that Britain should concentrate entirely on its empire as it was then constituted, and remove itself from all other responsibilities and interventions. Hence his support for appeasement (and for having nothing to do with Palestine); but the argument in the *Express* and London's *Evening Standard* was also sympathetic to a much-invaded, shockingly wounded Russia now seeking border security and reparation for the terrible damage within her frontiers.

It is also a surprise to find *The Times* taking a similar view. But the first leader-writer of *The Times* was an academic historian with a passionately pro-revolutionary background. Edwin Hallett Carr had been taken on *The Times* staff by Barrington-Ward, was to become the first British historian of the Russian Revolution – a five-decker study of enormous erudition as well as passionate commitment – and shared the editorial view that Churchill had been a wanton interferer in Russian affairs since 1917. Carr's confident prose criticised the Americans' anti-communism as ignorant (which it was) of European nuances and sympathies formed in wartime and out of vanished supremacies, and Bevin chafed under the criticism until the Russians did his work for him by their obduracy during the Berlin blockade of 1948–9 and their vicious coup in Czechoslovakia. By 1949 and the detonation of a Russian fissile bomb, the terms of NATO were drawn up and, for a long season, British press and British foreign policy remained tranquilly subordinate to the official calm and steadfastness of manner with which the Washington press and the White House concealed their bitter divisions and the personal obsessions constituting the stuff of foreign policy.

This settled composition of manner sheltering Washington's political commentators and the politicians who read them, fed them and were in turn confirmed by them during the long opening era of Cold War is rather drearily exemplified by a series of Alsop articles from the *Herald Tribune*. They display precisely the thoughtless mechanisms of such writing. It starts from and remains within rocklike assumptions about the omnipresence and justice of Cold War. It proceeds to mount what purports to be criticism by discerning American unreadiness for hotter versions of cold warfare, and takes up as consequence a nominal opposition (this is a Republican newspaper taking on a Democratic administration) by admonishing government for failing to keep up to scratch. Finally, it finds its news in differences of opinion, deduced, imaginary or inevitable between senior figures in the business, representing such differences as down to personal animus, status-jostling or ideological duels rather than rational disagreement on the handling of danger.

Such a structure of treatment may be found in most political editorialising and column-filling of those newspapers whose readership fancies itself for its political acumen, prides itself as being every bit as up to the mark in politics as politicians themselves, and whose class and professional responsibilities encourage it in a self-satisfied view that, dealing with those responsibilities as it does, it has brushed with power itself and could, if it came to it, give a neat little turn to the steerings of society which would do it no harm.

Joseph Alsop writes, in the opening paragraphs of a still-familiar portent:

Paris

There is one single, simple explanation of the sudden growth of tension, the seemingly unaccountable attack of nerves that is overtaking the Western world. We are imperceptibly passing into another period of acute crisis, comparable in some ways to the crisis period that produced the Marshall plan.

One cause of this new crisis is the tempo of Soviet rearmament. At London, it can now be disclosed, Secretary of State Dean G. Acheson gave the solemn opinion that the Kremlin's war preparations would at least reach a preliminary climax in 1953–54 ... The other cause of the crisis is the sudden realisation of the present weakness of the West. During the last two and a half years, Western unions and Atlantic organisations have been formed; imposing headquarters have been established; reams of top-secret paper have been turned out by platoons of inter-allied brass. Most people were lulled by all this activity ... The contrast between Western weakness and rapid Soviet war preparation has in turn produced the new crisis, which is essentially a crisis of will and leadership in the West.[25]

People wrote like this for decades. It was never even satirised. Joseph Alsop (and his brother Stewart) made a very comfortable living out of it. Joseph lived no less comfortably within this frame of mind and its expression as he lived without much fear that the endless invocations of crisis, the building up of conventional forces, the discovery of missile gaps, would ever burst upon them in the rude, incandescent form of nuclear warfare. Only two events broke open Alsop's sense of the safety and settledness of Washington life and forced something like raw feeling into his prose: the Cuban missile crisis of October 1962 and, thirteen months later, the assassination of the President.

Joseph Alsop was always the senior partner of the duet, but the long careers of both men betoken the rich certainties bestowed by American class privilege in a country still so earnest to disclaim the existence of any such thing. They indicate just how that social formation known as the WASP Ascendancy inhabited an impregnable redoubt. The splendid Boston houses and their fecund gardens, the clapboard Episcopalian churches, the Savile Row suits and Harvard education, the *Mayflower* and *Arbella* genealogies,[26] provided a detailed self and a stout public identity without a nice enough, gay sort of guy[27] like Alsop having to make any creative effort of his own.

Joseph Alsop's success indicates something else about America and social class: it is that even for ruling-class sons journalism was an always respectable career any time after 1919. This goes a little against the grain of Max Weber's strictly European placing of journalism on the map of status. Lippmann and Joseph Alsop, 'Sonny' Reston and conscientiously artist-intellectuals like Gore Vidal moved easily together as a class to whom the holders of power were familiar at Washington dinner tables and for whom the combined forces of art and liberalism composed a small world at the very centre of the great one. When Presidents as different from one another as Eisenhower, Nixon and Ronald Reagan kept the old WASP Ascendancy at bay, its members were censorious but unshaken. They might certainly differ among themselves – Vidal's tongue was feared, Dean Acheson's hauteur resented – but they remained inviolate. 'Society' as the sort of thing one used to 'go into' has fallen out of colloquial use, but the great simples of family money, education and dinner tables live on.

Joseph Alsop assumed the position of influence to which his inheritance entitled him, and had acquired during wartime a little experience with which to fill out the body of his tradition. He spent four years writing columns for the *New York Herald Tribune*, shed sixty-five of the pounds avoirdupois which threatened to kill him, before joining the Air Force as a press and intelligence officer, then to be interned by the Japanese when they overtook him at the capture of Hong Kong. The same old *suffisance* saw him through a short internment (he was repatriated as a civilian newspaperman), and saw him often back in China and India advising the great General Stilwell about what to do with the hopeless corruption of the Kuomintang and the invincible obduracy of the Chinese Communist Party. Finally Stilwell was sacked and Alsop's mighty mentor, the unbelievably square-jawed and Mount Rushmore-profiled General Claire Chennault, saw out time, and came back home in an ancient, rickety C-47 that he flew himself with trunkloads of loot (books, silks, marble figurines, porcelain, picture scrolls, precious stones).

Alsop, like Connor, went straight back to his column. He took on his brother Stewart as co-author of 'Matter of Fact'. They were copiously syndicated, infernally well connected, and those people in power Joseph didn't know he could always reach by way of his distinguished wartime acquaintance.

They enlisted as cold warriors right away. In spite of America's deep-rooted anti-communism, the principal correspondent about the USSR known to the newspaper-reading public was at that time a naturalised American from an English public school called Walter Duranty.[28] Duranty had been Moscow correspondent for the *New York Times* since 1919. He was an even more undisguised supporter of Lenin and the Revolution than E. H. Carr at the London *Times*. Throughout the course of his career and life (he died in 1957) he reported from an unswervingly pro-Bolshevik line the main historical events as necessary or inevitable steps in the great progress of still incomplete social transformation. He missed the famine of the Kulaks because he never left Moscow. He defended the treason trials and established, with a little help from the Manhattan Marxists of *Partisan Review*, the conventional argument on the Left that suffering had been unavoidable in a period of forced industrialisation, an abrupt foreshortening of the process of social development which included bringing literacy to the peasantry, all interrupted by the heroic defeat of neighbouring fascism. As a consequence of this compression of historical change the USSR was now, in the new jargon, a superpower, and although peaceful in its traditions, worthy of all due respect.[29]

Joseph Alsop put an end to all that. He even threw the two shameless British spies, Guy Burgess and Donald Maclean, out of his Washington house for talking dirty *and* anti-American. He got wind early of George Kennan's 'Long Telegram' which was to be so influential in shaping Cold War policy, listened in person to General Marshall's presenting his Plan (very unemphatically and badly) at Harvard, and concluded that the future of democracy depended on a combination of the dollar and the bomb. This simple device accommodated most of the foreign policy questions which the brothers addressed in the column in the *Tribune* and none of the domestic ones they, like Lippmann, consequently discounted. Joseph had had much to say in reproach of Truman and Louis Johnson for their supposed running down of US defences, and the country's unreadiness for war with the USSR. He knew from his personal friendship with George Kennan, by 1950 head of the Policy Planning staff at the State Department, that Kennan was asking commanders in the field along the line of Soviet-dominated frontiers where a Soviet attack was most likely. The popular winner was the Balkans; the least likely, Korea.

When a series of cross-border incursions and running battles by each side of the Korean divide finally became, on 23 June 1950, open hostilities, the press story was, and folk history remains, that this began with open invasions by the North. Such an account overlooks a number of inconvenient details about the Korean situation, including the fact that the country itself had never been a belligerent in the Second World War, had been brutalised by Japanese occupation during which one and a half million Koreans including women and nine-year-olds were transported to labour camps and a further quarter of a million abruptly conscripted into the coal mines, a notoriously radicalising occupation. Communism, already widespread because of its appeal to desperately poor peasants, had a good soil in which to grow in Korea.

When the country was portioned out in 1945 without reference to the people who lived there, the available leadership fell all too neatly into the ideological vacancies advertised for them. Kim Il Sung was a thirty-three year old stalwart of the Communist Party and a veteran of partisan warfare; Dr Syngman Rhee of Princeton had spent a well-timed exile in the United States, was dependably anti-communist and ruthless for power.[30]

Fanatic is as fanatic does. The United States demanded a joint declaration from the Soviets on the desirability of free speech in Korea; at the same time it suppressed committees of the people (often run by village elders of no political affiliation), closed newspapers, forbade trade unions, and assaulted the Left in thousands. When public dissent on a large scale broke out on Cheju island it was put down to the tune of 20,000 dead among the people whose island it was, known to the US as rebels.[31]

These savageries, dignified by the name of containment, became the standing orders of Cold War all over the east, practised vigorously by Britain and the USA and other imperial remnants alike. In Korea, Quemoy, Indo-China, Indonesia, Malaya and Borneo, the guardians of the liberal conscience – the great moral citadel built out of ninteenth-century history – supervised mass murder and eviction in the name of freedom. In return small groups of hard, pitiless and disciplined men and women swore never to rest or relinquish arms until they were either dead or victorious.

When Alsop went to Korea he knew nothing of this history. American troops a mere five years after their crashing victory in the Second World War were 'ill-equipped and ill-trained', whereas the Chinese troops whose leaders had so handsomely volunteered their lives in battle, and whom our hero never saw, wore plimsolls and cotton drill into battle temperatures of minus 20 degrees Fahrenheit.

It may be recalled that when the largely American UN forces first met the Koreans in battle they were driven quickly back in a rout and almost surrounded on the south-east tip of the peninsula at Pusan. In a truly astonishing stroke, the titan General MacArthur, then supreme commander in the Pacific, came to the rescue with a surprise landing well up the west coast at Inch'on. It was the least likely place in the country for such a move, with a massive seawall and a tidal lift of thirty feet. Alsop went with the army in their bucketing flat-bottomed landing craft. The defences were unmanned. The town was empty. Alsop interviewed MacArthur and was left bewildered by the man's utter confidence in his own superpower, his enormous vanity, his calm arrogance. When Alsop went home, to give him his due, he offered mild misgivings about those who believed the great general to be 'touched with divinity'.[32]

But Joseph Alsop was not a war correspondent. He was utterly of the world of Washington, believing, as the rest of its glittering political class did, that it was the centre of the world and that trifling quarrels at its dinner parties, minor vendettas and renewed love affairs had consequences for men sitting in tanks in Berlin and children starving beside the Yangtse river. They were in a weird way right, and so the form and content of Alsop's writing did its bit in thickening the political plot of the day.

On a couple of occasions he even infused a lemony tang in the concoction by speaking out and not for, and startled a President, it may be, into attention. He stood up for two or three men in danger of indictment during the Great Fear of anti-communism and the hysteria it caused to boil in national blood.[33] One was Henry Wallace, Roosevelt's Vice-President and something of an agronomist, whose sympathetic visits to China had given rise to perjurious claims among the frenzied that he too had been one of those treasonously inclined to 'lose China'. As even the *New York Times* allowed its reporting of these matters to foam a little in the summer of 1953, Alsop rebutted the charges in detail and in public hearing.[34] He made no difference and confessed himself 'surprised by the weakness of the press in the face of McCarthyism'. Nor did it make any difference when the victim was Robert Oppenheimer, formerly scientific head of the Atomic Energy Commission at Los Alamos, with Niels Bohr simply the world's most distinguished atomic physicist. He had had the wrong sympathies in the 1930s, was gauche and gauchiste in his friendships and in at least one liaison and, director as he was of the Institute for Advanced Study, saw his security classification humiliatingly removed, his wife named for political *mésalliance*, and Joseph Alsop try to defend him.

So there is something to be said for the often portly, sometimes reduced, conservative columnist. But he himself didn't understand how signally his own columns and his steady beating of the drum of anti-communism, nuclear might and atomic terror were themselves integral to the heavy atmosphere. Under its pall during Truman's second term of office, the Attorney-General arrested 300 people for deportation, and the judge in the case of Julius and Ethel Rosenberg sentenced the scared and shabby pair to death by electrocution and with a wealth of intemperate virulence which even startled God-fearing journalists.

This was only a moment before Alsop made a gingerly visit to see the French losing the Indo-Chinese war and to disburden himself of a few domino theorisations about the likelihood of communist victory, shillying on one side about the wrongs of European colonialism and shallying on the other about what pretty little spots Saigon, Bangkok and Rangoon were.

Alsop trod the stairs of the airliner trolleys down to the usual sequence of capitals – London, Paris, Moscow ('my vile little interpreter') – rather in Lippmann's wake though without Lippmann's calling list. When he came home the shrewd young men planning John F. Kennedy's skin-of-his-teeth victory in 1960 took him up and in, and Alsop confessed himself another conquest of the all-conquering charmer. Alsop had no inhibitions about sentences like 'the inward seriousness of the man was apparent now beneath the wit and charm',[35] or with equipping the young President with a wry grin and the usual doses of effortless vitality in spite of the pain in his back.

Not only that. In his columns, Alsop supported Kennedy's claim during the election campaign that there was a serious 'missile gap' between the two defenders of the world's only two faiths in 1960. Afterwards, when everyone on the inside knew this was nonsense but didn't care, Alsop asked Kennedy what would have happened if it had all been true. (I love this bit.) 'He briefly looked very grim and said, "Sometimes I wonder about that, and when I let myself do so I lose most of a night's sleep."'[36]

Alsop gradually became ineffable in the advice he was ready to tender the hero of the hour – not to give Fulbright the State Department ('too vain') and no to Senator Gore at the Treasury ('fashionably shallow').[37] Perhaps it was all excusable enough. Everybody subordinate to Kennedy but dependent on his favour reports themselves weakened at the knees by that combination of exhilarating and energetic charm, flagrant sexual allure, and the delighted possession of absolute political power. Kennedy didn't know that he didn't know anything about world affairs, but he did know the touchiness of his pride and his fixity of will. Most people who came close to these qualities accepted their consequences, but a columnist like Alsop could hardly do otherwise. He borrowed his own authority from his propinquity to the President, but he had to do so in prose that made a show of judicious detachment.

The Alsop column came out for getting rid of Castro, was embarrassed by the little *contretemps* in the Bay of Pigs in 1960, and from a not very informed distance backed the President in his terrifying showdown with First Secretary Khrushchev off the coast of Cuba in October 1962. Joseph Alsop went to interview President Diem of the so-designated Republic of South Vietnam, thought rather well of his guts and character, wrote in his column in the high style he sometimes affected that 'despite his virtues Diem saw with the borrowed eyes and listened with the borrowed ears of a madman.'[38] Kennedy was himself sufficiently of the same view to connive at his fellow-President's murder just three weeks before his own. Alsop bade his friend and patron magniloquent farewell in his column – 'the man perfectly formed to lead the United States of America' – and farewell also to the happiest days of his own life, adjunct to the power he had served, captivated by its actor, transfixed by its performance.

Joseph Alsop took happily enough to the celebrity brought him by the great good fortune of his fluent mediocrity. He coincided with official opinion and had no trouble persuading himself that such opinion was his own and therefore to be held with dignified and ardent conviction. Thereafter longevity in a prominent place, combined with unassailable self-confidence and a well-filled address book, led him to a fame and fortune it wouldn't be in the nature of such a man to consider unmerited.

The counterpoint of this book requires a different melody. It would be easy to prefer journalism of the leathery and sardonic Scot James Cameron to Joseph Alsop simply because he was of that class of journalists whose signature is set on his report in the middle of the physical action and well away from the conference tables of the grand strategists. Cameron took pride in his absence from the offices of coercive power. 'Being there' means for him and his kidney being where things are uncomfortable, maybe dangerous, and in any case where other men and women like oneself are living out the consequences of the master plan.

The distinction between eye-witness and strategist, however, will only serve to distinguish adventurers from opinionators, powerless from powerful, practice from theory. For the Oval Office, the Pentagon or the Bank of England are as much the scene of the action and a part of the field as the muddy roads and the blood-boltered bodies. If journalists are to explain our world to us and even, when it suits, remind us of the way it ought to be according to local ideals and principles, some of them must be on familiar terms with presidents and prime ministers. Some of them also had better be of sufficient intelligence to keep alive the hope that what is written may be read by the mighty, may inflect their conduct for the better, and will in any case give speech to some of those whose lives are so at risk from the doings of the mighty.

Cameron of course knew these truisms, but as a matter of temperament as well as ethics kept insubordinate company only with the subordinates. He had to hope (though not to believe) that the witness he bore to such company would be clear and piercing enough to be taken as evidence in the courts of history. Besides, he came to the job by accident and it only gradually turned into an avocation as his natural incredulity and *sotto voce* truculence sorted better and better with telling people what they didn't want to hear but did want to stop him saying.

I am no great propagandist of the virtues or values of the Press; nevertheless I hold its functions in the most jealous of consideration … it is possible to argue that the reporter engaged in serious affairs must be the people's eyes and ears; he must be the instrument associating people's government with people's opinion.[39]

It is rare to find Cameron as declarative as that. He came to journalism by great good luck and want of anything else. His mother died when he was a little boy, his father, a never-very-successful barrister in Dundee, made a sufficient living also writing competent little romantic novels while, always kindly and mournful, drinking himself quietly into an earlyish grave. James Cameron joined the Scottish *Sunday Post* in 1934 as a compound of reporter and subeditor of a kind impossible today, and after five years in the appropriately fabulous jostling, tumult and sheer physical labour of newspaper offices at that time, went to the *Scottish Daily Express*, and married on these diminutive prospects a Scots girl called Elma. He went almost straight from his father's deathbed to Elma's in childbirth: she sighed abstractedly as he arrived at her bedside, and died. He was left alone at twenty-eight with baby Elma as the fall of France was announced on the news.

He was turned down as unfit for military service and advised never to fly above 5,000 feet. So he spent half his life in aircraft on the way to the most dangerous places in the world, surviving Bikini, Korea, Malaya, Katmandu, most of Africa and all of India, while the soldiers whose doings he went to chronicle died all about him.

He was transferred from Glasgow to the *Daily Express*, and married Elizabeth, a staff illustrator (she drew the maps of the war reports). After making his way round assorted battlefields and bombsites of the war, he was despatched by his newspaper as one of a small group of journalists invited to report on the detonation of the fourth and fifth of the bombs which so satisfactorily promised to make all other bombs redundant since, if these new things were got to rights, there would be no more war because no more world. Even on the Pacific atoll of Bikini in 1946, as the Navy prepared to explode an atom bomb suspended a long way down below the deep blue sea, the experts weren't perfectly sure that when the bang came tidal waves would not sweep the hemisphere or that irrevocable fissures in the crust of the globe would not drain off the very ocean.

Cameron said himself that there was no other event in his career about which he had written more obsessively. His reports from the island were certainly unexpected as coming from Beaverbrook's *Express*, that great organ for the playing of the chords of Britain's world power marches. He enumerated in his bare prose the names of the American Navy ships moored for destruction, and went on to call upon the goats and pigs tethered in a 'little company of flesh and blood, standing reflectively in pens for their most abrupt and instructive dissolution'.[40]

Cameron was no pacifist, as he plainly said.[41] He had, however, come early to the view that these unspeakable weapons could be justified by *nothing*, and that a world which deployed them to maintain a condition it called peace was one whose balancing of craziness against stupidity could not be contemplated in a spirit of Buddhist detachment or with the blankness called objectivity by certain historians and journalists. Instead Cameron devised for himself a style of bitter resignation allied to a violently controlled sort of understatement, one which transpired either as hard jokes or, as in Korea, in the form of a terse and angry narrative.

> I still do not see how a reporter attempting to define a situation involv-
> ing some sort of ethical conflict can do it with sufficient demonstrable
> neutrality to fulfil some arbitrary concept of 'objectivity'. It never
> occurred to me, in such a situation, to be other than subjective, and as
> obviously so as I could manage to be. I may not always have been satis-
> factorily balanced; I always tended to argue that objectivity was of less
> importance than the truth, and that the reporter whose technique was
> informed by no opinion lacked a very serious dimension. It can easily be
> misrepresented. Yet as I see it – and it seems to me the simplest of disci-
> plines – the journalist is obliged to present his attitude as vigorously and
> persuasively as he can, insisting that it *is* his attitude, to be examined and
> criticised in the light of every contrary argument, which he need not
> accept but must reveal. There is a way of being scrupulous about this
> which every thinking journalist understands.[42]

This endless argument must sooner or later be resolved by abandoning the terms (and the false distinction they imply) 'subjective' and 'objective'. A truthful account will be selective as to significance, inclusive as to anomaly, vivid as to the facts of life, comprehensive as to the passions in the action. By such standards, the account will aspire to the condition of art where art teaches us to see things truly *and* as if we had never seen them before.

To stretch up to such a view is not to take a God's eye view of things, the 'view from nowhere' in Thomas Nagel's excellent phrase.[43] What Nagel intends is to criticise the idea that any human being may be able, in making moral judgements, ever to find such comprehensive vision. The moral view is always somebody's, located somewhere. Some views, however, take in a fuller prospect than others; some miss the prospect but find the tiny details; all may be less partial though never impartial, understanding rather than obtuse, decent rather than indecent.

Armed with such folk wisdom but anxious above all in such introspection not to 'turn into a howling bore',[44] Cameron patrolled the world for the *Express*, remarking as he did so that his famously tetchy and meddlesome lord proprietor never told him what to write or cancelled any of his reports for leaning as leftwards as Cameron's heart told him to do. Revealingly, however, when he was summoned home by the *Express* he found he couldn't bear to stay on its books. Being a journalist for Beaverbrook in England and reading the whole newspaper each morning was not something he could stomach.

When one day the Beaverbrook *Evening Standard* printed a brutally untruthful headline about John Strachey, a Labour Cabinet minister with a long-since-repudiated Communist Party membership in his past, and when, in its turn, the *Express* repeated the slander, Cameron resigned. For the only time in his life, he then took to the correspondence columns of *The Times* to explain why.

> Sir, Whether Mr Strachey did or did not publicly announce his moment of disillusion with the Communists is surely of less long-term importance than this: that we have now set the precedent for the purge-by-Press, which could end at last only in a race of people talking behind their hands, knowing that the words they said yesterday, in a very different world mood, are the words they may swing for tomorrow.
>
> Loyalty in every sense is a prerequisite in Cabinet Ministers, and newspapers have a right to examine it where they find it. At the same time one may wonder whether the best judge of political reliability is an industry whose own caprices of principle and accommodations of policy have seldom been marked over the years by a rigid ethical consistency. The loyalty-test, with the Press on the tribunal to link the names of a Minister and a convicted felon, is a troubling aspect of what – so far, happily – we do not have to call the British Way of Life.
>
> I have never met Mr Strachey, nor, indeed, seen him outside the House of Commons; I have, nevertheless, considered the issue involved sufficiently important to resign my own professional association with the organisation that initiated the witch-hunt.
>
> Yours faithfully, James Cameron[45]

Purge-by-Press. There's a lot of that to come. Rather less, however, of principled resignations by far-from-wealthy or secure employees who just can't stand their parent paper any longer.

The resignation puts a different slant on Cameron's studiedly sardonic misanthropy. Indeed, he turns out clean converse, a philanthropist with a detestation of human horribleness particularly as practised by those a long way from its horrible consequences.

When he left the *Express*, he was quickly – this man was known to be good – hired by the editor of *Picture Post*, Tom Hopkinson. *Picture Post*, long since gone, needs a moment's introduction. One might say that it started out as an English version of *Life* in the late 1930s. That is, its stories were told partly in black-and-white photographs, four, six or eight to a big folio page, each with quite detailed captions and with a longish version of the same story told verbally along the bottom of the page. But the stories, like the photographs, were chosen on the whole for what they told about the condition of Britain, and then of the world, to a readership with a lively social conscience, a modest patriotism and a more-or-less Labour-voting picture of that world which the beautiful pictures, taken by such geniuses of the camera as Bill Brandt and Bert Hardy, themselves authorised and ratified.

Cameron went with Bert Hardy to Korea. There he came very abruptly up against the deep and abiding purposelessness of the Cold War. Korea in the winter of 1950–1 was a terrible place. The fuel froze in the trucks and tanks; banging frost-bitten hands on something metal at night, a soldier could snap off a finger. United Nations officials had no authority to enforce Geneva Conventions upon the treatment of North Koreans by South Koreans, or even of South Koreans by their own countrymen.

Cameron had seen much of the conduct of the war by American and Commonwealth Brigade soldiers familiar to him from the Second World War. He was puzzled by the failure of the 'most ironclad and mechanical army in the world, with unchallenged control of the air and the sea'[46] to defeat large numbers of poorly equipped infantrymen with no tanks and little artillery trotting to battle in plimsolls. But that was the war set in train by United Nations led by United States determined to resist incursions by any military force likely to remind people of 1939.

The trouble was the utter incommensurability of suffering and victory; the pointless devastation of the grey landscape and the grey, blank, prefabricated townships which Cameron came so to dislike. The final trouble was the shocking treatment meted out by South Korean allies to South Korean citizens accused but unconvicted by the hideous tyranny of Dr Syngman Rhee's police and his grotesquely named Liberal Party. But then liberalism itself was party to his regime, and once again Cameron, and Hardy with him, found the gap between ideals and actuality so intolerably stretched that he split.

This grisly mob of men projected the war in special terms of human abasement. There were about seven hundred of them, and they were political prisoners of the South Korean Government – they were not prisoners of war; their uniform was a filthy and indescribably ragged kimono... They were skeletons – they were puppets of skin with sinews for strings – their faces were a terrible, translucent grey, and they cringed like dogs. They were manacled with chains or bound to each other with ropes. They were compelled to crouch in the classic Oriental attitude of subjection, the squatting, foetal position, in heaps of garbage. Sometimes they moved enough to scoop a handful of water to drink from the black puddles around them. Any deviation from their attitude brought a gun butt on their skulls. Finally they were herded, the lowest common denominator of human degradation, into trucks, with the numb air of men going to their deaths. I was assured, by a willing attendant anxious to make a good impression, that most of them were. Sometimes, to save inconvenience, they were shot where they were.[47]

Cameron took angry recrimination to the UN officials and was agreed with, held at arm's length, wrapped in the prose of non-interference, levered out of the office. The circumstances were well known; they were reported in the broadsheets; they were not merely filthy and disgusting, they violated the very principle for which United Nations and States had permitted 30,000 odd of their troops to be killed, let alone the estimated 3 *million*[48] Chinese, North and South Korean soldiers and civilians killed between 1950 and 1953.

So Cameron took his stand on the probity of the journalist and with his editor Hopkinson's strong approval and Hardy's horrifying photographs, wrote his Korean report to be published at the end of 1950 under the heading 'An appeal to the United Nations'. The special edition of *Picture Post* was duly plated and was at the rotogramme presses in Watford when the proprietor Edward Hulton (he of the photographic archive) stopped them, pulled the piece, and fired the editor.

Happily, a partisan printer pinched a proof and slipped it to the *Daily Worker*. Hulton's intention to avoid the embarrassment of being the owner of a magazine criticising the sanctity of Western political purposes could not, because of his own intemperate action and his denigration of his editor, have been more completely inverted. The British press got well and truly hold of the story, especially the *Mirror*, and as the *New Statesman* said, 'Mr Hulton's action provides unanswerable propaganda for the Communists.'[49]

Effectively the row finished off *Picture Post*. It declined into cleavage cover stories, its best photographers left and so did Cameron. Cameron hadn't by any means been alone in his reports from Korea – even the BBC in the casual, comradely tones of René Cutforth[50] – but the photographs, the quietly impassioned prose and the contribution of Mr Hulton made his the most famous, and this was because, contrary to conventional cynicism, it reported, as a matter of urgency and seriousness, a situation in which cruelty, injustice and indifference worked busily together to kill, starve and maim ordinary human beings whom we were supposed to be helping on the other side of the world.

What Cameron expressed was the sentiment of human solidarity,[51] and it was this slow burn which fired his journalism whether at war or during the many years he spent trying to discern historical direction in India's sometimes regressive emancipation, befriending the great Jawaharlal Nehru as he did so.

His last great coup came when he was fifty-four, and it was the outcome of his own perseverance. In 1965, as the American forces in Vietnam accumulated to well over half a million in strength and the name of President Johnson's Wagnerian bombing of the North, 'Rolling Thunder', became daily more of a deadly familiar resonance, Cameron won permission to visit Hanoi. He paid for his own trip and paid himself by publishing his reports as a freelance in the London *Evening Standard*. He was nobody's man but his own, and the authorities in Hanoi must have learned that. He had been there already, shortly before the crucial French defeat at Dien Bien Phu in 1954. He was known as a lover of India, an anti-imperialist for sure, but Scottish, bloody-minded, principled to a fault, a heavy drinker, eloquent on his day.

He told the whole story without varnish: the laborious tours of dull factories, the painful jargon of Asian communism, the intense military activities after darkness, the utterly exhausting labour under the heaviest bombing any nation had ever undergone over the half-century during which hand-held explosives dropped from the cockpit developed into the obliteration of Hiroshima and the 'interdiction' of Hanoi. Cameron set himself to make his *Evening Standard* articles[52] into a textbook for British readers, telling them what they probably missed in 1945, that the Japanese troops were rearmed in order to prevent native Vietnamese communists becoming the legal and accepted government; that elections were promised after the defeat of the French in 1954 and never permitted by United Nations negotiators not uninfluenced by the preferences of John Foster Dulles; that the communists in the South were from the South.

He chatted to President Ho Chi Minh and interviewed his prime minister, who said, unforgettably, 'Of course we can't vanquish the United States... We're not *trying* to vanquish the United States. There seems to be some preposterous belief in America that we are threatening them – a poverty-stricken little country like Vietnam! We are trying to get *rid* of them.'[53]

Ten years later, they did; but the price of the experience was, as usual, all that they had. Cameron came home, as he promised, to tell the British that the two Vietnamese leaders meant what they said. CBS asked him on to their programme 'Where do we stand in Vietnam?' and hated what he had to say; *Time* accused him of being a Vietnamese propagandist. Like others in our far-from-completed roll-call of journalists in Vietnam, Cameron turned out to be saying the right thing.

All journalists live on the line drawn in academic laboratories between participation and observation, doing and watching. René Cutforth in Korea was a doer, as near a combatant as made no matter, certainly as liable to be killed in action, as the phrase goes, as any soldier. By the same token, Joseph Alsop observing from Washington or James Cameron doing the same in Korea and Hanoi may well, as a consequence of something they wrote, have not just influenced what political leaders thought and felt, but affected how some fraction of that pale ghost, public opinion, would assign its support to a policy of war.

The third category of journalist, in other words, dodging between local colourist and grand strategian, is liable to be assumed by any writer at any time. This third person, involuntarily or otherwise, is dragged much deeper into both acting and observing than he or she ever expected. This is Martha Gellhorn in Spain, Ed Murrow in London, Albert Camus in Algeria.

It is also, and even more ambiguously, Whittaker Chambers in front of the FBI and the House Committee on Un-American Activities. McCarthy's is the name given to the period but there was grotesque paranoia everywhere, along with a chilling readiness to surrender freedoms and believe inanity. Arthur Miller's great play *The Crucible*, apple-pie American all through, shows in all modesty the vituperation of 1692 to 1953.

Whittaker Chambers himself, however, can't be accommodated within the simple moral emblems of *The Crucible*. He had sincere intellectual leanings, wrote vividly, garrulously, ardently, and timed one quotation to the moment:

If thou are privy to thy country's fate,
Which, happily, foreknowing may avoid,
O speak ...

He came from grisly domestic origins (kitchen brawls, homosexual father, alcoholic and suicidal brother) to make good at Columbia. He was an excellent translator, of Thomas Mann, of Proust, of – ha! – *Bambi*. Between 1931 and 1937 he rose to the top of communist journalism in the USA as editor-writer-organiser-marketeer of the party's literary journal *New Masses*, and married a Russian Stalinist.[54] He worked devotedly and on the hoof for six years on behalf of Russian intelligence, and then, frightened and revolted by the Moscow treason trials (and who in his position would not have been?), quit.

He got a job, a good job first in 1939 as reviews editor on *Time*, then in charge of its foreign desk. But he was a marked man, and as the delirious fever began to burn the blood of government, and as the squeeze was put on Chambers, he began – in the phrase of the day – to name names. Stardom is so central to the political economy of the United States that the history of anti-communist hysteria offers itself naturally as a series of starring parts, each played out, as you'd expect, in the courtroom. Alger Hiss becomes the large, dark silhouette at the centre of the stage; beside him Chambers, the Fool.

It is a premise of this book that its assorted spokespeople be taken as meaning exactly what they say. I do not see how one could carry out an inquiry into the history of ideas in any other way, and I take for granted that political journalism, whether in the case of Walter Lippmann or in the case of Cassandra, is a strong current in that history.[55]

By such an account, Whittaker Chambers, as he says firmly in his long autobiography,[56] knew exactly what he was doing and meant just what he said. Like at least two other journalists considered in this book, he called his book *Witness* but he did so with emphatically Quaker emphasis. When he quit the Communist Party he turned to Quakerism. You can say, if you like, that obscure forces within Chambers drove him equivalently to the mutual surveillance and abnegations of party or Meeting; or you can say that the secrecy and punitive autocracy of the party became so unspeakable that he sought relief in its opposite, the open witness-bearing of human possibility looked for but not demanded by Quakerism. His fellow Quaker in the Alger Hiss House hearings, Richard Nixon, was someone else pulled equally towards secretiveness and confession.

Nobody reading Chambers' *Witness* need look further for intelligibility in his actions than his own explanations. Given his experience, and then given the political atmosphere of America at the time of the House committee, his wretched tale is stuffed full with plausibilities of motive and intention. He not only had behind him the ghastly scenes of his boyhood, he had also worked closer than most of us to the proletariat, chipping out concrete recesses four feet below the live rails of the subway carrying a steady charge of 25,000 volts and having passers-by expectorate their tobacco juice on to the back of his neck.

Witness witnesses with zeal the appalling inner life and unsociable blankness of Communist Party duplicity and pointlessness in the 1930s. It is a handbook to a world well lost but one whose taciturn intensities help explain the horror and bewilderment felt towards it by all those on the outside. For six years Chambers took demeaning orders, pursued ludicrous party heresies and carried out trivial espionage before this stout, unappetising worm turned and, after a night spent staring out of the window, at the age of thirty-seven became a man again and prepared himself for the high calling of informer.

He is quite straight about this. 'The informer ... risks little. He sits in security and uses his special knowledge to destroy others ... the police protect him. He is their creature.' And then, 'Let every ex-communist look unblinkingly at that image. It is himself.'[57]

Chambers looked, and told. He named every name he could. The crux for cold warriors was the Alger Hiss case. But that came in 1947, over ten years after Chambers left the party, ten years in which he had risen competently through the hierarchy of *Time* and had made the book review section of the weekly into something remarkable, sprightly, alive to modernism, catholic in taste. He had as his deputy James Agee, himself a figure in American modernism, and his prime coup in the period was a cover story, in Henry Luce's *Time* magazine, on James Joyce and his baffling masterpiece *Finnegan's Wake*. The staff at *Time*, when Chambers's time came, just didn't believe he'd been a commie. He had been (a cue for psychological explanation here) a compulsive overworker who left the office at 3 a.m. for his midweek weekend at his farm in Maryland with his beloved wife and who, after heavy fat hit his heart and blood pressure, only reduced his fourteen-hour working day when he passed out. Once promoted to foreign editor and with a salary of $30,000, much quoted by enemies on the Left, he pursued, as one would expect and owner-editor Henry Luce would have required, an unremittingly anti-communist line, harrying and abusing those State Department officials and Treasury advisers – Owen Lattimore, Harry Dexter White – accused of 'losing China' and subsidising West European communism.

When Chambers finally received the subpoena of the House committee in 1948 the crucial case became that of Alger Hiss. Hiss himself still stands in an obscure position between innocence and guilt in the case history of American law. He was an assured Harvard lawyer, had been a senior civil servant in several offices of the State Department, a member of Roosevelt's entourage at Yalta treatying with Stalin and Churchill, and head of the Carnegie Endowment for International Peace. He was of almost-Brahmin deportment: Savile Row suits, Boston accent, New Deal formation, slim, tall, graceful, his beautiful manners tinged with savage class sarcasm. There are those who would say that Chambers's own admitted homosexuality was strongly attracted to Hiss, however much he protested uxoriousness.

That detail is, however, superfluous. Reading the innumerable reports of the hearings and the indictment, Chambers's own, Navasky's,[58] I come round to thinking that Hiss probably had been an active communist in the 1930s and that he had indeed, like Chambers and so many others, found membership intolerable, going on to great and patriotic things. But he lied about it and about passing documents of political delicacy, and went to jail for having held communist ideals at the same time as having kept faith with his anti-communist country.

Chambers himself plainly admired Hiss. He didn't press home any particular advantage, as he might have done under the torrent of counter-claims, abuse and smears to which Hiss's defence lawyers subjected him. Hiss was just the biggest name in his diary, and Chambers was on the long slide of witnessing, lubricating the chute with his florid, kitsch eloquence. Hiss at first failed to recollect Chambers's face and friendship. Then he did. Chambers held compromising letters typed, or so it seemed, on Hiss's typewriter. Hiss had passed microfilm to Chambers, and Chambers led two of the committee's heavies to his garden and, reaching triumphantly into a pumpkin gourd, held aloft the incriminating phials.

Twenty years later, the excellent Victor Navasky tells us drily, the three microfilms withheld from the courtroom for security reasons were prised out of the district attorney's office; one was blank and the other two carried high-tech information about naval fire extinguishers.[59]

Chambers's evidence was useful to the Right because they could link up communists with the liberals who backed Roosevelt and the New Deal, and must be done down at all costs. Chambers himself stayed much in evidence as a journalistic crony of the Right. But he tried to keep at bay some of the consequences of combining American anti-communist moralising and the journalistic halitosis which breathes it out, with an effort to ply the trade and retire to private life from time to time. He urged the virulent right-wingers, in particular William F. Buckley, who were starting up their house magazine *The National Interest*, to keep away from McCarthy's hoodlums and methods (they didn't). He had himself borne up under charges of drunkenness and insanity made in the courtroom and the complete certainty that these would be scattered across the newspapers whatever denial was made under oath.[60] At the same time, he had tried to explain to the House committee why he had joined the party and whereabouts its genuine appeal lay. Of course he was exculpating something of himself, but he did it decently enough. And he ended, in a trembling voice, 'I have testi-fied against Mr Hiss with remorse and pity, but in a moment of history in which this Nation now stands, so help me God, I could not do otherwise.'[61] Cant, maybe, but soulful cant.

He stayed in the limelight. Perhaps he hogged it. It was all he had, though he had money and a home. He continued to say Hiss had been and still could be a communist. He said it broadcasting on *Meet the Press*. Very slowly, egged on by the press (*Daily News* headline: 'Well, Alger, where's that suit?'), Hiss sued. *Time* and *Life* backed Chambers; all kinds of people chipped in for Hiss's expenses. Chambers tried to kill himself with fertiliser fumes. Hiss was found guilty of perjury and went down. Chambers wrote 799 pages of self-vindicating witness-bearing, fulsome, torrential, embar-rassing, believable. Alistair Cooke, who made a magnificent history of these events, wrote the last word about them first.

> Yet below the satisfaction of popular fears and desires, and the useful-ness of arguments we happen to have at hand, lies a deeper region of the mind which holds in uncertain equilibrium the springs of self-love and self-hate; where seas of spite are able to rise and flood the low gauge of self-respect and the surrounding plains of neighborliness and patriot-ism. Here the real wound would fester: whether it was the false accusa-tion, or the social betrayal of which this unhappy man had now become the public image; and somewhere in this dark region was tragedy enough, for all those who have had ideals and desires beyond, they dare to think, the understanding of their neighbors.[62]

There is much in Cooke's conclusion to illuminate the large, dark attic allotted to spy stories in the moral imagination of society (and therefore in the press) during the Cold War. As one would expect, without courtroom drama, British journalism ran its spy stories at a lower temperature than fever pitch and embellishing its effects with small snobbery rather than duels with Apollyon. The best of espionage in Britain were those two great novels of the early 1970s John le Carré: *Tinker, Tailor, Soldier, Spy* and *Smiley's People.*

They are a threnody sung over English upper-class idealism. The actual journalism was, as you'd expect, a seedy diminuendo from the tireless hand of one Chapman Pincher in the pages of the *Daily Express*, while, in the sister paper the *Evening Standard*, James Cameron was publishing his sympathetic reports from enemy headquarters in Hanoi.

Pincher won Reporter of the Year and of the Decade awards, ran his stories off and on for years and their faint echo – the 'fifth man' and all that – may still be picked up today. The books which came out of the articles work entirely by allusion and indirection to create a sense of startling revelation, now familiar from so much so-called investigative journalism, all in defence of those freedoms readers never for a moment supposed in danger.

This is the real difference on this side of the Atlantic. The Cold War was arctic enough for long enough: Berlin Blockade, the Soviet missiles pointing at London, Edinburgh, Birmingham, Cardiff, the unbroken trickle of refugees, the crowds in their thousands watching from behind the razor wire as nuclear weapons were wheeled by under a winter sun. But it wasn't fought in Britain with either hatred or persecution mania or sudden rushes of blind suspicion. This sort of stuff appeared, did its huffing and was huffed over, and was forgotten:

> Though Sir Harold Wilson now seems deeply perturbed by the extremist penetration of the Labour party, he was inclined while in office to dismiss warning about it by the security authorities. I understand that he was told how an MI5 agent had heard a Russian intelligence officer claim from memory that thirty-one Labour MPs were 'full Party members completely on our side and who will do anything to help us'. Wilson is said to have dismissed the information as 'reds under the beds' propaganda.
>
> MI5 has evidence from defectors to the effect that some crypto-Communist MPs are under such close day-to-day control that they are used to ask parliamentary questions calculated to damage the interests either of Britain or her allies. Soviet bloc intelligence officers are detailed to make a close study of Parliament and to make use of its privileges, wherever possible. They will frame an embarrassing question based on intelligence material and induce one crypto-Communist MP to ask it. A

second MP will then ask the even more embarrassing supplementary question.

Some of the MPs are even named – by their code-name – in KGB radio traffic. The late Konni Zilliacus was one of them, and Driberg was another. I greatly regret that, at this stage, I am unable to name others who are still alive and shelter behind the libel laws, as it is difficult to induce any intelligence source to appear as a witness, as MI5 itself knows only too well.[63]

How on earth could anyone take it seriously? Nobody could remember who was who in this thick, murky and muffled gossip, all got up in the snobbish baroque of the best clubs in London, the grandest houses in Belgravia, the fatuous titles and the 'highly placed sources'. The only people worried about espionage were the governmental departments of espionage, MI5 and MI6.

Even at this date, when surveillance is of necessity an international network of states seeking to entrap that most anonymous of enemies, the terrorist, we have hardly forgotten the absurd deference of the British towards the Americans, and we have rediscovered their chronic incredulity towards the rest of the world that anybody could hate them which may be why they proved so bad at espionage.

CHAPTER TEN

The Soloists: Living History on our Behalf

The Cold War was a lens through which to see the epoch. When wars of independence began or were resumed in remote places – Indo-China, Mozambique, Afghanistan – first one side, then the other rushed weaponry and war correspondents to the spot in order to make things worse by trying to slide a thin blade of advantage into circumstances none of their business.

Pretty quickly, any nationalist movement learned to protest its interestedness in ideology and thereby gain the weapons, the dollars or the roubles which would guarantee its seriousness and make entertaining its fantasies of victory. The tectonic plates grated along the line of Churchill's iron curtain from Stettin to Trieste, and were continued across Iran and Iraq, doubled back through the Sinai peninsula, ran across Afghanistan, crossed India by way of Tibet, turned south again along the two divides of Vietnam and Korea, coming finally to a halt on the coast of Chiang Kai-shek's sometime refuge in Formosa, now Taiwan.

The patrols of the journalists kept watch over those interminable frontiers, and if they went somewhere new, went to find the old news. This is no more than human, let alone literary. The subject-matter of a conversation, or of a novel, is conventional; it fits the frame of feeling of the day. For novelist or journalist to broach new subjects or to propose new feelings about old ones is to take a risk. James Cameron wrote differently about India, but then British and Indian writers had been writing about India for decades, so his little forays were allowable as a special kind of herbivorous rumination at the edge of the paper. Occasionally a quite different way of seeing broke the well-dovetailed smoothness of a newspaper's surface, as it did in France with Camus and Sartre, or in England with C. L. R. James.

But the two Frenchmen were intellectuals and Nobel prizewinners, so they had special permission marked out, and James wrote about cricket, so nobody noticed.

The big story of 1956, for example, was that two vast empires, the British which had reached the peak of its expansion in 1933, and the Soviet Russian which had barely arrived and was never consolidated, were beginning to break up. Although only recently emerged, with the aid of General Marshall's dollars, from near-bankruptcy, Britain threw a lost-empire rage in the Middle East, while in the self-same weeks the self-styled socialists of Poland and Hungary took so much and so suddenly upon themselves that they affronted their Russian patrons into sending in the tanks.

In Egypt, it will be remembered, so recently under British rule, the new president and sometime liberal-minded and modernising colonel Gamal Abdel Nasser and a group of like-minded officers had in 1953 thrown out the obese and venal monarch left behind by empire, and set about due independence. After the USA and Britain had put up the money to build the Aswan dam by way of helping Nasser's modernisation along, they took it away again. Congress wouldn't vote the money and, as the *Daily Express* put it: 'Does anyone in his right mind really *want* to give a £5 million present of British taxpayers' money to Colonel Nasser? If the Dam does not go up he may fall down. But why should we maintain him in power?'[1] Nasser promptly nationalised the Suez Canal. He was perfectly within his rights. The company was Egyptian; Nasser gave guarantees that shareholders would be compensated and the 1888 convention governing canal use carefully observed.

Back in London Anthony Eden had only recently assumed the prime ministerial throne not vacated by Churchill until he was senile and permanently drunk. Eden had been Foreign Minister for years, spoke Arabic (and seven other languages) fluently, possessed great charm, good looks, perfect conviction about the continuing might of his nation and had, it was said, a leaking bile duct apt to make him, well, bilious.

He lost his temper completely at his junior minister, Anthony Nutting, who had counselled moderation. Nutting resigned and observed the rule of ten-year silence before publishing his account of the crisis.[2] But some years after that, he was interviewed on such matters by Christopher Hitchens who asked Nutting if there were any juicy details he'd left out: 'He sat thinking for a bit; at length he said, "Well I am prepared to tell you that Eden didn't say he wanted Nasser destroyed. He said very emphatically that he wanted him killed. And, in fact, the idea of killing him was put to some senior officials."'[3]

The British were out of practice. Only three years or so later, the CIA was commissioned to draft an assassination plan with Fidel Castro as its target; they came up with the wheeze of an exploding cigar. But the true measure of this reminiscence is the distance it marks from 1956 in journalism. At that date no journalist would have credited such a tale, let alone been allowed by his editor to print it.[4]

Still less an irresistible sequel,[4] in which Eden summons Captain Basil Liddell Hart, Britain's most distinguished military historian and former *Times* military correspondent. He asks Liddell Hart to draw up plans for an invasion of Suez, and this Liddell Hart does, but has his first four drafts curtly returned by Eden for improvements. Extremely annoyed, Liddell Hart waits a day or two and then sends back again, unamended, the first draft. Eden calls him in and sharply rebukes him for taking so long. Liddell Hart then admits that the fifth draft, now entirely acceptable to the Prime Minister, is in fact the first. Eden flushes red; he throws a heavy pewter inkwell at Liddell Hart, spattering his natty off-white linen suit with large ink-stains. Liddell Hart, tall, slim, moustached, looks down at the damage. He rises swiftly from his seat, catches up a large government-issue wastepaper basket, jams it upside down on the Prime Minister's head, and stalks out.

It is a joyous little tale and, unlike today's prurience concerning ejaculations in the Oval Office, has political significance and therefore journalistic point. But alas, Liddell Hart kept it dark in 1956 and the British press dispersed into its usual formations in order to absorb the meaning of Suez.

The *Daily Express* ran the headline 'Red Devils go in. It's Great Britain again';[5] the *Daily Telegraph* expressed satisfaction that a jumped-up Egyptian colonel was being put in his place in a place which properly belonged to Britain anyway. The *Daily Mirror* did splendidly: the newspaper most of those in uniform on their way to Cyprus, Port Said and Aden were actually reading called the operation 'Eden's war' and demanded the resignation he had to write two months later. The progressive broadsheets lined up pretty much in a row, the *Manchester Guardian*, the *Daily Herald* and the *News Chronicle* severely critical, and the Astor family's *Observer* vehemently so, to such an extent that the paper lost a great deal of circulation for good, and printed letters of outrage from correspondents terminating a lifetime's readership.

The first week in November 1956 was, however, a hard one in which to balance judicious reporting in Europe, or indeed for one of the protagonist nations to know what rightly to feel about its actions. For the first time since the disgrace of Munich, Britain was split down the fissure represented by the newspapers. Bipartisanship in foreign policy stopped. Faced not only with the absence of any legality conferred by the United Nations but, more importantly, by the amazed disapproval of the United States, what was then undoubtedly the single nation of Britain found itself in a bitter family quarrel. A Gallup poll taken at the time of a cooked-up ultimatum by Eden to Nasser on 25 October found only 37 per cent in support of invasion, 44 per cent against. *The Times*, still the heartbeat of the ruling class, dithered hopelessly, the more so since Eden had actually confided his plans to Iverach MacDonald, the foreign editor,[6] who had told Sir William Haley, his editor; the two of them, shocked, one might say innocently so, were torn between loyalty to an elected Tory government which was lying to its House of Commons, and loyalty to honest principle.

Eden and most of his party pictured Nasser as an Arab Hitler. Eden plotted in secret with France and Israel in order to trump up an appearance of justification for the landing. He thought he had the backing of John Foster Dulles, but he hadn't. He assumed that the Labour Party would fall in faithfully, but it didn't. Its party leader Hugh Gaitskell broadcast his strong disapproval on BBC radio by constitutional right as Leader of the Opposition. Sterling poured out of Britain and the reserves were insufficient to buy it back. Eden appealed to Eisenhower for help and Eisenhower, running a tricky re-election campaign, turned him down. Eden burst into tears.[7] The advance south of Port Said was ordered to halt. In mid-November, young men and women piled into Trafalgar Square and for the first time since the 1930s a sometime officer class was beaten about the shoulders by police batons.

Suez, however, was not the only news. Earlier in 1956, three years after the death of Stalin, his successor as First Secretary, Nikita Khrushchev, had ventured some small criticisms of the monster tyrant at the secret annual conference of the Communist Party for all constituent nations. It was time for 'de-Stalinisation'; there had been 'excesses' and a much-to-be-deplored 'cult of personality'. The speech was, Khrushchev himself said, distributed to 'fraternal parties' and became easy to obtain in Warsaw and Washington. The communist neighbour nations began to stir. In Poland and Hungary criticism of blind discipleship towards Moscow was first whispered and then became audible.

In Budapest, Matyas Rakosi, robotic Stalinist, argued publicly with Imre Nagy, his liberalising deputy. An always active intelligentsia joined in on Nagy's side, still vociferous for socialism, but wanting it with a human face. New journals appeared overnight, run off illegally, circulated openly. Rakosi was sacked by Moscow, protesting crowds followed Nagy through the streets, the Petofi circle, a group of intellectuals named after a hero-poet of 1848, published a modest manifesto.

Their students promptly published an immodest one. It is heartening, in a history of political journalism, to note how often, when things are bad, the students take to the streets with the temporary newspapers they have just improvised, reckoning, with some justice, that in the streets of the city of reason reasonable citizens will read what they have to tell them and act accordingly. Without asking anybody, the students called for the withdrawal of Soviet troops, multiparty elections, a revolutionary return to the values of socialism. A wild excitement coursed through the city. The graffiti became wall newspapers, exhorting, admonishing, conscripting.

On 4 November, as British Canberra bombers finished off the last of Egyptian aircraft standing on Egyptian runways, Soviet tanks began their terrible screeching trundle in from the suburbs of Budapest. Hungarian generals known to support Nagy were arrested. The tanks swept away the feeble barricades the students and their supporters had assembled. The troops coming by carrier smashed into the national broadcasting station and as the piteous last pleas for help from the West leaked out into the ether, cut off the students and shot them down. No one knows how many Hungarians and Russian soldiers died. Recently declassified Red Army documents put their dead (including Hungarian police) at 750; the Hungarians reckon on 2,700 citizens killed, 196 of them children under fourteen.[8]

The news of an attempted loosening of Stalinist rigidity after Khrushchev's small show of emollience looked at first as though it would break in Poland. The Polish party leader, Boleslaw Biemt, died suddenly, of shock at Khrushchev's speech the savage joke had it, and the intelligentsia once again had its say, never more eloquently than in the pages of *Nova Kultura* and the voice of the brilliant twenty-six year old Marxist historiographer, Leszek Kolakowski. In a memorable article, 'History and hope', Kolakowski wrote, invoking as he did so 'a socialism of conscience': 'The world of values is not an imaginary sky over the real world of existence but also a part of it, a part ... that is rooted in the material conditions of life.'[9] The imprisoned former leader Wladislaw Gomulka was freed and, after a bullying exchange face to face with Khrushchev in which he promised that all treaty ties to the Soviet Union would be honoured, got his job back.

Once it was clear that Gomulka would indeed go forward gingerly with liberal reforms, the restoration of rights of Catholic worship, a fair price from Mother Russia for coal and steel, a wide-awake journalist at the BBC's

Panorama programme ('television's *Daily Telegraph*' as one wag put it) called Charles Wheeler turned his attention to Budapest.

Whatever was happening there was as fluid and murky as in Warsaw. On 23 October the students had marched to a city park in Budapest and torn down a gigantic bronze statue of Stalin, leaving only his boots on the plinth. The students took over the radio station while others, commemorated in a stirring newsreel, levered the Soviet star, big as a man, off the pediment of the main administrative building so that it swung out, toppled and, bouncing from the facade of the building, crashed into the street below. When students and factory workers tried the same thing in the town of Magyarova, they were machine-gunned. The Hungarian authorities, leaderless, asked for Soviet help and then, in a lull, the Soviet tanks withdrew.

Winding up BBC television machinery in those days took quite a while. The 35 millimetre sound cameras were heavy and cumbersome and the only two mobile ones were out of town. Wheeler and his small team (Hungarian broadcaster Georg Mikes and two cameramen) took off for Vienna under strict instructions from the BBC Head of Current Affairs not to cross the Hungarian border and to cherish the camera with their lives.

They accidentally smashed its tripod, which meant that, at nearly 50 pounds in weight, it had to be held by hand. They found that the secret police and the old party bosses had fled or, in a few cases, had been killed. People told them that the Russians had gone; formal government had dissolved into revolutionary committees run by twenty- to thirty-year-olds. When the Suez operation became distantly known about, the Hungarians were horrified. 'As they saw it,' Wheeler wrote, 'London and Paris were throwing away the moral authority that might have deterred Moscow from committing aggression in Hungary.' 'You'd better get out while you can', they said to Wheeler, 'before the Russians cut the Vienna road.'

Wheeler's team had been there four days. On Sunday 4 November, as they prepared their film, a celebration of a Hungary freed of secret police and government corruption, the news came in of eighteen Russian divisions pouring into the country.

Britain had its own corruptions. When *Panorama* went out the next day, an abominable, now disused rule obstructed any informed debate about Suez. The rule forbade broadcast treatment of any subject due to be debated in Parliament within the next seventeen days. Reporting Suez was cut back to poring over maps. Charles Wheeler had rewritten his story to include the frightfulness of the Soviet reoccupation and Nagy's taking refuge in the Yugoslav embassy. He is a handsome, shock-headed, rather leathery-faced man with considerable presence, and his plain, direct recital of brief triumph and bloody disaster, the first seen close up, the second reported (until he went back two weeks later to interview refugees), is a television classic. The manner of the man and the serious style of the house combined to make a model of newscasting. The authority of *The Times*, its partiality always concealed, had long passed to the BBC. Whatever its compromises, *Panorama*'s work on Hungary and Suez through November 1956 and again in Poland early in 1957 can still teach us that 'objectivity' and 'balance' as criteria of judgement need not lead to blandness and impotence. *Panorama*'s programmes exemplify the highest order of reporting, one in which grave narrative backed by careful filming and the uninterrupted eye-witnessing provided by those to whom these are matters of life and death assumes the absoluteness of established fact and the authority of history.

Writing about Hungary 1956, Timothy Garton Ash observes that: 'It is precisely the mark of great events that their meaning constantly changes, is forever disputed ...'[10] The first draft of history which Wheeler wrote and then edited at the time fixed something of that meaning: Kadar as the only man likely to steer Hungary safely enough away from absolute oppression by the USSR; Nagy as an ambiguous liberator; the Hungarian gesture for freedom as an unambiguous good, and the arrival of the tanks as brutal in both actuality and symbolism; the West as powerless in law and likelihood. Forty years on, Wheeler added another quiet speculation, to the effect that Soviet Russia could never be sure enough of the obedience of its allies to look in any war-waging spirit beyond their frontiers at Western Europe, and that to that extent habitual resentment and occasional insurrection in Poland, Hungary and Czechoslovakia helped to keep the peace.

It is dificult to believe that Soviet Russia, held in the fixed grip of Stalinism after Stalin, of reflex paranoia towards the capitalist democracies after years of reciprocal persecution, of poverty, hunger, corruption and incompetence, was ever likely to roll the tanks westwards. But, remembering that Gomulka himself told Khrushchev in 1956 that if the Soviet troops arrived, the Polish Army would attack them, it is fair to conclude that those frontier nations kept their hatred of the USSR and their longing for a better life as heavy weights in the balance of terror.

The year 1956 is a climacteric; like 1914, 1940, 1968, 1989. The list of all-dominating events is so definite that each has its distinct silhouette, even if we don't yet have the cipher to read the outlines. One consequence, however, of the colossal extension of daily news – the substitution (as

Walter Benjamin put it) of information for storying – is that mere eventuality overwhelms us. The wooden headlines cannot be reassembled as a narrative house one can live in. The opinionators are hired to do the construction work, to sort the timber headlines, the great girders of shock and event, the screws and shackles of individual actions, into the township of the present. Only some of them remain at work for long enough to be trustworthy as building contractors, issuing the drawings which can turn chaos into progress, the terrible messiness of human arrangement into a habitable present. These are the journalists of newspaper columns or newscasting programmes, who turn the present into history.

Such people are such a help, as much because of their longevity as anything. Their continuing across time is such a reassurance, their voices on the page and their features on the screen are so familiar that they become one of the family. It is not a trifling point to notice that respectable matrons may not infrequently have the photographs of kindly, mature newscasters – Walter Cronkite, Richard Baker, Trevor MacDonald, Kenneth Kendall – in a little frame on their sideboards.

These men, and fewer women, attach the items of the news and the stories which trail after them to a narrative thread. Lippmann did it, Murrow did it; for fifty-odd years apiece, so too have Walter Cronkite, Alistair Cooke and I. F. Stone.

These are three of the most famous of the several men and women to come who became trustworthy over many years. These are people whose manner and presence hold together the facts and a view of the facts. This seems to flout the precept about the absolute separation of facts and opinion. But in truth that separation is impossible to sustain. What happens in all journalism is that *style*, as much a product of the house as of the writer, sets the context in which the news is to be addressed. Let us say there are two types of grand soloists in this manner: dissenters and mediators.

My first soloist who matches up to 'the short twentieth century' is the dissenter I. F. Stone. His photograph turns up on few suburban sideboards. But he exemplifies in a vivid biography how a career may capture for itself a particular historic zone, of both actuality and its application. One went to Izzy Stone to find out what one couldn't possibly be told on television, and to discover or ratify how to feel about it.

He was a lifelong practitioner of the journalism of political outrage. It is a necessary mode of thought; and the niche it occupies depends on the prior labours of such as I. F. Stone, born Isador Feinstein in 1907, becoming I. F. Stone when in the 1930s he began to smell the reek of anti-semitism around him and changed his name, as much as anything, to protect his children.

I. F. Stone scribbled stories as soon as he could write, and published and circulated his own neighbourhood newsletter *The Progress* when he was fourteen. He went to the *Camden Courier* and on to the *Philadelphia Record* by way of Penn State University. He wrote prodigally and prodigiously. By 1933, when David Stern, the owner of both, transferred him from the *Record* to the *New York Post*, he was a regular contributor to the *New Republic* and to *The Nation*. He didn't join the Communist Party but was an energetic and well-known figure along the length of the broad, intolerant ranks of the Popular Front, the banner which waved over the many groupings of leftish politics in the thirties.

We have seen, in the case of Whittaker Chambers, the special and solitary agoraphobia induced by party membership, and Stone was too convivial, too impetuous also, too American to have enlisted. He used to call himself a Marxist Jeffersonian and there was something in that. But he was tainted by something in the air of the 1930s, holding on to Soviet Russia as a possible future for the good society even after the treason trials, even after the Molotov–Ribbentrop pact of 1939. In addition he was boisterously part of the frantic argufying of the thirties in the circles of Washington's intellectual life among the proletarians of culture. They cheered for the New Deal and for Roosevelt's stacking of the Supreme Court, and fretted whether the great charmer might yet turn into the great dictator. Whenever Stone and the family were broke, he swallowed his principles and wrote a piece for the *Washington Post*; the rest of the time – I don't suppose he ever had an unpublished thought – he wrote for a new middling-radical afternoon paper, called *PM*, with Popular Front sympathies and its roots in muckraking. Six, eight, ten hours a day he clattered at his typewriter and then dived out of the house on Nebraska Avenue clutching his copy, and if it was for *The Nation* catching the train up to New York to catch up with New York.

He cherished some of Orwell's fantasies about a peaceful revolution of good-hearted workers, but it was the kind of thinking he was no good at. What he stood firmest and best on was in defence of civil liberties on behalf of the Left and in attack upon the lies of power. The war for Stone, myopic and flat-footed, was waged by way of anti-fascist editorials. When it ended, he went on a commission from *The Nation* to Palestine and, his strong Jewish sympathies matched nicely by his sense of justice, wrote supporting, as 'nobler and politically sounder',[11] a binational state. He brought out a couple of books on his visit,[12] the first, *Underground to Palestine* including powerful descriptions of the innumerable legal and illegal ways, some of them taken by Stone, in which refugees from Europe reached the promised land.

With that short book of reportage, and its sibling *This is Israel*, he broke with simple-minded Popular Fronting and became his own kind of singular journalist. He thrived on snubbing the communists while defending their rights during Cold War and while keeping, as so many on the European Left did right up to 1989, a special enclave in his imagination where democratic principles could be waived for a season, pending the advent of full-blown socialism. At home, however contemptuous of the American Communist Party, he nonetheless unflinchingly opposed the detestable House Un-American Activities Committee. As he did so, and drawing on his experience of Palestine as it turned into the new state of Israel, he rejected the arrogantly self-absorbed hostility of the two super-power blocs. The saturating atmosphere of suspicion which pressed on the minds of both nations, at least in their governments, required them to insist on unconditional allegiance. What this lockjawed attitude could not allow was that many nations simply wanted to be free of this crazily high tension; the Yugoslavs, Israelis, Scandinavians, maybe Poles and Czechs before long, wanted 'their own little space in the sun'.[13] This feeling originated in the Hungarian and Egyptian crises and played itself out in Cold War uniform in the countries Stone names. Then people in Indo-China, and great tracts of Africa and Southern America, simply wanted to be *rid* of the superpowers. In 1989 the feeling mounted to its exhilarating *coup de théâtre*. In 2001, at the World Trade Center, it darkened with world menace.

It was the Korean War which unexpectedly provided Stone with the chance to prove himself an entirely new kind of scholar-journalist and to inaugurate a mode of investigation of which subsequently Noam Chomsky has proved his most direct and distinguished inheritor. His everyday journalistic labours as well as his passionate beliefs led him to keep an elaborate cuttings system from the newspapers and weeklies. This was routine. If nothing else it gave him a check on the consistency of arguments and sometimes of ethics levelled by journalists at politicians, at one another and at themselves.

He began to notice sharp discrepancies between how the High Command described the war and how journalists, even those strongly inclined to follow the line they were given by generals, reported what they found. The result was Stone's masterpiece, *The Hidden History of the Korean War 1950–1951*,[14] and the most precise and exactingly minute study of the accuracy of newspapers as well as of politicians which appears in our period.

Stone's method was all inferential. President Truman suddenly flew 18,000 miles to meet MacArthur on a small Pacific island called Wake immediately after two American fighters attacked a *Soviet* airbase sixty miles north of the Korean frontier and only forty miles south of Vladivostock. This was on 8 October 1950.[15] The Soviets objected, as well they might; they were not belligerents. Truman was known to have strained relations with MacArthur. The meeting lasted five hours. At its conclusion, the President said things had gone 'Perfectly. I've never had a more satisfactory conference since I've been President.' MacArthur, in Stone's word, was 'surly': 'All comment will have to come from the publicity man of the President.' Piecing all this together, reckoning up that those present included *all* Chiefs of Staff and Presidential Secretaries of State and War but none of MacArthur's staff, noticing that President and Supreme Commander were also alone together (with shorthand secretaries) for forty-five minutes at the outset, Stone deduced that Truman had needed to bring his full authority to bear upon his disobedient and arrogant commander, and that this was an urgent, indeed a dangerous necessity given the border violation.

Stone was quite right. In interpreting this minor episode so scrupulously he set a quite new standard for political journalism, one he followed all his life. The book is full of examples. When MacArthur's Eighth Army was in full retreat in late November, Stone added up a mixed bag of reports from the London *Sunday Times* and *Observer*, topped off with the scornful observation made by Peter Fleming in the *Spectator* that the Eighth Army's 'successful disengagement' (*sc* retreat) had left the 'Chinese Reds' (MacArthur's HQ phrase) 'with no more exacting role than sheep dogs'. A press correspondent had asked a senior officer what the military definition of a 'horde' was, there being, it seemed, hordes of Chinese. Stone quoted Fleming in reply: 'I can see no military considerations which would enable even the largest force of infantry to throw a modern army, supported by a large airforce and an unchallenged fleet, into the sea.'[16] Stone further deduced that the Chinese, having driven the UN army well south of the border, might be prepared to call things a day. But Truman had mentioned the atom bomb, MacArthur would have dropped it without compunction, Attlee had flown in high agitation to Washington to count Britain out of any such insanity, and world safety, Stone reckoned, was not exactly in safe hands.

It is matchless work. Even now it grips by the throat. It is however easy to guess that such reporting, when 33,629 Americans and 686 British were to die in action – 3 million Koreans and Chinese being for others, who could not even count them, to mourn – would bring its author only infamy.

So it is to the credit of his great country that Stone became, over the years, one of those legendary items, a legend and, even more solid, an institution. When *The Hidden History of the Korean War* came out other journalists and the government itself were quick to slur it and him as writing Soviet propaganda; but the book sold out, as did regular issues of *PM* with excerpts.

Nonetheless Stone became formally unemployable. It was 1953, McCarthy was raging on his way with no objection from a timid President, the Soviets had given the hair-trigger touchiness of the United States plenty to twitch about, and nobody wanted radicals in their columns. So, as Claud Cockburn had done in England, the unstoppable Izzy Stone started *I. F. Stone's Weekly*; it ran as long as Agatha Christie's *The Mousetrap*. He borrowed 3,000 bucks from a chum at lunch at the Museum of Modern Art, obtained the mailing lists from *PM*, placed advertisements in the progressive dailies, and signed up 5,300 subscribers, including Einstein, Eleanor Roosevelt and Bertrand Russell, at 5 dollars for the year.[17] The US Postal Service mailed it for an eighth of a cent a time,[18] Stone and his wife took a joint salary of 200 dollars a week, he wrote a page per day, scouring the dailies in order to detect the blurred and shadowy negative discernible in their clear black-and-white world pictures.

By 1955 he had 10,000 subscribers. Stone's political dedication drew steadily closer to Madison's *Federalist Papers* and, especially after Hungary in 1956, less and less optimistic about socialism. Already he was, at forty-nine, assuming the status of celebrity. Not that this took the edge off him. He started out as besotted as most journalists were with Kennedy, got wind of the Bay of Pigs debacle, and just before the missile crisis wrote under the headline 'Havana is the spark that could set off conflagration'; after things were over he set off for Cuba with gifts of medicines for the regime and was put straight into jail by grateful Cubans.

From 1957 to the assassination of Martin Luther King in 1968, the political issue in which decent-hearted journalism could make the most difference was civil rights and the state of the nation's racism. World politics has the thrill of power about it (one perfectly respectable reason why intellectuals, on the other side of the narrow bridge which gives access to power, are so preoccupied by it). But civil rights and domestic affairs respond to a palpable public opinion, one in this case still split by the Mason-Dixon Line.

Stone reckoned that change-of-heart politics needed 'a Gandhi' to lead it. Luther King promptly appeared and made his unforgettable speech at the Capitol in August 1963. The marchers were back and Stone was glad about it. A march for peace is, until it becomes warlike or meets hated opponents, a lovesome thing. Contingents from all over a country speed by bus or train, by foot or family car piled with children, strollers, picnic-boxes, to the capital. There they assemble in temporary little paddocks fenced round by official but movable railings, identified by felt-penned posters and carefully homeworked banners, and after inordinate, inexplicable delays patiently borne, are herded into a slow, slovenly, dignified procession into some vast and arbitrary concourse where they will hear their stars and leaders speak, and then go shufflingly home. These are the people bearing witness to themselves. They come to declare their bodily vulnerability and dedication to the cause in hand. The declaration only counts for something if enough people show up. Thus is public opinion become visible. The people's witnesses come along as well to reckon up how they've done, how many came, how this will play in the corridors behind the railings, up the Mall and in Foggy Bottom.

There were to be plenty such. As American involvement in Vietnam deepened, the basic training in the organisation of civil protest, learned in Mississippi and taken to Washington, served the leaders of the new leftist movements well. Stone was both source of knowledge and focus of dissent for bodies such as Students for a Democratic Society when, with another dozen acronymics, they began after the Tonkin Bay episode in 1965 to organise mass opposition to the Vietnamese war. No one was quicker or more dogged than Stone in his critical analyses of government statements or policy pamphlets. He arraigned the official case under what thereafter became the standard heads of criticism: that the US had dishonoured the 1954 Geneva accords; that it backed a corrupt and undemocratic regime; that plenty of those in South Vietnam supported the communists; and that communism was a rational set of beliefs for the wretched of the earth; that the weapons of the insurgents were less Chinese than American; that the domino theory would be vindicated, if at all, because of America's own efforts to prevent its fulfilment; that the USA, mightiest nation in the history of the world, was an abomination for its lying and cruelty towards those same wretched people it ought on the contrary to be succouring.

The *Weekly* became compulsory reading in and out of the circles of power. When the *New York Review of Books* started in 1963, it quickly turned into a dissident voice of some volume and penetration as far as the war was concerned. Robert Silvers, its editor, united Stone and Noam Chomsky in its pages, and their regular essays became the staple of the war resisters. Chomsky copied Stone's unremitting labours of scholarship, absorbing the big daily papers before 7.30 a.m., the *Congressional Record* over breakfast; both were men with prodigious memories and an acute eye for irregularity in what they read. The *Weekly* climbed to a circulation of 38,000 and in August 1967 the biggest march of all converged on the Pentagon with Stone, Chomsky, Norman Mailer and Robert Lowell in its vanguard and the armies of the night behind them.

The Pentagon march opened the most frightening and most commemorated years of civil dissent in America since the end of the Civil War. Throughout those twelve months Stone lived the lives of public radical leader and of dedicated and necessarily reclusive opposition journalist. The journalism itself reflected this cramming together of incompatible and mythic roles. It spoke in high rhetoric and yet with microscopic exactitude. In 'Nixon and the arms race',[19] Stone checks Nixon's declared policy against the record of the Senate's appropriations committee and the acute financial troubles of General Dynamics which was to manufacture the new F111, all as garnered from *Fortune* magazine. Following Robert MacNamara's admitted and expensive errors, Nixon had pledged himself to confirm the mistakes; the only consequences could be, Stone hoped, to make the country realise that 'at a certain point, in the awful arithmetic of nuclear power, superiority in weapons becomes meaningless'.

At sixty-three and after Nixon began secretly to bomb Cambodia, the centre of gravity in Stone's more rhetorical mode is caught by a *Weekly* headline, 'Only the bums can save the country now.'[20] He didn't like, he wrote, much of what the campus rebels were bawling, he didn't like policemen being called pigs, he hated hatred, and lifelong dissent had acclimatised him cheerfully to defeat. But, he went on, 'I feel about the rebels as Erasmus felt about Luther ... I feel that the New Left and the black revolutionaries [Stone thought of the two together] are doing God's work, too, in refusing any longer to submit to evil, and challenging society to reform or crush them.'[21]

It is impossible to be a famous and wealthy journalist and still be able to address a nation on an issue which divides it. Stone was lucky in having the life he had; he lived in a minority of one but was sure of his audience. He was also committed to the intransigence which certified such a life. This is not to say that Walter Cronkite and Alistair Cooke, the second and third figures in this chapter, lacked such principles, only that in speaking up for national continuity and largeness of heart they had to find a way of remaining non-committal about exactly the moral commitment Stone endorsed in the campus rebels and out of forty years soldiering in the same tradition. It is, however, testimony to the continued vitality of that tradition of Stone's radicalism in the nation at large and not just in the little enclaves of the American Left that he came to public recognition. There were always those for whom he could only be an object of obloquy, there were more for whom he became an object of veneration.

Stone kept on working. He closed the *Weekly* down for very tiredness at the end of 1971. But he became a contributing editor to the *New York Review of Books*, publishing his last essay in Victor Navasky's *Nation* in April 1987. Longevity does not promise reputation, although it is a help. By the late 1960s Stone had moved on to one of the pedestals reserved for public figures; it is a notable thing that this happened to a journalist like him and it is, I guess, only in America that it could happen at all.

I suggested earlier (with the help of Benedict Anderson) that the pages of a newspaper provide a kind of cognitive and sociable furniture upon which readers can temporarily sit themselves down in terms of history, geography, politics and passion. This is only true, no doubt, in so far as the newspaper in question sufficiently provides accommodation for its readers' minds. No single newspaper (obviously) could do such a thing for a whole people. Hence the divisions of class, labour, region, generation and so forth. Each newspaper serves, so to speak, as a light ballast with which to weigh down the readership and anchor it in a small stretch of water, one moreover commanding a sufficient view of the blue distances unvisited by but known to that same readership.

Drift and dragging occur when the newspaper fails its readers by not holding on to its society; it tells too many lies, perhaps, pursues a lost world towards which readers can no longer steer, the bearings have gone, the land is out of sight. When this happens, circulation may fall steeply or it may not – a paper may be utterly wrong but profitable – but by the tests of history a newspaper at such a moment has failed its readers by depriving them of history. It may leave them floating instead on vicious prejudice, arbitrary passion, sudden nightmare.

All newspapers must deal with such stuff and, if they have the finesse, turn them to account. But if they use these gases for their only fuel, they will steer off into craziness and triviality. They may make a living there. There are plenty of examples to hand in addition to *Sunday Sport* in England, the *National Enquirer* in the United States, *France-Dimanche*. But selling craziness is not the same as selling news-and-views, does nothing for the virtuous, truth-regarding citizen somewhere to be found in all of us, and falls outside our purview.

A wholly different set of reckonings and duties, however, come into play with the sort of national broadcaster of whom Bill Shirer, Ed Murrow, Alistair Cooke and Richard Dimbleby have been the towering prototypes. They emerged from the transformation of news reporting on the page to news broadcasting on the air, and in the process, as one would expect, gave authority to immediacy, to eye-witnessing and 'being there'. They saw what any intelligent observer would see (*not* quirkily, not 'personally'), accurately intuiting what each of them sensed the audience would want to have seen for themselves. In so far as authority, intuition and immediacy came together, the job was done as well as by the four examples I name. And these four were not just good, but astonishingly, continuingly so. They each are cases where longevity only confirmed dependability and trustworthiness.

When television came, a new quantity entered the effects. The news broadcaster was no longer a familiar, even well-loved *voice*; he or she was a half-body with a face as well. The newscaster became recognisable in public and the dimensions of celebrity were at once simplified and enlarged. A voice, after all, was attributable to the supreme authority of a station – of CBS or BBC; one knew of course that this was the voice of Ed Murrow or Richard Dimbleby, but especially during wartime each wore the authority of official truth-telling. During the decades that Walter Cronkite appeared on the screen, his authority was greater than that of CBS; it derived from the medium, from television itself, and to that extent Cronkite became one of the voices of the very nation telling its particulate membership what was going on. Alistair Cooke, by contrast, became a potent anachronism: through the non-visual medium of radio, it is his extraordinary achievement to have given his own voice and personality a comparable authority to Cronkite's. This has certainly been due to his amazing durability in office and the sheer length of life of the 'Letters from America'. Perhaps this is also due to his mid-Atlantic position, telling the English about the Americans, and their approving it at the same time. His very speech, now English, now American, suggests the intimacy of his relationship in both directions. It is surely impossible that there be another such figure, whereas Walter Cronkite must have a successor. It is *his* great achievement to have made himself, in response to powerful yearnings from his audiences in their millions, a quite new kind of character in society and in doing so to have written out a permanent role now indispensable to America.

Where Ed Murrow never really took off his uniform, Cronkite found in himself exactly the right, the simple, presence which his surging, localist and contradictory society discovered it wanted him to have.[22] He became, you might say, an individual embodiment of the key values of the Constitution, since *that* is the only ideal force capable of uniting so protean a nationhood.

Each accident of his life shaped him for this destiny. He was born in 1916, the child of a Missouri dentist and his handsome wife (who lived to her centenary), both of Dutch stock. Father went to war with his tray of implements and returned to move his family to practise in Kansas City, and to devote himself to serious drinking. Cronkite's parents eventually divorced but not before his father moved them to Houston, where Cronkite first encountered and learned from his parents to hate the southern racism which became the object of his unswerving public criticism. His attitude was shakingly confirmed when the black fourteen-year-old with whom Cronkite shared an ice-cream delivery route was shot dead as he transgressed a suburban segregation line.[23]

He was and remained tender-hearted all his life. It was as necessary a part of his character as the dash and enterprise with which he put out his unofficial high school paper *The Reflector* and cadged a job breathing in the smell of printer's ink and molten lead at the *Houston Post*. He dropped out of his physics degree at Austin and into the offices of the (Houston) *Press* deep in the Depression, and then back to the *Post* as second man on the crime beat, adept at the histrionics of the upright telephone, meeting the third member of the Bonnie and Clyde gang, and from there went to what was, in 1936, the biggest city of the wild west, Kansas City, to join the news staff of its just-started state radio station.

There Cronkite learned to translate the Morse code summaries of big football games sent out by Western Union into a simulation of live broadcast, shouting out the moves as he imaginatively transcribed them from three-line telegrams. Meanwhile his no less creative colleague blew a whistle, slapped a football and turned up the sound of a cheering crowd on the phonograph at likely intervals. It reads like the plotline of *The Sting*, and when, fifty years later, Cronkite described to Ronald Reagan the day Western Union's line went down and he improvised forty minutes of an unreported game, the President, as was his wont, appropriated and told the tale as his own within a month.

He accumulated the experience like savings in the 1930s and 1940s. He stayed in the west, did a lot more football in Oklahoma City, married a good-looking journalist, listened admiringly to Ed Murrow speaking from

London, and went to war in Tunis, London and Normandy as correspondent with United Press. He earned his medal ribbons crash-landing in a
glider during the huge three-decker airborne landing which terminated at
Arnhem in September 1944 – 'just remember, Cronkite,' his companion
shouted to him under heavy fire, 'these are the good old days'; he got home
after hostilities and was promptly posted, with his wife, to Moscow.

Moscow was as awful as everyone said it was, especially George Kennan
in the embassy.[24] The Russians were bullying, secretive, obdurate, incompetent. The plumbing didn't work. There was no food, even for American
journalists. Everybody spied on everybody else. The censors of what the
journalists despatched cut everything to shreds and replaced the original
with lies. Drew Middleton of the *New York Times* took to sprinkling his
copy with quotations from *Alice in Wonderland* to signpost their more
fanciful excesses. The Cronkites' apartment was searched, ransacked,
smashed up and left. Cronkite had befriended Jan Masaryk, friend also of
Murrow and Lippmann; the clever, cultivated, honest and eminent politician of the Czech Republic, in 1948 still a minister in a Communist-led
coalition government. Cronkite went to see him depart for an official visit
to Moscow and was warned off by the heavies. He called across to Masaryk,
'Au revoir!' 'Oh no, my friend,' Masaryk called back, 'Farewell.'

Cronkite went home and rejoined his Kansas City radio station, which
promptly commissioned him, on a shining new salary, to open a radio news
bureau in Washington. Two years in the capital and Cronkite was invited to
be newscaster for the brand-new CBS television station. From the start, he
hit upon the style which defined him; it was, after all, his own. He had had
to be a resourceful commentator on football games he couldn't see, he had
had editors who expected their juniors to memorise and smoothly to
rehearse all the main stories of the day without notice or hesitation,

> So the television ad-lib came easily to me, and I thought that this seem-
> ingly extemporaneous type of delivery fitted the concept of speaking to
> that single individual in front of his set in the intimacy of his own home,
> not to a gathering of thousands. My 'script' consisted only of a list of the
> subjects on which I would report, proper names I would need to remem-
> ber, and the occasional precise figure I might need. I crammed it all on
> a slip of paper I pasted behind the desk sign that identified the WTOP-
> TV news.[25]

It all makes one look down a bit disdainfully on the autocue. It also
makes beautifully clear just how experience turns into style, how man and

manner are blended into something well called integrity. Cronkite's quickness and calm, his readiness to turn the unexpected into a small news paragraph, his pleasure in human comicality and his strong, unexamined principles of individual sanctity and self-reliance, of unassuming liberty and presumptive politeness fuse in the excitement of the new job, new to him, new to the society, bringing simple, pleasurable fame pretty well overnight.

He revelled in the improvisations of the new industry, as when for instance CBS went all out to broadcast film made live at the coronation of Queen Elizabeth II in London in 1953, flying it back to Labrador overnight, down to Boston where it was cut, edited and broadcast with Cronkite's on-the-spot commentary intercut with Richard Dimbleby's, all by 4 p.m. eastern time. At just about this time, he was attending a political convention with the first president of CBS television news (the first person, Cronkite speculates,[26] to use the word 'anchorman'), when his boss turned to him suddenly and said, 'Well Walter, you're famous now. And you are going to want a lot more money. You'd better get an agent.'

In point of fact, Cronkite likes being rich but isn't so very interested in money.[27] He *is* deeply interested in those television processes which, in bringing him that fortune, have, he thinks, damaged the democracy expressing itself in the politics which is his living. His interest in this is moral rather than theoretic. Wealthy people, especially those who have made a lot of money in a line of work in which they started out young and poor, aren't usually very clear-sighted about their relation to their own success, but I believe Cronkite when he says he hadn't given the money much thought. Then he goes on: 'My misgivings about the sort of business I was in were well founded. This was show business, and as it turned out, down that road lay the perils of the star system and the million dollar anchors.' He never really identifies these perils, however, beyond some low-order ruminations about how most television reporting presents politics as the clash of wills and personalities, leaving out of focus the strong currents of historical force and moral issue.

His analysis won't quite do; it's a step towards the truth. And whatever the consequences for democratic understanding, let alone participation, Cronkite's way of reporting is now, forty-odd years after he put it together, a way of seeing the business of good or bad government on behalf of whole societies. If reducing politics to the taste of gossip and the smell of sex is bad for our ideals and principles, then we had better find some way to cross the ravine which gapes between the practice of power and the living of everyday civic life. By the time Cronkite finished as anchorman and

Barbara Walters had built a rival pedestal for an anchorwoman, the anchor was the figure on whom the people built an absolute trust. Cronkite as journalist-broadcaster sees the essential struggle as being between medium and messenger. Broadcasting ought to be a pure conduit for the passage of the clear waters of politics; politicians try to stain those waters in lush colours. They must be prevented.

All true, of course, and as Cronkite tells us,[28] it was Kennedy (no less) who – after a little contretemps but before he was elected – telephoned the president of CBS to remind him that he would have in hand the naming of appointments to the Federal Communications Commission. This kind of injudicious heavy-handing works *always* to the detriment of politicians. It obscures, in this corner of the story, that larger process whereby, immediately after John F. Kennedy's assassination, it was Cronkite's voice and face and manner which all unconsciously became the common reference point of the entire nation as it sought, in incredulous dismay, to catch together the shattered and incomprehensible glimpses of news in an intelligible narrative.

In a compendious reconstruction,[29] William Manchester reports Cronkite's first, bare announcement at 12.40 on 22 November 1963 (beating, as Cronkite remarks with pleasure, NBC by almost a minute), 'three shots were fired at President Kennedy's motorcade in downtown Dallas'. No gloss was put on the news. When Lyndon Johnson, not yet sworn in, climbed aboard Air Force One he went straight to the cabin from which he could hear Cronkite's voice coming, and when he arrived at the White House he found Pierre Salinger, the press secretary: Salinger watched 'Walter Cronkite remove, replace, and again remove his spectacles, a muscle in his jaw trembled violently. He confirmed the President had gone.'[30] Johnson turned to that calm mouth and those steady eyes, that nondescript-handsome, utterly familiar, American face, 'hoping that [it] would tell him what was going on',[31] while the rest of the nation did the same.

Cronkite stayed on duty that day for six straight hours, and when he was relieved by Charles Collingwood the colossal audience felt the pang of separation as from that best kind of senior, one with a touch of paternal authority but also of removal and mystery, whom one trusts to console and reassure, but trusts also to speak plainly and, it may be, painfully if the truth proves painful.

The connection between the private and public characters of a very well-known public figure is shifting but simple. The public character is a magnified version of the private one, with those attributes and accomplishments which constitute the grounds of fame detached, enlarged and projected on to the public screen without any of the blur, inconsistency and weight of those other details which taken together make another person so unassimilable to us.

In Cronkite's case, he brought off such a contrivance with a truthfulness and integrity amounting to genius. Partly, of course, and as I have suggested, his sheer longevity made for this completeness of self-presentation. But crucial to his achievement – one with definitive properties for all those who followed in similar positions – was that he was nearly enough *really like that*. The ethics he learned in his crowded, hand-to-mouth, supremely lucky and sufficiently historic apprenticeship gave his character both substance and essence when he became anchorman. Deep in that ethics were certain truths he held always to be self-evident such that, even when professing them in that manner of bluffness and *bonhomie* sincerely his own, they retained the gravity and echo which turn commonplaces into epitaphs.

When, therefore, as so inevitably is asked these days, someone demands in outrage why John F. Kennedy was allowed so lavish a licence for his unstoppable sexual escapades (Angie Dickinson: 'the most unforgettable fifteen seconds of my life'), Cronkite replies:

> In the sixties the Washington press ... operated on a rule of thumb regarding the morals of our public men. The rule had it that, as long as his outside activities, alcoholic or sexual, did not interfere with or seriously endanger the discharge of his public duties, a man was entitled to his privacy.[32]

These unimpeachable bromides were, in turn, impeached and violated in the notorious case of President Clinton and the White House intern Monica Lewinsky thirty-odd years after Angie Dickinson and Marilyn Monroe. The change is largely one in journalistic ethics and the shaping spirits of competition and profit, but one consequence for democracy is that anchorpeople, their private lives less under surveillance, are likely to be held in the hearts of their audience with more affection, esteem and familiarity than presidents or prime ministers.

Cronkite is, endearingly, both truculent and gratified by this development. He is truculent about Richard Nixon's campaign to denigrate the press as negative, self-referential, self-important, etc. etc., much of it accurate but not of Walter Cronkite; but then, quite without sanctimony, he is proud of the small stand he took in 1968 against certain of his own professional standards at the moment at which, even for the nation's anchorman, the Vietnamese war became insupportable.

Cronkite, true to that part of his role which assigned him duties of sensitivity to, *and* on behalf of, the heart of the nation, continued to feel up to 1968 that the United States was making a courageous and necessary fight for freedoms owing to all peoples when it counted its commitment in Vietnam as being covered by the Truman Doctrine. Nonetheless, after Kennedy had pledged in his ambiguous inaugural address 'to pay any price, bear any burden, meet any hardship, support any friend, oppose any foe to assure our survival and the success of liberty',[33] it was to Cronkite that he uttered a fateful qualification.

It was 2 September 1963 and the first time the CBS evening news filled a full half-hour slot. Kennedy gave them an interview at Hyannis to launch the enlarged programme, and Cronkite heard by way of friends in the agencies that the President would say something new and urgent about Vietnam. At that date there was no official military involvement but Kennedy had increased what was euphemistically called the force of 'advisers' to 18,000. Vietnam was still small beer and in any case Cronkite was fiercely opposed to his programme being used as a policy platform; 'it was definitely against my own code.'[34] Knowing that his interviewee could say what he liked in any case, he bided his time in order to judge what to edit after the interview was over.

Kennedy made an observation which has provided the text for all Kennedy-admiring revisionists who have subsequently tried to exonerate him from blame for the war and to claim that in 1963 he was beginning to consider withdrawal from Vietnam. He voiced a warning to President Diem that the South Vietnamese themselves wouldn't support the latest policies, and that there were limits to what America could do in a guerrilla war: 'in the final analysis ... [it is] their war. They are the ones who have to win it or lose it.'[35]

Cronkite went on visiting Vietnam between 1965 and 1968, attempting always to overcome the special treatment accorded celebrity by balancing dinners with William C. Westmoreland, general in charge of Military Assistance Command, or Ellsworth Bunker, the ambassador, against sallies into the field inside gunships or bombers. He was of the generation of newsmen shaped by the Second World War; he deplored the scatology and cynicism of reporters from Vietnam like Michael Herr, and he shed his illusions and his faith in his great nation's optimism and decency – the very values from which he drew his own strength and steadiness in his reporting – at first slowly, then all in a rush.

The rush came with the shock offensive launched by the guerrilla army of the South in Vietnam, the Vietcong, at the Indo-Chinese New Year, Tet, in 1968. Ten weeks previously General Westmoreland had told the National Press Club in Washington that 'the enemy's hopes are bankrupt. With your support we will give you a success that will impact not only on South Vietnam, but on every emerging nation in the world.'[36] On 30 January the People's Army and the Vietcong struck in every large town in the South bar one. The National Front had hoped for a spontaneous urban uprising to turn out the Americans. They didn't get it. What they did get was firestorm. The American war machine went berserk. In Saigon and Hue alone, over 10,000 civilians were killed as the choppers and fighter-bombers rocketed and blazed away at the thickly crowded shanties on the ground until the two capitals roared up in flames. All the time, the American public watched on television as the boys they had sent to save South East Asia for democracy did so, as a spokesman immortally said, by 'destroying the town in order to save it'. The two national news programmes at CBS and NBC were the main vehicles of such broadcasts.

The CBS president invited Cronkite and the Secretary of State for Defense James Schlesinger to lunch, maybe to reassure the White House and the Pentagon of the station's judicious objectivity. But Schlesinger, an unappetisingly arrogant man, chose to remind the broadcasters of their duties to patriotism, and for such a man as Cronkite, the reminder was tactless. In his turn and with angry passion, Cronkite reminded Schlesinger that patriotism is not a journalist's obligation and that in any case the value itself might be better defined in action as calling on one's country to live up to its own best self. Then he flew out to the siege of Hue, escaped with some difficulty, together with twelve marines in body-bags, and flew home determined to do his democratic duty in a way to affront the Pentagon.

He had once or twice spoken editorially on television, but strictly on professional issues. This time, 'speaking as a reporter' he spoke to the whole nation but for, as he hoped, its conscience.

I said: 'To say that we are closer to victory today is to believe, in the face of the evidence, the optimists who have been wrong in the past. To suggest we are on the edge of defeat is to yield to unreasonable pessimism. To say that we are mired in stalemate seems the only realistic, yet unsatisfactory, conclusion ... It is increasingly clear to this reporter that the only rational way out, then, will be to negotiate, not as victors, but as an honourable people who lived up to their pledge to defend democracy, and did the best they could.'[37]

He spoke also and directly to Lyndon Johnson, who was (and remained) a close friend. Johnson's press secretary, who was there, later recounted that he switched off the set, turned to the staff around him and said simply, 'If I've lost Cronkite, I've lost middle America.' Cronkite's own statement is a classic of middle America: 'We did our best; we must get out.' It was a lot milder than what the next generation of journalists were writing – Halberstam, Sheehan, Schell – and it was, no doubt deliberately, communitarian, healing, pacific. James Cameron and Martha Gellhorn were much more severe on the honour of the nation, the shocking injury done to democratic ideals. So Cronkite's statement hit the President all the harder for that. Making it made him the voice of unpolitical America, putting the best face on things for everyone's sake.

The reaction of one politician was to try to turn Cronkite into one of them. Bobby Kennedy pressed him, more or less ruthlessly, to run for Senate. Cronkite batted him away for the best of reasons, that thereafter all such anchorpeople might be suspected of seeking television fame to win senatorial power. He kept the main seat on CBS Evening News until he retired at sixty-five. He did more plain speaking on behalf of humanitarianism and old democracy, in South Africa and in his own Deep South. But his break to opinionising was unique. '[Murrow and Sevareid] were the editorial page; I was the front page.'[38]

He left office in 1981, and went sailing with the love of the nation in his sails. As he went he spoke a sharp curse over the insanely high salaries paid to anchorpeople when their juniors are laid off in droves, and, just as trenchantly, pointed out that his generation of journalists was part of the common people with whom they ate, drank, shopped, queued and died. They didn't come cruising into crises and take the microphone smoothly from the youngsters when the politics was lit in bright enough lights; fame and money did not cut out ordinary experience, as they have done since Walter Cronkite relinquished the role of the anchor which he first forged for his people.

While the Kennedy Administration dallied with Khrushchev over the imminence of a nuclear war detonated by Cuba, Cronkite connected the people to the tremulous and raucous hesitations of the President's crisis committee, Ex-Comm, and turned its uncertainty into the platitudes of order. When Kennedy was assassinated, Cronkite transformed fearfulness and incredulity into anguished composure. As the nation watched its own army's stupendous firepower incinerate the straw-and-wattle houses of some of the poorest people in the world, Cronkite for the first and only time changed tone and tack and spoke not to his people but for them, and for their sense of their own wounded humanity. Even then, he gathered together the sense of outrage and of due loyalty of his sundered nation, and gave it a single and conciliatory story.

Over an even longer period the voice of Alistair Cooke hovered over the mid-Atlantic and, in an accent soft-American to the English and all-English to the Americans, became, not unlike Cronkite, a talisman of political continuity, of wry, calm and reassuring sagacity about the unprecedented superpower which was his chosen nation. For over half a century, his unseen presence to his millions of listeners connected them to the history and politics made by the strange, enviable and inevitable Americans whose foreign ways and global predominance could be made so homely by the far-from-accidental coincidence of the English language.

You could say it was Cooke's destiny to find such a voice. It was certainly his shrewd and early choice. He was born in 1908 in the heart of northern industrial England, in the rise and fall of the close-ribbed streets of Salford. His father, a devout Methodist, was a skilled artisan and after the family moved to the holiday-taking headquarters of the working class at Blackpool, Cooke's family lived comfortably enough.

All the same, it wasn't a family capable of holding its exceptional younger son within its framework. He certainly wasn't going to follow his big brother into a butcher's business, neither was he going to be pinned to his class even by his own unmistakably class name. At twenty-two, young Alfred became by deed poll Alistair Cooke, and a transfiguration of the tall, handsome, willowy young man which began when he won scholarships to Blackpool Grammar School and then to Cambridge was fitted to the career which made him popular custodian of the shadowy special relationship between his two nations.

His biographer describes Cooke as 'his own invention'.[39] There are many occasions on which one might feel the invention of that particular combination of good-looking elegance, the perfect silver hair and golden tan, the lively prose and quiet voice, the intelligent play of his interest upon the mighty and lowly alike, the distance and cordiality to be a parody of the Englishman he learned to be at Cambridge. For well over fifty years he has acted as receptacle and generator of every triteness, every *bien-pensant* commonplace, every rock-solid prejudice which has made the *haute bourgeoisie* on either side the Atlantic what it has been and what it is.

Sheer perseverance and indestructibility brought off this singular achievement; add to them a kind of genius, a shaped and shapely prose, and an impregnable ego made only more so by years of psychoanalysis.

Cooke's one unmistakably great book, *A Generation on Trial*, 330 pages all written between mid-March and 12 May 1950, is so (I suggest) because its central characters, Alger Hiss and Whittaker Chambers, were themselves such elaborate contrivances of social construction. The confessional, voluble, passionate and histrionic Chambers and the removed, austere, charming but commanding Brahmin Hiss spoke alike to the two parts of Cooke's own public self. That hero and villain (and which was which?) had to play for their reputations under the theatrical lights of the courtroom only made the drama more piercing.

The occasion brought out the best in Cooke, an eloquent honesty about the ambivalence of history. More usually, Cooke's own ambivalence and its dangerous illiberalisms are overlaid by that gorgeous mellifluity which has for all of us and for so long made *Letter from America* the smoothest political commentary ever to drink down.

It was an act. That, however, is no put-down. At Cambridge his powers of mimicry and his social ambition found the best nursery it could have done in the Amateur Dramatic Club (the ADC), and by the time he graduated he was already the ideal recruit for the new public and political role quickly shaped for itself by the BBC. Not, however, that the corporation itself saw him that way.

He won what is still called a Harkness Fellowship, the name commemorating the open-handed donor who, in the interests of Anglo-American friendship and understanding, founded his fellowships to allow clever young men from British universities up to a couple of years of well-supported study and travel in their sometime colony. Cooke's ready and delighted seizing of opportunity made it easy for him to become American. He came home to importune the BBC to allow him to act as their American correspondent, won a few chances to prove he could do so, was viewed by his seniors at times doubtfully, but was nonetheless on hand, with a series of short-term contracts, to pronounce on British theatre, American films, traditional jazz (his lifelong passion) and Modernist literature, in which variety of ventures he interviewed T. S. Eliot, befriended Chaplin and, rather later, recorded a Duke Ellington session on disc for the first time.

He became sufficiently well known, but it was a precarious livelihood. He had to use his formidable charm to coax commissions out of an always coy and autocratic BBC but he always gave good value, was excellently trenchant (for example on the subject of the royal abdication in 1936) in the manner of Mencken, his admired journalistic model, and hit happily upon a blithe, affectionate and informative way with him when first given his own programme, *Mainly About Manhattan*, presager to the great epic of the *Letter*.

He married a beautiful New Englander, Ruth, of the honoured house of Emerson and having, with his habitual acumen in such matters, befriended the celebrated foreign correspondent of *The Times* Peter Fleming and his even-more-celebrated actress wife Celia Johnson, was handed an adjutant position to the grand benign figure of Sir Wilmott Lewis, *The Times* man in Washington. Being, by disposition and application, of chameleon powers of self-camouflage and with a toucan talent for unignorability, Cooke absorbed a *Times*-ish view of the world alongside that well-bred Americanness which saw with a Democratic eye Roosevelt's amazing gifts but kept the other eye carefully watchful in case such gifts were being made with honest Republican money.

He was viewed with comparable equivocation at home. By the time the United States went to war at the end of 1941 Cooke was a naturalised American. There were those who saw this as evasive of his patriotic duty. But Cooke had found his avocation early. It took the form of a dedication to the representation of the United States to Britain by way not so much of traditional literature, whether drama or the printed page, but of the new form of – let us call it in passing – 'cultural journalism'.

He was one key figure in the invention of that form and, not unusually, inventing the form meant inventing the formalist. He had, after all, to act up what he wrote down, and in doing so became the only possible performer of his own compositions. The BBC paid occasionally, *The Times* badly. He took a freelance column on the *Daily Herald* – it remains a paradox that Cooke spent his creative life as a decidedly conservative liberal and simple-minded cold warrior working for more-or-less progressive newspapers and the always throat-clearingly progressive BBC.

Cooke's was a peaceable and successful war. He became well known about Washington, friends with Sonny Reston and circle, rarely at home with child or wife, dropping in on America across those gigantic distances, always on the move, movingly so:

The night closes in and extinguishes Kentucky, pushes the war reeling away into memory, leaving you with the special timeless intimacy of driving at night. You have no goal, only a ploughing shaft of light on white cement and, to remind you happily of your own warmth, you hear far away the lonely call of a train. The little dead towns tick by like tombstones of a pioneer's past – Munfordville, Rowletts, Horse Cave, Bear Wallow, Good Night – and then you see a string of lights coming up above your headlights. It is Glasgow, and as good a place as any to stay the night.[40]

He was always away from home, but never an away-player. All the same and to his own extreme surprise, in 1942 he fell absolutely in love with Jane Hawkes, another beauty, a portrait painter and more his equal in forceful-ness than his wife Ruth. Her husband was away on active service where he died of typhus. Cooke married her and took on her two children and a substantial dowry including a fine summer retreat on Long Island not far from the Emerson family one he lost at his divorce.

By now, after the long shakiness of his settling in at the BBC, he was established as the voice of *American Commentary* (which became the fort-nightly *American Letter* in 1946 and at last, for over fifty years, the weekly *Letter from America*, in 1950). He was hired as correspondent in the USA by the *Manchester Guardian*, and he worked as unstoppingly hard as the best myths of journalism require.

His duty to America never fails. America made him, and he won't let her down in what he says. In the *Manchester Guardian* things are a bit rougher. The affection and the pleasant feel for domestic detail is qualified a little by something more profound, and more profoundly disagreeable which stirs in Cooke's soul. This is a hard example to take, but in showing him at his worst as a political journalist, it also reveals something deep and true about him.

It was 1955. The Cold War was freezing hard. He had written his classic *A Generation on Trial* about the battle dishonour of the anti-communist purge, and had done so with exemplary even-handedness as well as a lived engagement with its struggle between values and power. Then the Korean War came and Cooke, a long way off like everybody else other than the soldiers and his few fellow-journalists, diligently interpreted it according to Cold War protocols. By the time he was brought home by the *Manchester Guardian* to cover the British general election of 1955, any other politics than *realpolitik* seemed, as realists always say, utopian.

Cooke found Bertrand Russell (then eighty-three), who had written to him a year or two before to praise his journalism most handsomely,[41] speaking on a Labour platform for the first stirrings of the Campaign for Nuclear Disarmament. The occasion brought out not only Cooke's Olympian talent for condescension but also his distastefully robust contempt for visionary hopefulness, the immovable certainty of elite America about its own power, its weaponry, and the fact that comfort is well placed under the right bottoms. Finally, in a register quite alien to the *Letter*, he allows himself some heavy-writerly effects.[42]

A midget suspended against a huge Cinemascope screen, the last of the Whigs snapped his eaglet eyes under the white thatch of hair and flexed his arms at the elbows in a 'hey presto' motion, like a charming puppet straining for a miracle and in the act wobbling the tiny wire frame of his body.

Russell's wasn't the only body straining for a miracle. No journalist, no writer should write like this:

There was a great surge of applause for this sentiment, and the stolid housekeepers pounded their hands in the hope that belief would create its object. The noble and ageing lord himself was seized with the same emotion, and what practical steps we could take to … bully the great protagonists into loving each other, were forgotten in a long and poignant passage about the shining alternative to the world we know … He clenched his bony hands again, to grasp the vision that eludes us all, not least our legislators, and begged them to go away and bring about an era of 'happiness such as has never existed before … If we would, we could make life splendid and beautiful'.

He had done. The decent crowd clapped him all the way out on his careful legs …

Cooke's title for his piece was 'Lord Russell's modern apocalypse' and it is fair to say that, expectant as Cooke was of nuclear war, he hadn't much imagination, either of what such a war would be like, or of that feasible world in which cruelty and want have been diminished. Here, in the ineffable weariness, the shallow sadness with which those-who-know brush off any account of a juster world order which would undoubtedly reduce their privileges ('the vision that eludes us all'), he waves away his elderly prophet and 'the stolid housekeepers pound[ing] their hands' as so many wistful and (happily) ineffectual philanthropists.

It is not an endearing performance and it is not isolated. Over the years, Cooke was never loath to express uncomfortable opinions. They rarely, however, discomfited the received opinion of his friends, the powerful and famous. (That is what charm *is*: saying well what the wealthy like to hear.) Although he had often and pleasantly voiced criticisms of the injustices done to American blacks, when the Civil Rights movement really began to roll and Martin Luther King emerged as its rousing preacher-leader, Cooke wrote a series of articles for the *Manchester Guardian*, one of which ended all too sincerely: 'Thus we come down to the old question, which only the intellectual, the superficial and the foreigner far from the dilemma can afford to pooh-pooh, 'Would you want your daughter to marry a Negro?'[43]

Cooke's implicit answer is plain enough. Even half a century ago, it must have affronted some readers of Britain's great Mancunian-Asquithian tradition. Down in Alabama the marchers were gathering; up in the northern states were young white men and women preparing to work in the face of public vilification down south, and some of them would be baked into the embankment of a freeway for their pains. In Arkansas, the staff of the state daily braced themselves against their neighbours to stand up for the Constitution on behalf of other, only barely distinguishable neighbours, and to expect broken windows as a result. Meanwhile, in one of the *Letters from America*, Cooke spoke what was undoubtedly his mind, and did so with that show of candour with which ineradicable prejudice dresses itself in order to pass off as courageous objectivity what is actually revulsion:

> The Supreme Court's order not only imposes the quite harmless custom of working and playing with children of another race. It threatens to destroy the taboo which allowed them safe familiarity. I will not beat about the bush. It brings to all Southern parents the spectre of inter-marriage and eventual wholesale miscegenation.[44]

Across the wide extent of so unique a career it is hardly surprising to find some moments of malodorous self-disclosure. Cooke made himself into an English gentleman of a kind only capable of full realisation and complete success in America. Becoming such a creature, he then used his excellent intelligence and rare gifts of recognition to teach the English about the Americans. He couldn't have found a career more apt to his invention. Old English snobbery would have broken him down at home; new American ruthlessness would have polished him off if he had tried to meet it on its own terms. Poised between both, he turned his everyday detachment, his writer's ear and affectionate eye into the trick of his unrivalled purity of diction.

Only the big subjects of world politics were too much for him. Nuclear confrontation, black segregation, the war in Vietnam, they loomed up and his sensibility went tight and clenched. Old atavisms rose up in his gorge and he could only settle his stomach with conservative pieties. When he covered the British general election of 1955 for the *Manchester Guardian*, long strange to the country he recoiled from its urban scruffiness, its obvious and deep-rooted poverty, its stolidity, its absence of flair and dash, and in politics was drawn naturally to the charm, good looks, expensive self-assurance of the Prime Minister, Anthony Eden, who could so easily have served as a model when the young Cooke sat down to plan his forth-coming self. When, in 1965, the black quarter of Los Angeles known as Watts exploded in riots, Cooke denied that the burning shops and cars were anything to do with Civil Rights, itself so sedate and formalising a phrase with which to explain faces covered with blood or twisted with hate. Cooke said they were the product of 'envy', black envy of 'the white man's dainties', and the cure wasn't lots of federal dollars but such old-fashioned medicines as a 'full-time birth control programme, the return of parolees to jail, a couple of churches, a public works project, six playing fields and an army of coloured men in the police force'.

At first, it sounds like the implementation of a radical manifesto. It's more like the no-nonsense city councillor saying what government should do but he can't. Cooke's political commentary on the big events which broke open his composure was often edgy, even at a loss. Reporting on Vietnam over five or six years he kept his regard and affection for Lyndon Johnson, who had once in 1965 sat Cooke down at the Presidential desk and asked *him* to play President and say what he'd do in Vietnam. At the same time, he was openly distressed by the roar of American firepower over the Tet offensive, and called it an 'obscenity' in the *Letter* without being able to answer Johnson's abrupt question.

Politics, however, and thank goodness for it, is not just a long horizon of eventuality. Cooke's genius was for the continuities of everyday political life, and the polity as found in the most loving details of domesticity. Even when the Watergate crisis came along, Cooke refused to see it as critical or Nixon as responsible. He didn't like Nixon, but he disliked the routine detraction of Presidents much more. His propriety was rattled by the publication of the tape-recordings of all the President's foul-mouthed business in the Oval Office – the abuse of language shocked Cooke the writer more than the abuse of power – but he kept his tones level through-out his reports. They were so level that, in Nixon's last days, Cooke despatched his *Letter* by leisurely courier to New York and then back to the BBC in London, as so often, before the end of the action. (For years the corporation had chafed under Cooke's old-fashioned preference for this form of delivery.) With airy insouciance, as Nixon shook in solitude in the White House and stared at his resignation, Cooke came to the end of his *Letter* describing the state of affairs, and concluded 'the rest you know.' By the time it was broadcast, his audience did.

There had never been a political journalist like Cooke before, and it is safe to say there won't be one again. From time to time, the BBC grew restive with both the form and the author of the *Letter*, but not only was it monumentally popular, its sheer continuity also made it impregnable. The one thousand five hundredth *Letter* was broadcast in November 1977, the two thousandth in June 1987, the two thousand five hundredth (Cooke aged eighty-eight) in January 1997. His audience was ageing, no doubt, but devoted; it remained a lot younger than the *Letter*-writer. He recruited new listeners as they became old enough to dislike change, to feel enough things the same way, to move and be moved by that silky, friendly voice, those easy cadences, that known and knowable vocabulary.

That's what Cooke did. He brought together language, voice and feeling in a frame which fitted his story of the country which ran and runs the world of war, of Cold War, of post-Cold War. In that jagged and flame-torn landscape he found quite enough of such grand political absolutes as home, warmth, love and friendship to reassure his millions of listeners that these old names would see them through for a good while yet. He had blind spots for sure, and lots of nerve; he has sometimes haughty, always notice-able superciliousness. But loftiness in someone you admire for his wisdom is a help in feeling the same way, and Cooke never failed to add what was so true to his invented character, the warmth, the fondness for quiddity, the abundance of calm shed upon human action. Kenneth Burke once said that the comic vision (as opposed to the tragic) explains human nature in terms not of evil but of stupidity, and he goes quirkily on to define comedy as 'the maximum of forensic complexity'.[45] That fits Cooke.

Politically, such an attitude can lead you left or right. Cooke is a tran-quilly reactionary figure. But he did much for peace of mind, and much to keep in focus the greatest political values while also keeping the capital letters off them. His kind of journalism seems to me at its best when, as always a bit nostalgic, he praises in a *Letter* of 1972 his old friend the incom-parable golfer and Southern gentleman, Bobby Jones.

> I doubt there was a man, woman or child in America and Britain who did not know about Bobby Jones, the easy, debonair, modest Southerner with the virile good looks who came to have no more worlds to conquer and retired at 28, still an amateur. I make bold to say his feat of the so-called Grand Slam will not happen again because today golf too has turned into a money-making industry, and the smart young amateurs go at it like navvies.

It was a letter of farewell to Jones; I quote it as a farewell to Cooke.

Chapter Eleven

Adventurers and Constitutionalists: Vietnam and Watergate

Narrative history starts out on a big landscape populated by Men of Destiny in small numbers. Structural history works in the imagery of giant production, in which nineteenth-century machinery – boilers, pistons, compression chambers, oiled connecting rods, massive girders and stanchions bolted immovably together with heavy round rivets – thunders in unison to manufacture history, class struggle, capital, war. In the history on hand, the first men of destiny start the newspapers and their subordinates, hardly less colossal, write them. Then structures assume command, news becomes just another commodity, and the meaning of journalism in the latter part of the short twentieth century becomes synonymous with the dull repetitive business of news manufacture, broken down into the small sequences whereby reporting and opinionating reach the packed organisation of the page.

A narrative history of journalism can hardly ignore the heavy machinery, even after it has all got so much lighter. But at a time when all social explanation tends towards the structural, it is a pleasure to remark how much more crowded with journalists of distinction the landscape nonetheless became at just the moment when pietists were saying that things weren't what they used to be.

It was, as one would hope, a crisis of the republic which gave these young men and women their sudden prominence, but it was the pull of fame and the gleam of freedom which brought them into journalism in the first place. Journalism was, by the 1960s, a profession as much for the graduates of elite universities as it was for the traditional hero of old newspaper novels who worked his way up from cub reporter on the local paper to big crimebusting on a daily. As the figures who have trooped before us from the pages of the London or New York *Times* abundantly demonstrate, there has never been a shortage of men from either Cambridge. The grand ancestors had opened a new social space, prominent, well-lit, magnetic. Those who thronged towards that arena and saw its handsome pedestals had high hopes of the rewards of celebrity as well as of wages. They were fired, as like as not, by the literature they had read as students to want to write the prose of high art as well as of daily bread; and they craved the irregular hours, the autonomous timetable, the blessedly hard work, the zestful initiative, dash and flair all demanded of them in the glittering tales told of and by their seniors. Above all, young American journalists of 1963 had the good fortune to be presented all at once with a drama of national emancipation and with a dramatic new war in which to challenge comparison with Ernie Pyle or Martha Gellhorn, to each of which they brought their high American idealism, and at each of which they would win the eminence to carry them loftily up newspaper or network hierarchy.

Vietnam or Deep South provided the news of the nation for a decade and it was Vietnam which first summoned the flowers of new journalism, David Halberstam, Michael Herr, Gloria Emerson, Jonathan Schell, Peter Arnett, Frances Fitzgerald, Seymour Hersh and Neil Sheehan.

Every one of them came in the end to write in brave and uncompromising opposition to the war. Each found it necessary to contrive a quite new way of writing journalism in order to grasp and represent what was going on. Each stuck to the ideals of America's Constitution as they saw it embodied in the avocation of journalism. They went in complete and natural ignorance to Vietnam; they learned what they could about the country, its culture, its dynasties, once they got there, and they measured what they saw against the moral reasons they were given for their countrymen's being there in uniform in the first place. They then set out the discrepancies. They chagrined the military in doing so, and they only made a difference to the conduct of their government with inevitable gradualism and by way of persuading enough of their readers to feel differently and judge better about the nature of this hot war and its significance in the cold one. Government and military alike lied to the journalists and deceived themselves. But they didn't arrest them, their censorship was either light or incompetent but either way the stories came home, and the true history of the Vietnam War is not only clear and detailed, the moral judgements about it as voiced by the best journalists seem about right as well.

On 2 January 1963 Neil Sheehan, then aged twenty-five and working for United Press International (UPI), joined a unit of the South Vietnamese Republican Army near a hamlet called Bac, about fifty miles south-west of

Saigon. The unit had a US Army sergeant in attendance as adviser, and was being ferried into action by ten Huey helicopters. As soon as it engaged with the National Liberation Front and four helicopters were knocked out, the South Vietnamese soldiers took cautious cover and declined to move from behind the thick dyke holding in the rich mud and its sodden rice crop. In spite of the soldiers' objections, the adviser sergeant called down rocket fire on the dug-in positions of the enemy. As the napalm burned its huge orange bloom and the heat rolled back and hit the dyke where Sheehan was crouching, some of the South Vietnamese soldiers stood up to watch and cheer their victory. Two fell back dead. The Front had not moved.

The full enemy numbered about 350 men armed with light weapons. They were faced by a battalion, a company of armour, the remaining helicopters with their rocket and strafing power, and the fighter-bombers on call. They did not withdraw from the terrible heat of the napalm, or from the fury of aerial bombardment. They showed amazing discipline. When, with extreme reluctance, the South Vietnamese armour agreed to move forward towards the enemy position along the brush-filled ditches, the guerrillas drove them back by jumping out from their cover to toss grenades on to the tops of the armoured vehicles. When an airborne battalion was finally brought in, the parachutists were shot before they hit the ground. When the American advisers gave orders to shell the lines of retreat, the South Vietnamese, afraid of reprisals, fired four shells per hour.

The Front lost eighteen men, retired after dark in good order, taking their dead and their empty cartridge cases with them. The South lost eighty men, and some more the next morning when they shelled their own side. They wasted amazing quantities of plant and ammunition. Sheehan filed his report to UPI soberly. Early in 1963, the Americans began to lose.

He was one of a type. At his side, David Halberstam was just such another, former managing editor of the daily *Harvard Crimson*, and several years in Tennessee reporting the civil rights movement first for the Nashville daily then for the *New York Times*. In 1964 he won the Pulitzer Prize for his reporting from Vietnam, and when he came home he wrote the garrulous classic *The Best and the Brightest*[1] in which, with the insubordination born of his Alma Mater, he launched an analysis of the war not only in terms of the ignorance and incompetence of its battle strategists but also as a sociology of their political attitudes and intellectual presuppositions, as well as of the Washingtonian neighbourliness which made understanding their difficulties so impossible for them.

Halberstam's book started life in *Harper's* in 1968 as a long, careful and (at such a moment) insolent attack on McGeorge Bundy, second only to Dean Rusk in the State Department, sometime Dean at Harvard. There was a big fuss; Halberstam was almost unmade, and then made. When he had finished, at top speed and with a big enough advance to free him from other work, he had written a tome that combined the history, the sociology, the military intelligence, *and* the gossip of the capital with which to identify the very dinner party at which Dean Rusk yelled abuse at Tom Wicker of the *Times* for printing true stories about Vietnam denied by true Americans.[2]

You have to call it journalism, all 700 pages of it. Halberstam had done his battle training and carried its scars. Like Sheehan, he had followed Colonel John Paul Vann, best adviser of the war and veteran of ten years' service there, into action. He was utterly confident of his breezy shrewdness, picking surely on the corporate characteristics of the power elite – Johnson, MacNamara, Rusk and company – while discarding qualities he knew were irrelevant to running a country at war. He didn't want a novelist's but a journalist's eye; in this case a journalist with every bit as much social *savoir-faire* and class confidence as his political superiors. Good journalism (to adapt George Orwell) is written by people who are *not afraid*. In the end, Halberstam's admirable opposition to the war was based in his own conviction about his rightness and (like his enemies) the superior rationality of his frames of mind, the card-index detail and notation of his character analyses.

In this, as in all his powerful and impressive journalism, he was a complete Washingtonian, even down to his blithe way with a cliché. Dean Rusk, Secretary of State, 'quiet man of enormous self-control, his ambition carefully marked'; Robert MacNamara, Secretary of Defense, 'taut, controlled, driving ... he pushed everyone, including himself, to new limits ... time was of the essence ... it was action, decisions, cost effectiveness, power'; General Maxwell Taylor, 'articulate, presentable ... cool, correct, handsome and athletic':[3] these crisp cameos speak eloquently of the world which is Halberstam's subject-matter. It is how his politicians speak of others as well, and the journalism in which it figures with such a pleasant accuracy is not without irony or kindliness (far better this than Joseph Alsop), and its insights are those of *arrière-pensées*. What matters is to have been right, and then to have been decent.

It isn't a bad precept for a journalist, a politician or a graduate of Harvard. Neil Sheehan, like Halberstam, took his principles from the Constitution and as his ideal of professional conduct, a determination to attach a strong and excellent patriotism not so much to the flag as to the *Federalist Papers.* In the United States, the flag hangs at the back of every courtroom and its authority takes its strength from a written ethics of law. A great deal of American journalism during and since the war in Vietnam was conducted with lawyers in the offices of the broadsheets; and the vindication of the discoveries Sheehan and men like him made and the truths they told would be in lawsuits compelling the United States government to abide by its own legal ethics.

There is no such redress available in Britain, or indeed in most states of the European Union. The contribution of what I call here the constitutionalists of American newspapers to making the world a better place is solid and unmistakable. Their inquiries took them, by way of their learned disillusionment, from the honest conviction that the Cold War was a just one, and that the Americans were right to raise its temperature in Vietnam, to the certainty that nothing could justify the waste, the killing and the aerial bombardment of which they watched the headlong increase between 1965 and 1972. Indeed, the consequences for the Vietnamese were even worse after the departure of the US Army and as the bombing authorised by Henry Kissinger became more and more excessive, as well as spreading, secretly and illicitly, to Laos and Cambodia in time to destroy those nations also, once official hostilities were replaced by revanchism.

The natural framework of inquiry for a journalist like Sheehan was to try to measure the gap between what he saw and heard was going wrong and the official statements. In this he was much helped by his country's genuinely liberal principles as enshrined in its laws. Nobody, not even government, could keep dark those matters ruled by judges as open to public scrutiny and debate and as not threatening the safety of the realm.

Sheehan was a carrier of that great tradition of American journalism whose members went so naturally from Ivy League to one of a handful of national broadsheets. Harvard's formal code is to honour the nation's ideals and the university's code of exact and truth-telling scholarship, but Sheehan found the traditional way of criticising what the state told him quite insufficient to the historical moment, and to its crux in Vietnam. He had to find a quite different method of journalism to handle not only the state's licentious mendacity but also its wilful self-deceit. Sheehan's runaway bestseller about the Vietnam War, *A Bright Shining Lie,* is the product of that new form of journalism designed not only to report on both the Cold War and the Vietnam War but also to turn the constitution of the state against the state itself.

Sheehan had arrived in Vietnam in 1962 at the age of twenty-five to report the war during the most confident years of US involvement, while his country was taking over the role of the French. He worked for United Press International in Saigon until 1964, did eight months in Jakarta for the *New York Times* at the start of the civil war that was to lead to the massacre of the Indonesian communists, and went back to Saigon for the *Times* for a third time from 1965 to 1966. Then he was posted back to Washington to cover the executive end of the Vietnam War in the Pentagon and the White House – 'investigatively', as people started to say around that time, because there suddenly seemed to be so damn much we did not know that called for investigation.

So it was to be expected that when Daniel Ellsberg, in one of the more important attacks of conscience during the Cold War, came to his proper conclusion in 1971 that the secretly truthful papers kept in the Pentagon on the conduct of the war should be made public, he contacted Sheehan.

Ellsberg by then was a senior Pentagon official with a star career. He was that Bostonian character the romantic puritan, a hard-working man of passionate commitment, intense feelings and no less intense conscience. He was extremely bright, a member of Harvard's Society of Fellows, a Marine officer for three years, and one of the Rand Corporation's secret architects of nuclear war plans. After working with the head of anti-insurgency and undercover operations in Vietnam for two years, he had gone back to Rand and the Pentagon, dismayed beyond words by America's inability, and his own, to turn Vietnam to those virtuous means and ends that were his country's only justifications for being there. When in 1969 he read the forty-three secret volumes of what would come to be termed the Pentagon Papers (and being Ellsberg, as Sheehan observes, he read them all), he became convinced not only that the war whose affairs he had prosecuted so zealously in 1965 had gone badly wrong, but that his country was wrong to wage it.

He had smuggled the strictly confidential documents past the security desk and photocopied them, gradually accumulating a full 7,000-page collection of papers. In early March 1971 he had waited for hours one night at a Washington hotel to talk to the man closest to him from Vietnam, John Paul Vann, formerly Lieutenant-Colonel, now a civilian with general officer status who was in virtual command of an entire region of South Vietnam and its army corps.

Vann, however, had other fish to fry that night and never showed up. Ellsberg went to the house of another friend in the capital, a confidant entirely different from John Vann. The friend was Neil Sheehan. After a conversation that lasted almost until dawn, Ellsberg and Sheehan made the decision that would lead the President to use all his power, mixed with his taste for personal revenge, to press for a conviction of Ellsberg for treason. Their decision would put the *New York Times* in the dock as the traitor's accomplice and would end with the historic judgment of the Supreme Court that publication of the Pentagon Papers transcended the interest of government and was vindicated by the Constitution, the highest interest in the land.

Sheehan was the quiet, upright, precise and implacable hero of the story: without beating his breast, either publicly or privately, he pressed his colleagues towards what he argued was their civic duty. He helped a great and, at times, complaisant newspaper to live up to its professional standard. And he protected his sources – that is, he betrayed nobody. The man who had already won a civilian medal in Vietnam for 'conscience and integrity in journalism' was endorsed in his action against the state by the official foundations of civil society; he was awarded a prize for 'excellence in investigative reporting' and his newspaper won a Pulitzer Prize.

In the nature of so American an episode, Sheehan no sooner had his hands on the Pentagon Papers than the *New York Times* lawyers took them away. Their blithe revision of this corner of our history is that it was all their affair anyway and that, as one lawyer puts it: 'Sheehan was unsatisfied with his reporting assignments and his prospects at the *Times* seemed limited. Getting his hands on MacNamara's secret Vietnam history may have been a way of resuscitating his reporting career and his chances of becoming a *Times* editor.'[4]

It's not much help trying to write history as the result of human motivation. We shall reach a better understanding, as this study insists, if we interpret people's actions as expressing their most simply determinable intentions. Such a method may leave us with unexplained residues of passion and incoherence, but it has the merit of finding reasons in what was intended as reasonable action.

By this test, Daniel Ellsberg wanted to bring the significance of the secret Pentagon Papers out into the forum of good old public opinion. He had met Sheehan in Vietnam, been immediately struck (as most people were) by his seriousness, his care with detail, his fastidiousness about judgement, and then much impressed by a long review-article of Sheehan's discussing with ardour and principle the suitability of war crime trials held by American courts to try American offenders.[5] The particular instance in everybody's minds just then was the burned-out village of My Lai, first known to the troops after its incineration by Zippo lighters as Pinkville, and then under both names for the abominable and pointless murder of its hundred or so inhabitants, all of them old men, women or children, by a bunch of trigger-happy infantrymen commanded by one Lieutenant William Calley.

One of the writers most responsible for keeping 'Pinkville' in view was also at pains to emphasise its strictly symptomatic rather than its critical nature. Noam Chomsky is the most astonishing example in these pages of the scholar-intellectual whose ideals and whose gifts (in his case gifts of quite momentous stature) drove him at an epic moment of his country's politics to occupy the moral centre of national debate. Ellsberg, Sheehan and Chomsky – German Jew, Irish and Russian in their distinct and American genealogies – the first two from Harvard, and Chomsky the author, at twenty-nine and at MIT, of a subject-altering and highly techni-cal essay in linguistics which was at the same time an affirmation of human creativity as evinced in every human being's capacity to invent new sentences.

Compelled by character and events alike, Chomsky became the nation's most celebrated intellectual who, like all those taking such a role, perforce became a much-cited journalist. Intensely productive and gifted with remarkable powers of memory as well as of organising multitudinous data into intelligible patterns, Chomsky wrote essays that captured and focused the tumult of distress, anxiety and angry opposition to the Vietnamese war which boiled over in American universities after 1965 and President Johnson's decision so vastly to increase the drafts sent to Vietnam. Whatever the pretext – and Johnson's, as is well known, was a trifling and perhaps trumped-up engagement between the US Navy and a North Vietnamese destroyer in Tonkin Bay – the true text for Chomsky and his allies was the brutal assertion of American power and the self-serving servility of American scholars who accepted lucrative contracts to help arrange the incarceration or the extermination of some of the poorest people in the world.[6]

By 1971 Chomsky had already been arrested on charges of civil disobedience and had become the indefatigably central figure in a network of dissenters taking in both the scholars and people like Ellsberg, elite members of state policy-making, and Sheehan, leading light of the new generation of journalists looking to inherit the seat of Lippmann, Alsop or Sonny Reston. Alongside these men, themselves of some hauteur and substance, the lawyers ranged themselves, each with his considered politics but with a larger allegiance to the noumen of the law and the Constitution which was its stately home.

Those with the most to lose were the journalists. (The individual who lost most, on principle, was Daniel Ellsberg.) Some of them might have had their freedom at stake, all of them had the future of their newspaper, Sheehan maybe both. In any case, after his night talk with Ellsberg he still didn't know what kind of story this was. Abe Rosenthal, managing editor of the *New York Times*, supported the war; Sonny Reston, like all the grand columnists, was personal friends with assorted of the mighty who had been in Johnson's Administration, particularly Robert MacNamara who, as Defense Secretary, authorised the compilation of the Pentagon Papers and ordered that they be kept to a limit of fifteen copies.[7] On the title page of the *Times's* special edition of the series they published, they append a list of the *Times* staff who, under the direction of James Greenfield, foreign editor, wrote and edited and, in Sheehan's case, photocopied an undercover version of the volumes over which the President ordered full legal battle to be joined.

After Ellsberg came to give him warning of the story, Sheehan went for advice to the house columnist, Tom Wicker, and then to Sonny Reston, a Washington figure as well known, as judicious and as politically conventional as his rival, Joseph Alsop. Wicker, indeed, hailed Reston as 'by anyone's measure the most prestigious and respected reporter in Washington' and in so deferential, clubbable and keenly prestige-studying a city such a *Times* columnist as Wicker would know Who Was Who.[8] Reston waved Sheehan on.

Sheehan himself has always refused to say how he actually gained access to the Pentagon Papers and who left him in a position to photocopy the four most revealing volumes. If Ellsberg handed them over personally, then, as a state employee and signatory of a secrecy affidavit, he was liable to imprisonment. But he was absolutely convinced that public opinion ought, for the common good, to know how badly the war had gone and how comprehensively its failure had been concealed. It is a measure of the place of journalism in the history of modern society that such a man thought this, and that a journalist like Sheehan was there to receive him.

So he left Sheehan with the secret Papers, forbidding him to do what, the moment Sheehan was alone, he did, which was copy them on a slow old 1971 copier, 7,000 typescript pages one sheet at a time, all conducted across a long weekend in a little hire-shop in Bedford Town.

The *Times* had the evidence. The editor, Rosenthal, was with Reston convinced it should publish. He was deeply conservative, he believed the domino theory, and he supported the war; but he saw at once that the Papers showed how Johnson's whole administration, and Kennedy's before him, had deliberately misled the public, and how Nixon, coming to power in 1968, had continued the deception. Rosenthal was in addition anxious about the proper and necessary privacy of government and he guessed that the government – *any* government – would try to prevent publication.

He and his journalists backed publication. Rosenthal resolved to resign, no less, if his publisher forbade it. In the event, Reston, the senior professional on the staff, persuaded Sulzbeyer the publisher to go ahead and dictated by open telephone line a flyer for the series entitled 'The MacNamara Papers'. The story duly broke on Saturday, 13 June 1971. It was three months since Sheehan had spent the weekend in the Bedford copy-shop, but no one leaked a drop. It was the scoop of the century.

The affair was in the hands of the White House Counsel John Dean first thing on the Monday morning. From then on the planned ten-parter was in and out of courtrooms at various levels of seniority in America's legal supremacies until 30 June. On that day, the nine members of the Supreme Court handed down their judgment.[9] It was not a straightforward dispute, rightness of disclosure versus wrongness of subterfuge; the issues included the possible endangering of troops on active service; there could be no doubting the importance of due secrecy as a necessity of power. The quality of counsels was moreover, according to the outspoken David Rudenstine,[10] expensively uneven.

Three of the nine Supreme Court judges ruled that courts themselves, let alone newspapers, should defer to the executive branch on all matters of national security. The other six gainsaid them, and at this distance from the ruling, one cannot read what Justice Black concurring with Justice Douglas wrote without hearty applause at the retaking of a liberty, and with open admiration at the majesty of the prose. Quoting James Madison's magnificent First Amendment, Justice Black set down this:

In the First Amendment the Founding Fathers gave the free press the protection it must have to fulfil its essential role in our democracy. The press was to serve the governed, not the governors. The Government's power to censor the press was abolished so that the press would remain forever free to censure the Government. The press was protected so that it could bare the secrets of government and inform the people. Only a free and unrestrained press can effectively expose deception in govern- ment. And paramount among the responsibilities of a free press is the duty to prevent any part of the Government from deceiving the people and sending them off to distant lands to die of foreign fevers and foreign shot and shell. In my view far from deserving condemnation for their courageous reporting, *The New York Times*, *The Washington Post* and other newspapers should be commended for serving the purpose that the Founding Fathers saw so clearly. In revealing the workings of government that led to the Vietnam war, the newspapers nobly did precisely that which the founders hoped and trusted they would do.

The *Washington Post* had muscled in during the action. Ben Bradlee, then managing editor, had with his publisher Katherine Graham already set out to make it as much the national paper of record as the *New York Times*. Philip Graham, publisher until his suicide in August 1963, framed the ambition and opened his campaign, it will be remembered, by purchasing Lippmann as the paper's columnist for a stupendous price in 1962. But there was a long way to go. The most vivid legend of the *Post*'s eventual success, Ben Bradlee himself said, when the Pentagon Papers came out, 'we found ourselves in the humiliating position of having to rewrite the competition.'[11]

Not for long. There were spare pages of the Papers to be found round Washington that June. Ellsberg contacted Ben Bagdikim, the *Post*'s national news editor, who flew down to the capital from Boston with 4,000 pages in the first-class seat beside him. The *Times* was abruptly silenced by injunction. The affair became a straight, thrilling race between old brigade and new hussar. Bradlee was recommended inaction by the *Post*'s lawyers. Naturally a reckless man, he was bursting to publish, especially with the *Times* temporarily in the punishment box. He phoned Katherine Graham. Still on the phone, she turned to the family and *Post* lawyer, Fritz Beebe, who wavered. Then she turned quickly back. 'OK, I say let's go. Let's publish.' Bradlee dropped the phone, shouted the news to his waiting colleagues, who cheered wildly.[12] The *Post*'s first version of the Papers appeared on 18 June.

It was a cinematic moment. It confirmed the *Post* in its new elevation. The government duly invoked the Espionage Act and the *Post* entered the dock with the *Times*. The courtroom windows were hung with blackout material – perhaps, Bradlee wondered, in case of the KGB lipreading on the other side of the glass – and those arraigned had first to be given security clearance having already violated security.

The *Post* joined the *Times* in victory and in scorn for Justice Wilkey who foamed in assumed outrage at the damage done to the safety of soldiers by the disclosure of decisions taken at least seven and in most cases ten or twenty years before. It was a landmark in both the local newspaper history and in the larger history of Cold War. It marked those years, between 1967 and 1973 or so, when the populations of the newly imperial United States and of the depleted imperial powers in Europe found their feelings towards their governments turning to mistrust. A lot of political sewage began to come to the surface and drift inshore. At the same time, more and more individuals, unconcerted and disconcerted, began to disbelieve the grand narratives of the day with which they were supposed to hold together the quiet desperation of private lives and the tides of human progress. The press, reporting, mediating, inventing these processes, found that its new task was to subvert officialdom, rebut confidence, corrode belief. This was the work of investigative news journalism.

So Sheehan wasn't finished with Vietnam, and neither were the other reporters. In a transformation already familiar in this book and in any case a necessary sequel for the understanding of its politics by society, he turned his Vietnam reports and, by implication, the depth of his knowledge of the Pentagon Papers into the book he called, quoting its leading character, *A Bright Shining Lie*. It is a prime document in that corrosion of belief and its concomitant change of feeling which I mentioned. In an intuitive flash, Sheehan took a single, indicative *figura* – the silhouette of a biography – with which to contain and explain the Vietnam War.

John Paul Vann became one of the very few Americans to study and understand the pattern of Vietcong warfare and, later, the strategy of the North Vietnamese army, to grasp the corrupt incompetence and straight-forward cowardice of the Saigon government's high command and its troops in the South, and at least for several years, to name as such the self-deluding character of American policy. Vann made his observations close up and, because he was a bouncy bantam cock of a man, insisted on describing them faithfully and very audibly to his seniors and, even less forgivably, to reporters.

The cockiness was shaped by his class origins in illegitimacy, maternal drunkenness and the grim poverty of a childhood in prewar Norfolk, Virginia. Vann's bounce and verve carried him to senior levels in the army. The same characteristics were apparent in his desperate eagerness to please, rule, and seduce women of any age or appearance, a predisposition that marked Vann's file and prevented him from being promoted beyond colonel. His wretchedly unhappy wife and children in the United States were unaware of his two mistresses and one child in Saigon.

His promotion blocked by his past, Vann returned to Vietnam as a civilian in 1965 but became so important to the policy of Vietnamisation that he rose to senior command as a *civilian general*, the first in American history. By the time he was killed in a flying accident in 1972 he had fallen fully into line with the American policy of bombing the enemy to pulp and blindly hoping for the best.

Sheehan spotted how fully Vann's *figura* embodied the meanings of the Vietnam War. Vann's career threw into vivid relief the little that was right and all that was wrong with the war and could do so as a gripping story: the individual man or woman caught up in the swirl of history, the struggle for territory or for freedom, the battling to make sense of life or death as one or the other knocks down the door.

Sheehan's genius was to see how much that one life could be made to carry. The steady centre of his subject was a man. Sheehan, from his job as a journalist reporting for the country's most important newspaper the country's most important news of the day, knew all the men whose seniority and power Vann tried to bend to what he believed to be his nation's best purposes.

It couldn't be done. Speaking in a way he never does in his great book, Sheehan said to me:

By early 1968 many of the US soldiers were demoralised. Not the Marines, they never went to pieces, but the rest did. There weren't any mass mutinies, but whole units were on the edge of mutiny. There were plenty of fraggings. Junior officers had to negotiate with the soldiers. They might say, 'You're out on patrol' and get the reply, 'No way.' There was a limit to what they could order, and if the officer didn't agree, they'd kill him. In 1965 there was no dope and all the soldiers believed in anticommunism. So did I; when I went out I was a pure cold warrior. By 1969 people were stoned in the field.

Sheehan went back to Vietnam after Vann's death in 1972 and found the broken grove of trees around Montagnard graves where Vann crashed in a storm. Sixteen years and 900 pages later he published what was, effectually, his last testament as a reporter.

The journalist, like the historian, tells us how things are *and* what they mean. Sheehan caught and expressed a widespread American feeling that the nation had done wrong, and with that shocking openness of disposition that is the best part of the American character insisted that its wrongdoing should be acknowledged. After all the hard and unforgiving judgements that must be made of America's conduct in the war, there is something lastingly impressive about the fact that the country should have found and listened to a chronicler like Sheehan.

Sheehan's book, so difficult to classify, so heavyweight in any case, is nonetheless one of a multitude. In assigning him to the constitutionalists' party, I do so in part because of his central role in the affair of the Pentagon Papers (themselves the definitive first draft of a history of what the Vietnamese call the American War). But the man is through and through a constitutionalist by disposition; his journalism speaks eloquently of this. It was moreover a trait shared by a group of reporters who became more than newshounds precisely because of their writing about the war. Halberstam was naturally one such, and with him Homer Bigart (of the *Times*), Ward Just (of the *Post*), Gloria Emerson (also of the *Times*), Peter Arnett (*Associated Press*), Philip Caputo (*Chicago Tribune*). It is perhaps invidious to name so few where the politics of the day and newspaper competitiveness alike demanded that any national organ have a reporter on the spot. For there were, as Knightley notes,[13] simply crowds of reporters there.

Alongside the dailies and the stringers were ranged such as Jonathan Schell, whose long essay-length reports for the *New Yorker* matched in stature and effect such classics of journalism history as Gellhorn's for *Collier's* in the Second World War or great originators like Lincoln Steffens. Besides Schell there were others who, after 1965 and the Tonkin Bay incident, came to bear witness on behalf of the best America had been against the worst the country could now do. Gellhorn herself, as we saw, flew in on such a pilgrimage, and so did Mary McCarthy, novelist, princess of the *Partisan Review* and its partisan politics, *grande dame* of the New York intelligentsia, who like James Cameron from Britain and like Noam Chomsky went to Hanoi, the enemy's capital, and wrote with passionate sympathy and, it may be, idealisation of the suffering and courage she saw there.

Finally, there were the dozens of policy scientists and anthropologists come to make their academic careers, or to destroy them, by writing their reports and analyses of the success or failure of 'forced-draft urbanisation' (herding peasants into concentration camps), 'neutralisation and pacification programmes' (annihilation of the Vietcong), 'counterinsurgency government restructuring' (getting rid of communists).[14] The Vietnamese war was not only the most reported war in history, it was the best attended experiment in social and political science that academics have ever known. It is worth noticing the extent to which journalists and social scientists shared, exchanged, distorted and raided one another for both facts and theories. What is then there for the taking is the truism that all facts live in a context of values from which they cannot be disembedded without making them meaningless.

The journalists in Vietnam found this out, according to their particular moral allegiances and much faster than the social scientists. It was in 1963, at Ap Bac, that Sheehan and Arnett first noticed the gap opening up between what they saw and how official sources assessed the progress of the war. By 1965, the public demonstrations had begun to gather force at home in the USA and the journalists had begun to wonder how much they were being lied to either by men who knew how badly things were going or by men who were deluding themselves. By 1968 and the Tet offensive, itself a military defeat for the communists but a hideous victory for the Americans, very few journalists could still believe that the expenditure, the slaughter and the destruction could ever match up to any moral or political end.

Societies as powerful as the USA change their minds and their direction with the massive cumbrousness of an aircraft carrier. The journalists anticipated this slow, tremendous change. The constitutionalists, the broadsheet dailies and the literate magazines did so, one can say, first and most vividly.

Such is a journalist's duty. It is to see and judge swiftly, the compulsions of byline and deadline unignorably present. Heavy on the writing of journalism weigh the nature of the readership, the gravity or frivolousness of the organ itself, the ferocity or nervousness of editor, owner or publisher, the invisible atmosphere, solid as air, of culture. Vietnam, above all as Chomsky pointed out,[15] was a racist war in which mass murder was made much easier by enemy males being small, flat-featured, olive-skinned and clad in black pyjamas. To find new ways to write well about it and, as well as getting duty done, to come out highly placed in a competition in which so many writers were jostling for notice took some doing.

To bring off a little local triumph some journalists moved from an analysis grounded essentially in the ethics of constitutionalism – of holding the government to its own Bill of Rights – to one which shortened its moral horizon to the urgencies of everyday warfare. Constitutionalism, after all, could hardly handle the complexity of the political circumstance: the tangle of obligations assumed in 1945 and arrogance corroborated by the defeat of the French was too much to sort out other than by a simple edict to withdraw unilaterally. The United States, on this view, had no moral business interfering in a civil war. Such a position, adequate as far as it went but with nothing to say to tyrants, left the constitutionalists with their own country as the centre of attention, and its government as the object of moral analysis.

The adventurer-journalists, responding in part to a readership which wanted to know what its sons and husbands were doing in the war, and in part I guess, to adventurousness in their own temperaments, looked for news where news was always, if repetitiously, to be found: in the noise of battle.

Sheehan, of course, does this but does it by pointing John Paul Vann's ghost at the War Cabinet in admonition. Michael Herr and Gloria Emerson set themselves to write two very different but non-constitutional kinds of report, Emerson, rarest of all, accompanying and talking to South Vietnamese infantrymen as they fled in rout from the fearsome fighting in Laos early in 1971.

Herr turned himself into a reporter as close to American soldiers as possible. This meant that he not only learned their language, but spoke it as well. To do so was to violate convention and to use routinely scatological language hitherto forbidden in the magazine column. He became fluent in that terse, monosyllabic, brutally foreshortened language of grunts and gooks; of lucking out and fucking up; of good shit, bad shit, and a noble shit; of ass, bastard, cocksucker and motherfucker, as well as having off by heart the dustbinful of acronyms, technicalities and unintelligible digits which have always made military argot so rich and strange. Rich and strange and funny and *savage*. A steel helmet is a 'brain-pot'; 'hell sucks'; 'Schnitt Zips'; 'rack the flak', all alongside the staccato unstoppable rap of black and white streetwise big night stridesmen.

It was a daunting language for readers of Herr's *Dispatches*[16] and it will do to mark the change in journalistic register. Herr combined the dignified periods of the *Times*, the terse telegrammatic summaries of the agencies, the friendly quotidian of radio and the fuller cadences of a remembered literary canon in such a way as to find ample accommodation for low-down dirty and high-up tech versions of what the Army really said in action. It's a rainbow effect in Herr's writing but it not only brings the war world very close, it makes possible a new relation between news and history, between the swirl of events and the individuals swirling in them.

You can't ask more of reporting than that, and of course it wasn't Herr's achievement alone. But he was one of those who made the most of it. He had wangled some sort of freelance deal out of *Esquire* to go to Vietnam in 1967 at the age of twenty-seven. *Esquire* no doubt anticipated something of the kind of thing he had written for *Holiday* magazine when he left Syracuse in the early 1960s – a little aquaplaning in the Mekong Delta, street-colourful prurience from Saigon about pimps in wasp-waisted suits, prostitutes with their cataracts of long black hair, ice-cream parlours with cocaine counters in the back. All that sort of thing. But as Herr said himself, 'actual youth had been pressed out of me in just the three days it took me to cross the sixty miles between Can Tho and Saigon.'[17]

From then on he was the writer in whom the soldiers themselves most clearly *heard* their own lives and speech in the war vividly represented. He spends no time looking at the moral horizon and nothing much on the pity of war. That is, he says little in his writing about distress arising from the sense that all these things need not be happening. All his attention goes to what *was* happening, and this makes for a very direct kind of reporting. It is not a report of any complexity and it is curiously empty of feeling. But the likelihood is that he was in fact, like the soldiers themselves, emptied of feeling. This means that when the report of some small event forces itself on us in an unignorable way, feeling spontaneously spills out into the open.

This happens when the company he is with is taking a break to open its compo ration tins, only a city block away from heavy fighting. A little ten-year-old came up to the Marines. He was laughing, jerking his head strangely, his eyes fixed in a ferocious glare. He had been driven mad by the shelling, and jumped up at the men, big, powerful blacks they mostly were, 'going for their eyes ... until a black grunt grabbed him from behind ... "C'mon, poor li'l baby, 'fore one of those grunt mothers shoots you," he said, and carried the boy to where the corpsmen were.'[18]

They were in the ancient city of Hué during the siege and the frightful battle in which the Marines retook the ruined city and the shattered palace of the Annamese monarchs where Malraux had been forty years before. Herr watched himself back at base, eating hamburgers, five of them, and ordering a dozen, then eighteen brandies from the peasant waitress, and then going outside to see the casualties piled in the truck going up to first aid, and

Sometimes ... the more seriously wounded would take on that bad color, the gray-blue fishbelly promise of death that would spread upward from the chest and cover the face. There was one Marine who had been shot through the neck, and all the way out the corpsman massaged his chest. By the time they reached the station, though, he was so bad the doctor triaged him, passed him over to treat the ones that he knew could still be saved ... The doctor had never had to make choices like that before, and he wasn't getting used to it.[19]

This is the style and the manliness bequeathed to the trade by Mr and Mrs Hemingway. The dry final comment releases as much feeling as it suppresses; it is how Herr sees what is happening and, pretty likely, it is how the Marines saw it also.

It is a good way of writing, making for a perfect journalism because it is so faithful to his close-up seeing. It is just how objective reporting should be; it is faithful to the selected facts, it is without opinion; it is vivid and immediate, it transcribes directly what people said; it has an author and one feels a bond with him, but he has only a few characteristics, principally his trustworthiness. You turn away and make your own mind up about what you have just read.

There was a lot of that kind of journalism about Vietnam and Michael Herr was probably best at it. He was there, I say, for the adventure of it; for the hell of it, come to that. Because he was intelligent and could write well, his reporting registers plainly what it is for adventures to go wrong and to imprison the adventurer in horror. 'A fat Marine had been photographed pissing into the locked-open mouth of a decomposing North Vietnamese soldier.' So Herr sees that too, and passes it on.

Gloria Emerson had first gone to Vietnam and Cambodia in 1956 when she was twenty-six, had gone more quietly adventuring, and the country had rooted itself in her heart. So when the *New York Times* sent her back during the war, and she did a two-year stint from 1970 to 1972, she was somewhere she loved, a traveller returned to another home, and so could hardly bear what she saw. She suffers terribly at what she sees and tells us of, and it seems to her as though the beauty of what was being destroyed in Vietnam and Cambodia had only been made visible by its destruction. Trying to absorb the extraordinary force and breadth of feeling which she discovers and releases in so many Americans during and after the war, she is first filled and then distended by torrents of passion, of loss and hate and bafflement and regret that is not to be assuaged. Crammed with such distress, she writes it out of her as much as she can, her words and the words of her always agonised interlocutors tumbling on to the pages of *Esquire, Playboy, Harper's, New Times* and the old one which sent her first.

Gloria Emerson takes the unspeakable miseries of the Vietnam veterans into herself, cannot rest, and it is nearly too much for her. In the book in which she collects and rewrites her remarkable journalism,[20] she roams the battle front and then, back home, the whole of the United States and writes down her interviews volubly, the tape-recorded words of those she spoke to, and what they ate while or after she spoke to them (this white-haired judge who believed in people living together in harmony and his chopped egg salad with olives, that private soldier on patrol feasting on fruit cocktail, boned turkey, spaghetti, but not on apricots which are unlucky).

She puts everything in, one veteran's favourite poem (Owen's 'Dulce et decorum est'), another's odd anecdote about the FBI, the long, agonising account of John Young's eighteen years as a prisoner in the north, a transcript of the interrogation of another soldier who complained formally to the Defense Department about American atrocities. Finally she talks with one or two of those who were present at the 1968 Democratic Convention when the young rioters forced the nation's self-mutilation on to its television screens; and at the end of it all, she includes Eugene McCarthy, the sardonic, intelligent, bitter and generous Senator who sought and lost the Presidential nomination relinquished by Johnson in order, as he prayed, abruptly to stop the fighting and the bombing without any more dishonourable prating about ending it all honourably.

So Emerson, tall, willowy, her beautiful heavy hair falling forward over her face, trod her nation's dead patrol and recorded its injuries as if they were her own. It is a lugubrious, intolerable pilgrimage. The pilgrim goes out on an adventure-with-a-destination; it is a solemn journey but she never arrives anywhere, except perhaps to find a love for both countries.

Emerson took on the weight of a nation's misery. It nearly broke her in half (she hates and disbelieves diagnostics of the emotions). She tried an impossible kind of reporting, one which fills itself with the words of others. It restores speech to those officially silenced, unheard, powerless. It publicises privacy. Doing so, it cannot leave these voices without a context. Fearful of imposing upon them significance they would themselves not accept or understand, Emerson can only place her spontaneous texts in the context of a national wretchedness.

Perhaps it is better to be a trouble connoisseur with all your own voice than a collector of other voices. James Fenton, one of the few Englishmen in Indo-China for any length of time, was one such, weighing up many deaths alongside his own terrific liveliness, making poetry out of journalism all the same.

He was – is – a man with an insatiable curiosity and a comically morbid zeal for hot water, like his friend Christopher Hitchens.

Fenton has something of the old imperial explorer's recklessness in him; he is touched a little by the wing of the Victorian Richard Burton, with the taste for the dark and smelly spots of the globe first turned into art by Joseph Conrad. The new class of adventurer-reporters which he joined had grown up under the shadow of the bomb, had learned young and at university to disbelieve governments, had cut its literary teeth on W. H. Auden and Ernest Hemingway, kept its politics by and large to itself, but went to look for the answers to its questions well away from the capitals of the old countries. It also coincided in its literary flowering with a recrudescence of that odd literary genre, the travel book. But where once the travellers went to be amazed by the exotic, the wild and the untamed, this new brigade went looking for trouble with no baggage train and a frugal vocabulary.

I suppose such men and women would once have been players of Kipling's 'great game'; certainly they looked for wars and rumours of wars under the tutelage of the superpowers, and stayed to stare at the heart of the action and tell their readers – readers of the *Wall Street Journal, Saturday Evening Post, Granta, Grand Street,* the *New Statesman,* the *Nation* – of what happened to the wretched of the earth when, at the edges, cold war turned violently hot and children lay dead in the fields.

James Fenton took an English upper-class education and its occasionally radical conscience to this experience, and turned the mixture into poetry and a blend of rumination and reportage for which the precedent is more the travels of Robert Byron in Afghanistan than George Orwell's in Spain. That is to say, the politics of the Pacific rim was for him not so much a place called choice where he would make his commitment plain in action – as Orwell did in Catalonia in 1937 – but rather a way of judging the distance between politics and consequence and of living as close as he could get to the people on whom consequences fall.

For James Fenton this wasn't a matter of pretending to put on grace in virtue of his closeness to the misery of others, one of the less attractive attitudes struck by conscience-stricken journalists. He was a non-protestant non-combatant. He wanted to be *there*, and to keep his nerve by unrelentingly seeing the funny side of things.

> Nonetheless, I wanted very much to see a communist victory. I wanted to see a war and the fall of a city because … because I wanted to see what such things were like. I had once seen a man dying, from natural causes, and my first reaction as I realised what was happening was to be glad that I was *there*. This is what happens, I thought, so watch it carefully, don't miss a detail … The point is simply being there and seeing it. The experience has no essential value beyond itself.[21]

To render experience-as-for-itself he could, as he said, 'invent my form as I went along';[22] moving like an old-fashioned traveller in antique lands, he would live as they did and recover 'reporting in its natural state'. By doing so, he could stick to what he really saw and lived through and avoid the orders of those 'horrible old men obsessed with the idea of stamping out good writing'[23] who, for him and for me, did so much to build the mortuary of journalism.

He had a good start in life. He was born in 1949, son of the chaplain at Oxford's loveliest, most Venetian college, Christchurch, where he was a student. At Oxford he won, naturally, the Newdigate Prize for poetry and came of age as it were in 1968; already he wore the brave badges of poet, reporter, traveller, bohemian, socialist.

He left and became a journalist-poet, worked for the *New Statesman*, Britain's hardy leftish perennial, and in 1973 was awarded a grant on which to travel and write poetry. The Paris peace accords had just been signed providing for the withdrawal of US troops and a ceasefire which no one observed and he went to Vietnam where there would obviously be trouble. He would take the socialism with him, but guardedly, as one who knew that the ultimate victory of the Vietcong would not bring in its train the good society but would at least be a just outcome, whatever happened afterwards. When the revolutionary government finally took charge in Saigon, why then, as Fenton ironically noted of his old self, 'it might then take its place among the governments we execrated – those who ruled by sophisticated tyranny in the name of socialism.'

Off he goes to Saigon, to a war that has lasted longer than the twenty-four years he has been alive, and where 'Saigon cast you, inevitably, into the role of the American.' He tries to help a baby drugged to within a few inches of death in order to summon up pity for its state from passers-by and alms to its mother's bowl. The taxi ignores his fervently well-meant instruction and takes the baby to a respectable witch's house who cures it with a little toothpaste. In self-righteous (self-amused) rage, he gives the mother money and goes.

Wherever he goes, he metamorphoses into the inept bystander drawn into the action against his will – an old English trope. He travels on to meet the Khmer Krom, the border Cambodians, makes an interrupted journey over broken roads and bridges, reckons that officers of the Thieu regime 'were no better and no worse than anybody else in the world' and talks memorably to a couple of cops.

They said it was very difficult to combat the Vietcong, because they used such crude methods. 'Crude?' I asked. 'Yes, crude.' The word was spoken with a dreadful scowl. 'What do you mean, crude?' One of the officers explained. It was these frogmen. They didn't use proper equipment. They just put a clip on their nose, tied on a bit of rubber hose to breathe through, attached stones to their feet, and walked along the bottom of the river. They had found from intelligence sources that that was how they had blown up all these bridges. It was impossible to see them coming. It was all very crude. I had to agree with the officer. It did sound pretty crude. But why didn't they do the same thing in return? Why didn't the Saigon troops go walking around on the bottom of the rivers attacking Vietcong positions? The officer looked at me with utter contempt. 'That would be quite impossible,' he said flatly.[24]

After some scary stuff on the border dodging gun-runners and staying with monks in a religious dosshouse, that was Cambodia. Fenton gave the parents of a paralysed baby some 20 dollars – all he had; the baby was the child of the cook in the sort-of-monastery. The parents came back and tried, ardently and at length, to give Fenton the baby. He could care for it far better than them. He refused. That, too, was Cambodia.

It was the end of 1974 and Fenton was back in Vietnam, holding rambling conversations with shy officers in the dark 'who told you one thing by night but begged you not to remember it the next day' and led Fenton to his rule of Crespuscular Journalism: 'believe nothing you are told before dusk.' Yet looking for stories in the reporter's way was hardly what Fenton was up to. He wasn't really 'looking for' anything; he was a kind of wandering tale-collector for whom way, truth and life were in the detail of what happened.

He would tell by selling his stories to any editor who would listen. They included the *Washington Post*, Britain's new *Independent*, the *Guardian* and eventually Bill Buford's remarkable British magazine, tailor-made to Fenton's purposes, *Granta*.

He very much wanted to meet the almost-victorious Vietcong, now under new initials as the PRG or provisional revolutionary government. So he drove vaguely around the war zone until he found some Northerners, smart and clean, in the Central Highlands and then, satisfied, went back to a 'fortified Club Med belonging to the South' where the girls were tucked up in the bunkers beside their officers. The trouble with conventional war correspondents is that they think military action is the only action and in Vietnam there was less of that than met the eye.

Fenton's stories are like those of a kindly and inspired saloon-bar anecdotalist. He will talk to anybody. He could write the same book as his *All the Wrong Places* about prowling round England, were it not for the fact that being in the wrong place and missing the official action, or at least the official statements about the official action, means that he was in the right place to find the battiness of ordinary life still going unrepentantly on in modern wartime, whether the comic battiness in question was that of a garrulous *cyclopousse* declaiming Lamartine or a member of Cambodian royalty.

Fenton, as we saw, was at the fall of Saigon – the right wrong place, all right – and stayed on unruffled for weeks after the last green helicopter lifted off the roof of the embassy on a billion TV screens. He took a book or two from the abandoned building but couldn't bring himself to take a framed epigram by Lawrence of Arabia: 'Better to let them do it imperfectly than to do it perfectly yourself, for it is their country, their war, and your time is short.'

Then they came. They behaved very well.

> I was very very excited. The weight of the moment, the privilege of being a witness, impressed itself at once. Over and above my self-conscious-ness, and the trivial details which were made all the more interesting by the extraordinary nature of the event, there was the historical grandeur of the scene.[25]

He was unquestionably in the right place alongside the real thing.

But he had his responsibilities, as I have mine to him. He was there by choice as well as by vocation. Obviously, as he says, he was testing his own bravery by being there, as well as his honesty about what it all meant. Both qualities come out of danger pretty well if, as he also admits, you let him off the political opportunism. He has a stab at making judgement too, his master's voice sounding from *The Shield of Achilles* in the background.

> The villages are burnt, the cities void;
> The morning light has left the river view;
> The distant followers have been dismayed;
> And I'm afraid, reading this passage now,
> That everything I knew has been destroyed
> By those whom I admired but never knew;
> The laughing soldiers fought to their defeat
> And I'm afraid most of my friends are dead.[26]

James Fenton is a disconcerting guide to the Pacific in the last two decades of Cold War. Like all good poets, he makes his moral meaning out of his poetic style, in his case the flat, plain style of anecdotes culled from the edges of historical moments.

He came and went from the Pacific. For two or three years at the end of the 1970s he wrote the weekly political column for the *New Statesman* and was brutally funny. He had a year or more as theatre critic for the *Sunday Times*. But opportunism will out, and planes fly from Heathrow to Manila as well as to New York.

So he dropped in on 'the Snap Revolution' which overthrew Marcos in the Philippines during 1986, pinched a couple of Imelda Marcos's hand-towels when the palace was looted, and chatted to the communist guerril-las in the hills about watching *Rambo* on their Betamax. When he also turns up in Kwangju in 1987 to remind us of the tear-gas, the beating-up of students, the singular nastiness of the much-mentioned, capitalist-inspired miracle of South Korea, then it is clear that Fenton's mocking masquerade as joker-drifter had served its day to the end of the Cold War. A good half of him belonged by then to the Pacific rim. He compiled his big stock of quiet, comic anecdotes. He backed the books which brought newly uncom-fortable truths[27] out of Cambodia and Vietnam. He put his money in a little self-subsistence farm in the Philippines.

The other half of him belongs a mile or so beyond Magdalen Bridge in Oxford. He became the university's Professor of Poetry and, leaving the wrong places behind, found the right one as a self-made art historian of great prowess and gardening correspondent to a British Sunday.

When America's leading poet Robert Lowell met America's leading novel-ist Norman Mailer at the most memorable party of Cold War opposition ever held by radicals, Lowell said, 'in his fondest voice, "Elizabeth and I really think you're the finest journalist in America",[28] to which Mailer, twinkling and prickling all at once responded, 'using Lowell's nickname for the first time, "Well Cal ... there are days when I think of myself as being the best writer in America."'

They had both shown up for the vast march of anti-Vietnam War protesters which massed along the Potomac and closed upon the Pentagon at the end of October 1967. Lowell, one might say, was there to speak against the war, not only on behalf of the family name and its towering Bostonian authority, but also on behalf of the humanism of letters which he incarnated for the crowds who came as well. Mailer was spokesman of a much more raffish and multitudinous collective of writers-and-readers, first (no doubt) among its equals but emerging from its dense and smelly ruck as the man who is at home with the underside of society.

So there they were, the two of them, constitutionalist and adventurer, but interchangeable with it, for Mailer had turned up in his three-piece suit and regimental tie and in the guise of unofficial officialdom as a veteran of the war against the Japanese and world-famous chronicler of the fighting, author on the first hand of *The Naked and the Dead*, on the second – the day before, as it were – of *Why Are We in Vietnam?*, and on the third of all the boiling and pouring and high-spirited and downright dirty-minded journalism collected as *Advertisements for Myself* and *Cannibals and Christians*. So Mailer's authority came from his own immersion in literary, scatological and physical adventuring, as well as by his blasphemous remoralising of his people's antique Constitution and his urge to use it as an indictment of the godless rationalisations of the Pentagon's death-delivery men.

He had done everything a dustjacket could require: 'sodajerk, usher, flat-painter, rifleman, *Story* magazine, *Cross Section*'[29] and English literature at Harvard. He was a famous drunk, an eager boxer in fashionable salons and at gatherings of New York cultivation, a constant husband to several wives and therefore effortfully carrying an intolerable burden of alimony, and a man with the gift of irresistible charm and of insanely plausible, copious theorisation.

These were qualities uniquely fitted to making this public dramatisation of the American crisis into a journalism which demanded art as the guarantee of its truthfulness. Ed Murrow's reporting of the air-raids on London or even James Cameron's descriptions of nuclear bomb trials on Bikini could count on the facts of the case to match its truth. Justice hand-in-hand with a seemly courage in London in 1941 turned news into history in a single draft. Horrific physics and natural incredulity did the same for an underwater bomb. But this time, Mailer had to make a story into history out of unintelligible human milling about. So he gave his amazing book[30] the subtitle 'History as a novel, the novel as history' and in doing so laid claim to being first and best writer of what Tom Wolfe dubbed 'the new journalism'[31] (Wolfe smartly included himself among its best examples) and what we might call, with academic ambiguity, 'the re-presentation of the historic'.

However that may be, *The Armies of the Night*, like Malraux's early novels or *Homage to Catalonia*, gives us the case of a book read immediately by those who were there and those who were not but who in both cases wanted urgently to know what it meant and could discover the truth from nobody else, certainly neither from television nor from the hateful condescensions of *Time* magazine with which Mailer laconically opens his reporting.

Mailer himself, as everyone knows, moves through the action in the third person. Full to his brim with bourbon, he speaks impromptu, perhaps boringly, to a packed little Ambassador Theatre, lends himself to the enormous, slovenly dignity of the march, sprints in a quick, portly manner past the guards, is gratifyingly arrested, held in custody along with Noam Chomsky, appears before a US Commissioner magistrate defended by a lawyer friend in lemon-coloured trousers and a scarlet shirt, is sentenced to a few days in jail but then, after a wonderfully funny account of some legal legerdemain, is released on bail and appeal, and leaves the courtroom to begin, at once, on his remarkable high literature-journalism.

He has to be, he decides, novelist, reporter and historian in one. He has to write in the third person not only for old objectivity's sake, but to put down vanity (all is vanity to the good novelist, but vanity is the source of so much of the pleasure novelist and reporter must both give). His huge subject is, once more, America, and he loves America even while hating the mediocrity it has released in a tide upon the world.

Mailer does everything a modern novelist can do who acknowledges his duty to the truths of journalism. Time and again he draws back from the teeming crowd brimming with its individual obsessions and terrible heartache in order to see it as a large part of the redeemable soul of America. Standing up the slope of the mall above Washington boulevard, he sees a protester put a match to his draft card – not a slight thing to do, as thousands discovered – thereby to a federal document requiring the holder to present himself at its will to the military. Burning the draft card was the defining gesture of insubordination by those liable to conscription during the war, the ultimate appeal to the freedoms guarded by the Constitution in spite of the unconstitutionality of the act. Mailer sees the little flame joined by many little flames, and sees also in the sight the reminiscence of other camp-fires along the Potomac just a century before.

> The light of the burning card travelled through the crowd until it found another draft card someone else was ready to burn and this was lit, and then another in the distance. In the gathering dark it looked like a dusting of fireflies over the great shrub of the Mall.[32]

He sees them all with the eye of God and then hurtles back down through space to do his seeing up close and his little bit of suffering for the common weal. So he lines up on the march and finds the nation's history written on the faces of the US Marshals lined up in their turn in readiness to make the arrests.

The faces of all too many had a low cunning mixed with a stroke of rectitude: if the mouth was slack, the nose was straight and severe; should the
lips be tight, the nostrils showed an outsize greed. Many of them looked
to be ex-First Sergeants, for they liked to stand with the heels of their
hands on the top of their hips, or they had that way of walking, belly
forward, which a man will promote when he is in comfortable circumstances with himself and packing a revolver in a belt holster. The toes
turn out; the belly struts.

Mailer can do this sort of thing all day and better than anybody else. Can
one see the history-fashioned soul of a working class in a cluster of faces
and bodies? Reporters try – why not? – and Mailer is best at it.

He does the same with his own army, the night watch, and its crazy
kaleidoscope of uniforms, Foreign Legionnaires, Turkish shepherds,
Roman senators, Martians, Moonmen and a knight clanking about in full
armour, finds them lovable in their way and maddening, above all *records*
them in the rich, vivid coil of his interminable sentences, historical specu-
lations, phrenological jokes, all quickened by his sense of his genius and its
vitality this splendid October day.

The book is a masterpiece and assumes an easy place in the Pantheon of
Journalism. On any definition of the form except that we require it to be
printed on a broadsheet it does what the best journalism should do. It
describes with incomparable liveliness a singular political event; it *compre-
hends* it for us, enfolds it as a huge story in a circumambient history known
to readers but recast for these new, these *novel* purposes; it holds together
many and one, the many-headed multitude that is, with the class struggle
they embodied (not for nothing is Mailer an old leftist), the one nation in
its amazing unity.

Having invented the form for himself, he repeated his success the following summer, this time as (pretty well) straight journalism. Commissioned
by *Harper's* he wrote the reports which appeared first in its pages, second
as the book[33] which stands as sequel to *The Armies of the Night*.

His sheer productivity over those ten months is astounding. Two full-
length books written in so short a time, and the turbulence of the day
stopped and silhouetted in classic American prose. This time he spends
much longer face-to-face with the authenticities of political power. Being
Mailer, he interprets power-in-action (political action being largely in the
performances of language) as the expression of moral character, and so
when he listens to Eugene McCarthy he hears the man's heart beat and the

Democratic Party's dull indifference all around him. Mailer feels compassion for the certainty of McCarthy's defeat, together with a touch of distaste for a politician for whom human stupidity fermented a sour, caustic flavour in him which came from the solitariness of being in the right. 'If there was a grave flaw in McCarthy, it came out of some penury of his own spirit; too bitter even to express his own bitterness, it leaked out of the edges of his wit, turned as punishment upon his own people ... and leaking, seemed to get into the very yellow of his skin ...'[34]

Mailer sets McCarthy down in the stately, tedious, gripping gavotte of party nomination, then he goes out into the street. The dance of the politics formalises the melodramatised hatreds and high idealism of the five-day battle between the police and the protesters. Not that the protesters, as we have seen, wore one uniform. Mailer is marvellously sensitive to the many inflections of the New Left, the Students for a Democratic Society, the innumerable sectarians of initialled Marxisms, old-style members of the Communist Party, shaggy prophets from the Yippies, the straight socialists, the Resistance, each with a picture of the good society fixed in their gaze, free love, free sex, free money, free marihuana, free access to the media, and all of them fired with a crazy courage to run the gauntlet of Mayor Daley's hate-maddened policemen, mobilised to *hurt* the goddam students who so revoltingly violated flag and domestic decorum and the masculine rules of sex.

Mailer watches them flood into the city's concourses and mass about the speakers; he knows every one of the speakers, often personally, and gives a snatch of speech to Allen Ginsberg husky from tear-gassing, to Terry Southern, William Burroughs, Rennie Davis, Jerry Rubin, Tom Hayden, all the glittering stars of a revolutionary, change-of-heart, unrepeatable galaxy long since exploded into tracelessness. Mailer looks down from the top floor of the Hilton and sees the students proving that whatever it was making them refuse their draft, it wasn't lack of bravery; he watches the delegations to the convention tramp the ballroom floor to the Battle Hymn of the Republic; he folds pious hands over the doomed nomination of Hubert Humphrey, 'the candidate least popular and least qualified by strength, dignity, or imagination to lead',[35] while outside the students chant in humiliation of the wretched man, 'Dump the Hump, dump the Hump.' As the convention folds slowly in on itself and the spectre of a society coshed and cajoled into order by the weight of police truncheons on shoulder-blades fills him with fear, Mailer feels himself move once more from observer to participant in a mighty event whose consequences no one yet foresees. 'Reporters', he notes, 'live happily removed from themselves',[36] but this reporter has one hell of a self to contend with. 'Liver disease', he thinks as he goes back on the booze, 'is the warehousing of daily shame.'

So he gives a speech to the massed ranks of the demonstration, undiminished after four days, 'as good a speech as he had ever made', and the hearty, still affectionate crowd bellows back, 'Write, write. You're right, baby, do the writing.' He's arrested, twice, unjustly, for incipient affray. His true farewell to an incomplete event is spoken over the memory of Bobby Kennedy, hot redeemer or doomed, simple victim of his own decision to force America to see its own irreconcilable injustices, either way loved 'by a river of working-class people [who] came down to march past Kennedy's coffin ... this endless line of people had really loved him, loved Bobby Kennedy like no political figure in years had been loved.'[37]

Mailer goes adventuring and ends holding on to the Constitution, 'not much to bet on,' says a veteran, 'but all I can think of.' After 1968, the Pentagon Papers; after the Papers, Watergate. For years the framework of a political journalist's inquiries was set by the effort to measure the gap between the moral necessity of the founders' principles and the political actuality of their disregard. From, say, 1957 onwards this practical, sometimes activist measuring went on in the generation-long struggle over civil rights, as it switched back and forth from other demonstrations and filthy murders too, in Mississippi and Arkansas, up to Washington and Presidential orders and uncertainties about what to do in the main streets of the South.

By definition, the journalist's vocation calls him and her to the action in the street. Civil rights are violated and upheld first of all in the street, in the segregated diner and trolley-bus. Given those vast American distances and the intensely local lives they enclose and keep apart, the story of journalism and civil rights will be a story of local newspapers, their courage or cravenness. In the very middle of the generation which went to school under the protection of the National Guard, turned out to have its head cracked in Chicago, and calmly lived for eight years under a folksy film actor stifling all impulse to reform, the biggest street story of half a century's political journalism broke, so quietly as to be almost inaudible, on 17 June 1972. Its consequences were constitutional, for sure, as well as hugely personal for all the leading figures right up to the President. They were just as large for the shaping narrative of journalism, of newspaper circulation wars, and for the coming to birth of a quite new kind of polity, one in which the industrial manufacture and sale of news for profit, the telling of truth to itself about itself by a society, and the everyday making and taking of political decisions all become inextricably intertwined, indeed, mutually embedded.

Watergate serves to mark the advent of such a polity, every bit as much so for all the other democracies of more-or-less liberal capitalism as for the United States. Watergate fulfilled the ambition of Katherine Graham the publisher and Ben Bradlee its managing editor to make the *Washington Post* a daily of equal, national, status to the *New York Times*. Watergate made the two reporters, Bob Woodward and Carl Bernstein, aged twenty-nine and twenty-eight that June morning, into myth-heroes of their profession. It put political corruption, always a likely instrument of states with their reasons, at the heart of the question of governmental legitimacy, and sent reporters frantic to follow the reek of money through the sewers of society until they could make their own name and fortune by smelling it out in the wrong pockets.

That Woodward and Bernstein get so much of the historical credit in popular memory for the Watergate story is doubtless a result of the incomparable film of *All the President's Men*, and the fact that their parts were played by two of the most famous film stars of the half-century, Robert Redford and Dustin Hoffman. But from the start – as the two main reporters on the case make clear in their book[38] – there was a *Post* team on the story. After Katherine Graham and Ben Bradlee themselves, there were Howard Simons, managing editor, Harry Rosenfeld, metropolitan editor, Barry Susman, city editor, the immortal cartoonist Herblock, and Al Lewis for twenty-five years the *Post*'s police reporter who went to work in a regulation police sweater. There were yet others, including the editorial writers and those assigned from time to time to the mammoth and dreary tasks of sifting forgotten documents and trying for days to obtain unilluminating interviews. Even in Woodward's and Bernstein's classic account – entertainingly rebranded in a recent edition as 'the original novel' – the overwhelming impression is of months (over two years) slogging away in files and on endless phone calls after distantly possible leads and obdurate witnesses, finding a thin trickle of a story which ran away into the sand, assembling a narrative pitifully short on evidence, barely circumstantial, riven by gaps and corroded by official denial. They were sustained as much by pride as anything, by what Bradlee used to call 'the defensive crouch',[39] a trophy awarded to reporters 'clinically unable to admit they missed a story' or, in his case, unable to relinquish a story to which he had given his newspaper's good name.

Bradlee, as the District of Columbia well knows, is a figure of tremendous dash and vivacity. Strikingly handsome, deplorably youthful even in old age, he brought to the executive editor's desk his Harvard degree, wartime heroism on destroyers, resurrection from polio, a lifetime in journalism including years on the *Post* when it was a mere local, a job as press attaché in Paris for the US Information Services (loved Paris passionately so stayed on for *Newsweek*), long and close friendship with JFK, a terrific zest for life, especially life's women, and an all-American vocabulary, vivid, foul-mouthed, manly, cheerful, charming, to go with everything else.

Bradlee saw Watergate as a *Post* story at once. Woodward went to court the morning of 17 June and heard a small group of cheap crooks arraigned for burglary at the Democratic Party's headquarters in the lavish Watergate apartment block overlooking the Potomac, where the party was preparing for the 1972 Presidential election. Woodward heard one of the burglars confess to a connection with the CIA. This was obviously a metropolitan story and Rosenfeld put Bernstein on to it as well, in the nick of time to avoid his being fired for a certain nonchalance towards his expense account as well as an overenthusiasm for the company of women.

Bernstein, following a hunch by following the fresh crisp hundred-dollar bills found on the burglars, went down to Miami, American capital of all well-fleeced, well-fed, sun-bronzed burglars speaking Spanish. He found a direct connection between the cash and a Republican fundraiser for the Committee for the Re-election of the President (given the acronym CREEP), one Kenneth Dahlberg, who had simply handed money over for the committee to use as it pleased under the direction of ... and here, as everybody of a certain age still remembers clearly, the question, *Who? Who* paid burglars to derail political rivals? was put in a series of mounting crescendoes by the *Post*.

The Republicans dismissed the connection with contempt. Bradlee and his men *knew* (Bradlee's word)[40] they were lying. In a moment of rich satisfaction for the two journalists and for the readers of their book, they transcribe Bernstein's notes typed in great agitation immediately after he had telephoned John Mitchell, Attorney General of the United States and therefore keeper of his nation's political legality, to ask him to comment on a new allegation Bernstein had written up for the next morning's *Post* that Mitchell controlled the secret fund and its payments.

Mitchell:	'JEEEESUS. You said that? What does it say?'
Bernstein:	'I'll read you the first few paragraphs.' (He got as far as the third. Mitchell responded, 'JEEEESUS' every few words.)
Mitchell:	'All that crap, you're putting it in the paper? It's all been denied. Katie Graham's gonna get her tit caught in a big fat

wringer if that's published. Good Christ! That's the most sickening thing I ever heard.'

Bernstein: 'Sir, I'd like to ask you a few questions about ...'

Mitchell: 'What time is it?'

Bernstein: 'Eleven thirty. I'm sorry to call so late.'

Mitchell: 'Eleven thirty. Eleven thirty when?'

Bernstein: 'Eleven thirty at night.'

Mitchell: 'Oh.'

Bernstein: 'The committee has issued a statement about the story, but I'd like to ask you a few questions about the specifics of what the story contains.'

Mitchell: 'Did the committee tell you to go ahead and publish that story? You fellows got a great ballgame going. As soon as you're through paying Ed Williams and the rest of those fellows, we're going to do a story on all of you.'

Bernstein: 'Sir, about the story ...'

Mitchell: 'Call my law office in the morning.'

He hung up.

Bernstein and Bill Brady, the night editor, called Bradlee at home in bed. 'Leave everything in but "her tit",' Bradlee instructed, 'and tell the desk I said it's okay.'

The *Los Angeles Times* ran an interview with the stooge set on guard across the street during the break-in. The *Post* was agonised to miss it but it confirmed the combination of mistrust, hatred, the avaricious hoarding of power and the criminal megalomania which gripped the minds and spirits of the President's men, even those closest to him, even the President himself. The names the *Post* reporters were collecting – Howard Hunt, the undercover operations coordinator, the happily named Donald Segretti, a Nixon lawyer with a taste for political espionage – edged ever nearer to the Chief Executive.

Woodward and Bernstein were working on the fine edge of legality. Bernstein obtained credit card records on Segretti from a sympathetic and nameless acquaintance in the company. Woodward, himself hired by the *Post* in the first place because, among other reasons and even if he wrote lousy prose,[41] 'he knew a lot of people', had regular recourse to a secret 'source' whom he met after dark in the corner of a multistorey car park. In the jargon of the trade, this shadow spoke only in 'deep background', has never to this day been identified (except to Bradlee) and was known to

Rosenfeld and the *Post* team only as 'Deep Throat', the majestic sobriquet of a fairytale specialist in fellatio whose most urgent sexual responses were placed below her tonsils.

Deep Throat would never allow himself to be quoted but was never wrong. He kept Woodward and the *Post* on track, led him to the trail of slush-fund dollars dropped by the finance chairman of CREEP, Maurice Stans, his deputy, Jeb Magruder, and assorted others, all of them hiring crooks to commit crimes. Deep Throat implicated John Mitchell, he described the several ways in which leading Democrats were mendaciously vilified in a series of foul operations by the hoodlums on the Nixon committee. On 10 October 1972, the *Post* published its fullest story on Watergate so far. It ran to sixty-five paragraphs. It listed the slanders, the squalid disruptions, the bribery and petty crime routinely practised by Nixon's stooges with the sole purpose of retaining power. Bradlee had the deep satisfaction of equalling the score with the *New York Times*. 'There are many, many rewards in the newspaper business, but one of the finest comes with reading the competition quoting your paper on its front page.'[42]

Two weeks later the *Post* and its pet reporters were gleefully charged by the White House team and its dim, tubby little press secretary Ron Ziegler with a serious mistake as well as with crude partisanship. In a schoolboy evasion which he must have known would eventually be caught up with, the Nixon committee's finance chair Hugh Sloan had emerged from a grand jury testimony able to declare that he hadn't implicated Bob Haldeman, Nixon's immediate adjutant, in the shady dealings with the money. Since he seemed to have done so in conversations with Woodward and Bernstein and had been duly reported as placing guilt at the President's elbow, this was a heavy blow to the *Post*.

No other paper had named such powerful names. The White House set its hounds baying at the *Post*. The *Washington Star-News* reported that the President's special counsel, Charles Colson, had in train a campaign to break the newspaper once the election, in which Nixon would win every state bar Massachusetts, was easily won: 'We're really going to get rough. They're going to wish on L street that they'd never heard of Watergate.'[43] Even the incomparable Katherine Graham, steeled by her partnership with Bradlee during the courtroom drama of the Pentagon Papers, 'was feeling beleaguered ... during these months the pressures on the *Post* [from, among others, Joseph Alsop and Henry Kissinger] to cease and desist were intense and uncomfortable.'[44] Readers were writing directly to her as publisher, charging her, as did the creature-Senator Bob Dole, with bad journalism, bad faith, lack of patriotism and loss of impartiality. For a woman whose close friends even then included Ronald Reagan, Lippmann, of course, as her columnist, Isaiah Berlin, Lyndon Johnson and Henry Kissinger, charges of anything so vulgar in Georgetown as partisanship were hard to bear.

She wrote to John Ehrlichman, a personal friend although Nixon's senior adviser on domestic affairs. She was at pains, she said, to rebut Senator Dole's very public and widely reported accusation that she personally 'hated Nixon', but also to reaffirm the principled position she stood for at the *Post* that a publisher does not shape a newspaper's editorial line according to her 'personal feelings and tastes'. She wrote on the matter with exceptional dignity and truthfulness, qualities unassumingly confirmed by her exceptional (but not absolute) immunity as a public figure and of a class eminence somehow untouched by the brutal rivalries of American politics. I mention this by way of marking the contrast with the ownership by Rupert Murdoch and Robert Maxwell of once honourably even-handed British newspapers, and the discernible adulteration of what she called in her letter to Ehrlichman 'the highest standards of professional duty and responsibility'.

These are phrases and cadences made filthy with dishonest use. But not at the *Washington Post*. Kay Graham stood by her editors and reporters because, however much all other newspapers drew away from hers, she believed they had discovered something evil-smelling and important.

On 27 October the *Post* was joined by much-welcome company. Walter Cronkite insisted that CBS Evening News give a full fourteen minutes to the Watergate revelations by the *Post*, in spite of the fact that it was a story without strong visual imagery or documents and with nobody prepared to go on any record, least of all a record watched by 30 million citizens.

Gradually, however, the story stalled. The President, re-elected in November, looked safe for four years. The CBS News report had given the *Post* a bit of solidarity but nothing new. Woodward and Bernstein tried to reach the grand jury hearing Watergate evidence but were frozen out. Only in March 1973 did they make a break and this time it was in more or less open court, when Judge Sirica, due to sentence the Watergate burglars, disclosed that one of their number, James McCord, a tall, bald and incongruously benign CIA officer, had written to the judge from jail alleging danger to his life if he turned informer, but nonetheless accusing his seniors of ordering him not to inculpate them, of their perjury, and of his utter mistrust of attorneys in the pay of a Justice Department he accused of venality.

The entire national press heard Sirica out. The *Post* was, at the least, vindicated in its lonely tenacity. The President's press secretary, the appalling Ron Ziegler, had to acknowledge shiftily that he might unintentionally have made 'inoperative statements'. Bob Dole went very quiet. Kissinger held up pious hands, ineffably rebuking the press for 'its orgy of recrimination'. The Senate set up its House committee under the chairmanship of the venerable, thick-textured Southerner, Senator Sam Ervin, and with non-stop televising of its proceedings, the nation became one vast society reporting to itself and sitting in judgement on what it heard.

It was, I think, unique and the nearest thing modern electronic society could get to Athenian democracy. For the representatives of the people, Ervin's all-male committee, turned out to be amazingly good at the task assigned them by that people. They showed remarkable stamina, pertinence, judiciousness and indifference to their own preferment. In front of the television, the colossal audience *took part* in the proceedings; its millions of members watched the searching out of the criminal and horribly foul-mouthed circle of toughs, including the President, which ran their country for personal satisfaction. Then the people debated the meaning of what they saw, firmly endorsing that the House Committee would do all they could wish.

It is hard to leave alone such a stirring and fulfilled coincidence of journalism and democracy. The *Post* fairly earned its Pulitzer. Quiet testimony turned into high drama. A country whose Constitution aspires to order not just the legality of political conduct but its ethical significance as well had its moral appeal upheld. Deep Throat warned Bradlee, Woodward and Bernstein that the vengefulness of the President and his henchmen knew no limits and that their lives might be in danger. But at the end of June the President's junior counsel, John Dean, already promised jail by the President if he did so, testified fully to the full involvement of himself, his seniors, of Mitchell, Haldeman and of the President in the whole repertoire of underhand, lying, poisonous and cowardly practices by which those rogues bought their power and repaid their enemies. Out of the shelves of reports of Dean's long week of testifying, in his expressionless mesmerising monotone, to his own part in things, self-convicting, self-exculpating, sycophantic as he was, the report in *Time* with no byline will have to serve to represent the prevailing tone and accuracy with which American journalism treated the high theatre of the moment caught, for most people, on tiny black-and-white screens in offices, banks, hairdressers, grocery stores, petrol stations.

Time's opening summary is unbeatable.

Now the grave charges against the President had passed a point of no return. Carried with chilling reality into millions of American homes and spread massively on the official record of a solemn Senate inquiry, the torrential testimony of John W. Dean III fell short of proof in a court of law. But the impact was devastating. As President, Richard Nixon was grievously, if not mortally wounded.[45]

The cover headline was 'Can Nixon survive Dean?' As Alistair Cooke put it, 'the rest you know'. Two weeks after Dean's testimony, tipped off by Woodward, the Ervin Committee called one Alexander Butterfield, White House security head and naval officer. He disclosed that all discussions involving the President were tape-recorded. The evidence for all that the *Post* had disclosed from the hoarse whispering of Deep Throat and the fragments and scraps out of which Woodward and Bernstein had confected their accurate reports was undeniably present on hours and hours of routinely recorded, classified and carefully preserved tape.

Nixon held on for another full year through one appalling, hysterical and humiliating defiance after another. He withheld the tapes, he made deletions from them, he shocked the nation with the coarse brutality of the conversations transcribed from them,[46] he sacked the lawyers determined to see him sacked, and in the end Senator Barry Goldwater led a Republican deputation into his reclusive, paranoid sanctum and, on 9 August 1974, Walter Cronkite on behalf of the nation saw him out of the White House and into his final Presidential helicopter, looking, as Clive James put it so happily, 'like a cake in the rain'.[47]

CHAPTER TWELVE

Fictions (2): The View from Somewhere

Professional ethics seek simplicity. The coming of professionalism effected the reconstitution of social structures worldwide in the twentieth century. When Max Weber was meditating on the vocation of politics as the First World War ended and his nation faced revolution, for all the triumph of irrationality, vengeance and atavism he could see about him, he was prophesying a very different victory in the world.[1] It would be the victory of super-rationalisation conducted by a quite new figure in the cast of contemporary characters, the manager-bureaucrat. Weber took time out to define the best version he could imagine for this new role; a clear-minded, efficient, law-abiding, master of the files and keeper of their anonymity who would combine justice with attentiveness in a way to ensure the smooth administration of modernity.

At the same time, however, he saw his vision under a darkening sky. These machines of rationalisation would, he wrote, prove to be our 'iron cage' imprisoning the natural freedoms of the everyday world, demanding preposterous surveillance, ensuring intellectual and emotional incarceration, turning the purposes of society into mere adjuncts of its own systematisation. Later sociologists, supremely Jürgen Habermas,[2] have watched Weber's prophecies come true until they see a society in which the 'life-world' and the 'systems-world' are forced apart for very survival's sake, but in which the systems-world is forever encroaching on life and seeking to dominate it.

The boundary marked on either side 'private' and 'public' has been one, often ineffectual, way to give real life a bit of breathing-space; 'professionalism' represents one effort to moralise the amoral and lifeless realm of cost-effectiveness, managerial hierarchy and administrative authority. By its lights, the professional conducts himself or herself according to scrupulous principles of personal detachment, absence of self-interest, the careful application of impersonal techniques and skills attributable in their subtlety and precision only to the formality of the parent institution (school, hospital, government agency, department store, newspaper, TV station) and never to the passions and moral purposes of the individual.

For the journalist in modern politics, professional ethics taught that, in the tired formula, facts were sacred, opinions separate, and news transparent. The virtuous journalist reported on the plain truth, came with no previous convictions, refused nationhood, spoke not even for common humanity but in the voice of the Martian. He or she saw what they could and reported what they saw. Such enlightenment would illuminate posterity rather than politics; for professional reasons, the journalist informed a public opinion without public membership.

As the several biographies of this book indicate, from Walter Lippmann and Martha Gellhorn to James Fenton and Joan Didion, the best journalists square their human allegiance with their feeling for truth, which we may as well think of as natural. Alasdair MacIntyre once wrote, in connection with his view that each human being turns the storytelling faculty of mind to shaping an intelligible biography out of the facts of individual life, 'Man ... is not essentially, but becomes through his history, a teller of stories that aspire to truth ...'[3] In a more earnestly personal admonition, Henry James once wrote to a dear friend: 'Don't, I beseech you, *generalise* too much in these sympathies and tendernesses – remember that every life is a special problem which is not yours but another's, and content yourself with the terrible algebra of your own.'[4]

We had far better understand what the best and the worst journalists wrote as a struggle with that algebra (which takes in the ethics of professionality) than in terms of some abstract duty to and concrete dereliction of facts and objectivity.

These lucubrations preface a second look at the fictions which, as much as the facts, shape journalistic narratives. They have changed since the first batch. They have become less local, more universal. In a paradox, however, they are also more provisional, less generalisable. They presage a different structure of feeling as framing an epoch, the epoch (let us say) of end-of-Cold-War, which proves to be a lasting moment of radical uncertainty, a welcome end to global terror, a terrifying advent of global fragmentariness. This same structure, therefore, is compounded of the mistrust of power; the necessity of self-determination; the distillation of a professional style and its forms out of the exigences of a personal situation and its commissions; the sharp awareness of professional situation (boss, dead-lines, circulation, byline) and a new acknowledgement that making sense of it all and keeping up a wardrobe of decency have to be worked out on the job. Waugh's moral fastidiousness and *idiot savant* in *Scoop* or the moral putting-down by traditional American values of the two villains in *Sweet Smell of Success* are quite inadequate when it comes to Cold War and post-colonial journalism, its high fame and publicity, its low deceits and treachery.

It takes a big novelist, a big talker with the swank, the intelligent vulgarity, the great wit and good humour, the sheer gregariousness of Saul Bellow, to create a pair of journalists capable of judging the two civilisa-tions standing off on either side of the iron curtain, announcing the terms of the future even as, in spite of themselves, their enmity begins to drain away. In *The Dean's December* Bellow devises two eminent journalists as characters capable of reporting the frightfulness of civic life on either side of the Cold War divide.[5] His main character, a middle-aged dean in a substantial college, is married to an eminent astronomer, an emigrée from Romania, and is transfixed into immobility by his vision of two cities, here and there. He tests himself faithfully to see what life in either Bucharest or Chicago can hold, especially for the poor, and although he belongs unequivocally to Chicago, he cannot see how anyone could live a decent life in either. This is the pass and these are the desolations to which Cold War brought us.

His December is spent in Bucharest, waiting on the deathbed of his mother-in-law, Valeria, once health minister in the regime. He has little place in the busyness of the threadbare, elderly, pious ex-bourgeois womenfolk who bustle about his wife and prepare dutifully for the meagre obsequies. He moseys about the cold apartment in the ancient, heavy building, drinking plum brandy and reckoning up his two home towns.

Back in Chicago he has left a commotion caused partly by his pursuit through the courts of the footpad murderer of one of his students, partly by articles he has published in *Harper's* about the dire straits of the old place. *Harper's* is Bellow's deliberate choice for essays by an Albert Corde, sounding exactly like Saul Bellow, in which he terribly affronts received opinion by disavowing the correct idiom and inventing a mad wild wind of a language in which to describe the metamorphosis of Chicago into Gomorrah. Bellow, supreme fictionalist of the end of the epoch, sprays voluble theory everywhere in the essays, extensively (dazzlingly) quoted in the novel, making his hero mad at the world and therefore (necessarily) slightly mad in himself. He speaks with tongues. He becomes subject, as he puts it, to 'fits of vividness', in which he sees the individuals he reports on in his articles with preternatural physicality – 'the hillocky man … the cannonball head' – and releases them into his headlong, florid prose, himself 'somewhere in fever land', while downtown, 'in higher circles of influence, people may have been saying, "What's with this Professor … His pilot light is gone out."'[6] Bellow's hero-dean and journalist interviews leading characters in the city's internal life – the head of a hospital for the savagely poor, a criminal lawyer whose practice takes in cases of unimaginable abomination, a millionaire meatcutter and city boss of obsidian hardness, an utterly honest prison governor fired for cleaning up the prison rackets. Corde understands that political journalism of this kind can only deal in 'Personalities, scenes, feelings, tones, colours'; revelation is pointless. What would it reveal? The toughness of the city? The wealth of the rich and the fact that the rich deal in money? This is the glory of cities, not their shame.

He meets up in Bucharest with an old school friend. This is the other journalist, Dewey Spangler, a hotshot, a prodigy, known to millions. The name (this being Bellow) is allegorical, part the great American pragmatist philosopher, part the star-spangled banner, part the *weltschmerzlich* author of *Decline of the West*. For Albert Corde, Dewey's column was 'too statesmanlike and doughy': 'He was trying hard to be a Walter Lippmann. But Lippmann had been the pupil of Santayana and the protégé of potentates at an age when sharp-toothed Dewey in an undershirt was still shrieking and grimacing at his mother.'[7] All the same, Dewey, with his diverticulitic bag, 'his decent seniority of aspect … his short, fleshy trunk and spherical, overfull, overfructified face'[8] is allowed to tell his old friend all that is wrong, that is impossible with his journalism. Dewey has *such* aspirations. 'Above the Walter Lippmann bracket to which he aspired there was the André Malraux bracket.'[9] So he tells Albert how journalists simply cannot cut loose with a lifetime of anger, veer off the topic of feral and starving children into Gianbattista Vico and his theory of custom, cannot fall in with cranks like the environmentalists ('You're cranky enough already'), shouldn't go all super-expressive, metaphorical, and all of this without humour, no touch of old Mencken, 'you gave 'em hard cuts, straight across the muzzle.'[10]

It's obviously no good being a Spangler, or even a Lippmann. He deals in big initials, NATO, USSR, the Gulf. It's all too sedate, orderly, well upholstered. It misses out altogether on the rocklike difference *and* the drunkenness of things being so various. Corde checks out on Spangler. He looks back at Chicago, tries to see it by the light of the American Idea.

Chicago is a maelstrom. Corde's student had gone out on a hot city night in bare feet to look for dirty sex. He had been chased to his apartment by a black hood and his skinny termagent of a girl. His terrified wife was locked in an inner room. He was half tied up and in a fight shoved through a ninth-storey window. Corde is accused by the loony student Left of making racist trouble. His college stands by him, wincingly.

The detail of the murder links up with his researches into the cesspit life of the undercity. Dreadful tales of rape and cruelty catch up with him, all embedded in the crazy struggle to eat, to live, to shoot heroin, to find sex, surrounded by the city's unbelievable and filthy waste. Corde looks away and sees Bucharest instead.

Bucharest is even worse. Bellow gives to the familiar litany spoken over the dreariness of communist Europe a Dickensian zest and particularity. His Bucharest has suffered a recent earthquake (as it had when Bellow wrote his novel). Its houses have heavy wrought-iron-and-glass doors, pitted stucco walls, rats lie flattened on the road, there are rusty trams, cast-iron sinks, croaking pull-chain toilets, lumps of rubble, withering cold. All dealings with the bureaucracy have to be primed by cigarette bribes, the exchanges handled by one of Bellow's new city species, this time a Romanian called Traian with Zapata moustache wisps, bulkily built in an orange bomber jacket and high-heeled boots.

There is a malevolent colonel of the Interior department who obstructs all the efforts of Corde and his wife to visit the dying Valeria. He is a 'braided-whip sort of man', correct, sharp, hard as nails and probably sadistic, probably evil. In spite of him, the faded old birds of Valeria's circle flutter about, keeping up their barely fledged appearances. Valeria dies, there is a grim funeral.

Corde and his wife go home. Bellow counterposes to the colonel the native sons of his native city, Chicago's 'men of power, devoid of culture, lovers of money, fearlessly insolent – Lyndon Johnson bullies', and he counterposes to the shabby, defiant lovingness of Valeria's funeral a party in an exotic penthouse sixteen floors up, overlooking Lakeshore Drive, of course. It is a lavish birthday party with champagne and sturgeon, the guests on the way to elderliness but groomed and dyed and sunburned and fit. It is given for the household's dog, a Great Dane, gleaming and lugubrious.

Bellow and Corde together take the dog's party in high style. They give the dog birthday presents, what the hell. This is America, and Corde likes the people. He's sixteen floors up from the city and well away from its terrors and dirt. It is all a bit reminiscent of the story told by Arthur Miller about coming back from a writer's conference with Norman Mailer and, thinking of the Russians quarrelling, intensely declaiming their poetry, implacably brave and *against* their state, Miller says, 'Jesus, Norman, but doesn't it make you glad to be an American?' Bellow can also be trusted to take full responsibility. He has looked *so* hard at Bucharest and Chicago, he can say the same sort of thing. His hero, having resigned from his academic deanship, is resolved to return to fight the good fight as a journalist. But Bellow leaves him with his astronomer wife at Mount Palomar, faces tilted to the cold stars, mucky human life out of sight and, for a while, of mind.

Bellow counterposes two types of political commentator generated both by the politics of modern city life *and* by the structures of production in the press and on television. The trouble is that while there have been many journalists alongside Dewey Spangler treading in the footprints of Walter Lippmann – Joseph Alsop, James Reston, Anthony Lewis, Lars Erik Nelson in the United States, Louis Heren, Hugo Young, Nora Beloff, Neal Ascherson in Britain – there have been very few attempting the eloquence, the super-expressivity, the immersion in the lower depths of Bellow's hero, Albert Corde. Perhaps Corde is a version of Tom Wolfe's new journalism, and it must be the case that Wolfe himself, for all his unremitting condescension towards any rival, has felt the high hot rhythms of Bellow's prose run through his veins. Certainly such a piece of his journalism as 'the Electric Kool-Aid Acid Test' *sounds* like Corde but without the desperate compassion, the keen sense of the mad absoluteness with which other people are so, well, *other*.

Perhaps Norman Mailer is a sort of Albert Corde, and certainly Mailer, being (like Bellow) a great novelist as well as an adventurer-journalist, wants to live as dangerously as Corde, to find out the little motors which drive Mayor Daley's cops or Jerry Rubin's Yippies, to speak for the super-expressive universe with all these fizzing monads in it. Joan Didion drily declines the expressive side of things but no one can miss the calm courage with which she sets off into the depths of the pit in order to find out what's going on down there, or the artistry with which she makes meiosis tell so much.

So there is something to the idea of the new journalism and we shall see more of it later. But only a Mailer or a Bellow can invent it on the page, and the fictional myths of the epoch after *Scoop* or *His Girl Friday* settle for solving the algebra whose equations have on one side the quantities of news reporting and due objectivity, and on the other the values of personal decency and human connection. The movies are the fullest of these puzzles, but it is obviously easier to follow through the stages of solution by way of the explicitness of a novel.

Raymond Williams's *The Volunteers* will serve this purpose well. Williams, an Anglo-Welshman and one of the leading intellectuals of the Left in the years of Cold War until his death at the age of sixty-six in 1988, uses this admirable novel for a dramatisation of the moral collision between a journalist's professional obligations and his political allegiances.

The action is set in Wales and England a dozen or more years or so after 1978, when the novel was published. In a national economic crisis, there has been a coal strike, the army has been mobilised to move fuel stocks and a coal-wagon driver has been shot and killed, maybe under orders from a Cabinet of National Unity. At a huge demonstration in Cardiff against emergency measures as well as of outrage at the killing, the government minister suspected of its authorisation is publicly punished by being peppered with shotgun pellets fired deliberately low into his shins. The hero of the novel, a Welsh sometime leftist and reporter specialising in political protest and fantasy guerrillas, is put on the affair, ostensibly to find the origins of the marksman, but impelled by his own past to connect the minister to the dead loader.

Lewis Redfern partakes of and deepens the story and living myth of the solitary, resolute, ingenious reporter with a complete cynicism about political motives and a knowledgeable contempt for politicians. Williams himself knew intimately the bitter sectarianism of the non-parliamentary Left, and his hero Redfern is set to be dry and stinging about his former comrades: 'In the competitive situation of the factions in [Marxist-Leninism], there is a constant bidding-up of aggressive lines and I had seen some such [threatening] phrases about virtually every prominent right-wing politician … as if saying it did some good and might even make it happen.'[11]

It is worth pointing out that Williams wrote the novel at least seven years before the national miners' strike in Britain, which lasted from early summer 1984 to spring 1985 and which was broken by Mrs Thatcher's Tory government amid widely televised scenes of hand-to-hand and brutal fighting between strikers and police which deeply shocked and divided the nation. The miners were routed, the union split and the industry was finished as a consequence, but the nationwide struggle gathered and concentrated in itself all the political yearnings and class hatreds of a century of British history.

So there is striking prescience in the action of the novel, as well as unavoidable anachronisms and, to anybody with a heart to feel, affecting idealisations. Redfern reads a beautifully written report on the death of the loader (it is perfect journalism, of course; Williams wrote it). 'I stopped and shifted my speed. I read it as it came.' When he finishes, he is displaced, lost, 'as if I was moving in two ways, two places, at once'.[12] Moving through him are two currents, both irresistible: the flow of the reporter's energy towards his story and the high tension of political solidarity.

Either way, his feel for his subject makes him realise that the assault on the minister's shins was a *staged* affair. Demonstrations dramatise a constellation of ideas. The shooting demonstrated retribution from a wounded class and nation. It symbolised its opposition, its scorn, its daring. Redfern found in the amused contempt with which the protesters planted phoney clues, and in the calculated callousness of the shooting, a mind 'somewhere inside them [with] an unusually hard edge; a certain settled bitterness; what I thought of, indeed, as an older kind of bitterness.'[13]

Redfern recognises it and welcomes it. Using his press card and his reputation, he connects the injured minister and a well-known radical of the same age, once a Labour MP, now head of an international political aid agency. He connects both, by careful reportorial backtracking, telephoning, memorisation, flashes of insight, to the union leader on duty at the coal-yard on the day the loader was shot. The ex-MP is pitilessly drawn. He is handsome, energetic, newly remarried to a very much younger, ice-cool and beautiful wife, writing a new political classic *The End of Social Democracy*. He is at bitter odds with the eldest son he abandoned from his first marriage, who turns out to be the mind behind the attack on the minister.

The hero pursues a beautiful young woman, a sprinter with the speed to have got away from the shooting. He finds *her* links to the underground, presses her with presumptuous questions, she turns on him.

'You're filthy,' she said.

It took me by surprise. As she spoke she turned away and hurried along to a bus-stop. I could have caught her up and gone on with the questions. But I didn't manage it. I had no real need, I would get nothing else from her, but it was more than that. I'm used to hard words, it's my trade. But 'filthy', just like that; just a quiet, ordinary word in the street, from this vulnerable girl with her pink shirt and her long yellow hair. It wasn't easy to take.

But now I did tremble for her. She would get the breaks again.[14]

It's a good moment. He asked for it. It brings us much nearer the present when a lot of people might have occasion fairly to say to journalists, in or out of politics, 'You're filthy.' The jolt sends Redfern to look at bullet-holes at the coalyard, to see the dead man's young widow, to find something important shifting deep within him, 'more than in the head, in the nerves and stomach'. The story of the two shootings, and the location of each press upon him urgently. He can hold off neither the story nor its history. The privilege of distance conferred by his standing as reporter, his mobility, the ease with which he can hire a car and drive out of those lanes on to the smooth wide expressways which circle the latitudinous globe, all these desert him. There is neither the time nor the space of detachment. Not just the hardness of the facts but of the feelings also hit him, as they say, in the face.

Williams is trying to catch something about the politics of the late and post Cold War world which only a bare handful of the super-expressive journalists, and no one else at all, have even noticed is there to be reported upon. His hero-journalist (now called by his agency, in a good joke, a consultant analyst) glimpses but cannot grasp the truth that political people are now so riven by the contradictions of things that they 'are inhabited by radically divergent potentials … their ordinary active condition is profoundly divided.'[15] All they can do is live with these divisions, and then live in and by them as circumstances either allow or demand.

It's damned hard to write political journalism answering to such conditions. The more Williams's journalist finds out the less he can do. Through a long series of clipped, hard, contained conversations, Redfern tracks Mark Evans, the big international aid agency radical, by way of his surprisingly tough young wife to an authoritative position in an underground radical movement pledged to penetrate and subvert, over many years, the old enemy of old corruption and its settled place on the commanding heights of capitalism. The movement calls itself The Volunteers.

Redfern's work and way of talking puts one in mind of the Watergate inquiries; but he is far less innocent than Bob Woodward. The range and depth, the ruthlessness and indifference to *anything* but money and power on the part of the enemy is, however, the same. As for Redfern, when *he* has to meet them, the mighty and mighty powerful head-on, he goes all awkward on himself while covering up his own discomfiture by braying unuttered abuse at them in the halls of his own mind. '*It's at the edges like these that we all learn a style.*'[16]

He talks to Evans. At length and politically. He notes the divisions, the hard, sharp, clever, impatient man, the genuine sadness at an awful, hardly improvable world ('the long sighing of the just; the mature, sad consciousness of non-intervention').[17] He is several moves ahead of Redfern. In an excellent novelistic twist, the hero is put down by the superior strength and intelligence of his quarry. Evans wrongfoots him consistently; is open where he would be expected to be shut, truthful about lying, active and radical after years of all that mature sadness. So much so that the journalist, poised to zoom in, to break lives and stories, to make secrets public, finds his so-called style, cynical, incisive, unshockable and so forth, blocked, misdirected. Old urgencies drift up from deep inside him.

He has to stop. He has to think. He even has to refuse 'the usual piquant self-disgust' as well as the self-pitying satisfaction of that 'cool ... and alienated intelligence'.[18] Evans has seen right through him anyway; he's the hard one, Redfern the clear. But Redfern knows before Evans that the political cover of the radical movement, the Volunteers, has been blown away. He warns Evans of his danger. He has rejoined the other side, the right (the wrong) side.

Evans sees this swiftly. He and his elder son, hard men both, are at bitter personal odds but still politically in sight of one another. Evans *père* gives Redfern the documents assigning responsibility for the shooting in the coalyard. Redfern finds that he, the coolly objective, reputable reporter, has agreed to present the papers at the public inquiry. He's got the full story now. It's a story of political failure and the opposition it calls out. Evans says to him in the blunt, hard way of conversations in this book: 'We are rotten with failure, all of us rotten. You must know this, you particularly.'[19] Redfern has rejoined the opposition but, as Evans tells him, not exactly as a Volunteer. 'I'd say you were more a pressed man.' Redfern finds the 'line between observer and participant, that I'd always theorised, had been turned ... effortlessly ... And not by his force, as he said. By my own momentum. By my own style.'[20]

It is an epigraph for this book. Or better, perhaps, for its last four or five chapters. The line is turned. The easy stand-off between action and involvement, subjective and objective, is held only by self-entrancement or blurred by the tears of self-pity (itself endemic). In Williams's little fable, however, radical probing and hard but empathic interpretation meld in a style. Style presses on the man. It makes him go home. Heaven knows what kind of journalism it would make him write. He's beyond that, when the story ends.

Saul Bellow's journalist or Raymond Williams's? The fictions of journalism, since, say, the Vietnam War or the Chilean coup against Allende (for the USA) and the degradation of the British miners intensified mistrust of politics, have repeatedly crossed the line between personal passion and professional action, and made permeable the separation of public and private ethics. Very rarely have these fictions found it possible to embody a style of life (let alone of writing) which would dramatise and reconcile mutual exclusions. But it is something to have recognised that change in feeling structures and in the way emotions inform events and reform experience, such that a journalist makes once again the commonplace discovery that action changes you even while you report it.

The fictional character who lives this change is as often a policeman or a doctor as a journalist. But the policeman has legal obligations of an unignorable kind, whereas the journalist, that glamorous, opaque figure, is making the call on behalf of us, ordinary people.

Ordinary, however, is as ordinary does: in extraordinary politics, the ordinary journalists can only do their best. In a decent film like *Salvador*,[21] the feckless journalist played by James Woods is already compromised by a shady past, a devout, loving but already once abandoned mistress, let alone by drunkenness and sponging. He finds in San Salvador what is always plain to see; there is American duplicity, a decent enough ambassador, a crooked anti-communist staff. He attends involuntarily the assassination of the saintly Archbishop Romero who had, in historical fact, accused his communicant government of shocking cruelties and injustice. 'American diction in this situation tends towards the studied casual, the can-do' but, as two actual ambassadors 'believed, the situation in El Salvador was bad, terrible, squalid beyond anyone's power to understand'.[22]

The James Woods character, closer by far to terror and squalor, lives in a frenzy of impromptu rescues, punctuated by brief erotic idylls. His friend and ally, an intrepid photo-journalist, is killed at the front of guerrilla fighting. Woods covers what he can, for the pay and out of a casual cynicism about American diplomacy which, even if it were published, would be of interest only to the people living their desperate lives in Central America. Honour rooted in dishonour, he tries to smuggle his mistress into California as his wife. She is turned back at the frontier. He is trapped by the style of his life, all right; his journalistic, fast-talking, kind-of-gallant American style.

The Killing Fields[23] comes from the same ethical provenance. It became more celebrated than *Salvador*, partly because the political difficulties of that country are still so unsorted, partly because its subject-matter lay so heavily on the conscience of the Americans after Nixon's and Kissinger's illicit bombing and invasion of Cambodia in 1970 caused Year Zero and the terrible slaughters by the Khmer Rouge which are at the centre of the action of the film.

Sam Waterston, towering, black-bearded, imposing as always, plays the prize-winning American journalist, Haing Ngor his Cambodian assistant, both leaving the country at the very last moment, as the Khmer approach Phnom Penh. When the assistant and the American lose touch, the movie becomes a straightforward journey into the inferno for the unhappy, courageous Cambodian by way of bamboo prison cages immersed to nostril depths in the river and house-high heaps of human skulls. Meantime the journalist does what he can with obdurate officials, social panic and acute physical danger to get his friend and colleague safely back. The story ends happily, as it did in life.

Nobody would oppose its moral stance. Journalists should stick by each other and be supported by those who entrusted them to find out and tell us what was happening in the most dangerous places on earth. There is a hint of criticism of those Americans who left allies, friends and lovers behind in Saigon in 1975, but Waterston puts all that right with his massive anxious integrity. The demands of journalistic collaboration exact the duties due to fraternity and to the blood-brotherhood of soldiery. No ethical difficulty about the public–private boundary there.

All the same, these two and many more movies play on both sides of the boundary; they largely conclude that any journalist, being human, must live the human obligations and bonds on each side of the line and at the same time. This is, I suppose, a dramatisation of the old canard that asks whether you report (or photograph) the carnage, or try to help stop it. Easy to answer, of course, if everyone is in uniform as they were in 1945; less if 'it isn't your war.' Modern political journalism, as far as movie-makers are concerned, is often about warfare and always about the untrustworthiness of governments. This is, as a convenience of narrative grip, easy to explain. It is also expressive of an epoch which saw the sensational headlines of the end of Cold War, the crowds in the squares of the capitals of communism – Prague, Warsaw, Bucharest, Budapest, the breaching of the Berlin Wall, the hideous suppression of the same hopefulness in Beijing.

So one serviceable British movie configures the dual forces of this simplified journalism: the omnipresent, distorting force of abstract power and the no less pervasive force which pushes the journalist off his or her perch and into the normal messiness of that somewhere from which a view – a view of how to live and what to do – must be found. In *Welcome to Sarajevo*[24] Stephen Dillane plays the actual ITN reporter of the Serb-Bosnian war and the 1992 siege of Sarajevo for whom reporting was at first the attempt not so much to understand the political puzzle of how on earth the war could possibly benefit the Serbs, but simply to transmit the horrific actuality of ordinary shoppers being sniped at and killed in a European city once well known to tourists and now smashed up by furious bombardment.

Some of the best – the most factual and immediate – journalism of the end of the century came out of that decade-long war; one thinks of Misha Glenny, Mark Danner, Maggie O'Kane, Martin Bell. But in spite of the books which issued from their work,[25] that journalism was largely a matter of describing military deathliness and civilian death in tones of incredulity and then reporting the inadequacy of UN or US or European efforts to win some kind of tenable settlement. The strategic commentators were left either in indifference or at a loss; the journalists on the battlefield described faithfully what they saw and summarised sceptically what they were told.

Welcome to Sarajevo silhouettes such incomprehensibility, and the rushed, reeling passage through it all of a no-more-than-normally coura-geous man. It shows us corpses, wounds, the terror of being lost under fire, the terror of being suddenly robbed, of one's money for sure, of one's life quite likely. Then, following the facts, the film abruptly closes the gap between bemused headshaking at human horribleness and the sharp pain of direct sympathy. Stephen Dillane (playing Michael Nicholson) finds an abandoned nine-year-old girl in distress, cares for her, spirits her illegally and to her joy out of the country, adopts her, makes her an extra child in his happy family. 'The great emotional crises of modern life are fought out in silence' says W. B. Yeats, and when Dillane, who does his job with a sort of clenched, impassive anguish, tells his wife in a few syllables that they are to accept this new daughter, she is just as brief and contained in response. The film approves with a full heart the breach in the dykes of professional detachment, and uncomplicated moral support gushes through from the audience.

In America there has always been a popular narrative trope in which the big organisation (rancher, corporation, state institution) threatens the brave, unaided individual. What arrives, and crosses the Atlantic, in the last quarter or so of the twentieth century is a new certainty in journalistic mythology about the corruption and mendacity of power in the state, and a new emphasis upon the truth-telling necessity of the Fourth Estate. Public opinion, that protean ghost, may be damned hard to locate in social structure and historical passage, but there is no doubting the materiality and busyness of, as they say, its providing agency, the press.

The result, I suggest, is that more and more of the films about political journalism are founded on the compelling absoluteness of established fact. It is a help to dramatic effects if the facts themselves are also celebrated (or notorious) in their factuality. Of no film about journalism has this observation been more urgent or more trite than of *All the President's Men*.[26] We know the men already; we know the book, its leadenness as well as its grip. The proposal for the movie began with Robert Redford at the offices of the *Washington Post*[27] – terrifying poor Bradlee and his fellow-editors by telling them that they would figure in the story under their very own names – introducing Bradlee to Jason Robards, due to play Bradlee with much of the original's combination of jaunty recklessness and thoroughgoing responsibility to the newspaper's reputation. Dustin Hoffman turned up in the newsroom for two weeks and proved so complete a mimic of Bernstein's voice that even Woodward was taken in. Bradlee's fourteen-year-old daughter had a star-struck dinner with Robert Redford; and Howard Simons, the *Post's* managing editor, was so affronted by the diminution of his historic role in the story that he became estranged for years from his old friend Ben Bradlee.

Simons was right to feel slighted; that's art for you. These are the things that happen when your life and its unheroic action (taking, in this case, twenty-six months to live) is pressed into the intense and dazzling frame of two and a half hours of movie magnification. Redford, Hoffman, Robards, certainly the dominant characterisations are long since superimposed in public imagination upon the features and characters of the men who did the job of discovering that the world's mightiest nation was run by a bunch of dim, foul-mouthed and paranoid gangsters. Redford and Hoffman now incarnate for the young hopeful the ideal form of the investigative journalist.

Nor does the film traduce what the true journalists actually did. It configures the long, disappointing encounters with refusal to talk and with dislike of being questioned. It dramatises the childish catechisms of verification ('hang up on me if what I say is wrong,' 'just nod if one conspirator's name begins with M or N'). It shows us, with a rare combination of prosaic fidelity and imaginative power, the fear of retribution among ordinary clerical workers and two junior journalists. It catches the ways in which all those whose work is even vaguely political have their virtues, their dutifulness and their hard work enlisted in forms of life dedicated to calculation, indirection, evasiveness and an opaque manoeuvring for a thin edge of advantage located between truth and mendacity.

The film renders this condition finely. But it is both history and genre; so it culminates in the pure American success which crowned the efforts of the *Washington Post*, vindicated the Fourth Estate as guardian of the Constitution, and turned Redford's and Hoffman's good-looking, youthful and unformed representations into Woodstein, the composite myth-hero of the political journalist, protector of the democratic faith.

It is a splendid movie, endlessly watchable. It inaugurates, moreover, an epoch in which politics on film takes the form of documentary drama. In documentary drama, the convention is that power lives in fierce tension with the threat of revelation. The journalist, like Chomsky's intellectual, threatens to disgrace power by disclosing its self-interested lies and corruption. If things are bad enough, power is dismissed, as Nixon was. Otherwise, the threat may be enough to cause power to act a bit more on our behalf and a bit less on its own.

Three movies remain to exemplify this new-old genre according to which real history, rearranged to suit box office receipts and dramatic form, is dressed in the antique authority of myth and the brief aura of glamour. The first of these is not a glamorous film at all. It is Andrzej Wajda's *Man of Iron*,[28] an almost factual, almost fictive documentary describing the occupation of the Gdansk shipyard in Poland by the sometimes legal, sometimes banned trade union Solidarnosc – Solidarity.

The film follows a well-known television journalist, afraid of and suborned by the internal security forces, as he seeks access to the shipyard, meets an old friend from his sometime radical past, and is introduced to one of the workers' leaders, Lech Walesa's lieutenant, the man of iron principle and resolution whose faithfully socialist father was shot standing up for his own picture of socialism in the desperate year of insurrection in 1970.

The journalist has the dogs of secret police at his heels. They want his access to the radicals and they want the pictures he has shot. One of their number, hard, assured, eating grossly as he bullies the hero, shows us their fearsome jaws. The iron man is not broken even though his wife is imprisoned and interrogated; she speaks her calm and lovely intrepidity to the journalist; and she is released. The journalist, small and unimpressive (the difficulty for us is to understand how he ever acquired his reputation), quavers and wavers and finally, unobtrusively, goes over to Solidarnosc, camera and all. He enters the shipyard. He films the partial victory of the union.

The moral of *that* is the reiterated necessity of the view from some-where. For a Pole, at least, but probably for any journalist,[29] the only way to tell the story of Solidarnosc was to find solidarity with *somebody*, and as long as you were safe from their attentions it could hardly have been with the secret police or their employers. If this is a truism, it picks up new vitality for the truthfulness of the documentary and its following the nervous, now cowardly now brave movement of the journalist's soul from their side back to ours where he began. He loses his job, of course, but wins an audience.

Losing one's job is a token of journalistic probity, of having chosen principle over advancement or safety; of having seen the view from some-where and counted it a vision. As with the men of the *Washington Post*, so with the story of Donald Woods, editor of South Africa's *Rand Daily Mail* in the darkest days of black opposition to apartheid in the 1970s.

In *Cry Freedom*,[30] Richard Attenborough, heir to David Lean as the only Big Picturemaker left in British cinema, takes Woods's noble story and, so to speak, elevates it into a huge sculpture in the style of English social democratic realism. It is an admirable tradition, and produces his most affecting film. But its effect depends upon our sharing its moral framework (as who could not? one asks, but is then faced by the sharks of Afrikaner intransigence). As in most of the films I am taking, the moral choice for the audience on behalf of the journalist is an easy one. Not for Donald Woods in his life, of course: he lost his job, his house, his money, his native land; he and his family were threatened, his children injured, his wife (beauti-fully played in the film by Penelope Wilton) terrified at the worst moment almost to desertion. But the drive of the film drama demands of him the stand that Donald Woods truly took. Behind him are lined up all the heroes of theatre who stand up for human dignity against the monsters of power-without-value: from Sophocles' Antigone to Arthur Miller's John Proctor, these characters will not move; they give their names. In Attenborough's film, Woods is taken from his editorial desk and raised to their eminence.

What helps to raise him up is the moral power of the black activist who becomes his friend. Steve Biko is played with Biko's own calm beauty, his courageous good humour and courtesy by Denzel Washington. His body was, in fact and in the movie (though we aren't, to our relief, shown the dreadful beating which mortally wounded him), battered to death. Unconscious and dying, Biko was put in the back of an estate wagon and driven without doctor or stretcher over 700 miles of dirt roads to Pretoria. He was dead on arrival. Kruger, the chief of police, announced on television that he died on hunger strike. A huge crowd turned out for his funeral, Woods and his wife among them. Many thousands were turned away.

Attenborough does this kind of scene splendidly. The crowd sings in slow, lovely harmony the words of the liberation anthem; Woods joins in shyly, surprising and pleasing the blacks about him by his halting knowledge of their tongue. Then the film follows him to suspension from work, to house arrest, and his escape across the border to Lesotho disguised as a priest, followed in the nick of time by his family. South African fighter planes appear as they overfly South African territory. The fighters turn away.

Telling the story of Attenborough's film is, allowing for its statuesque narrative, the same thing as telling Donald Woods's own story. But its position in this chapter – celebration apart – is intended to confirm that shift in the mythology of journalism which split open the division between professional code and human sympathy, between politics and ethics, and what is more, recast this bit of boundary transgression as morally excellent. Woods (Kevin Kline) begins the movie as the classically liberal editor who sees black protestation as incitement to violence, but hasn't yet learned either about the state's effectual monopoly of violence, or of the same state's ruthlessness with truth and with those who oppose it.

Biko taught Woods these lessons, mostly by example (this is the only glib part of the movie). Attenborough reserves the most shocking example of the state's murderous hatred for the very end of the film (released, it should be remembered, three years before Nelson Mandela). He screens another crowd scene. It is the infamous shooting down of a boisterous multitude of joyfully disobedient schoolchildren doing what all schoolchildren want to do, refusing school; on this occasion, however, in the name of black resistance. Seven hundred of them were shot dead as they ran away from policemen armed with heavy repeater rifles. It was 1977, the day before yesterday.

My last, recent example of the way movie-makers mythologise journalism will serve to emphasise the post-Watergate theme: that journalists do their duty best when they expose the lies of power, and that they do so not only in allegiance to truth but to human solidarity as well.

The Insider[31] is another dramatised documentary, telling the true story of one Jeffrey Wigand, a medical scientist and company vice-president who blew the whistle on the tobacco companies' chief executives swearing on oath that their product was not addictive, and that they didn't dose their cigarettes with additives to ensure that brand loyalty really did run in their customers' bloodstreams. Russell Crowe plays Wigand, the decent, honest but unexceptional hero who faces up to dismissal, the loss of home and marriage; Al Pacino the ex-*Ramparts* radical now producing CBS's *60 Minutes* with his rugged rock of a face avowing his integrity.

The tobacco companies threaten CBS with appalling legal costs; CBS bends before the gale; Pacino takes his story to the *New York Times*, whose editorial reproaches the network with the impregnable name of Edward R. Murrow; the scared hero sees his duty through and is voted schoolteacher of the year in his new vocation. The individual defeats the corporation, and Pacino resigns because CBS let him and his man down.

The moral is the same as that of *Sweet Smell of Success*, but with fifty years more experience on its back. The two and a half good men (the half being the CBS anchorman, heir to Cronkite) win, but lose their jobs all the same. Integrity, truth and human health win out, but only just. The antibodies of American homeopathy aren't as strong as they were. If journalists are part of the immune system of the body politic, the heavy toxins of capital have weakened them badly.

The distinction between history and myth is harder and harder to draw.

CHAPTER THIRTEEN

Rights and the Right: Difficulties with Democracy

A newspaper is not a person. Like all social institutions, however, it has aspects of human personality. In any case, the mental habit of giving individual attributes to human collectivities is so deep-seated that history would be even more unintelligible than it is without such help. All the instruments of political organisation must treat institutions and corporations as well as nations as autonomous agents. The legal system can only function by ascribing purposes and intentions to institutions; the great canopy of international order will only stay up if vast agglomerations of peoples count themselves as one will and agree, however, sullenly or haplessly, that that will be expressed by a handful of representatives.

Newspapers therefore may be spoken of as having characters and personalities. It makes sense to give them mind, intelligence, passion; to speak of their duties and conscience. It is a straightforward judgement to discern their expression of their social class membership, the way in which they speak in a voice belonging to this or that segment of society. Such a voice magnifies or parodies its segment of the audience, but it must for the very sake of circulation remain recognisable. In so far as the order of society may be thought of as democratic, the voice of a newspaper does what it does to speak up and for its corner of the people and what it wants from its rulers.

The voice of a newspaper is, however, a multiple thing – heteroglossiac, in the jargon. One listens for its most characteristic tones and inflections in its editorials, at least where the broadsheets are concerned. But even in the broadsheets, the ideal of *balance* as between different moral and political perspectives means that the readership has to do the balancing for itself, tuning in and tuning out to certain contributors until each reader, in the trifling bustle of the day, matches news and views to those feelings which count for him or her as being sane.

By this token, a newspaper helps you keep your social balance. Doing so is rather more than is expected of the entertainment business which is how Rupert Murdoch once roundly characterised the stuff he bought and sold to one of his editors he was about to fire for disagreement with such a view.[1] No doubt there are plenty of days on which even the most serious-minded and public-spirited citizen doesn't open a newspaper, and for people whose work is less a matter of words on the page or the green screen, and the pushing of the paper in either case, reading the newspaper is of correspondingly less account.

Nor is it possible to determine the quality of people's emotional or intellectual life from the quality of their daily newspaper. The papers have to guess at what their readers want, and give them something anyway. In the familiar metaphor which defines a culture – that vast tapestry of stories we tell ourselves about ourselves – as being a conversation, the voices of newspapers may be said to figure as the loudest colours rather than the pattern of the picture.

These platitudes being what they are, newspapers and news broadcasters continue to serve as the most powerful storytellers of the day. The rulers turn to them to find out what to do next; the ruled discover what will happen to them as a result. It is worth adding, moreover, that paper retains its dominance over television screen and radio airwaves. Whatever we do at the moment with the thrills of individualised electronics, broadcasters read the morning newspapers in order to decide what goes out over the air and before your eyes.

Naturally, the so-called information flow from news writing and reading to audiences of the powerful and powerless is broken and reassigned by all kinds of influences. It is probably impossible to model these,[2] although any rational critic, let alone a radical one, keeps up a healthy respect for conspiracy theory, an abiding loyalty to the poor in their losing battle with the rich, and a lively readiness to find out the injuries done by the powerful to those below them with lower status and higher principles.

In this nursery diagram of the virtues, the editor is all-important. This is so whether we mean by 'editor' the traditional figure at the head of a newspaper or the television programmer who allocates the daily content, the hierarchies and classifications of subject-matter (news, features, editorials) and decides when one moves to the other, when comedy turns into tragedy. Back in Geoffrey Dawson's day, the editor of the London *Times* was only intent on his relationship with political power. The readership trusted him to stay tuned to the governing class, and he learned by virtue of his own initiation the unbreakable protocols and styles of language which maintained that class in office.

By the time we reach Harold Evans's *Times* of London the editor has become a much more protean as well as powerful and (at the same time) precarious figure. Sometime round about 1965 when the circulation of the *Daily Mirror* hit its legendary 5 million, the class divisions of Britain began to shift. It wasn't that they became any less important or exclusive – not at all – but that their hierarchies became more nuanced, certain boundaries more porous, some entirely new social characters joined the competition. The settled allocations of heavy old labour began to disperse. By the mid-1980s, shipbuilding, coal-mining, stevedoring, iron-smelting and the manufacture of automobiles had pretty well vanished, along with those calm, confident, heavily built and blue-overalled men who constituted working-class identity. Unemployment began to rise steeply again for the first time since 1939 and its precipitate was deposited around the old industrial conurbations as the new, so-called underclass, desperately poor, members of no trade, footloose, bored, feared.

This twenty-five year transformation was further lubricated by the arrival of a smallish but unignorable crowd of black immigrants from old empire. Six in every hundred British have a variously dark skin as declaring ancestors recently departed the Indian or African continents and the Caribbean archipelago. They too were conscripted into the genteel frictions of British class struggle, while at the same time the officer class found itself invaded by some new, pushy and surprisingly senior recruits who had made a lot of money in property and banking and commodity trading, bought Georgian vicarages and Jacobean farmhouses, and barged their way through such symbolic doors of the ruling class as the Atheneum, the cricketing haven of the MCC and the Houses of Parliament.

This bit of off-the-peg sociology[3] is the context for a terse theory of the role of the editor as embodied in the impressive and moving career of Harold Evans, known to everyone as Harry. By the day he took over at *The Times* it was no longer the voice of the British ruling class. For a century or more *The Times* acted to affirm and confirm its readers' gravity and their place of responsibility where things really mattered. Reading the London *Times* counted you into the central conversation of the culture and as auditor to its power elite. It was a sign of membership for them and aspiration for you.

That this was no longer so marked out three changes: first, in the judgement of its editors about the relations of news as serious business and news as light entertainment; second, in the switch in attention on the part of proprietors, Rupert Murdoch especially, from dabbling in the business of politics like Beaverbrook and the Rothermeres to the strictly businesslike business of making money on an international scale (itself a pretty political business in any case); third, in the disappearance of Britain itself from that pedestal on the world stage beneath which *The Times* acted as its more-or-less official interpreter and genteel microphone, to a much lower stand at the edge of things with a little throng of newspapers offering to mediate government to its special corner of the class still taking an interest.

Harry Evans's career is nonetheless far more than a token of that old chestnut of Dean Acheson's, Britain's loss of an empire and misplacement of a role. It catches up the great themes of journalism: truth-telling for the public good and thereby defeating public bad hats; editorial artistry, diplomacy and ethics in the delicate balancing of a great newspaper's attitude towards a nation and then towards that nation's governing class; above all, the editor's definition of the integrity of his newspaper and of himself whether either is threatened by the costly weight of litigation brought by institutions of great wealth, by the apparatus of a government's secret services, or by a proprietor for whom the word 'promise' has no content at all.

Evans was born in 1926, first son of four of a steam engine driver from Crewe, in those days the headquarters of the railway industry in the north of England. His father moved to Manchester, where Harry grew up; he was clever and duly won his scholarship to grammar school, gaining social promotion, a degree at the University of Durham, a Harkness Fellowship studying foreign policy in Chicago and at Stanford, and going straight on to a subeditor's job at the *Manchester Evening News*. He rose like a rocket through the industry and at a mere thirty-two was appointed editor of the *Northern Echo*, 'sitting in the chair of the great nineteenth-century editor-campaigner W. T. Stead'.[4]

The *Echo*, then as now a pillar of the best kind of local British daily, was quartered in Darlington, County Durham, reporting local matters, engaged with national ones, nobody's creature, part of a brotherhood including (for instance) the *Arkansas Democratic Gazette* (with us in a moment), stitching together the stuff of communal life and the trade-winds of change. Evans began as he meant to go on, with a prominent campaign to obtain a posthumous pardon for Timothy Evans, a retarded wretch hanged for murders committed by the assured hobby-killer John

Christie. It was the moment, slowly arrived at, when the British Parliament was edging itself towards the abolition of the death penalty.

The *Northern Echo* fought a lone campaign and won. The then editor of the *Sunday Times* (Denis Hamilton), shortly to become editor-in-chief of Times Newspapers, made Evans his chief assistant and, a year later, when Evans was only thirty-seven, editor of the *Sunday Times*.

Evans was an editor with strongly intellectual leanings. The Timothy Evans campaign had been a deliberate attempt to run and build a news story out of the protracted leisureliness and recursive procedures of a powerfully personal as well as symbolic lawsuit. The police, the legislature, and the human passions each provokes and subdues have been the stuff of journalism since journals began. But they work in spurts, and the quick blaze of violent events (murder and riot) and solemn sentencing (the slammed-shut cell door, the snapped neck) are all that illuminate the tedium of defence and prosecution briefs, the principles of justice and mercy.

So Evans was devising a difficult kind of journalism in his campaign-building. Matching the abstract principle of justice to the dead against holding on to his young and old readership was a tricky and extended work of editorial art.

It became his characteristic achievement. The *Sunday Times* was a gigantic opportunity. The millionaire Roy Thomson, another Canadian press owner like Beaverbrook, this time with pebble specs and an interest in politics only so far as meeting the mighty went, touchingly foreswore interference with his editors by way of a small printed oath which he would take out of his wallet. He and Hamilton handed over the most senior organ in the British Sunday press, and Evans took it straight into campaigning investigative journalism.

His first triumph was a campaign, his second an investigation. In the first, he rode out the initially discreet, subsequently heavy-handed persuasion of the state itself in order to be first to publish the candidly personal diary memoirs of Richard Crossman, the Labour Cabinet minister who had recently died. Crossman made a virtue out of a gossipy nature and found public good in recklessness. All the same, there was no reason to array personal embarrassment in the shrouds of the D-notice, Britain's state injunction forbidding publication as inimical to security.

Evans manoeuvred assorted selections from the diaries in front of the Cabinet Secretary, who ruled on publications. Evans showed him a 'eunuch version' of one of the spicier passages. The Cabinet Secretary (Sir John Hunt), as is the way of such men, returned it after long obdurate negotiation, with Crossman's widow, with ex-journalist Michael Foot MP, who was Crossman's executor and by now (1974) himself in the Cabinet, as well as with troops of lawyers, all in attendance. Hunt stipulated that the *Sunday Times* must undertake to clear everything with him giving seven days' notice and with every likelihood that he would clear nothing and be all too ready to impose a thirty-year ban on the diaries.

Evans received this instruction on Thursday 23 January 1975. It required that the undertaking be in Hunt's hands by Monday 27 January. On Sunday 26th, the *Sunday Times* published its first, uncut extract. Thomson and Hamilton concurred. The state was duly defied.

Hunt took it mildly, asked to see subsequent extracts, was sent copiously too much material, and set conditions and deletions. Evans jigged, dodging some conditions, disobeying others, staying out of jail with sudden concessions, until finally he reached the account of the celebrated Cabinet meeting of 1966 at which the Labour government resolved to devalue sterling and necessarily cause an acute monetary crisis. When at last the *Sunday Times* was taken to court, the law was adjusted but the paper went free.

Democratic trust failed to break down after the revelations. Evans's belief in the value of informing public opinion and quickening its debate was vindicated by sales of the *Sunday Times*.

When Evans first took over at the paper, he had reorganised his staff of reporters and set aside one group for the purpose of collaborative investigation into subjects which looked promising. Evans set the 'Insight' group, with Bruce Page and Phillip Knightley[5] as key members, to pursue the always prurient, limitedly important topic of British communist spymasters, specifically Kim Philby.[6]

Whatever the high ideals of communist brotherhood which undoubtedly fired Philby at Cambridge in the late 1930s and, it may be, lent themselves to such bravery and dedication as he showed with the Special Operation Executive during the Second World War, he no less certainly betrayed to their death several hundred British, American and, if they were caught trying to defect on their own government's moral bankruptcy, Russian agents.

All British governments concealed what he had done after 1946. Evans's men found it out, in part because Hugo Young simply but studiously read the publicly open Congressional records in Washington. Philby was a KGB senior of anti-Western intelligence while being British head of anti-Soviet intelligence. Evans ran the story, D-notices were posted, the intemperate Foreign Secretary George Brown became intemperate, Philby himself offered the *Sunday Times* his memoirs.

Evans declined; damned if he'd 'reward treason',[7] not trusting Philby anyway. He called off his men, leaving them to write their book and conceding to Chapman Pincher a meal of sanctimony about Philby in the *Daily Express*. For Evans has, in spite of knowing so intimately the heavy male warmth of English ruling class clubs-and-lunches and these as providing, you might say, the bread-and-butter, kept faith with a more remote integrity, taken perhaps from his father's footplate. He saw that what was at stake in the rush to wrap up the story was 'class solidarity and inefficiency', and the exasperating and pointless secrecies of a disgraced secret service which could only be better for being less secretive.

Alan Bennett once observed that 'the trouble with treachery nowadays is that if one does want to betray one's country there is no one satisfactory to betray it to. If there were, more people would be doing it.'[8] The enormous system of lies and false crises and sexual tattle around the espionage business was kept up as much by newspapers and television as anybody, until its utter hollowness was made visible by cracking open the Berlin Wall. What the researches of the Insight team showed more than anything was that that same system was so used not to keep at bay real enemies, but to silence and mislead our people and, not incidentally, to betray some of the best of our past.

Evans brought the best out in his readership and, in enlarging it, showed that the spectre of public opinion was indeed capable of materialising once it discovered in a newspaper the materials for its own self-education and self-definition. The *Sunday Times* under Evans's editorship pursued the details of the McDonnell Douglas DC10 which crashed out of a clear sky above Orly Airport and killed 346 people. Only a pointlessly severe semantics of the adjective 'political' would keep this particular newspaper campaign out of our purview. The story forms itself out of the elements of the lying and self-protective corporation, Lloyd's underwriters and lawyers trying smoothly and desperately to silence the families of the dead with a nicely judged but unexcessive cheque, the first wavering then extinguished interest of Congress, absorbed as it was by Watergate and bored by compensation disputes, and *Sunday Times* journalists photocopying confidential documents from all the parties busy blaming one another, and spiriting them from the headquarters of the inquiry on Wilshire Boulevard in Washington.

A door-catch design on the DC10 was faulty. The corporation claimed to have corrected the design when it hadn't. The *Sunday Times* was following its story on to alien soil, was accused in court by one of the defending lawyers of being 'an evil in the way of a fair trial', being, the ineffable lawyer went on, even then under stricture from the House of Lords for effrontery towards a firm called Distillers. Only Harry Evans's faith in American fidelity towards alien rights kept his newspaper without deviation to the path of the story, its duty and a deeply gratifying victory.

McDonnell Douglas, General Dynamics, and Turkish Airlines caved in and paid up in May 1975. Evans was at last able to turn his attention back to a much longer-running story demanding stamina adjusted to exclusively British tests of obfuscation, procrastination, the protection of the wealthy, and the slow, wanton and justiceless harrowing of individuals with no money to prise out what was owing to them for hideous malfeasance on the part of omnipotent pharmaceutical companies.

In the 1960s more than 500 babies in Britain, and 7,000 others world-wide, were born with shockingly deformed, attenuated or non-existent limbs. The condition was caused, as everyone still recalls, by their mothers having been prescribed a morning sickness antidote called Thalidomide made and marketed by the giant liquor, spirits and pharmaceutical company, Distillers. Eleven years after the birth of the children, trivial sums had been offered as compensation to the distraught parents and often helpless children. Evans decided to force their plight in front of his readers and his nation. 'Publication of any material that might prejudice the legal proceedings would violate the law of contempt of court. This was why there had been silence in the press and Parliament for a decade. Everybody had forgotten about the Thalidomide children.'⁹ Evans, in a manner exemplary to his less intrepid fellow-editors, risked imprisonment and took his owners and newspaper once more to the courtroom. The orders he gave his journalists and, even more importantly, James Evans, his lawyer, was to obtain sufficient compensation for the children.

Phillip Knightley, with great persistence, won access to the documents in the case. Distillers blocked parental interviews in the press. Grudgingly, they eked out the smallest compensation they could get away with. The parents were only squeezed out niggardly sums by way of endless letter-writing, form-filling and testifying. James Evans, the lawyer, handed Harry Evans the draft of an editorial leader. In a way exceptional for a lawyer, he sketched an argument in which the law appealed to was not legal but natural. The case for compensating the children damaged by thalidomide was, he said, clinched by the absoluteness of their *moral* claim.

Harry Evans followed his namesake's advice in a strong editorial on 24 September 1972. Distillers promptly withdrew their £600,000 worth of advertising from the paper. The moral argument studiously avoided all questions of legal liability on grounds of negligence. The Attorney-General passed it. Distillers issued a writ. A Labour MP, Jack Ashley, himself deafened by an operation which went wrong, pressed questions affirming the priority of moral over legal justice in the House of Commons. The government, naturally trying at first to fend moral questions off as outside the scope of politics, for once had its moral duty thrust upon it by the House and came up with a decent cheque for the families affected by thalidomide.

Distillers remained obdurate. The *Sunday Times* published the names of their biggest shareholders in order to persuade the shareholders to instruct the board to pay up. The *Guardian* ran a quotation from the biggest such shareholder, the Legal and General assurance company, whose chief executive agreed that corporations had moral responsibilities and should act as moral agents in society. In January 1973 Distillers agreed to pay what was needed, though it took another year to do so. In an exquisite touch the Treasury proposed to tax the money to the children, but the Prime Minister had the bill covered.

Evans, being the man he was, 'could not accept the High Court's narrow view that the discussion of public affairs was always at the mercy of a single writ, issued as they are as a mere formality in the course of any serious human conflict'.[10] He set himself and his newspaper to fight the case for press freedom in such matters as far as the European Court of Human Rights, and told the Insight team to find out whether Distillers really had tested the dreadfully useful pregnancy drug as common caution would dictate.

It has to be said that it was those newspapers whose unquestioned instinct would be to defend capital and its corporations from any moral restrictions on the freedoms of money that insisted that Distillers had done all they should. The *Daily* and *Sunday Telegraph* (Sir Peregrine Worsthorne, editor and defender of the faith) said Distillers followed normal medical practice.

They hadn't, and in a protracted investigation the *Sunday Times* established that truth in the face of predictably egregious rulings by the Law Lords ('dwelling on the peculiar horror of this particular case is apt to cloud judgement'). The *Sunday Times* was finally and ringingly vindicated by the European Court as having pursued matters 'the clarification of which would seem to lie in the public interest'.

Much of a nauseatingly sanctimonious kind is spoken by newspapers of their freedoms to go anywhere and say anything. But no one can doubt that, in disclosing the actual processes of medical scruple neglected by Distillers, in forcing the moral dimension of liability ahead of legalism, and

– not least – in upholding the age-old charge against the law that its majesty is too often sluggish, inhuman, egoistic and merciless, the *Sunday Times* stood for the best the press can do in defence of a country's best ideals.

The thalidomide-Distillers case is a happily simple and prominent instance of the press acting for the people to hold together the morally necessary and the merely regulative aspects of any rule of law. That is the purest version of the function of political journalism, and since the British were not deaf to their consciences and since they were only going to pay a little into the kitty by way of the government's subvention, they eagerly bought the newspaper which was doing this good work for them.

The affair brought publicly heroic status to Evans. He deserved it. Along with the DC10 inquiry, the Philby investigation and plenty more, it also won him what was then the pinnacle post of British journalism, editorship of *The Times*. When he quit the job twelve months later, the extraordinary longevity of its standing, the calm authority of *The Times* and all its long witness to the vagaries of the British ruling class had ended more abruptly than anyone yet understands.

The sudden crumpling of a cultural and political authority is not a slight matter. *The Times* had its several pomposities and egregiousness. It was wholly conservative. It opposed reform and obstructed social improvement. It was invincibly inegalitarian. As one celebrated intellectual leftist burst out, 'I simply will not begin the day with these people in the house',[11] and one is at once sympathetic. But continuity, unshakeable self-satisfaction, a calm habit of command, moralising the defence of the way-things-should-be-done are necessary to the foundations of any society, and its leading newspaper commemorated these attributes. Besides, Evans himself had other instincts and convictions; his *Times* might have been one capable of helping Britain steer a better course through the economic storms of the last twenty years of the twentieth century than the crazily self-righteous helmswoman who did the job.

The newspaper industry was, as Harry Evans approached appointment to *The Times*, being steadily strangled by its print unions. It is a well-known and disgraceful story, however much one would habitually take the side of hired labour against the power of ownership, and of manual print-setters forced into redundancy by new technology which took their jobs and enlarged the profit of those who dismissed them. The print unions, under the old system of production, 'were effectively sub-contract[ors] of shopfloor control',[12] and they handled their contract with the crudest venality. They kept their own timesheets and pay records; many of the names on the pay sheets were false; men were paid twice over, overtime was credited with the freedom of cups of tea, long-dead individuals drew their wages, and any editorial changes caused by sudden news stories breaking were blocked at once by bargaining obstacles, and ended up at a much higher and harder price. Sudden and arbitrary strikes disrupted production so much that after Evans's departure the great *Times* itself was closed down for a year in a kind of retribution.

While Evans was still at the *Sunday Times* he learned that Rupert Murdoch was negotiating with Roy Thomson to buy all the Times newspapers. There were other bidders and Evans himself was proposing to put together a trust whose trustees could ensure press independence; it was to include national trade unions. Denis Hamilton, Evans's ally, supported Murdoch against the trust consortium. The *Guardian* was interested in a co-production deal.

It makes an intensely contorted narrative for anyone who is neither a millionaire newspaper-purchaser nor a journalist. What is plain, however, from Evans's autobiography and another half-dozen press histories,[13] is that Murdoch himself was contemptuous of the guarantees he undertook, broke promises with perfect cynicism, and kept a heavy hand on the back of his editor's neck whenever the fancy took him.

So did Northcliffe, so did Colonel McCormick and Randolph Hearst; so did Robert Maxwell. Murdoch is probably the best of that bunch, certainly the most ruthless, the most scornful of the bonds of human entailment: affection, sympathy, generosity, probity.

When it came to it, neither the unions nor the *Guardian* had the money to stay in the consortium. Other bids came in from a sea-freight mammoth called Sea Containers and from Rothermere's group, but they quickly lapsed. Murdoch was out in front. In a long interview with the board of directors, he agreed that editors would be appointed by the board as a whole, not by the owner, and would make strictly their own decisions about the editorial direction of *The Times* and *Sunday Times*. Murdoch was modest, proud of his achievements and proud of his new acquisition also, seriously aware of the place of the two great newspapers in British life, clearly loved newspaper life for itself. He was also charming in his rather saturnine way, genial, cheerful.

The deal was fixed. It left Murdoch owning Times Newspapers. The acquisition would leave him as proprietor also of the *Sun*, the *News of the World* (and large overseas holdings), clearly vulnerable to the attentions of the weak-kneed British equivalent of American anti-trust legislation, the Monopolies Commission. The Tory Minister, one John Biffen, accepted the imaginative adjustments his department effected on the figures and waved the purchase through.[14] It was, as Evans said, 'the steal of the century', but when the chapel of the National Union of Journalists at *The Times* and *Sunday Times* asked its members for substantial contributions to fight the decision in the courts, well, as one *Times* man said, 'the size of every man's soul is a little smaller than his mortgage.'[15]

Murdoch's sometime Australian and bloody-minded republicanism went rapidly through the familiar mutation required to make very rich and powerful men into enemies of the people while singing a populist chorus. He berated his editors for having 'commies' write their columns, he sacked senior subordinates in three-line letters, he never forgot a grudge or forgave an enemy. Having appointed Evans to *The Times* in 1981, he went (for a space) easy on the unions and came down hard on the twelfth editor of the two centuries of the paper's life. (Murdoch has, at the time of writing, appointed another five since then.) He badgered Evans to despise in print the newly formed Social Democratic Alliance of 1983, to disparage the monarchy, to support Mrs Thatcher in all things, especially where her actions meant redundancy in what Murdoch strongly believed was an overemployed, overstaffed, overpaid and self-deceiving political economy.

Murdoch held the beliefs of routinely right-wing economism, domestic conservatism and moral philistinism, all of which revived in such surprising combinations in Europe and North America during the 1980s. In themselves, as we shall see, they are unexceptionable enough in any longer historical perspective, however briefly repellent and rebuttable. Held, however, by the highly visible owner of *quite* so many newspapers, they proved more coercive of attention. Evans himself wondered once or twice whether Murdoch laid his manner on so thick by way of a joke – 'two kinds of politician in Africa, both chimps, only one has charisma'[16] – while being so unfaltering in pursuit of the money. Murdoch's apparent veneration of *The Times*'s special standing in English society was entirely subordinate to the profits which, he believed, followed increased space given to sport and leisure pastimes.

His politics were simple-minded, crass and vulgar. Evans headed off his desire to reduce *The Times*'s editorial position and coverage according to these qualities, and he admired Murdoch's astonishing power of accounting, holding the figures in his head, jabbing them down on an envelope.

It was 1981. Murdoch's audacious dealings in international media were, not for the last time, in peril. The neo-conservatives, so styled, were speaking with increasing confidence in Reagan's America; the President himself at his first press conference on 30 January spoke with nonchalant sincerity and his peculiar blankness of an enemy 'who would commit any crime ... lie ... [and] cheat' and whose only goal 'must be the promotion of world revolution and a one-world socialist or communist state, whichever word you want to use'.[17]

Evans dined with the dogmatic Mrs Thatcher who so admired Ronald Reagan and was so admired by Murdoch. He left his long spoon at home; Murdoch, ranting on about the economics about which, like so many businessmen, he understood so little,[18] even while following profit with an infallible gambler's nose, harried Evans to despise all liberals in or out of government.

Evans's defence against Murdoch's unrelenting pressure upon his editorial balance was his parliamentary correspondent Frank Johnson, who followed the antique drum first beaten by Disraeli when a political correspondent under the nom de plume 'Taper'. Energetic disrespect towards all those absurd enough to speak in the mother of parliaments was Johnson's method, and heavy jocosity flavoured with downright abuse his manner.

Johnson was an early sighting in Britain of the fledgling right-wingers of the press and, although Evans and his deputy Charles Douglas-Home sustained a moderate criticism of the Thatcher government, his well-known columnist Fred Emery was only one of the voices on the paper keeping it moving steadily starboard, rightwards, in the wake of what Denis Healey called 'the great she-rhino'.

Evans's end at *The Times* came, as Denis Hamilton had bet him it would, after a short twelvemonth. The tale is instructive. As the plentiful examples in newspaper history show, there have always been proprietors who expected their newspapers to express the boss's view, and who have used their ownership to further their own or their favoured candidates' political careers. Harold Evans's is the first case, however, in which an unusually intelligent and successful editor with strong political convictions and an exemplarily virtuous allegiance to journalistic freedom is put down and driven out by his proprietor's will-to-profits, by his absolute indifference to the public significance of a privately owned newspaper, and by his apparent deracination from the contexts and history of this or any other society. His significance is given by how light he travels, so if newspapers are for sale, and if buying them requires an Australian to naturalise himself an American, then he will, as Murdoch did.

Murdoch provides a more compelling illustration of the politics of newspaper baronies than the more raucous example of his contemporary, Robert Maxwell. Maxwell was cast in the role of old contemptible among press lordlinesses in that he recognised *no* limits, no limits at all, on what political mischief a rich crook can get up to. As everyone now knows, the Department of Trade and Industry, finally proving rather a long way behind their reputation,[19] concluded as early as 1971 that Maxwell was 'a bully and a domineering personality', unfit 'to exercise proper stewardship of a publicly quoted company'. On the symbolic date of 5 November 1991, Maxwell himself apparently came to a similar conclusion, although one may be sure that he was rather more embarrassed by insolvency than disgrace, when he tipped himself, all eighteen stone of him, off his yacht and into the Mediterranean.

As soon as he bought the Mirror Group in 1984, Maxwell had insisted he be authorised to sign any cheque on his sole signature. He joined Murdoch in the successful war of destruction upon the corrupt print unions, and from the start of his ownership freely plundered the pension fund of the Mirror Group's employees for ready capital to spend on various share-purchasing ventures. Many of these forages were illegal, as for example when he secretly bought Mirror Group shares in order to push their price back up. Meanwhile he used the *Daily Mirror* to print lies about the leadership of the National Union of Miners which forced the union to split during the year-long strike in 1984–5.[20] At the end of his stormy and psychopathic career, with his sons and heirs cowed and complicit, he could not pay for his borrowing; the group collapsed, taking the pensions fund down with it, and Maxwell drowned himself.[21]

Murdoch, by contrast, no less of an authoritarian and as little of a compromiser as the brigand (who never rivalled him), was strictly legal in his business dealings, but at the same time brutal and cynical. He humiliated Harry Evans so that he quit. He insisted that the paper meet a strict budget without telling his editor what it was, but fired him anyway. He issued flat edicts about the authorisation of trifling expenditures without reference to the editor.

Murdoch claimed the paper was losing too much money. Denis Hamilton, whose position in the chair of Times Newspapers helped hold Murdoch to his always elusive word, deserted. Murdoch assumed the chair. He kept up his personal fire at the editor for his purported political softness, although goodness knows *The Times* was still as solidly, old-fashionedly Tory as it was bound by its history to be. He broke his pledges to his board of directors one by one: he brought direct influence to bear on Evans and on individual journalists; he prohibited appointments made by the editor; he tried consistently, sometimes with success, to ensure that *The Times*'s American reporting worked through his own US news bureau; he originated stories, first appearing in the *Guardian*, that Evans was to go. Finally and with complete insolence towards the conditions of purchase, Murdoch moved the ownership of the two titles *The Times* and *Sunday Times* into his News International company, was again given craven approval by the minister concerned, John Biffen, and told Evans to keep quiet about the move.

He asked for Evans's resignation. At this point Evans's own story disintegrates into a flurry of those muffled, coldly bloody-minded and ultimately executive meetings-over-lunch in the best London clubs. The national directors were, of course, affronted and ineffectual, Evans's deputy sympathetic and treacherous (he succeeded to the job), Murdoch himself lethally non-committal in public ('You must ask Harold Evans. It's not for me to say anything'),[22] relentless in private. Evans resigned with a ringing last leader on editorial freedom, a well-earned public statement in front of the cameras, and a very large cheque.

Murdoch softened Evans's departure with large doses of the old oil, then decamped with both titles to the horrible Bucharest-style headquarters surrounded by razor wire down at Wapping, locked out the unions, brought in the new technology and profitability, bought out any journalists left with principles (including Robert Fisk and Hugo Young).

So it was that the thing was done and *The Times* done for.

Harry Evans went to America, became American, and rang up new success as editorial director of *US News and World Report*, of the *Daily News*, rival to Murdoch's tabloid *New York Post*, and as an optimistic historian of his new country.[23]

When Evans arrived in Reagan's America, he found a country in which the new forms of monetarist economics allied to cultural conservatism and a concomitant religious observance had found embodiment in power, in enthusiastic new journals and in the very marked, indeed dauntingly unattractive self-confidence of an elite minority now of a mind to call in question the founding fathers' originary liberalism. To be a liberal, in their vigorously no-nonsense realism, smacking its lips with relish at the thought of the reassertion of American power in the face of the commies, was pretty well to connive at the sapping of that virile and patriotic manliness which was what the Federalists' Constitution truly intended to idealise.

Newspapers and periodicals are so required by the exigencies of competition to strike postures and take up attitudes that they are, more than most forms of written or broadcast expression, prone to posturing.

The ascendancy of the Right[24] in Reagan's America was blown along by more than its fair share of these attitudes because of that law of social dynamics which exacts from each particle in the field a discharge of energy commensurate with its size. Thus the energy of each journal or broadcast channel must oppose itself to the energies of other, mutually bombarding particles if it is to survive. In this theory of the social field, the new Right must discharge new energy in order to move at all.

It is the great French sociologist, Pierre Bourdieu, who has most completely theorised the competitive market of intellectual life (including political journalism). His theory[25] gives us leverage on the cases in point. He contends that all thought, like all other activity within capitalism, is competitive. That is to say, the thinker braces himself or herself against opposition and defines a position within a field of particles, like an electronic field. Thus the recrudescence of right-wing commentary, which took its chance with the advent of a similar politics as Ronald Reagan and Mrs Thatcher came to power in 1980, followed the slipstream of energy released by their assumption of office. This change allowed those who rode that energy to carve themselves a temporary swathe of space-time, and fill it for a little with their hum and buzz. Some of these were natural scions of the Right, that is, little energy bundles who entered the competition equipped by class and money to make their charges in that direction. Others felt the latent force of the field and bent their energies at a new, amenable angle.

As it happens, we have a peculiarly candid and rather well-written account of this process by one man who bent himself in just that way and fired himself off at the new right angle. Norman Podhoretz[26] was born to a Jewish family and went, at barely seventeen, to Columbia in 1946. He was a star pupil of Lionel Trilling, himself the star teacher of English (and world) literature as the storehouse of recorded values, values which spoke up, moreover, for a classical liberalism as the one dependable home of passionately dispassionate, interestedly disinterested, non-political politics. Such literature taught the poise, maturity and sadness over human misery which forbade radical conviction and conduced to quietist domestic decencies.

In the aftermath of fascism and amid the robotic obedience of Stalinists, it wasn't a bad creed, and Podhoretz was confirmed in it by graduate study in England's Cambridge under Trilling's senior partner-competitor, F. R. Leavis, the hawk-featured opponent of pretty well everything in what he so accurately styled (in conscious periphrasis) 'technologico-Benthamite civilisation'. Podhoretz completed his compulsory military service, and joined the staff of the radical-Jewish-Trillingite monthly *Commentary* as an assistant editor. He wrote for the *New Yorker* and the *Reporter* as well; he was a bright new commentator-about-town, anti-communist perforce, but leftish in liberalism, much more political than Dr Leavis would have approved of, dedicated indeed to making a moral aesthetics, with its deeper plumbing of life's depths, stand in for politics.

What gradually happened to Podhoretz was not only that his anti-communist hatreds were deepened by what he saw as the bad faith of the fellow-travelling leftists still struggling to believe in the possibility of the coming-on-earth of the heavenly Socialist paradise, but that he also wanted to avoid the obscure decorum of a life spent in careful academic book-making. He wanted to act in public, and the only way for a writer of limited talent to do so in New York was by writing contentious political commentary.

Podhoretz acknowledges his craving for celebrity. Indeed, he published a book, which first appeared in the monthlies, frankly entitled *Making It*. Less endearingly, he sees his as an entirely merited success. Not only that. It must as a matter of form be a feature of the leftist apostate that autobiography should confirm the rightness of moving right, and that apostasy was compulsory once one had, against all odds and in spite of the dim vision of everybody else, seen the truth clearly however dark the sky. In our times, it seems, breaking ranks and making it are actions heavily seasoned with sanctimony and inordinate doses of malice.

Sanctimony is sugary and malice salty. Of the two, in journalistic gossip, which is on the whole about people the readers know as celebrities but not as acquaintances, salty is the better taste. But it is a surprise nonetheless to find Podhoretz sprinkling salt on the tail of Lillian Hellman twice in the same pages and both times about a book whose moral point even devout anti-communists could by 1979 agree with.[27] In *Scoundrel Time*, Hellman roundly condemned the scoundrels who, having once been idealistic communists and having renounced such ideals either in the name of reason or of self-advancement, named the names of others who did the same thing but kept it dark. Taking the Fifth Amendment was an always available if financially constricting choice. 'Scoundrel' seems a mild enough term for creatures, whatever their creative gifts, who named the names of others; but not for the apostate.

So Podhoretz takes in a wide arc of detestation when he stigmatises Lillian Hellman for her 'natural middle-brow audience – now swollen by the rising tide of feminists ...' and for her 'prose style – an imitation of

Hammett's imitation of Hemingway, and already so corrupted by affectation and falsity in the original that only a miracle could have rendered it capable of anything genuine at this third remove'.[28]

This was the tone of Podhoretz's monthly column in *Commentary* by the early 1970s. There he was, 'having such a good and happy time'[29] 'loathing the Soviet Union ... and the fact that its system included a hatred of Jews'[30] that he could enlarge the goodness and happiness of his time by using his column (to the great satisfaction of his publisher) to defend the increasingly indefensible state of Israel as 'one of the few democratic countries in the world and the only one in the Middle East'.[31]

Commentary became one of the two house journals of the neo-conservatives. It is placed on the spectrum of political beliefs accordingly, and Podhoretz is, in the small world of the American intelligentsia and its active sphere of influence in Washington, well known, sufficiently respectable, noisy to a degree, plaintively aspirant, offensively defensive. He is significant in these pages as standing for a political position which put on quite an air after 1979, counting itself absolved from all criticism by eventual victory in Cold War. But he tells us rather more about the importance of the toady in the politics of the last superpower.

Fifty and more years ago, the columns of such as 'Beachcomber' in the *Daily Express*[32] were placed at the bottom of the editorial pages as a kind of sump into which the political prejudices of the lower middle classes could be drained through a filter of genteel malice, snobbery and complacency. As the press came to feature more and more largely in the minds of the powerful and in the shaping of action, political gossipmongering – always pleasurable whether mischievous or sycophantic – was found to be more and more congenial. When Podhoretz published yet more of his columns as a still less attractively titled book, we hear the parasite's accents at their most repellent:

> Here, in what is for me a rare submission to the principles of affirmative action, which dictate that I should strive to achieve greater name-dropping 'diversity', I will single out Henry Kissinger and William F. Buckley Jr ... we have managed to join forces as a dissenting minority of 'heretical' intellectuals who are trying to break the virtual monopoly that the worst ideas of my ex-friends hold ... over the cultural institutions of this country.[33]

This gets it all in. Drop names just to jeer at affirmative action, but drop them all the same. Then hold on to the trousers of what was, for several years, the second most powerful suit in the world, but prove not to be a toady by pretending its occupant is a heretic and that together 'we' will beat up all those bleeding-heartthrobs who are taking the country to the dogs.

William Buckley was second in that unholy trinity of which Podhoretz claims intimate membership. Henry Kissinger, I take it, is as elephant to these field mice. They claim acquaintance across the dinner tables, no doubt, but their true position on the arc of journalistic significance is as speaking for a florid, aggressive but largely uninfluential cadre of political opinionators which cultivates *outrance* as its preferred mode of expression.

It has its direct equivalent in its mirror images of the old Left. It is no doubt true that, since 1989, the collapse of actually existing socialism and the end of Cold War, it has been increasingly difficult to assign great precision to the stand-by terms Left and Right. I. F. Stone, it will be recalled, described himself as a Marxist Jeffersonian, and in so far as the rich economies are still the battlefield of sporadic class struggle and that only the observance of a more or less Jeffersonian tabulation of rights is likely to protect the poor, the small, the old and the out-of-work, then his self-designation, like Norman Mailer's 'left-conservatism', has plenty of running in it.

Stone or Mailer, in any case, stand in a very different relation to political efficacity than do Podhoretz and Buckley. Stone did the mind-breaking labour of a journalistic genius to find and nail down the lies of government. Mailer explained to a whole generation what its crazily flamboyant, incoherent and inarticulate actions meant both in their own lives and in their nation's history.

The point and meaning of a commentator like Buckley is to reassure a wealthy, middle-aged and politically ineffectual fraction of American club-class businessmen that they have a voice at court. This is not for one moment to say that his version of American conservatism has no consequence at the heart of things. American Republicanism has had pretty long runs throughout the twentieth century and on into the twenty-first. Its main executives have been on nodding terms with Buckley and nod approvingly to hear his lucubrations. Buckley's involuntary meaning, however, is to gather up, concentrate and distil the foaming expostulations of his sympathisers into a pungent after-dinner liqueur. Kissinger at his most ruthless would never have consulted a Buckley or taken his great expectations seriously.

Buckley's main journalistic preoccupation is therefore to keep himself busy and visible: to address business dinners, to turn out 10,000 words of controversy per week, to edit his magazine, to keep a toady's touch upon the sleeve of the mighty and, among all this, to embody the good life of the handsome, wealthy, silver-haired, bronzed and cultivated Republican it is the purport of his political journalism to celebrate.

No wonder, then, that his books are sprinkled with self-congratulation, uninhibitedly quoting reviews of his own work – 'never sloppy prose', 'my book *Airborne*, such an unusual success' – sprinkling the pages with name-droppings (Reagan, Charlton Heston, Howard Hunt), and this in a book shamelessly entitled *Overdrive*[34] and giving his admirers a detailed diary of one week's overdriven overwork in which the flight never lands with a minute to spare before he takes his seat at the opera or at the table in La Caravelle.

It is a mystery how, other than by rubbing flanks in the bars and biers of the right clubs, Buckley could win endorsements from Evelyn Waugh, Murray Kempton and – ha! – Alistair Cooke.[35] When he turns to address an international episode – an unquestionably major one, the shooting down by Soviet fighters of Korean Airlines flight 007 on 31 August 1983 – this is how Buckley begins:

> After the first flush of horror American leaders began asking themselves: What were we going to do about the execution of 269 passengers, including thirty Americans, one a congressman? Some of the relevant data:
>
> From the beginning, there had been from the Soviet Union nothing but a succession of lies. The Korean aircraft had not responded to signals, the Soviets said (false). The aircraft had not obeyed instructions (false). The aircraft was obstinately headed deeper and deeper into Soviet territory (false). The Soviet plane hadn't in fact knocked it down (false). If a Soviet plane had done so, it was not acting under instructions (false).[36]

The Soviet action was, like so much of their military-political conduct throughout the Cold War, frightened and abrupt. If they had known the offending aircraft was a civil airliner that had got lost, their cruel reaction would have been not only beyond all bounds, but quite inconsistent with their policy over the several years since Brezhnev came to power. It seems likely they lost all judgement, having been prevented by its special technology from identifying the airliner correctly and believing it to be a spy-plane.

There is a journalistic battle to arbitrate in the matter of KAL 007. Buckley was writing a mere week after the event. By the time R. W. Johnson finished and published his investigations[37] it was eighteen months later and the peculiar horror of the incident had faded (the Lockerbie bombing of Pan Am 002 at Christmas 1988 burned on in the social imagination into the next century). Johnson is able to rebut each of Buckley's easy shouts of 'false'. His conclusion is as follows.[38]

The Korean pilot in question was the airline's most experienced veteran (with combat experience into the bargain). If he were simply lost, as opposed to doing a little espionage on the side for the USA, he would have had to make an incredible series of mistakes as well as explain an extraordinary sequence of misconduct.

Flying so very deep into Soviet space, his aircraft would have brought on bright avenues of electronic detection systems tracking the alien for all of its 365 miles of deviation. He would have been able to take back a map of the surveillance alert network for hundreds of miles, the lines of detectors winking on his copy like the streetlights of a great city.

This pilot scrapped his computerised flight plan, took on dangerously too much fuel, manually programmed a new flight plan, made a ten-degree mistake in course (which the two partner computers declined to identify), and switched to automatic pilot without checking that he was on course, thus breaking the most basic of civil airline regulations. Then he lied to ground control about his whereabouts, put latitude but not longitude figures into his computer, and left his cabin for *five hours* without explaining why to his officers (and they in turn had to stay mum about all these known errors). When the aircraft was hit by a Soviet rocket and flew on for twenty minutes mortally wounded, all three officers had to agree not to send out the international Mayday signal. The pilot then flew, while at an inexplicably low altitude, at speeds that might have torn the wings off his craft, and went on doing this after his plane had been hit by a rocket from a fighter that flew all around him, buzzing him with threats that he ignored for several minutes. When he did take evasive action, he also lied about his manoeuvre to ground control.

It's a baffling as well as a hideous tale. Its use by William Buckley has exemplary force, which is why I have stolen some time from hindsight in order to rebut it. His is a fine example of journalistic insincerity. There's always plenty of that about, but it is here the more repellent for working up and working off an anti-Soviet feeling clearly inextricable from something close to satisfaction when the case in hand involves the kind of not-so-sudden death dreadfully easy to imagine. There isn't a word to classify such feeling, caught between shameful pleasure and shameless self-righteousness, but it is worth mentioning that even the Brookings

Institution historian subsequently thought that 'the United States (as evidenced in bipartisan congressional expression as well as administration statements) seemed almost to welcome in the tragedy an opportunity to belabour the Soviet Union with hasty charges of savage barbarity.'[39]

It is the function of journalists like Buckley to turn up the volume of sanctimony at moments of international crisis. The fault is compounded by the man's celebrity. He becomes a virtuoso of Right-feeling passion, exaggerating its tempestuous expression, like the pianist playing Liszt, for the benefit of the audience in the dark. He enfolds their feeling and gives it gesture and flourish. This is his role; eloquently histrionic, radically dishonest, the line of such journalists stretches out to the crack of doom.

The deep difficulty of such writing is the problem of action. The prose works to keep temperatures high, sinews stiffened, eyes blazing and all that. The trouble is that nobody in the Cold War wanted it to turn hot. So however much the patriotic militarists called the nation to its colours, nobody wanted to start marching. Even during the Vietnam War, during which the *National Review* went perfervid in its bellowing of support and its hatred of the opposition, and when half a million young Americans were in uniform and the average age of the corpses was nineteen, it was hard for the zealots to close the gap between desire and action.

Historic action remained at home, where it belonged. The Vietnam War was acutely a question of action for the Vietnamese; the Americans just wanted to go home. They had a war there, too, as it happened, a bit less bloody, a good deal more urgent. This war was certainly fought with slogans, as well as with boots and knives and ropes. It was the race war, and for once the journalists could find what they craved on their doorsteps: a significant public action, one which touched the central meanings of the polity and one moreover about which all citizens wanted the news, wanted at their best to know what to think about it, knew at their worst what they thought without knowing about it.

In the condition of localised knowledge necessary to understand a family row, the man or woman you want to listen to is a local. You couldn't do better than Bob Douglas. If you still want to make your appeal to the best moment of post-Second World War optimism and change of heart, he's your man. He can stand for the mind of the South at its most steady, upright, liberal; he makes it possible, indeed, to understand how democratic liberalism remains a livable creed even after its many contradictions and its suppressed cruelties have been forced into the open.

Douglas was born in Arkansas in 1924, *not*, as he puts it, in a family of 'haters', and in any case he saw how completely the Second World War changed everything. He served on the US carrier *Essex* and was aboard the vessel while it acquired several of its fifteen battle stars, came home with the magnificent GI Bill in his pocket, went to the University of Arkansas and then joined the staff of the *Arkansas Gazette*[40] for the rest of his working life.

Arkansas was the most mildly racist of the southern states and lived out with a certain blitheness the notorious paradox that the South was, until segregation was overcome and elderly well-pensioned Republicans moved in their millions down into the sunbelt, solidly Democrat in its suffrage. It meant that when principle came to knock at the door, the southerners really had to choose between the southern party's deep-rooted attachment to its Confederate past, its historic enmity with Lincoln's victorious Republicans, and the very precepts which constituted democracy itself as at once a political system, a legal enforcement and a moral perspective.

For Bob Douglas there was no difficulty. He had seen twenty black gunners killed in the anti-fascist war on the *Essex*; his new boss and editor, Harry Cashmore, six foot two and big with it, was a mass of unfailingly liberal instincts and had a powerful, simple way with plain prose put to the task of drawing a picture of a 'new South'; the owner, J. N. Heiskell, son of a Confederate colonel, was no liberal but he kept stoutly to the word of the law. Their combination was more than enough to fire up an already high-minded young journalist with as high ideals for the conduct of his avocation.

After the landmark lawsuits, *Brown v Board of Education* in 1954 and *Boynton v Virginia* in 1960, enforcing, respectively, desegregation in school and on public transport, the Freedom Riders came to town, the 16th Street Baptist Church in Birmingham was blown up while its children were in Sunday school,[41] and young Douglas joined his editor in 'the most exciting place in the world'[42] to write out the news and editorials, on desks propped up with wooden orange crates, on behalf of freedom. The circulation fell but not their position or their prose. There were no bylines; the journalists were the newspaper.

Governor Cherry, who supported the law, gave way to Governor Faubus, who didn't. Faubus was a demagogue in something of the mould of Huey Long, had been labelled communist in the *grande peur* and now called out the National Guard to resist the law and ignore school and transport legislation. Cashmore, Douglas and the *Gazette* stood steadfast athwart the law. The site of the battle and its honours won by the schoolchildren and the *Gazette* was Little Rock High. The newspaper's switchboard was jammed with calls, a 'toxic cloud of hate' hung low over the office roof. The town's Chamber of Commerce, respectable heart of civic society, closed its door to the newspapermen. The governor himself not only backed but fronted a boycott of the *Gazette* and he told what by then was a mob drunk on racial hate, on invincible self-righteousness and on liquor, that they didn't have to obey the law. The *Gazette*'s men held the editorial line without flinching. By 1961 the battle was won in Arkansas, and the unpredictable rhythms of popular sentiment surged away along its submarine channels to boil overground again in Mississippi and Tennessee.

Governor Frank Clement of Tennessee was a straight and vociferous segregationist. In Nashville, for example, ten years after the Supreme Court's ruling on *Brown v Board of Education*, there were barely 800 black pupils in previously all-white schools.[43] Staged desegregation was dissolving into procrastination. A devout and radical black priest called Jim Lawson, who had a prison record for conscientious objection to military service and was much influenced by Gandhi's doctrine of passive disobedience, was holding classes in political activism. Its unlikely locale was the local diners. A few years before, the youthful and handsome Martin Luther King had organised a boycott of the segregated bus services in Montgomery, and his victory over the company was the first battle of the new republic. Lawson's people, carefully schooled in courteous immobility, asked the store managers in question why they, black citizens, were refused a cup of coffee at the lunch counter in a store from which they could purchase any other goods.

David Halberstam, whom we have already found a year or two later in Vietnam, had left the editorship of the *Harvard Crimson* lit with something of the same fire as brightened the face and heated the blood of Lawson's gallant militia of 124 black students. So Halberstam came to join the staff of the *Nashville Tennessean*, to hammer his own name into its 'flinty editorial integrity',[44] its character so well recognised locally that the reporters on the *Tennessean* were standardly referred to as 'nigger-lovers'.

The press in Nashville, as in Little Rock, split under simple headings but in contradictory styles down the lines of white racism and white liberalism. The *Nashville Banner* was hated by black Nashville on the excellent grounds that, under its explosively reactionary publisher Captain Jimmy Stahlman, it opposed any trivial step towards black emancipation, described anybody who pressed such a step as an outsider and black extremist, and threatened to sack any reporters found near the lunch counters at the scene of the town's biggest story.

The *Tennessean*, under the dauntless, edgy and aggressive editorship of Coleman Hanwell, reported all the news with plain, uncomfortable fidelity.

Hanwell, Halberstam tells us, understood 'as few editors in the South did at the time, the transcending nature of this one story', and Halberstam, Northerner come South to make his name rather than his fortune as *the* journalist of the struggle, was assigned as principal reporter on the story.

So he was there, at the front of the small throng of local people one sunny summer morning on the courthouse steps in 1960, when Diane Nash caught Ben West the mayor just sufficiently off-balance to tip him into ending lunch-counter segregation. Mayor West was a decent enough liberal trying, as was his duty, to sail before every political wind no matter from which quarter it blew. He should have been an ally of the *Tennessean* but, by some old accident of local history nothing to do with the great issue of the day, had fallen out with it. The *Tennessean* harried him and the *Banner* bullied him and once he had joined the two departure lines at the airport into one, he left racial emancipation to make its own way without requiring anything very much from his office.

So he did what all politicians do when faced by irreconcilable conflict and set up a committee to deplore and debate it. During its ruminations a leading black lawyer in Nashville, Alexander Looby, an active supporter of lunch-countering, had his sleep violently interrupted one morning at 5.30 when a large bomb was tossed through his front window. It blew apart his house and blew out all the windows of the training hospital across the road. Astonishingly, Looby and his wife came out unhurt.

Halberstam was out on the street as soon as he heard the news. The protesters were well ahead of him. They already had a meeting called for six o'clock in the morning. The meeting resolved to march to the courthouse, in silence. The bomb went off too late to catch the local dailies. The protesters had to hope for the best as to calling out their small number of the faithful, the large body of the sympathetic.

They needn't have worried. By the time Halberstam found the march and followed it to the courthouse, there were 4,000 rather than the usual 400. The crowd sang 'We shall overcome'. The mayor came out to speak to the crowd with no better idea than to soothe and disperse it. Diane Nash, sometime beauty queen and, at twenty-one, diffident, convinced, brave, already arrested, fingerprinted, bailed, pressed the mayor to turn a platitude into a precept.

'Little lady,' the mayor answered, 'I stopped segregation seven years ago at the airport when I first took office, and there has been no trouble there since.' That, he thought, should end it.

But she was too nimble for him. She had one more question. 'Then, Mayor, do you recommend that the lunch counters be desegregated?'

'Yes,' he found himself saying. She had ambushed him morally.[45]

Halberstam stood a few paces away, scribbling it all down. The *Tennessean's* banner headline read 'Integrate Counters – Mayor'.[46] Halberstam's report on the bombing and the march conformed, without byline, to the house style. The newspaper told the story and allowed the facts to settle into their own order. Objectively as one might say; at least unless you read the *Banner*.

There was still a fearful road ahead of the Freedom Riders, the Civil Righters, the Black Movement. Mississippi would burn its own heart, and Alabama would kill Sunday schoolgirls, but those two newspapers in Arkansas and Tennessee serve to remind us, like Harold Evans's *Northern Echo*, of the truism that moral issues which look easy from a long way off take plenty of nerve closer up; that locally is where all of us, except an extremely peculiar and unappetising class of the international elite, live; that the local paper is an archive of our local memory and that, whether it stands on the right or the wrong side, it speaks the words which bind a habitation and its name to its values. Once the *Tennessean* ran its headline, the mayor was held to it. An utterance became an action. Among all the expressions of print, and after all the reservations about the effects of media have been made, newspapers cause things to happen, for good and ill.

To matter in that way, David Halberstam simply had to report what he saw and heard in the plainest possible idiom. There was no gap between him, his newspaper and the readership. This could only be true for the local journalist. If you wanted to close the gap between yourself and the action, event and reader, then as the century turned, a clutch of journalists turned themselves out of doors and into the kind of adventurer James Fenton or Norman Mailer had to become. They had to find the immediacy of things by looking over the shoulders and under the feet of those whose mere presence defines an event as news. Rather than news, they made personal experience into history.

It was Tom Wolfe who, as is now well known, first spotted and configured this different way of writing journalism, then duly canonised it, with himself squarely at its centre as its first evangelist, in *The New Journalism*.

For rising thirty years since it first came out in 1973 the anthology has served as a textbook for journalism courses. Allowing for the delirious self-congratulation of its editor, it also characterises with some subtlety what Wolfe hails as a quite new kind of novelistic reportage, every bit as experimental as the heroes of modernism in the novel, much more actual and vivid than that kind of political journalism practised by the 'paralysing snoremonger' Walter Lippmann who:

> for 35 years seemed to do nothing more than ingest the *Times* every morning, turn it over in his ponderous cud for a few days, and then methodically egest in the form of a drop of mush on the foreheads of several hundred thousand readers of other newspapers in the days thereafter.[47]

Wolfe, entranced by his own examples of his own prose, tells us how to write in this unprecedented way, with lots of new words and onomatopoeia ('Varoom! Varoom!'), lots of screamers, lots of crazy unstoppable torrential no-punctuation *sexy* metaphors ('thrust bras stretch pants honeydew bottoms eclair shanks flaming little buds'). To these high-pitched pyrotechnics, he adds a deadly knowingness (you'll never catch *him* out taking a seat he might have to pay for) allied to a coarse preference for injuring those who won't answer back, while hiding behind those who will. His is the politics, one might say, of the jeerer from a safe distance (his essay *Radical Chic*, for instance) or of the fearsomely eloquent, funny, dandily dressed (that white suit! that fedora!) old-fashioned coward.

He fairly sears an image in your imagination, amused, amusing, outrageous of course (this from his novel *A Man in Full*): 'She wore some sort of go-to-hell white pants that were very floppy in the legs but exceptionally tight in the crotch. *Exceptionally!* There was an astonishing crevice.'[48]

But Wolfe is only serious about never being serious, except, of course, by way of keeping up his never-expressed, rigidly kept prejudice in favour of himself and his neo-conservative hedonism. He does, however, give credit where credit is due – not to Norman Mailer whom he pretends is a rival, but to Joan Didion.

Didion is the heroic traveller-journalist of the last thirty political years. She was born in California, in San Romera in 1934 where her father was in the US Air Force. So the Pacific is Joan Didion's stretch of wide water and it holds her. She is pulled out towards Hawaii, beyond the Frontier, the last state of the West and the first stage of the archipelago which leads into the East. She travels down the seaboard to the wretched semi-states of the countries that live at the edge of her country's enormous and casual wealth. Her imagination works in the dense heat and thick air of Honolulu, Guam,

San Salvador, Los Angeles – Melanesian and Spanish names. When she goes to Miami she finds a Hispanic and Caribbean city, a city mirroring the form and structure of cities the other side of the equator, gleaming obsidian skyscrapers holding in their cool wealth, the mad rout of the poor in the stinking streets behind.

The battle honours of the epoch look a long way from these hot gates; but here too the busyness of paying for politics, losing money, hating communism went avidly forward, leaving eyeless corpses rotting on tips and cars burned out black beside the road; equipping countless hard-faced young men with M-16s, and giving dark and beautiful women seated at glossy dining tables their plump fervour, their creamy dresses and heavy gold bangles.

The modern political artist works in such images – corpse dump and dinner tables – and the resulting journalism searches out a politics to connect the two. The puzzle is, once again, to measure the gap between minute, pleasurably subtle observation, which she is so good at, and the content and meaning of action. For Tom Wolfe, the observation of behaviour, restoring flagrancy to the unmentionable, is all there is; political meaning is then assigned by habit. For Didion, the almost physical difficulty (she is a very shy woman) is to detect what is being *done*. Standing in the dark, anxious to discover how in her nation public figures might lead worthy lives one could admire and even emulate, Joan Didion has to feel with her fingertips for what she can find.

The exiguous task she sets herself and, by implication, the political journalist is to follow little flames of belief and conviction and see how they fire up individual or collective conduct. It is to seek out the secret allegiances of lives lived in a glare of publicity, and to feel the heavy weight of such big, blunt and disobliging words as Democracy or Success as they press upon and split open the little creatures so effortfully carrying them about.

Thus, in her novel *Democracy*,[49] she finds the shreds of the master-value in the mean lives of the rich and successful family in which the father just misses the Democratic nomination for President and the grandfather murders his daughter. The subject of the novel, the victim of Democracy, is the chasm in the heroine's life between her vivid hope for 'eccentricity … secretiveness … emotional solitude'[50] and an everyday routine made up of photo-opportunities. It sounds like a cliché: public figures lack private lives; the yellow press drools over this banality every day. Didion notices how certain individuals check out of public vision to make what settlement they can – it isn't much, it's all a human has – a lover seen ten times in ten years, and once or twice, a seat on the 747 flight from Honolulu to Hong

Kong leaving at 03.45, 'exactly the way she hoped dying would be, dawn all the way'.[51]

Joan Didion married the writer John Gregory Dunne in 1964, published a couple of novels, *Run River* and *Play It As It Lays*, which did passably well, while she and her husband took any assignment which came up. The Vietnam War was the big story, and Dunne returned from a visit on behalf of *Time* convinced the war wasn't winnable. Didion, she says, went on thinking like many people and for a long time that the war was all just part of the responsibility of being a great power, 'that a border war was better than World War III. Until one morning in 1968 it came in a flash as if I'd been asleep all that time that stuff just didn't add up, that everybody was lying.'[52]

Joan Didion amply discharges the poet's duty as an unacknowledged legislator, counts as her jursidiction the whole American continent, in particular where English and Hispanic voices, bodies and bank accounts meet and mingle. She went to a film festival in Colombia, where films cannot be wilder than life, and began to wonder how on earth the North and South of the continent had gone such different ways. The subject she was looking for found form in certain private lives lived in Central America; it was impelled by the North American soldiers, industrial plant and dollar bills in every local capital going south and west. She wrote her way to the frontier, until west turned to east, and her flights were called to land in Jakarta, Bien Hoa, Singapore, Guam.

No writer can write out the long connections which give shape to that dim omnipresence of a potential subject. She has to find an image or two. For Didion (as for Hunter Thompson, who was on board), it was the image of the giant green helicopter lifting off the roof of the American embassy in Saigon in 1975.

The helicopter took its place beside the rich, slightly two-faced people in Honolulu she was interested in; while listening to their dinner-table chat, while reading a few of the government's official policy statements, while lost in mean streets in San Salvador, 'it came to me it was all about *contracts*'. Behind political action gleam and wink the contracts, miniature and potent as transistors. Human purposes are quite obscure and transitory; contracts, however, have direct consequences.

Joan Didion alights on the gap between love and politics. She doesn't even want to talk politics, not because it is unimportant but because the political conversation of mankind so garbles the facts and is so fixed and false a set of exchanges that there is no point of entry or point in making an entry. 'Things that might or might not be true get repeated in the clips until you can't tell the difference,'[53] her heroine of *Democracy* says.

So Joan Didion flies from one horrible spot to another, not at all looking *for* something, but looking at things, appalling things, for which, repressing her shudder by an act of will, she has braced her frail body and terse speech.

She speaks in a true American voice which is also all her own. 'All a poet can do today is warn': completely unlike Saul Bellow and his florid, garrulous, Dickensian prose, she too reports that there is no speech in which to report the beastliness of men to men and women or an incredulous tone adequate to the monumentality of American self-deception.

She goes to Salvador and finds her image. It is a body-dump. 'Terror is the given of the place', and so she goes to the Puerta del Diablo to look at the numb aftermath of terror:

> bodies … often broken into unnatural positions and the faces to which the bodies are attached (when they are attached) … equally unnatural, sometimes unrecognisable as human faces, obliterated by acid or beaten to a mash of misplaced ears and teeth or slashed ear to ear and invaded by insects.[54]

She holds horror in place by the tight-lipped reticence of a style which assigns its author, like all good styles, a moral position in a political world. At the Puerta del Diablo she finds a man teaching a woman to drive a Toyota pick-up along the very rim of the steep and dreadful tip. Three children were with them, playing in the grass above the vertiginous cliff littered with 'pecked and maggoty masks of flesh, bone, hair'. The fear of the Left drives American action in Salvador, the magnetism of the contracts heats the blood of the Salvadorians. Boredom, as anywhere, is dissolved by violence.

Salvador could not be such an unspeakable place without hearty and lavish American efforts to make it resemble the best of Miami. Her sense of this discrepancy puts acute strain on Joan Didion's manner, both her physical presence and the presence of her prose. She was in Salvador in 1982 and she reports faithfully 'the mechanism of terror' which held her tight in its grip while she walked carefully and courageously about, Conrad's *Heart of Darkness* in her pocket. At the same time, alongside terror in a car casually boxed in by expressionless toughs armed with G-3s ('I studied my hands') or terror in the dark beyond a porch with a candlelit dinner table, she quotes the unyielding cheeriness, 'the studiedly casual, can-do, sheer cool' of US statements about this awful place.

'There are no issues here,' a smart Salvadorian told her, 'only ambitions,'[55] and that seemed about right to her. If you dropped the usual political analysis – leftist, rightist – and you saw American or Russian weapons in the hands of state killers as part of the intricate machinery of terror, then you can only conclude that a shopping mall like the image of an oasis, crammed with gilt goodies and bright bathing towels, is hardly a rampart against communism. If you also concluded, as Joan Didion did in 1982 after a visit to the San Salvador morgue (easily arranged, the door stands open), that life there was untranslatable into Washington's language, then you'd have to look out for a quite new story with which to understand the third world, and its old facts of filth and murder.

Faced with Ronald Reagan's or John Kennedy's tall tales, Joan Didion turns to open contempt. She went to Miami, capital of Cuban Florida, in 1985 and 1986. I would say she went to add substance to her horrified sense of the *irrelevance* – the entire lack of purchase – on the part of received wisdom, received facts and received ambassadors to the nightmare life-in-death of Central America, to the pratings about democracy and elections, the busy plotting of the Left.

She found substance, as always, in images. She found it in 'the waking dream' of the city, where José 'Coca-Cola' Yero is arrested in charge of a posh boat called *The Connection,* 1,664 pounds weight of unrefined cocaine, two Lamborghinis and a million-six dollars in cash. She found substance in the young woman, four of whose toes are blown off when a bomb goes off under her accelerator. The sheriff's office says to the local paper and says pertinently, 'she definitely knows someone is trying to kill her. She knew they were coming, but she didn't know when.'[56]

Somewhere at the back of that story is the good sound of the author's laughter. But these are the bits and pieces of inner-urban American life, and not vignettes of ideological conflict. What sends Miami mad and red-eyed, both among the harbour drug-and-gun dealers and the jewelled, white-suited rich in the Omni hotel, is Castro's Cuba first, and gringo perfidy about Cuba second.

Kennedy had promised to help, had accepted the flag, and then had failed them at Cochinos Bay; twenty-five years later, Reagan had sincerely mouthed the lines written for him, 'We cannot have the United States walk away from one of the greatest moral challenges in postwar history.' In between, the Miami Cubans had plotted and bought weapons, from time to time murdered one another, and lived the life of nationalist exiles, forever drafted in a war forever on the edge of starting.

Virtually every sentient member of the Miami exile community was on any given day engaged in what was called an 'ideological confrontation' with some other member of the Miami exile community, over points which were passionately debated at meals and on the radio and in the *periodiquitos*, the throwaway newspapers which appeared every week on Southwest Eighth Street. Everything was read.[57]

Incomprehensible to national American politics, 'where political positions were understood as marginally different approaches to what was seen as a shared goal', the ideological finessing was and is part of the preparation to enter the moment of political redemption in a purified and vigorous state. It is a typical discipline of redemptive politics and if, as became horribly clear in Manhattan on 11 September 2001, these are unending, we had better know what to do about such acolytes.

What Joan Didion found were well-dressed, well-read citizens with overseas interests and the conviction that they had been traduced by seven administrations, which had manoeuvred Cuba and Miami in and out of world and Washington policy for strictly Presidential ends. Thinking the Miami Cubans right, liking them rather 'in spite of their tendency to bomb one another', leaves Joan Didion as a voice calling softly from somewhere on the road, while despising American politics and politicians, and reporting in her tense, laconic voice the appalling facts and the appalling people, with nothing much to bet on except a few exiguous truths, and her tenacious scepticism.

It is in *Miami* and *Democracy* and in a long meditation on Washington[58] that she adumbrates a bitten-off sort of theory of postmodern politics. The world boils and seethes, and the Presidential team organises world media attention around 'issues' and this or that 'focus', first putting something front and centre, so that it is much-mentioned, then pulling it back when people have had enough. In Miami or Los Angeles it may be that the right people will also step forward to dance to their tune when it is played, but then again maybe not. A good President, played by rather than playing to the orchestra of issues and ethnicities, gives everyone a dance, sufficiently on cue.

She is driest, tersest of all the 'new journalists', in the essays on Washington. Things are falling apart all right, she says grimly, 'but not as fast as I once thought'. She treats the pretensions of the Reagan White House with her usual inexplicit derision, letting the feeling gather unnamed around the preposterous quotations. She detected in these rich people a new and horrible elite, entirely confident about their running of the world, 'devoid of social responsibilities precisely because their ties to any one place had been so attenuated'.[59]

Once in a while she covers the main story like all the other journalists. She follows a Presidential campaign and looks down into the abyss which separates all these breezily self-confident men and women setting up the daily spectacle, and the actual messy life being led by everybody else. The assumption made by the busy men and women is that the Presidential story 'should be not just written only by its own specialists but also legible only to its own specialists'.[60] It is this voluntary amputation which separates them from the citizens and opens an abyss the features of which fissure every one of the wealthy nations. (In poorer nations the boundary is marked out by truncheons and rubber bullets.) Campaign success, as Joan Didion was one of the first to notice, is achieved by 'inventing a public narrative based at no point on observable reality',[61] and by persuading a bare sufficiency of the electorate to march to the drum of old loyalty and public duty.

In a glimpse of another politics she sees Senator Jesse Jackson, handsome leader of black America, chuck his necktie into a cheering crowd. There was another story somewhere there, indiscernible but 'because … grounded in the recognisable' exuding 'a powerful glamour for those estranged from the purposeful nostalgia of the traditional narrative'.[62]

Theorists of contemporary democracy call mournfully and without conviction for the restoration of civil society and the re-creation of a public narrative capable of sustaining it.[63] Joan Didion's bleak achievement is to have written a political journalism-become-art which shows so vividly how empty of plot and vicious of circumstance are the insubstantial pageants currently staged in a masquerade of active democratic politics. No one can figure out the remainder: the filth, the broken syringes, the dead babies and living skeletons, the young men schooled to mass murder and their own suicide.

CHAPTER FOURTEEN

Fame is the Spur:
News without History since 1989

'Literature is news that *stays* news,' wrote Ezra Pound. Political journalism has hopes that its news may be turned into literature. The political journalist, in other words, builds a life out of an avocation and a way of writing out of the house style, a handful of well-known examples, a body of professional precepts, and such an ear for prose as nature may have provided and an apprenticeship may have taught. The political journalist has to fashion enough consistency of vision to be able to tell a story which will hold up day by day. The strong tradition of the trade is such that politics still gives off a glow of seriousness; hence those who practise it can keep the brutality of a Maxwell and the cynicism of a Murdoch at bay. That same tradition also binds together practical method and personal virtues. The French journalist and Nobel prizewinning philosopher–journalist Albert Camus remarked in his book *The Fall*, 'When you have no character, it's necessary to give yourself a method.'

The method of this or that political journalist depends, as we have seen, on the tasks set by the editor, on the moral style of the newspaper in hand, on the pressures of the competition and the cultivation of the readership, on the happiness or otherwise of historical opportunity and the size of the story of the day. With a few gifts of their own, the honest journalists make themselves a method out of these bits and pieces. Add to them a few trade mottoes about hunting down the facts, the stupidity of those in power and their predictable predilection for concealment and lying, some old truths about natural resentment in the face of bullying and mendacity, and it is encouraging to see how methodicality may conduce to virtue, and how tradition and its duties may turn a byline into a character.

This has been my theme. Since 1919 inaugurated the century of political spectacle, the big sights of that history have been projected on to vast screens for everyone to see, and even the mere words of the epoch have been read and circulated to millions at high speed and in simple headlines.

Learning what sort of person to be in these circumstances has been a process much influenced by fame, and social systems have responded to high spectacularity by placing great authority in appearances. Fame is the aura of familiarity which radiates around the wholly inaccessible representation of the celebrity. We know who they are but we cannot reach them. (One reason why people try to touch the famous person is to overcome this lack. But even if they manage it, the touch can only disappoint.) The practice of politics in the era of political spectacle – from the rallies of fascist or communist dictators to the confetti-covered nominations of presidential candidates – has been to dramatise its ideas in a show of symbolism. The everyday conversation of politics, conducted with politicians on television and in newspaper reports, caught in the newsreels of Pathé Pictorial or Movietone news, fixed in the imagery of *Life* or *Picture Post*, is interpreted for us as a clash of high ideals, a comic or tragic 'constellation of enshrined ideas'.

The phrase belongs to Clifford Geertz, and Geertz contends that *any* politics is best understood as the dramatic symbolisation of its dominant ideas. The symbolism, on this account, is not a system of deception whereby the mighty dazzle the oppressed, or a stage contraption with which 'to clothe the engines of privilege in the rags of virtue': 'The dramas of the theatre-state, mimetic of themselves, were, in the end, neither illusions nor lies, neither sleight-of-hand nor make-believe. They were what there was.'[1]

The subject-matter of political journalists is the meaning of this symbolism, and their calling is to interpret it faithfully and critically. Given that the politics of the world framed by the several ends of empire scattered between 1919 and 1989 was made so internationally visible and audible by masses of people watching and reading mass media, the journalists, it seems, are as much makers of history as the great dictators and masters of ceremonies.

The whole form of life which moves across the world stage in the character of the journalist involves a great deal more, therefore, than the revelation of lies and the telling of the truth, however central to all dramas these slices of action may be. The dignity of the man and, more latterly, the woman of letters attaches itself also to the political journalist. History men and history women therefore cut a bit of a figure, nothing loath. However much it remains the case, as Weber told us at the outset of these chronicles, that the journalist is glimpsed by the readers with one dropping and one auspicious eye, the auspices and their rewards have steadily mounted as the years wind on. Journalists may now win enormous celebrity and corresponding salaries. Inasmuch as the popular narratives of the job teach its newest recruits and undergraduates how to live, then those narratives fairly shine with fame and money. Fame spurs them onwards; money may console them; each is in thrall to the master symbols of the day. The journalist must serve and serve up the official ideals of democracy: success, say; attractiveness, niceness, resourcefulness; integrity, independence of mind, softness of heart, and so forth. Intelligence, even; candour ...

There is a limited number of ways in which the contemporary journalist may present and respect these values in the symbolic biography of a career. It has been the point of this book to enumerate some of these, and to tell their story as capable of animating emulation in journalists to come. A journalist, like anybody else, has to combine opportunity and disposition as convincingly as possible. To work for the BBC in the time of a just war is a happy chance; at such a time you certainly should be able to stand up for modest courage and a decent society in calm prose speaking of both; if you can't, journalism isn't for you. To be a reporter in pursuit of sexual self-indulgence in the private life of public persons is rather less likely to give you a chance to test the principles of your nation's history in action, and you may have to conceal this weakness with a lot of rhetorical hoo-ha.

The political journalist is split between the commands of ideology on the one side and the belittlings of pragmatism on the other. Big ideas and value-names call imperiously for attention; soluble difficulties beckon in the corner of one's eye. The historical epochs from 1919, by way of many small wars, one big one and a cold one, offered themselves for analysis in terms of the grand ideas of the metropoles. Journalists as different as Orwell and Murrow in world war, Neil Sheehan or Jonathan Schell in Vietnam, could invoke Lion and Unicorn and Constitution without the music going flat. A smaller corner of history, like the misery of deformed children or the cruelties of unemployment, calls out different allegiances and another way of telling. Harold Evans, for instance, made with his journalists' help a simple appeal for moral justice on behalf of the children damaged by thalidomide; Seamus Milne found out that the *Daily Mirror* had slandered its own people, the coal miners, during the British strike.[2]

These are the two ways of writing political journalism: the necessary flourish of ideas, the slow struggle for achievable improvement. Neither seems to be of much importance to the moguls of media, but saying so merely identifies a standing contradiction in the structure of public communication. Newspapers and news broadcasting deal in the commodity form of audiences; they sell readership to advertisers. They are also and at the same time instruments in the formation of the political will, and teachers of a nation about its own condition.

To learn to be a good political journalist is, therefore, to learn that ideas and values are at the behest of intelligent human beings, not the other way round. The most shocking events of the past hundred years were caused, one could readily say, by giving ideas their head so that those who did so went off theirs. The history of journalism is not very encouraging in this respect. Let us say that political journalism is at its most respectable when it turns ideas into instruments to think well and with, and criticises politicians pungently and openly for using ideas instead to madden a species with their power.

Thus far, so trite. There are not, however, so many ways of doing this. The last clutch of our biographies suggests how, in the aftermath of the ideological cacophony which filled the airwaves during Cold War, the political journalist does what he or she can to turn ideas to human benefit; to shape a plausible narrative history out of the shapelessness left by the deflation of ideologies and the uncomprehended shadow of terrorism; to give a speaking part to inhabitants of local history who had too frequently been marched to their destiny by catchwords; and to do all this in a decent prose. English needs to be kept up, and with the daily prints so copious the task is these days as much in the hands of the journalists as of the authors of formal literature.

No doubt that has been true since the invention of the public sphere in the eighteenth century. The information revolution began with the coming of the book, and the loud, bitter conflicts of the nineteenth century over the ownership and legality of the free press subsequently set in motion an argument, quickly gathering itself into a tradition of critical thought, in which the honest and outspoken journalist is driven by his or her principles of labour to oppose employers (let alone the readership) whenever they try to dictate what the staff should say.

Habermas remarks[3] that the classical defence of the Fourth Estate against old power politics is, precisely, that the free press keeps debate open, opportunity mobile and freedom of thought in sufficient health. The trouble is that as the press and the broadcasting technologies are more and more concentrated in increasingly few pairs of hands, then the great viziers of ownership make appeal to liberal freedoms in order to accrue to themselves the power believed to flow from public media privately administered.

The moral of this last chapterful of true parable-biographies is that nonetheless neither the owners nor those holding official power have things all their own way. No doubt the rise of the million-dollar anchor-person has done much, as Walter Cronkite said, to pull the individual concerned away from the ordinary life which is truly subject and object of the news. It is damned hard to keep active faith in democratic systems and with working lives if you live the removed, intense, madly luxurious and crazily overworking schedule of celebrity journalism.

Much sanctimony is spent by the journalists themselves on the topic. For reasons we shall touch upon, 'scandal politics is the weapon of choice for struggle and competition in informational politics',[4] and such scandals, starting from the Watergate burglary, turn upon the tight knot of interest where sex, money and the hoarding of power are twisted together. All the same, it is worth pointing out that when journalists are set, like Jack Burden in *All the King's Men*, to dish the dirt – 'there's always something' – to find out exactly who is on the take and who is giving it out, they are themselves hardly ascetic in the rewards to which they consider themselves entitled. In a conscientious blowing of the gaff on family secrets, Nick Cohen runs through a brief list of salaries in journalism by way of indicating what a very long way from the readership its stout defenders live.[5]

The figures quickly date, no doubt, and rise on an elevator of share options, luscious perquisites and other ways the rich have of concealing and congealing wealth. All the same, it is a pleasure to learn that, in Britain, at the turn of the millennium, Paul Dacre, the then editor of the *Daily Mail*, protector of the class faith of millions of small home-owners and put-upon screen-operators, was paid £637,000 apart from chauffeur-driven car and company credit card, while the doughty editor of the *Evening Standard*, Max Hastings, bore up under a mere £400,000 per year. The best-known gossip columnist of the day, Richard Littlejohn, went to Murdoch's Sky TV for £800,000 in 1997, while it is, as we know, the television interrogators who really get paid the celestial sums. In Cohen's report, the estimates of BBC contracts for such as Kirsty Wark and Jeremy Paxman stand at 'between £750,000 and one million' while for a limited number of appearances on the circuits of political chat-show-with-audience-participation, David Dimbleby is paid £300,000 a year. Dimbleby, eldest son of the earliest master of BBC political anchoring, was for many years owner of a large number of local newspapers. Rather callously, Cohen adds that the sports editor of the *Richmond and Twickenham Times*, which Dimbleby owned, was paid £7,800 in the year 2000, a rate well below the official poverty line and the minimum wage.

Hiding in these cursory figures is something important which Cohen puts down to the 'Murdochian system' or, more generally, what has been described by Edward Luttwak as turbo-capitalism.[6] For such a system, cutting the staff, stepping up the hours, breaking the unions and marketing the product ruthlessly, together constitute the dynamics of manufacture. Such an economics began to declare itself on either side of the Atlantic round about 1980, and was incarnated by the three giants of its underworld, Ronald Reagan, Margaret Thatcher and Helmut Kohl. In journalism, the tide of money flows only across the executive and celebrity floors. There is a close, inevitably financial sympathy between owners, editors, stars; their business is selling the channel or the paper to the audience. They will only retain their rewards by holding down all other costs and pushing up, by any means possible, the numbers of those who will watch or read.

Once the celebrities lose ratings, they sink traceless. As long as the smell of success sweetly pervades things, editors, anchors and owners can dine together.

It is an old image of the capitalist enemy on the Left. But it keeps its force. Cohen concentrates his argument in a rich old English anecdote.

At the 1997 Labour Party conference [just after the party won its biggest ever election victory] Prime Minister Blair was being lunched by the *Daily Mirror*. The conversation turned to Gordon Brown's decision to freeze the pay of his Cabinet colleagues. Piers Morgan [editor of the *Mirror*], who was probably earning three times as much as the Prime Minister, found the differential hilarious. He chucked a £20 note on the table and bellowed, 'Here, Tony, buy the kids some toys.' The note lay on the table. Silence descended. It takes a man of extraordinary crassness to bring out the hidden nobility of Alistair Campbell [the Prime Minister's Press Secretary]. Morgan was that man. Campbell picked up the crumpled offering and straightened it out. 'Why don't you give it to charity, Piers?' he asked quietly.[7]

In Britain and America – and across Western Europe as well – social class has become more simply measured by money over the past fifty years. I cannot doubt that in so far as journalism, in print or on television, still answers to its duties to inform public opinion and shape popular sentiment in the name of reason and virtue, then present wage levels will tend to cut its few beneficiaries off from discharging those duties well. Gross inequality is bad for human sympathy; lots of money sedates the imagination and renders inaccessible the lived experience on the other side of the cash. Tom Wolfe and P. J. O'Rourke would hoot, like Piers Morgan, with heartless mirth at such pieties. There are times, however, when the laugh is on the laughing.

'Political democracy,' Castells says roundly, 'as conceived by the liberal revolution of the eighteenth century, has become an empty shell.'[8] States, he claims, are becoming fragmentary; power is moving upwards in the direction of transnational federations and life interests are coalescing downwards in the direction of localities and regions. The straightforward connections between national governments and nations ordered in distinct classes, sending their currents through journalism, are stretched, broken or attenuated.

It was always thus. Diagnosticians of the shattered present overrate the tidy past. But it is clear that the way in which human clusters define and antagonise one another is once more on the move, and that journalists presently lack a ready political narrative within which to situate stories, explain action and find meaning. The break-up of former Yugoslavia, the attempted secessions of parts of Indonesia and Sri Lanka, the inexplicable civil wars of central Africa, above all the hideous destruction of the New York World Trade Center, all offer recent examples of political news which journalists struggled helplessly to explain; they could only describe what they saw.

We can then say, very roughly, that the grand commentators with their large salaries become those who report on the undemocratic politics of the large new federations, and another class of journalists, less well paid but with a far from anonymous signature, go to the regions and report on local life and the many deaths scattered across it. In Britain, for example, for some years and at the time of writing, men like Jeremy Paxman and John Humphrys cross-examine *on our behalf* the representatives of the national government for whom European federation will prove the crux of future politics. In the USA, Peter Jennings does less of the interrogation and more of the gathering and ordering of the hierarchy of news items into an intelligible framework. One of Cronkite's heirs, he sings a similar song about the way in which the network ratings competition, clean new technology and dirty old dollars have cut off reporters from experience. The CNN journalist flies in, catches up a microphone, stands in front of windowless houses and bombed-out buses, brings into order the chaos of mere events with a few calm sentences, and flies out. As Jennings himself said, 'they're speaking from they don't know where.'[9]

What would it be like to divide the labour of journalism into these two realms of global vision and local anecdote? Can we find, in the passing present, journalistic career exemplification which may become a tradition capable of shaping the profession for its own good? Capable of resistance to the bullying of bosses and the corruptions of cash? Let there be four types.

The first and most commendably old-fashioned is sibling to the adventurer. He or she is a bit of a desperado. Ryszard Kapucinski is one such, born a Belarussian in Pinsk in 1931, indigenously a Pole in Warsaw during the Nazi occupation, hired as a journalist at eighteen because there were so few intellectually minded Poles left around, taught himself English by reading, dictionary in hand, *For Whom the Bell Tolls*.

He was fully equipped for legend. He became a wanderer, travelling down the track of any wind that blew through him, mostly towards Africa. Going nowhere in particular, he always ended up where the revolutions were revolving; in one year alone seventeen new African countries emerged from old empires. He read omnivorously as he wandered, and fashioned both a political anthropology and a singular journalism which he dubbed 'literature on foot'[10] with which to realise and comprehend the troubles he'd seen, the illnesses survived (emerging from the coma of cerebral malaria to see the unhallucinated features of Idi Amin gazing at him), the interminable waiting for a last rickety aircraft out of a shelled airport (Luanda), a man in Tehran singing – 'Allah Akbar' – in such a fine, carrying voice that Kapucinski follows him,[11] and so do others, many others, until there is a crowd – a crowd draws a crowd says Canetti – and the crowd is expressing something about itself. Its politics is in its crowdedness.

His most typical story, untypically told for the most part in direct quotation from the participants, is of the fall of Emperor Haile Selassie in 1974.[12] A group of middle-ranking officers under one Major Mengistu and styling themselves the Dergue encroached more and more upon the Emperor's power with demands for constitutional change, and then, bit by bit, with open abuse. The once-sacred name of the Emperor was defiled in the streets. The aged, aged man fell more and more silent, ordered callisthenics for his court, stroked the unchanging black marble everywhere in his palace, fed his birds and pet wild beasts. He left his court alone as, one by one, his court left him. At length he was alone with one servant, Kapucinski's confidant, inevitably ancient, immitigably loyal.

The officers of the Dergue came and demanded the Emperor's money in order to take it away and nationalise it. They found it in thick little wads stuck with sellotape to the underneath of the great Persian carpets. The Emperor murmured, 'If the revolution is good for the people, I am for the revolution.' The officers led him out to the pillared portico of the palace. There was no Rolls-Royce, only an old green Volkswagen Beetle. He clambered into the back past the tilted front seat, and was driven away. 'It was so, my gracious sir,' says the solitary servant. Kapucinski has done with another revolution.

Kapucinski, wandering Pole, is perhaps a survivor from an earlier journalistic epoch, and at the same time brother to Joan Didion and James Fenton. John Simpson, a second wanderer,[13] speaks in the cut-glass accents of an old boy of St Paul's School and in the received register of classical BBC impartiality. He is irresistible. Born in 1944, brought up by his divorced father as a Christian Scientist, he proved a handsome sportsman, a low-key intellectual, went to Cambridge to read English literature and emerged, married to an American portraitist, to join the BBC and live the contemporary version of that nineteenth-century English hero, the scholar-explorer-adventurer-soldier.

His soldierliness is largely a matter of being in the wars and soldierly company rather than carrying a weapon. But something about him, reckless and attractive and not without an endearing conceit, combines with the unrepeatable good fortune of working for BBC political news in its happiest decades to turn him into an apologetic and fearfully courageous reporter of a kind to stir one's blood and keep up faith in the future of such work.

He doesn't miss much in the way of trouble. He learned about the word early, in Belfast and Dublin between 1971 and 1975. Soft-hearted as well as hard-edged, he hated from the start a republican cause which caused two young women to entice three young men into a blind alley to be shot through the brain stem, let alone the loyalist one which detonated two terrible bombs in Dublin one May afternoon in 1974. Simpson saw 'an old man sitting calmly looking at the remains of his smashed leg, which was pumping blood, and ended with a piece of protruding shin' alongside an 'apparently eviscerated woman',[14] and muted the rawness of these sights in the decent drabness of BBC prose: 'I saw a woman's body lying on the pavement, covered with a coat. Close by an old man was being attended to; his leg was injured fairly badly ...'[15]

Simpson did well in Ireland, went via dullish days in Brussels and then at the behest of Charles Wheeler, indomitable model in such matters, to the Angolan civil war.

He tells an exuberant tale, as you might say, objectively. Time and again a gun is poked into his stomach or the side of his head, held by a variety of psychopaths or very jumpy, spotty youths: in Kinshasa, Teheran, Belfast. He has interviewed Sakharov in Moscow, Khomeini on his way home. He's still here safe and sound; it was a near thing once or twice, but Simpson is angrier at the Tasmanian reporter who cheats him over the story of the execution of a dozen mercenaries than he is at the trigger-happy gunslingers roaming the danger-spots.

During a year in South Africa he made friends with Biko and Donald Woods, paid homage to the hero's dead body, was extremely clear in his reports about his own admirable principles – clear enough to upset the authorities – but quite without compromising the BBC's impartiality. Perhaps I should add, in another attempt to sort this difficulty, that values speak in their eloquence as much in the sequence of a story as in the selection of the facts, and just as plainly in the silence of what is not said. He interviewed Winnie Mandela – corroded but magnificent – and just afterwards, arrested for speeding, talked his way out of custody with a sergeant-enthusiast of stained glass making.

John Simpson's is one great roaming success story, lovably so, especially when it went a bit wrong. Having been neatly wrongfooted by John Humphrys for one job, he took the next best, which was political editor for BBC television news. He disliked the absurd rotas and heavy conventions of the Houses of Parliament and found his own disposition quite unsuited to its regularities. Like James Cameron's before him, his wandering life as a foreign correspondent was what he loved, who he was. Even so, he found a place in his heart for Mrs Thatcher as 'queen of the doorstep interview'[16] even when she so exasperated him that Bernard Ingham, her press secretary, kicked Simpson hard on the shin to make *her* shut up.

It makes an epic story, one of our times. Simpson was eventually sacked from presenting BBC news (he had criticised government policy during the military action in the Falklands of 1982) and promoted to diplomatic editor the same day ('the BBC does these things with unparalleled brutality').[17] He had by now, it seemed, moved a little out of immediate life dangers, in spite of being present to film the disinterring of the skulls and skeletons of hundreds of Argentinian 'disappeareds'.

Somewhere – while watching Israelis kill Lebanese civilians with phosphorus bombs, I think – he says, 'I couldn't bear to watch it any longer.' But he can. He has to. He acquired for himself some kind of senior roving brief, and patrolled the stations of the sudden end of the Cold War in 1989, turning up at the fall of Ceausescu in Romania and at the awful maintenance of the old order in Beijing.

In Beijing and the summer of 1989 several thousand students piled into the biggest empty space to be found in the capital, Tiananmen Square,[18] built themselves a plaster-of-Paris Statue of Liberty, and settled down in little bivouacs to wait for the government to resign. Western news and camera teams poured in, Simpson's among them. The Chinese People's Republic had been on the softer, less arctic edges of Cold War for a while, and looked as though it would tread an appropriately inscrutable path towards the market economy.

Not everyone in the square was a student. There were workers from nearby factories, piratical with their red cloths tied around their heads. People had brought their little children to stare at the sudden, temporary settlement of untidy campers. At night the darkness was speckled by little fires all over the square. There were no public lavatories and an acrid smell of urine.

Small groups of riot dispersal units from the army had already tried to clear the square, but their shields and batons were no match for the thousands of students with bricks and bottles, so they went away. The square was packed and busy and throbbing with excitement. John Simpson, roaming around after losing touch with his film crew, suddenly saw hundreds of figures standing stock-still around a lamppost. Out of an old-fashioned loudspeaker bolted to it came these words: 'Go home and save your life. You will fail. You are not behaving in the correct Chinese manner. This is not the West, it is China. You should behave like a good Chinese. Go home and save your life. Go home and save your life.' The people listened. They did not move.

The tanks came sporadically, as though they had no coherent orders. One vehicle was only a light armoured carrier with a small squad of soldiers in it. A corner of the crowd turned into a lynch mob as the carrier ran down several people, grinding limbs under its tracks. It stuck on a block of concrete. The crowd yelled and swarmed on to the helpless vehicle, recklessly pouring gasoline everywhere, dropping Coke bottles of blazing gas down its flues. The vehicle caught fire. Simpson goes on, unforgettably:

> The screaming around me rose even louder: the handle of the door at the rear of the vehicle had turned a little, and the door began to open. A soldier pushed the barrel of a gun out, but it was snatched from his hands, and then everyone started grabbing his arms, pulling and

wrenching until finally he came free, and then he was gone: I saw the arms of the mob, flailing, raised above their heads as they fought to get their blows in. He was dead within seconds, and his body was dragged away in triumph. A second soldier showed his head through the door and was then immediately pulled out by his hair and ears and the skin on his face. This soldier I could see: his eyes were rolling, and his mouth was open, and he was covered in blood where the skin had been ripped off. Only his eyes remained – white and clear – but then someone was trying to get them as well, and someone else began beating his skull until the skull came apart, and there was blood all over the ground, and his brains, and still they kept on beating and beating what was left.

Then the horrible sight passed away, and the ground was wet where he had been.[19]

They say the lynch mob was not students; the students sang the 'Internationale' and stayed in the open spaces of the great square and vowed to observe Taoist non-violence. But the smell of blood was in the air, and the soldiers were enraged at their comrades being torn to death. They came back in a massed phalanx with bayonets and machine guns and squadrons of tanks in battle order, and the students and the mob died together, crushed or shot. Once again, communism provided the televisions of the world with living images of its valueless power, power that came down like a fist on its children and smashed their lives out, all because they didn't feel the same about things as their fathers, and wanted to say so.

Simpson remarks in his autobiography that his BBC report on Tiananmen Square hadn't 'an ounce of emotion in it' whereas 'Kate Adie's was very different … full of emotion… While mine was perfectly accurate it had nothing of the real feeling of what had taken place. Hers did.'[20] Simpson changed all that with what he wrote for *Granta*.

Simpson's story betokens the powerful urges of the contemporary political journalist. He loves fame, adventure, the pace of his travels, the levity and gravity of history. He went hunting terroists in Afghanistan in 2001 concealed under a *burqa*. He stayed to bear witness to the curiously sporadic deathliness of the war. Not able to say much, he kept up the corporation's great name for laconic truthfulness.

The millenarian has visions of Utopia, and quite right too. Each broadsheet newspaper hires an occasional millenarian columnist, one whose vision of paradise is matched to the social class, age group and political inclination of the house constituency. Most such writers are millenarian in negation. That is to say, compared to their picture of the good society, they find themselves consistently horrified: on the Right by modernity, permissiveness, lack of respect for age and authority, sexual indulgence; on the Left by international capital, by racism and imperialism; urbanity notwithstanding, William F. Buckley is a Right millenarian: *his* good society was situated in a big house with coloured servants in Charlottesville while Teddy Roosevelt was President.

Most millenarians, it is true, live in transports, often of rage. But millenarian is not a term of mockery. It identifies those journalists for whom certain aspects of the world are intolerable and whose vocation it is to say so. There is then bound to be a question of sincerity. To maintain as moral posture a consistent appearance of steadiness in all circumstances, of sobriety of judgement, quiet regret at human folly or accident, quiet satisfaction at happy endings or beginnings is one thing. These are the manners of the regular television presenters and columnists, and their conviction of a more or less rational and moral world in turn convinces us. To appear or to write always in a spirit of outrage, of sustained condemnation at human wrongdoing is plain exhausting. The space held open on the features or international news page and in the schedules for the expression of rage and outrage is kept available first in response to the newsworthiness of human cruelty or negligence. People ought to know about such things. The same space is also an ideological sign. Moral outrage is marked as a necessity in a particular frame of belief and value.

The good liberal, for example, is in part defined as such by the belief that the one worst thing is cruelty.[21] A liberal newspaper hires a journalist to mark the sign of the belief by reporting the ample instances of cruelty to hand. This is the work of the millenarian. A first choice for the job for many years was the Australian John Pilger.

When Pilger was named Reporter of the Year in Britain in 1974 the citation said: 'John Pilger's field is the world and his subject humanity. His material is factual but his expression of it powerfully emotional, his contribution to present-day news reporting unsurpassed.' This definition of the subject-matter is so wide as to be vacuous and to call Pilger's treatment 'emotional' similarly vague. His subject is the cruelty shown by the strong against the weak, and his passion, conveyed with unrelenting urgency, is less a burst of outrage at evil or, indeed, derisive condemnation of mistakes (though both are present), than an invincible righteousness.

Righteousness, our Bibles tell us, is a breastplate to be worn against one's adversary, the devil; Pilger wears his armour like a Puritan. Righteousness may turn into self-righteousness, and that, in the trade of journalism as of politics, is a consequence of celebrity as well as of the demands of ideological competition.

The power of Pilger's television journalism derives from that admirable and moving strand in the socialist tradition which keeps solidarity with human suffering. He was born to parents believing in such a duty, in Sydney in 1939; the fine egalitarianism of the Australian Left provided Pilger with the straightforward, two-sided narrative which fired his journalism. From the beginning he took the side of the weak against the strong, the poor against the rich, the small against the large, and did so in a plain, forceful, necessarily simple-minded prose with a political framework to match.

He started out in the tranquillity of Australian journalism but went to seek his fortune, like so many bright white youngsters of the Antipodean, in London. He joined the staff of the *Daily Mirror* in the 1960s, when it was at its peak, admired its straight Labour politics and blunt way with language, and took his training, his socialism, his crusading passion and his highly photogenic looks to political television in 1969.

He was and is a man of imperturbable confidence both in his abilities and his opinions. It made him unignorable and hard to employ. In 1974 he got his break. The British commercial station ATV gave him a series, with Pilger's surname as its simple title, and it ran for three years, establishing him as a crusader-advocate, one man who would take big, difficult, political topics and face those in power with their failure to observe even the most elementary versions of truthfulness and justice.

The air was full of such voices. The year 1974 saw Nixon's slow and ugly withdrawal from the Presidency, largely the result of the *Washington Post*'s investigations; the previous years had seen Harold Evans's thalidomide campaign at the *Sunday Times*; the Pentagon Papers victory; the certainty of US involvement in the Chilean coup which overthrew the democratically elected Salvador Allende; the extensive allegations of British complicity in Vietnam and support for the illicit bombing of Laos and Cambodia;[22] all these things had combined to make scepticism about and outright mistrust of governments and their public statements very widespread. Pilger cast himself as the star of scepticism and, in doing so, devised with his producers, in particular David Munro, the new-looking form of the 'personal viewpoint' documentary.

The rubric was intended to ward off charges of tendentiousness. If a programme expressed a 'personal view' then objections to a lack of impartiality could be dismissed, the requirement made by the Royal Broadcasting

Charters for balance could be set aside for a moment, and strong feeling and commitment became permissible.

Pilger is, in his television persona, immune to doubt. His winning good humour, his human sympathy, his moral simplicity, let alone his forceful- ness and needful egotism, made him an irresistible presenter, once his producers had been persuaded of the subject. All the subjects were, more- over, high temperature news. Pilger picked the very topics which the demands of impartiality – a word, Pilger himself says, 'now almost Orwellian in the perversity of its opposite meaning'[23] – caused customary political programmes to treat much more gingerly.

Impartiality, it had better be added, retains moral force. It is one theme of this book to insist on the inextricability of the facts and the values, but a misgiving one might properly have about Pilger's style of protesting journalism is its implication that impartiality is another name for deferentiality.

Nonetheless, one cannot doubt Pilger's record of dropping squarely on those subjects about which governments least wanted discussion and which they most wanted to obscure. He began in Vietnam in 1970 with 'the Quiet Mutiny' for ATV's *World in Action*, a programme examining the collapse in morale, the recourse to hard drugs, the murder of officers, all afflicting US forces in Vietnam.

From the start Pilger was apt to treat topics as though no one had ever dared mention them before. Anthony Hayward, his chronicler, inanely claims that in 1970 viewers in Britain and America had seen little criticism of the fighting.[24] The mark of the programme's success was, for Pilger and his producer, that it gave rise to angry rebuttals from officialdom. It's not a bad criterion. It was a powerful bit of television, propaganda in so far as the propagandist has no doubt about being in the right and sees the writing of history as an act of rhetoric rather than of the record.

Record, reason, rhetoric: they are never readily told apart. It is Pilger's distinction to have made so many programmes whose rhetoric *makes us feel* he is right. He did it with François Ponchaud's astounding book on Cambodia, Pol Pot and the Khmer Rouge[25] (without giving the French priest much credit), and the programme was overwhelming. Pilger spoke from the side of horrifying pictures of starving and agonisingly sick children shown with unremitting steadiness. It was screened in October 1979. It released a little surge of public charity and a large spasm of public sympathy. Thus political journalism has political consequences. It makes history. In making this history, however, Pilger is compelled by something unyieldingly self-righteous in his disposition to act overmightily in making a film of protest on behalf of the undertrodden. When criticised by Clive James's otherwise eulogistic reviews for not acknowledging the North Vietnamese contribution to human misery,[26] Pilger made free with accusations of McCarthyism. It is clear now, and has been for a long time, that, as one would expect of so disciplined and ruthless a politics, the North Vietnamese were fully accomplished at their own forms of oppression.[27]

There is something important here about the intellectual habits of millenarians. In order to hang on to a vision of a feasible paradise, they have to deceive themselves about the character of those whose side they have taken (Buckley and Podhoretz do the same). The lapse may be absolved where so much is strong and moving and on behalf of so desperate and needy a cause. But if the self-righteousness will out, the cause is then damaged.

In an unimportant interview in March 2000 with a senior UN official on Pilger's documentary 'Paying the price: killing the children of Iraq'[28] – a subject Pilger made his own – his interviewing method, for a man now over sixty and world-famous in his role, is surprisingly heavyhanded. The issue at stake is the sanctions the UN applied to Iraq in order to forestall the country's manufacture of nuclear and biological weapons. Their immediate consequence was that children would die for want of ordinary medicines.

Pilger [to Peter van Walsum, UN Security Council Chair of the Sanctions Committee]: ... Why aren't there sanctions on Turkey which has displaced something like three million Kurds and caused the deaths of perhaps 30,000 Kurds? Why weren't there sanctions on Turkey?

van Walsum [after a long pause]: Yes, well, there are many countries that do things we are not happy with, but this is the situation which has come into being due to the invasion of Kuwait and that is the explanation for it.

Pilger: Do you believe that people have human rights, no matter where they live and under what system they live, that the human rights belong to the individual?

van Walsum: Yes.

Pilger: Well, doesn't that, if you apply that to Iraq, don't, then, the effects that these sanctions have had, documented by the UN itself – aren't they violating the human rights of literally millions of people?

It would be just as illuminating to add the stage direction after Pilger's entries, 'without a pause', and it is hard to escape the conclusion that Pilger is more interested in discomfiting his interlocutor and forcing him into hesitation and periphrasis, than in exposition or even persuasion. He knows he is right and he wants to win.

Such manners force themselves on the millenarian. Pilger casts himself, as he must, as the lonely dissenter. But he is famous, very well paid, and always at work. Fame makes him scant his references and work less carefully for his arguments. He hasn't time; but then neither have the dying wretches for whom he speaks so bluntly. In the end, one has to mute one's inevitable but sporadic irritation with Pilger's grotesque pretence that all state leaders in the West are crazed child-murderers. Exasperation has to give way to the concession that for a spokesman on behalf of the victims of avoidable misery to be famous and garrulous and extravagant is to add weight to those on the side of justice. If I wish, as I do, that the famous profile and rueful smile were less regularly in the picture, the price of such self-denial might well be an increase in suffering and cruelty.

Pilger the protestant and righteous man would likely be scornful of the homemaker. Walter Cronkite lived and limned this character into being, and we can't really do without him (pretty well exclusively 'him', so far, unless you count Barbara Walters). The homemaker, at his best, speaks or writes in the cadences which put a form around the day, the week or the epoch in such a way that we, readers or listeners, are comforted and confirmed in our capacity to carry on with living. Where Pilger can shake us until we tremble, the homemaker, like a good parent, gathers the tumult of the world into an intelligible order and tucks us in with a firm hand.

I intend no disparagement. The instruments of public communication have given us as never before an hourly picture of the turning world. The quiddity of news manufacture, the competition and fevered profit-seeking of the organs of news distribution have classified ordinary experience as compounded of death and destruction, crisis and catastrophe. It is no wonder that we turn to journalists who hold a steadying hand out to us and gather the suddenness of events into a comprehending account. We turn our own, inevitable story-making habit of mind to the same ends with our immediate lives. We are reassured when, in the name of the great world and the powers to whom we have consigned our safety, a familiar and trusted figure appears on the screen and calmly puts at peace the quarrelsome homunculi who are supposed to be running things.

The same magic is worked by the best columnists and editors, each according to his ideological stripe. In Britain, Hugo Young speaks in the *Guardian* a calm, scornful commination over the political babel and, writing some of the best prose liberalism has seen since John Stuart Mill, transforms the angry lineaments of disputing ministers into the march of time and nations either trekking away from or towards progress. Like so many of the worthies in these pages, Young is a formidable historian; his judicious and caustic biography of Margaret Thatcher is a classic contribution to the history of popular sentiment.[29] Hugo Young serves to identify something central to the difficulty of writing serious political journalism in the past hundred years, above all since the end of Cold War. It is a process that may be headed, 'the accelerating desuetude of narrative'. I borrow the idea, if not the phrase, from Eric Hobsbawm's history of the twentieth century, already invoked with respect.[30]

Hobsbawm says that the present is marked by a loss of explanatory narrative. The stories we have with which to theorise the way of the world no longer cover the heaps of information, or assuage the depths of anxiety we feel. The *grands récits* have disintegrated: fascism, communism, Christianity. As politics mounts to the upper reaches of globalisation and contracts downwards to the little sphere of the locality, there may still be plenty of nationalisms around, but the nations who attach their flags to them are less and less perpetual and coherent. The religious faiths which profess the finality of fundamental adherence – Sikhism, even doctrinally non-fundamental Hinduism, above all, Islam – do so, it is contended, as much to dispel the suspicions of encroaching unbelief as to announce anything changeless about their continuity.

Turbo-capitalism is to blame for all this, no doubt. It unfixes faith, work, class and neighbourhood. But that won't stop it, not for a long time. Meanwhile, the narratives which justify the continuity of generations (inheriting work or property), the sanctity of membership (the neighbourhood, the trade union, the family), the plenty of nature (the globe as an infinite resource of food, fuel, water and air), and the significance of one's own death (remembered as a step on the way to the greater prosperity of one's children)[31] all cover many fewer of life's eventualities and persuade us all less and less of their explanatory reach.

With a shortage of stories, the journalist as a storytelling sage is more and more put to the test of knowing what to say. The large confidence of the opinionator-editorialist becomes attenuated and spectre-thin. People can see through him. The best of them cultivate hesitation, provisionality; they look to as short a horizon as is both moral and rational.

Hugo Young is one such. In America, so until his premature death was Lars-Erik Nelson of the New York *Daily News*. In the fifty-odd years of his journalistic life, Victor Navasky remained a homemaker-in-opposition. His generation-long editorship of *The Nation*, the only national American left-wing weekly, and thereafter his assumption of the office of publisher, gave him ample opportunity to study the unlikelihood of the socialist paradise ever coming about. All the same, that principled leftism could be held up as the impossible, desirable future from which to criticise the present. Leftism became one site from which to imagine the better conduct of the present, and Navasky was a lifetime custodian of that imagination. In this, he was much like his contributor I. F. Stone but, unencumbered by the heavy sanctimonies of Western Marxism, he could deploy the common-places of socialism – so much detested by so many of his compatriots – to remind the larger society of its own best parts and what was due to social justice and equality, socialism's bravest tenets, on their own account and as recognised by all Americans.

In Britain, a trio of men can serve to represent the comfortable many-sidedness of the homemaker. In November 1981 John Cole was appointed to the position of political editor of the BBC, holding the position for eleven years. He was an Ulsterman with a far from conventional BBC background: he took his degree by correspondence course from the University of London, spent eleven years on the *Belfast Telegraph*, and only joined the Corporation at the age of fifty-four; he spoke with a pronounced Northern Irish brogue, softer than the accents of more assertive Ulstermen but unmistakable. He first caught attention at twenty-one on the *Belfast Telegraph* with a chance interview with Clement Attlee on his way from Sligo to Fermanagh. Attlee dictated to him a careful statement rebutting a rumour in the *Observer* that the partition of Ireland was to be ended.

So Cole came to fame in the old-fashioned way with years in the neigh-bourhood of Belfast, quiet enough in those days, before leaving to make his mainland reputation by working his way up the *Manchester Guardian*, first as Labour correspondent, then (in 1963) as news editor, deputy editor and after 1975 deputy editor of the *Observer*. True to the tradition in which Cole had been brought up, true also to the man's exceptional and principled good humour and likeableness, the *Observer* printers, still working hot metal presses in 1981, 'banged out' the departing deputy editor by crashing their heavy metal rulers on the metal-topped tables, while a house (Irish) bagpiper played a descant over the racket.

The political editor of the BBC is not an anchorman like Cronkite. He is the televisual equivalent of his print colleagues, but his editorials are largely improvised and, of course, his name and face, unlike theirs, are nationally known and recognisable by every corner of his audience. BBC news tells a nation about its political condition, not about an individual class, still less a ruling elite. The political editor must have known that elite personally, must not (by statute) favour any political party, must speak in a formal, simple language about often very intricate matters, must love the political life and must be prepared, to a degree not found in other journalists' lives, to take the phone calls wherever he or she may be, disrupt vacations, quit hospital early (Cole suffered a burst duodenal ulcer and a heart attack and *still* resumed work), go without sleep.

In doing all this, seriously but not solemnly, humanly living an inhumane schedule, Cole became, so to speak, the well-loved author of a long-running comedy of manners-in-politics. Naturally, the drama of which he summarised the plots and the characters had to prove true even where he allowed himself to anticipate the action, as he did the fall of Margaret Thatcher. His historical novel of manners reported and organised the lived drama of events. It did so, largely, in terms of the individuals observed, for that is not only how people make political history intelligible to themselves, it is how it happens.

No doubt everyone overestimates the importance of the individual in causing great events. Such an overestimation is at the heart of that political liberalism to which the countries principally discussed in this volume principally subscribe. The volume itself turns on the axis of this belief; it is a sequence of interwoven biographies. The distinction of a journalist as good as Cole is that reporting on the individuals and their sometimes savage differences of opinion, his lively sense of their historical connection to institutions larger than themselves – party, trade union, department of state, nation or neighbourhood – never failed him, nor did his courteous respect for the office whatever he thought of the official.

Consequently, it is to do him no more than justice to point out in what general esteem and affection he was held by the nine o'clock news-watching class (millions of them), just as it is a measure of the man that when he was stopped in the street by strangers it was, as often as not, to be recognised as a weather forecaster of vaguely similar appearance and very similar voice: 'it was my habit at such encounters to spread cheerfulness by predicting sunshine all the way.'[32]

On the screen, no one was in any doubt who he was, particularly if he was wearing, as he invariably did for outside broadcasting, his elegant but ageing grey herringbone topcoat. The duty to which he brought his unselfconscious creativity was to be, as I've put it, political homemaker to the nation, and to fill the role by turning himself into an evening storyteller.

It has always been baffling that 'home' is never a concept which rates an entry in the lexicon of political science even though it is the central life value for most people in all societies. The exigencies of the old enemy 'turbo-capitalism' have done much to thin out the meaning of 'home' in our political vocabulary. Mobility, dispersal, unemployment, retraining, casualisation all do their usual work in dissolving our membership one of another. In so far as we are all, willing or not, political beings, the political editors of page and screen do much to give solidity to the concept by telling us a coherent story of those to whom our votes have assigned the duty to look after us. No one in Britain has done the job for a larger audience or better than John Cole.

Margaret Thatcher was a politician who did much to give her name to the most headlong and destructive-creative version of turbo-capitalism. Cole was the product of the great liberal duo of newspapers, *Guardian* and *Observer*, the author of a book called *The Poor of the Earth*, and no Thatcherite. Nor, in spite of Denis Thatcher's casually expressed view to him that everyone at the BBC was a Trotskyist,[33] was Cole anything other than an ardently gradualist liberal of that version in Britain which gives its heart to a fair-minded and egalitarian picture of the common good. Richard Hoggart puts 'fair play' at the centre of the civic virtues as understood by modernity, and if the phrase sounds a trifle flat and low in the catalogue of goodness, it may nonetheless be as passionately upheld as it was by John Cole.

He never held it more aloft than in the *coup de théâtre* which was a peak of his broadcasting life; it usefully illustrates the storytelling role of those in his position. During 1990, more and more of Mrs Thatcher's cabinet ministers expressed themselves exasperated beyond measure not only by her summary disregard for their views, let alone their responsibility for the work of their departments, but also by the increasing virulence of her opposition to the slow, small steps of the European Union's development of continental integration. Her Chancellor of the Exchequor, Nigel Lawson, resigned; so did her official (but powerless) deputy, Geoffrey Howe. Her strongest opponent was the ex-minister, Michael Heseltine, who had been first to resign, sweeping out of a cabinet meeting in uncontainable affront at her overriding his authority once again.

Cole had been largely responsible for the convention of answering live and impromptu questions from newscasters on camera. During these dramatic days, he pieced together from his sources, all of them senior, and from his excellent wits, what turned out to be a wholly accurate story, carefully sustained as to drama, intelligible as to motivation (especially with regard to Michael Heseltine), correct as to prediction (he forecast, against the odds, John Major's victory in the party's leadership election), sympathetic, even, to the end of the career of the central protagonist in whom he saw much for others to admire but who was too much opposed to his own key values for him to like. All the same, as she went, he essayed – at his presenter's invitation – a sudden (premature, as he said) estimation of her place in British political history.

> Leaving out the Churchill wartime coalition, hers was one of the three landmark administrations of the twentieth century: the liberal government of Campbell-Bannerman, Asquith and Lloyd George which began in 1906, Attlee's Labour government after the Second World War and hers. Because she was the longest serving Prime Minister of the century, she has her place in history. What precisely that place was will remain controversial, because her policies have so bitterly divided the nation.[34]

Cole was always sharply aware of the gap between what politicians said in private (and to him) and their public utterances. He was no less aware of the difference between the persona adopted by a politician, and the same confection as magnified, distorted and attributed by the media. His great storytelling achievement was to stretch his prose across these spaces without offending probability or damaging the shape of the story.

Two other homemakers expand the category backwards and forwards in time. Cole worked in the present. Phillip Whitehead worked eventually in the past, though he spent several years producing *This Week*. But it is his television histories which count for us here, by way of emphasising that making a liveable politics is a comprehensive and practical venture, privy to a whole nation; it isn't easy, except by way of the moral, to distinguish between the storymaking of the comedy of political manners as told by John Cole and the retelling of the world tragedy of the Second World War as devised (principally) by Jeremy Isaacs and Whitehead's powerful predecessor series, *The Day Before Yesterday*. *The World at War* counts here as political journalism because it came at a timely moment in the reconstruction of postwar Britain and came, moreover, from the generation too young to have fought (Whitehead was born in 1937 and served for a year in an imperial regiment of the British Army) but which had its imagination forever shaped by the war.

Isaacs persuaded Thames TV to make a colossal investment in research and filming, recovering unshown cans of wartime film, some of it shot against orders and in extreme danger, and finding and listening to protagonists whether momentous or unimportant (in Whitehead's case finding and recording Hitler's adjutant and his secretary). They devised the simple, novel form which now defines their innumerable imitators: old black-and-white newsreel footage, talking-and-reminiscing heads in colour, a first-rate script on voiceover (preferably a famous voice – in the case of *The World at War*, Laurence Olivier's), with a specially written musical score to match (Carl Davis's).

With this immediately accessible form and the amazing content collected from a year and a half in the newsreel archives, along with finding and coaxing into speech so many dozens of remembering and tormented participants in the epic, *The World at War* was broadcast in twenty-six weekly episodes in 1974. By the time this unprecedented and gigantic venture was ready it had gathered in an unrepeatable collaboration a generation of the best in the British trade, Neal Ascherson and Stuart Hood among the writers, Peter Batty and David Elstein among the producers.

The point at issue is that the programme was conceived as a wholesale reordering of the national imagination, a transformation for the genera-tion after the war of the way it thought about the war's significance, using the popular narrative to explain the country to itself. The series restored Soviet Russia to the centre of the action, followed in a detail quite unfamiliar to the British the Americans' Pacific campaign, weighed up once more the issues which exploded at Hiroshima and burned up Dresden, taught a nation the lesson that the future emerges only from the past, and that the European past between 1919 and 1945 still shaped the passions and directed the purposes of Cold War, European alliance, and multiplication of nations.

Such television history is, I therefore claim, indistinguishable from political journalism. Whitehead's work stands here as vindication of this. In subsequent programmes – a self-appointed series for which Whitehead's private title was 'the Great Dictators' – he produced televised biographies of Ronald Reagan, Margaret Thatcher, Nixon, Stalin and, in a series of remarkable triptyches, the Kennedy dynasty: father Joe, and the two dead brothers Jack and Bobby; the Nehrus: Jawaharlal, Indira, Rajiv; the Churchills. In each case, you might say, Whitehead took an individual biography by way of illuminating the plain truism that history makes us as we make it. The truism, however, takes on the force of absolute truth only when it is dramatised in particular instances. Stalin, for instance, was by 1990 (when Whitehead's series was broadcast) beginning to drift off the edge of the social memory. The programme reminded old sentimental

Stalinists still to be found coaxing old fantasy into new hope just what a monster the old brute was, while teaching those who had never learned how deathly an experiment the USSR turned out to be at his hands.[35]

Whitehead understood and visualised what it is also the preoccupation of this book to illustrate: that most of us try to follow the march of time by way of individual figures picked out from the crowds trooping past. Biography and its significance is the vehicle of everyday and unacademic historical understanding.

We make our historical home out of those life-stories of our neighbours which are comprehensible. If a few of the stories concern neighbours with power or glamour, that too makes sense. From a rather different political position, Timothy Garton Ash takes up from Phillip Whitehead the reinterpretive task of making a home in history. In many ways, Neal Ascherson would serve my purposes better,[36] particularly as his politics sort so much more happily with Whitehead's and the ingenuous Fabianism of this book. Garton Ash, however, also does his rewriting of history by way of the journalism of big events plus biography, and this makes him as methodically simple-minded as I am.

Garton Ash's journalism starts out from the rebellious occupation of the Gdansk shipyards in 1980 by the new, hardly legal trade union Solidarnosc. His provenance lay in a fierce anti-communism learned at Oxford and consolidated as a journalist on the *Spectator*. He spoke Polish, German and Czech fluently – rare attributes on either wing of British political journalism – and he told the rousing story of the ultimate victory of Solidarnosc as a triumph of a national assertion of individual freedom silhouetted by its heroic leader, Lech Walesa, and helped on towards a duly Christian democracy by a no less heroic Polish Pope, Karol Wojtyla.[37]

To his joy (and who would not share it?) Garton Ash went on to chronicle the end of the Cold War in what has come to be known as Central Europe (with some striking exclusions and occlusions: no Romania, still less the Ukraine). The best story of the lot Garton Ash was able to tell at first hand. *The Magic Lantern*[38] narrates the events in the theatre club in Prague in which the playwright-intellectual Vaclav Havel brought down the old, horrible regime of Gustav Husak, and his dull obdurate clique which had killed the Prague Spring of twenty years before. The photo-lithographed daily *The Free Word* was published from the Magic Lantern itself and sold out daily before breakfast. Czechoslovakia (as it still was) ruled itself pretty well by popular assent to what Havel and the Civic Forum told the crowds each night in Wenceslaus Square. Garton Ash saw it all and told it well and gleefully.

Thereafter, as the title of a recent collection of his journalism indicates, he set himself to turn a ghastly present explained in terms of a blood-stained past into a safely liberal and capitalist future.[39] He does so plainly and without cant. He stands looking down at the Krajina[40] soon after Croatia had swept it clear of Serbs, weighs up the savagery the Serbs meted out elsewhere, and he hopes for the best.

A history of the present, Perry Anderson says, cannot be written as journalism – or not, at least, the journalism of episodes, cameos, elegies to leading characters, however courageous. The greatest journalism considered in these pages – Mailer's, let us say, Orwell's on his day and Joan Didion's on hers – *is* so good principally because it combines a rendering of immediacy with the provision of reasons. There simply is no history without episodes and characters, while some at least of the causes and consequences can only be discerned on the spot. Immediacy is not a lower value than causal explanation in historical interpretation; it is just as much a part of moral understanding. Politics is the drama of symbolic action, and only comprehensible if you know what actually happened.

The malcontent journalist, my fourth contemporary type, sings an old refrain to our general theme. He or she is as likely as not to be a straight intellectual and therefore with the simple duty to *oppose*.[41] In the nature of the market competition of ideas, the malcontent is assigned a niche along-side the millenarian, bought up and distributed to powerless members of the comfortably off, conscientiously disquieted bourgeoisie. To whom else, nonetheless, may the malcontent speak? He or she comes on to the platforms of the media with a sardonic tongue, a bitter taste in jokes, the cynicism of Diogenes and, if successful, the enviable aura of celebrity. These, however, are no more than obstacles to be overcome, difficulties to be carried with grace, never more gracefully than by Christopher Hitchens. He speaks with the angry disdain of a man whose anger would turn at once to generous happiness if only things were all right.

Hitchens is here cast as malcontent, a type invented for Elizabethan drama by John Marston's Malevole, Shakespeare's Jacques or Fool, a part by now playable only by a journalist. Hitchens is supremely English but lives in America; was at Oxford with James Fenton a little before Garton Ash, a public (private) schoolboy with early allegiance to certain sectarians of exhilaratingly theoretic Marxism but, at least after graduating, without any corresponding delusions about the imminence of revolution. As I approach my coda, Hitchens is called forward to play for me the role of contemporary hero-journalist, for he commands a daunting acquaintance with the politically powerful and wealthy on either side of the Atlantic, with the dissident intelligentsia almost anywhere, with the literature of politics and with literature *tout court*, which he loves with an easy reference and an open self-surrender that of themselves rebut any charge of vanity.

Like ordinary news journalists (and like Ascherson or Garton Ash) Hitchens has collected his battle honours. In 1989 and on Christmas night, stuck in freezing fog at the Austro-Hungarian border just pierced by the first surge of liberated migrants in clattering old Ladas, Hitchens was told of the execution of Ceausescu. He set off for Transylvania.[42] In the middle of Count Dracula's forest he meets a blood transfusion unit; there are happy crowds on the road and in Timisoara, where the tyrant's end began with mass demonstrations; there are the corpses of his last retribution before the punishment fitting his crimes. Hitchens sees plenty more blood, some of it squelching in his shoes at the morgue, gives away some packets of lump sugar he is carrying to hungry children, and gives up calculating the numbers of the dead.

There is no shortage of trouble spots in Hitchens's collected journalism:[43] Nicaragua, Cuba, Angola, Zimbabwe, Grenada, Baghdad, Lebanon, Palestine, Palestine again and again. While he always hopes to find the Left coming out having morally had the best of things, his journalism acquires its style at that edge of things where preparation for the worst is the only sensible precaution. As he leaves revolutionary Nicaragua with a low-order hopefulness we now know to be not quite prepared enough, he reckons up the moral quality of the revolution and the outstanding threat to it waiting a little higher up the atlas:

Nicaragua has logged six years of revolutionary government after half a century of the Somozas and more than a century of humiliating colonial subordination. It has done so with hardly any vengeance or massacre – capital punishment has been abolished, and some Sandinistas now say they wish they *had* shot the Somocista Old Guard instead of releasing it to reincarnate in Honduras and Miami. It has not avoided all the mistakes and crimes of previous revolutions, but it has at least made a self-conscious effort to do so. The Stalinist bacilli are at work all right, but they do not predominate as yet, and there is nothing that says they have to. Perhaps one should beware, anyway, of biological analogies. On the shirts and badges of the American 'advisers' in Honduras is a monogram that predates Marx and Lenin and, probably accidentally, has an echo of an earlier Crusade. Emblazoned with a skull and crossbones, it reads: Kill 'Em All – Let God Sort 'Em Out![44]

Dry horror is part of Hitchens's stock-in-trade, along with open contempt and madly cheerful mockery. If these do not sound transparently attractive qualities, perhaps one should recall the prevalent tone of sycophantic over-respect with which Washington journalists largely greet power-in-residence. Washington is this expatriate Englishman's home town, and loving in his way both England and America, he reserves for both his strongest scorn, his detestation of dead old snobberies in one and bright new corruption in the other. Not to be missed for those with a relish for the manners of Jonathan Swift are a few of his observations on the British yellow press. He is writing of the Murdoch daily, the *Sun*, the tabloid whose best-known political comment was the headline 'GOTCHA', daubed across the sinking of the Argentine warship, the *Belgrano*, with all the men aboard during the Falklands engagement of 1982. Hitchens notes, with his chilling calmness of manner, some of the newspaper's most horrible bawlings to its readers, to join 'rape and castration' phone-ins on one hand, to smack their lips at 'classroom crackers' (under-age girls with over-age breasts) on the other, to hunt down (in Kelvin MacKenzie's delicate phraseology) 'botty burglars and bum bandits' in public life. Hitchens concludes with a poignant question. He remarks with that unshockable relish which is his best and necessary self-protection that 'the cretinisation of the press – the replacement of gutter journalism by sewer journalism – is an enthralling [topic]' but that neither the hands of its journalists nor its often-dismissed editors are the guiding ones. 'The most absorbing question [is] ... what does Rupert Murdoch want – out of politics, out of journalism, out of life?'[45]

Hitchens writes like this about England, which matters so little, because the condition of England's journalism is of more than national importance. But he writes about America, which matters absolutely to the entire world, with a caustic, hilarious condemnation of its political excesses exactly because what it does with the can-do brutality of unimaginative childishness threatens the lives of so many of the globe's more helpless inhabitants. He does so, moreover, with precision. There can be very few journalists with so particular and manifold an acquaintance among the powerful *and* among all those at the receiving end of political disaster. In his recklessly candid indictment of one of America's most powerful officials ever, Henry Kissinger,[46] Hitchens draws with fateful accuracy on the unknown history of the CIA in Chile, of Kissinger's collusion in the murder of a Chilean general called Schneider and his siding (in telephone transcripts) with General Pinochet. Kissinger's ruthlessness in negotiating with the North Vietnamese is fairly well acknowledged, if not the plotting and double-dealing with which he surrounded it; and very little indeed has circulated about the honest doctor's deadly duplicity in the quarrel between Greece and Turkey over Cyprus in 1974.

When he braces himself to face the biggest and most horrifying story of the new millennium, the suicide bombing of Manhattan which immolated 3,000 people in September 2001, Hitchens starts characteristically from Peshawar in 1979, where he was looking for a driver to the Khyber Pass in order to see how the Red Army was, like the British Army a century before, failing hopelessly to put down the local insurgents. He finds one who knows the geography, the politics, and the music of Dire Straits. 'My guide in Peshawar', he notes, 'was a shadow thrown by William Casey's CIA, which first connected the unstoppable Stinger missile to the infallible and inerrant Koran.'[47]

Hitchens is our spokesman in these pages for the moment of turmoil inaugurated by the World Trade Center incineration, which – with a very deliberate spectacularity on the part of the killers – handed political journalists the puzzle of a lifetime: first, how to recount facts everybody could see, and second, how to fit them in a story nobody could tell. The bafflement, as well as the rage and anguish, of that moment pour off the end of this book. Hitchens forswears any recommendation but not, in his sharp, fluent, unaccommodating way, judgement.

For once, he agrees with the rulers of his two nations about the cause in hand and the need for opposition: what he wants to make, caustically and passionately, is the right moral judgement.

> There is no sense at all in which the events of September 11 can be held to constitute such a reprisal, either legally or morally.
>
> It is something worse than idle to propose the very trade-offs that may have been lodged somewhere in the closed-off minds of the mass-murderers. The people of Gaza live under curfew and humiliation and expropriation. This is notorious. Very well: does anyone suppose that an Israeli withdrawal from Gaza would have forestalled the slaughter in Manhattan? It would take a moral cretin to suggest anything of the sort; the cadres of the new jihad make it very apparent that their quarrel is with Judaism and secularism on principle ... They regard the Saudi regime not as the extreme authoritarian theocracy that it is, but as some-thing too soft and lenient. The Taliban forces viciously persecute the Shi'a minority in Afghanistan. The Muslim fanatics in Indonesia try to extirpate the infidel minorities there; civil society in Algeria is barely breathing after the fundamentalist assault. Now is as good a time as ever

to revisit the history of the Crusades, or the sorry history of partition and Kashmir, or the woes of the Chechens and Kosovars.

But the bombers of Manhattan represent fascism with an Islamic face, and there's no point in any euphemism about it. What they abominate about 'the west', to put it in a phrase, is not what western liberals don't like and can't defend about their own system, but what they do like about it and must defend: its emancipated women, its scientific inquiry, its separation of religion from the state. Loose talk about chickens coming home to roost is the moral equivalent of the hateful garbage emitted by Falwell and Robertson, and exhibits about the same intellectual content. Indiscriminate murder is not a judgment, even obliquely, on the victims or their way of life, or ours. Any observant follower of the prophet Mohammed could have been on one of those planes, or in one of those buildings.

He remains sombre about the likelihood of intelligent conduct among political elites, cold and grim about the certainty that what he calls Islamic fascism is an enemy for life, as well as an enemy of life. His is the commentary of the outsider-intellectual, looking out not for policy but for clarity. His long, tightly coiled sentences are intent on teaching his reader what to think and how to feel. In the face of so much moral hypochondria in the Anglophone press of that moment, Hitchens speaks as bluntly and resolutely as any of his political leaders of what irreducible values must be defended (and hadn't been): social freedom, scientific thought, the secular state.

The political commentator cannot get everything into 1,200 words, though too many try. The journalist-intellectual must, as the point of his or her avocation, speak uncomfortable truths; to oppose for sure, but to hold to life, the necessary word, and to old humanism as the foundation of new dissent. Hitchens forbears to say what he thinks should be done – the besetting self-indulgence of a powerless intelligentsia mesmerised by power. He forswears blame, another such indulgence. He names the blankness of cruelty on one side, idiocy on the other, and mere innocence among the pitiful bystanders.

At the time of writing Hitchens is everywhere, paid most for his contributing editorship to *Vanity Fair*. The appointment may be indicative, for surely no one – *no one* – can keep up his pitch of indictment or his magnificent prose – *and* bear up under the glare of publicity and the sweet susurration of fame all around him? He will prove the key test of Cronkite's dour predictions about the wounds dealt to journalism by money and celebrity.

CHAPTER FIFTEEN

Epilogue:
For Continuity

When Islamic terrorists flew their living gasoline bombs into the World Trade Center on Manhattan and the Pentagon in Washington on 11 September 2001, they broke the biggest story since the end of the Cold War. News, politics and culture collided in a frightful explosion, and that explosion announced the opening of a new world epoch.

It is of the nature of terrorist actions that their meaning is obscure. They are meant to be. In his brilliant excursus into the interpretation of terror, Roger Poole suggests[1] that the human instrument of terrorism deliberately withholds the significance of the action. The body is the locus of all our ethical experience, and the terrorist's body is invisible – at most, masked, hooded, running for cover; on Manhattan, destroyed in the same flames as the victims. The contexts of meaning – gesture, expression, movement, speech – were deliberately suppressed, and this in order, precisely, to block explanation. That fear is greatest for which we can provide no meaning. The sudden noise in the dark, the unidentifiable menace in the shadowy city, the detonation which rips without warning through a bus, a café, and then, unimaginably, through 110 floors of the two tallest buildings in the world, are more frightening because less intelligible than some of the darkest deeds of world war.

It is unusual for news and politics to coincide so abruptly, particularly since the frames of customary political interpretation could hardly be made to fit. Commentators and reporters alike had to improvise such frameworks from the bits and pieces of methods roughed out for more commonplace eventualities. So, to begin with, they collected the tales of survivors and embedded them in what they could count on as the trustiest of their national values.

The results were pretty good. The *Los Angeles Times* began its leader on 11 September with the terse flourish, 'Buildings collapsed. Democracy stands', and then, with grim relevance, pointed out to its people that until this moment, American society had proceeded without hurt on its own soil except for the self-inflicted wounds of civil war, and that its foreign policy had been founded on this formidable base of stolid indifference. The *New York Times* added, the same morning, that 'it is important to consider the hatred it took to bring this mission off' and the *Boston Globe*, acknowledging 'the cruel ingenuity' of the terrorists, the vast spectacularity, perfect shapeliness, and abominable simplicity of the event, put at the centre of its editorial argument the necessary, clinching opposition to the invisible enemy of everyday democratic practices: freedom of movement as well as of belief; freedom of election and the easy tolerance of American civic life. The American press wasn't going to name, on such a day, the disfigurements of its polity, still less the conduct overseas, some of it blameless, much involuntary, which gives so much fuel to the 'philosophical hysteria' the great journalist-novelist-travel-writer V. S. Naipaul long ago detected in contemporary Islam.[2] Reporters reached, as naturally they would and should, for the reassurances of domestic heroism among the firefighters, for examples of stalwart resolution in their history (Pearl Harbor), and for the nation's abstract but inviolable commitment to justice and the retribution it entails.

It took – as well it might – a journalist on the *Palestinian Chronicle*, Robert Jensen, to provide the lead that same morning towards an interpretive context for the atrocity. 'For more than five decades,' he wrote, 'throughout the Third World, the United States has deliberately targeted civilians or engaged in violence so indiscriminate that there is no other way to understand it except as terrorism'.

Jensen was writing from the heart of political darkness. But it was notable that a more virulent strain of straightforward anti-Americanism transpired in portions of the British broadsheet press. The BBC lived up to its mighty reputation squarely. John Simpson, as we saw, was immediately reporting by videophone from a hard-to-determine front line, and the corporation put its long experience and remarkable powers of co-ordination and timing to assembling a daily circuit of plainspeaking and scrupulous reporters in every scene of an uncontrollable action, stretching from western capitals to middle eastern dirt roads. If it cannot be said that CNN came up to this standard, it is because their spokespeople command so much less eloquent as well as less neutral a prose. The catastrophe of 11 September 2001 pointed an antique moral: that political journalism is good in so far as it is well-written, and that first drafts of history are as liable to cliché and to sanctimony as later ones are to smell mustily of the academy.

This self-righteousness was what was most in evidence on the flanks of the old Left in both Britain and the United States. Its advent brought out a home truth about the field of journalistic production; it is that dissent is held in place by its opposition. In order to oppose, in particular to oppose on behalf of the powerless, the established ramparts of dominant power, you must always be in the right, and they – your enemy – must always be in the wrong. Without this tension, dissent loses its bracing antithesis. The danger, of course, is that such dissent abandons rational critique and lapses into routine vituperation and, by extension, hypocrisy. Relativising the great historic gains of human rights and freedoms of western history in order to find moral credit in the sternness and inflexibility of absolutist Islam, the Left refused to acknowledge exactly those intellectual comforts and the material ease that made it possible for its members to voice its criticisms.

There was plenty of hypocrisy about at the time. There were journalists and commentators – John Pilger, Robert Fisk and even Noam Chomsky among them – for whom their routine incredulity at and dislike of professional politicians in the usual party stripes led them to a casual invective and unexamined derogation quite unsupported by the facts. Stuck for specialists who spoke Arabic, newspapers reached for their novelists. One Ahdar Soueif, writing for the *Guardian* (on 6 November 2001) reported without demurral that, in Cairo, 'nobody believes that Americans went into action in Afghanistan because of the events of September 11', that military action was a way of tightening the American grip on desert oil, after which *bêtises* the writer asked rhetorically, echoing what he claimed to hear all about him, why the British Prime Minister 'is rushing around with such zeal? Why does he look so pleased with himself?'

The mood of mistrust which, one may claim, was inaugurated by the covert foreign brutality of Dr Kissinger and the overt domestic criminality of President Nixon in the 1970s, has produced a popular mood and a political journalism to match in which politics becomes a pointless game, and politicians mere sharpers at the gaming table.

This is the obverse of Islamic dogmatism. As Howard Jacobson, another novelist-journalist and one of rare trenchancy, put it: 'If there is a flaw in democracy, it is this hankering after the certainties of undemocracy. If there is a weakness in civilisation, it is nostalgia for barbarism. It has become a commonplace of recent times that we will not find, because we do not know whom we are fighting. A more pressing problem, it seems to me, will be finding ourselves'.[3]

The terrific jolt of that first day of the new kind of mega-terrorism took a while to find a room in the house of fictions built for our cognitive and emotional accommodation by our journalists. One can discern a threefold process, following three threads spun by predecessor journalists for the hundred or so years of their trade.

The three such threaders are three distinguished journalists from three generations of the trade. The first and most senior, Seymour Hersh, we have met already in Vietnam and in passing pursuit of his inquiries into the shooting down of the Korean airliner by Russian defences in 1983. But he is an old grandee of investigative journalism whose cautious, gradual but damning researches[4] into the lethal career of Henry Kissinger set quite new standards for the painful, essential work of journalism to subvert scoundrels and affirm a sustainable civic probity.

Hersh has long had unrivalled connections in Washington. His work at this end of his mighty, almost forty-year career has been to report all that he can find out of what his government knows and does about the Middle East, sometimes with government complicity, sometimes not. The *New Yorker*,[5] hospitable as ever to the best political journalism around, leaves him to spread himself over 2,500 words, and Hersh sounds out the shakiness of the royal foundations below the factious power of the house of King Fahd. At the same time, Hersh logs the arrogant unpreparedness of all those enjoined to secure the nation's security, and the nervousness and indecision with which the nation's generals and their legalistic henchmen were so painfully learning to fight the new kind of sporadic war. Hersh's conclusions are bleakly pessimistic; he discharges a first duty of the journalist; finding little for our comfort, he discovers what we could not possibly discover for ourselves, and tells us what it is. He is faithful to his science, which is the history of the present.

Hersh's first mate is the youngster of the trio, an Englishman, Tim Judah. He is in the mould of Peter Fleming except that he writes on both sides of the Atlantic. He is heir to the adventurer tradition, reported in detail from the war in Kosovo which, in the last year of the old millennium, completed the final breakup of Yugoslavia. He had long been a journalist in the region, spoke Serbo-Croat, had lived in Belgrade, wrote for the *Daily Telegraph*, *Guardian* and – at greatest length – for the incomparable *New York Review*.[6]

He followed the same forms in his work in Afghanistan as he did in Yugoslavia. He moved easily between the obligatory self-deprecation of *being there* and the sure deployment of big strategic tropes. 'As I sprinted for shelter and fell into the deep dust of the trenches, the crowd of accompanying soldiers broke out in hysterical laughter, before taking cover themselves'. He correctly predicted large-scale defections from the Taliban, then the Islamic fundamentalists ruling the country by gun, whip and masculine cruelty; he met the brigand leaders, perforce the allies of the United States; he talked to schoolboys pressganged into the line by the Taliban, sneaking home under threat of death by night, and he met the fifteen-year-old regent-commander of 300 Uzbeki soldiers (from the northern zone adjacent to Uzbekistan of the former USSR). The fifteen-year-old looks forward to victory, and going to London. Judah added up how things were likely to end, stuck to his moral duty to hope, and kept his appointments, not with destiny (he doesn't write that sort of prose) but with the best of a bad job.[7]

The third of the trio is not so much an officer on the same ship as commodore at the admiralty. He is Michael Ignatieff, fifty-something novelist, journalist, intellectual, chat show chair, finely titled professor of the practice of human rights policy at Harvard. He doesn't – in the vapid phrase – 'call for' consequences. He foretells them. He is invincibly optimistic. In round and stirring prose, he says, 'We can contain terror, but we cannot eliminate it. This is not a defeatist thought.' Terror can be blockaded, deprived of money, its grisly hosts prosecuted, isolated, if necessary bombarded. 'This is not victory. This is risk reduction.' Briefly he summarises the frame of mind of modern *jihad*, 'the fantasies of violent expulsion of the infidel', the sweet daydream of the cleansing of all-Arab corruption. Changing these hate-filled, monochromatic imaginings will take more than the BBC World Service and aid parcels dropped from the sky.

To describe what it will take, Ignatieff calls up a vision of the international settlement of 1945. What history requires of present leaders, whose power and representativeness only we ourselves can call to order to ensure their trustworthiness, is a politics compatible with their own professed ideals and our own formal principles of political action. It is a politics of moral consistency, one which would 'stop remaining silent when Arab states oppress their citizens ... stop pretending that our foreign-aid budgets are all we can afford'. And he ends:

So victory in this war will mean something more than feeling a little less afraid and becoming more astute about risk management. It will mean doing something real about the hatred of millions of people who feel excluded from our abundance and our freedom. Towards the hatreds of those who engage in terror, there is only one response. But towards those whose lives we could actually improve we owe it to them, and to ourselves, to act. I don't know whether we will know when we have won this war. I do know it is a war we have not even begun to fight.[8]

This is bigger music than most journalists compose. It is the last quotation in this book, so it is not inopportune that Ignatieff's eloquence and his appeal to the best in our societies is made for a life-and-death occasion. In a condition of intermittent terror and localised, sporadic warfare, the citizens of a peaceful, wealthy country read what is being done to other, poorer peoples to protect home comforts and, on a good day, local ideals. At the same time, they look apprehensively out of their windows at harmless stratocruisers overhead, and torment themselves with nightmares about poisoned water in the tap from which their children are drinking, or five kilograms of plutonium strapped to the belly of the ordinary-looking student with a dark moustache and liquid eyes.

The journalist goes off on our behalf and to more casually dangerous places. Sometimes he or she gets killed, sending the news back home. The obituary columns are full of those who have died doing political journalism, died *for* political journalism on occasion. I could tell the ambiguous tale of Veronica Guerin, crime reporter in both parts of Ireland, where as much as in Salvador or Chechnya crime is synonymous with politics, who was shot dead in 1996 while waiting at traffic lights by a hit-and-run motorcyclist in Dublin. She had already been wounded and threatened, she had lived very dangerously, she loved danger, she courted it, they say, she put her small son in it, she knew and told a lot; what *was* she up to?[9] There are simpler tales of saints and martyrs who go to the world's end and the sea's jaws to bring back the politics of other people and who die or risk death doing so. Nicholas Tomalin of the *Sunday Times* was blown up by a mine in the Six-Day War in the Middle East; the Iranian Farzad Bartoft of the *Observer* was executed in hateful revenge by Saddam Hussein for pressing his journalistic researches into Iraqi weaponry too far; I cannot doubt that one private hero of mine, Lars-Erik Nelson, died of overwork; the Frenchwoman Elisabeth Schemla pursued with her informants the horrific abuse by Algerian fundamentalists of their own disobedient womenfolk to a point at which she could fear the *fatwa*; Robert Fisk, now of the *Independent*, forced off the *Times* at the time of Murdoch's takeover, made himself into the wholly unyielding, cordially self-righteous, and always steady reckoner of the body-count in Palestine and of the monstrous injustices enacted by the Israelis upon their inconvenient neighbours amid so much hand-wringing ineffectuality by American journalists. He was almost beaten to death in Afghanistan for his pains. If he *has* nine lives, he has risked them all too regularly.

This book contains a mere handful of the tales still to be told of journalistic conscience, recklessness, truth-telling, courage and the rest at a time when so much journalism is no doubt every bit as bad as Cronkite or Hitchens or you and I say it is: bad because trivial, mean-minded, clunking and clichéd, unresearched, ignorant, barbarous, uncivilised, lying and cowardly ... we could all go on going on about it. 'Journalists', people say contemptuously or dismissively, 'there's nothing in the paper ...'

This book speaks up for the best, as any tradition *defined* as the best selected from amongst the worst people can do and write, is bound to do. This is how a tradition composes itself and teaches its children to grow up and live well. There are shameful tales collected here as well, for the sake of balance, maybe, and for the saltiness of a useful malice without which the exemplary biographies would come out savourless. But largely, I have looked for and found tall, exemplary tales of brave journalists, fine writers, high steppers, good lives; and a few satisfactorily bad ones thrown in, to lend colour.

These names, sometimes their faces as well, brought home to us our history, made us at home in that history and called us to action when home was threatened. In so far as they kept a good prose and were faithful to a sufficient ethics of their exiguous trade, then – in the small number of exceptional cases I present here for wonder, for admiration, for relief that one only has to read and not write the words let alone gather the facts – they group themselves at my arrangement and on my plinth in their modestly heroic attitudes.

They and we deprecate heroism, in the modern way. All the same, these journalists write the daily prose which keeps the blood up in the ideals we live for and the principles we live by. Politicians may traduce those great names and potent words; journalists mustn't. In this canon, they mostly don't. The more or less famous men and women I praise in these pages have nothing much to be ashamed of. They told the truth about what they knew and what they believed; they wrote as well as they could as fast as they could; they made up as handsome and generous a circumambient story about how the world was going as squared with the facts; they abjured sycophancy and disrespected the mighty on suspicion. Until recently, they weren't even very well paid for doing so; even now, plenty go short. No doubt they drank far too much, and numbers of them screwed up families, lovers, selves, commissions and stories. But in the essential, at times idealised form in which I have recounted these brief lives, these particular writers found a way of working, of reconciling the pleasures of art and life, of desire and actuality, which did them and their times a lot of credit, and they kept us who read them well enough satisfied in our unassuageable hunger to know what on earth is going on.

Notes

Chapter One *First Lady:* Martha Gellhorn

1 Martha Gellhorn, *The Face of War* (New York: Atlantic Monthly Press, 1988), p. 179.
2 Gellhorn, *The Face of War*, p. 180.
3 Gellhorn, *The Face of War*, p. 180.
4 Gellhorn, *The Face of War*, p. 184.
5 *Face-to-Face* interview, BBC, 1994.
6 *Face-to-Face* (1994).
7 In Michael Schudson, *Discovering the News: A social history of American newspapers* (New York: Basic Books, 1978).
8 Lincoln Steffens, *Autobiography of Lincoln Steffens* (New York: Norton, 1931), p. 171.
9 The debate is analysed in relation to the practice of academic history by Peter Novick in his *That Noble Dream: The objectivity question and the American historical profession* (Cambridge and New York: Cambridge University Press, 1988).
10 Quoted from her conversations with Martha Gellhorn by Mary Blume in *Côte d'Azur: Inventing the French Riviera* (London: Thames and Hudson, 1992), p. 117.
11 The letters are reprinted in Martha Gellhorn, *The View from the Ground* (New York: Atlantic Monthly Press, 1988), pp. 10–32.
12 Gellhorn, *The Face of War*, p. 13.
13 Gellhorn, *The Face of War*, p. 23.
14 Carlos Baker, *Ernest Hemingway: A life story* (London: Collins, 1969), p. 371.
15 Ernest Hemingway, *By-line: Selected articles and dispatches of four decades*, ed. W. White (New York: Simon and Schuster, 1998), p. 259.
16 Jeremy Harding, 'No one leaves her place in line', *London Review of Books*, 7 May 1998.
17 Quoted by Jeremy Harding, 'No one leaves her place in line'.
18 Gellhorn, *The Face of War*, p. 41.
19 In 'A program for US realists', reprinted in Hemingway, *By-line*, pp. 290–3.
20 Gellhorn, *The Face of War*, p. 52.
21 Baker, *Ernest Hemingway*, (1969), p. 452.
22 Gellhorn, *The Face of War*, p. 90.
23 Gellhorn, *The Face of War*, p. 93.
24 Gellhorn, *The Face of War*, pp. 119–20.

25 As Phillip Knightley seems to recommend in his nonetheless classic study *The First Casualty: The war correspondent as hero, propagandist and myth maker* (1985; 4th rev. edn, London: Pan Books, 2000).

26 In Gellhorn, *The Face of War*, pp. 183–225.

27 Gellhorn, *The Face of War*, p. 231.

28 Gellhorn, *The View from the Ground*, p. 295.

29 Gellhorn, *The Face of War*, p. 278.

30 Graham Greene, *The Honorary Consul* (Oxford: Bodley Head and Penguin, 1973).

31 Gellhorn, *The Face of War*, p. 316.

32 Harding, 'No one leaves her place in line', p. 30.

CHAPTER TWO *Cautionary History:* Lords of the Dance

1 Max Weber, 'Politics as a vocation', in *From Max Weber: Essays in sociology*, ed. and introd. H. H. Gerth and C. Wright Mills (London: Routledge and Kegan Paul, 1948).

2 Weber, 'Politics as a vocation', p. 96.

3 Weber, 'Politics as a vocation', p. 96.

4 Weber, 'Politics as a vocation', p. 97.

5 The phrase is Eric Hobsbawm's in the celebrated final volume of his great series, *The Age of Revolution: Europe, 1789–1848* (1962); *The Age of Capital, 1848–1875* (1975); *The Age of Empire, 1875–1914* (1987); and finally *Age of Extremes: The short twentieth century, 1914–1991* (London: Michael Joseph, 1994): 'short' because it encloses the three world wars; the third, for all it was the cold one, nonetheless saw twice as many fatalities as the first.

6 Elias Canetti is the first, indeed the only writer, to analyse the different ways in which crowds have lost or taken political power, in his *Crowds and Power* (1960; Harmondsworth: Penguin, 1981).

7 Weber, 'Politics as a vocation', p. 98.

8 Weber, 'Politics as a vocation', p. 99.

9 This example is taken from Harold Evans's millennial essay, 'What a century!', *Columbia Journalism Review* (Jan.–Feb. 1999), pp. 27–37.

10 Here, as so often in these pages, I follow James Curran and Jean Seaton in their anti-mythologising classic, *Power without Responsibility: The press and broadcasting in Britain* (5th edn, London and New York: Routledge, 1997), see chs 2 to 5 in particular.

11 Curran and Seaton, *Power without Responsibility*, p. 10.

12 Curran and Seaton, *Power without Responsibility*, p. 31.

13 The canonical (and moving) analysis of such journals is of course Richard Hoggart's in *The Uses of Literacy: Aspects of working-class life with special reference to publications and entertainments* (Harmondsworth: Penguin, 1958), ch. 4.

14 Especially Nicholas Garnham in his *Capitalism and Communication: global culture and the economics of information* (London: Sage Books, 1990), ch. 2.

15 I take much here from Raymond Williams, in his 'The growth of the popular press', *The Long Revolution* (Harmondsworth: Penguin, 1963), but follow Curran and Seaton in identifying owners not advertisers as the true inventors of the modern newspaper.

16 Williams, *The Long Revolution*, p. 227.

17 For Northcliffe, see T. Clarke, *My Northcliffe Diary* (London: Gollancz, 1931); A. P. Ryan, *Lord Northcliffe* (London: Collins, 1953).

18 Quoted by Stephen Koss, *The Rise and Fall of the Political Press in Britain* (London: Hamish Hamilton, 1984), p. 167.

19 Quoted in Koss, *The Rise and Fall of the Political Press*, p. 207.

20 Koss, *The Rise and Fall of the Political Press*, p. 269.

21 Koss, *The Rise and Fall of the Political Press*, p. 279.

22 Matthew Engel, *Tickle the Public: 100 years of the popular press* (London: Gollancz, 1996), p. 98.

23 Quoted in Curran and Seaton, *Power without Responsibilty*, p. 48.

24 The whole story is told with relish by his friend, admirer, correspondent and political enemy, A. J. P. Taylor, in his *Beaverbrook* (London: Hamish Hamilton, 1972), pp. 121–7.

25 Quoted by Engel, *Tickle the Public*, p. 103, from the *Daily Mail* editorial, 30 Nov. 1923.

26 Quoted in Engel, *Tickle the Public*, p. 103.

27 Curran and Seaton, *Power without Responsibilty*, p. 52.

28 I take the phrase 'structure of feeling' from Raymond Williams, who first sketched out its usefulness in *The Long Revolution*. See also my biography, *Raymond Williams* (London and New York: Routledge, 1995).

29 Gunther Barth, *City People: The rise of modern city culture in 19th century America* (New York and Oxford: Oxford University Press, 1980).

30 Walter Benjamin, 'The storyteller', in Walter Benjamin, *Illuminations* (London: Jonathan Cape, 1970), pp. 88–9.

31 Ian Watt, *The Rise of the Novel* (London: Chatto and Windus, 1957).

32 I take this point from Rolf Lindner's admirable study of the beginnings of sociology in urban reporting, *The Reportage of Urban Culture: Robert Park and the Chicago School* (Cambridge: Cambridge University Press, 1990).

33 Lindner's point, *The Reportage of Urban Culture*, p. 11.

34 Elizabeth Cochraine, writing as 'Nellie Bly', is credited with being the first woman reporter, certainly the first star in the role. She wrote for the *Pittsburgh Dispatch* and then for Pulitzer's *World*, first as a muckraker then as a travelling correspondent. See R. Ross, *Ladies of the Press* (New York: Norton, 1974).

35 Herbert Shapiro (ed.), *The Muckrakers and American Society* (Boston: Beacon Press, 1968), p. 3.

36 Walter Lippmann, *Preface to Politics* (New York: Mitchell Kennerley, 1913), p. 12.

37 George W Juergens, *Joseph Pulitzer and the New York World* (Princeton: Princeton University Press, 1966).

38 This point is made very well by Paul H. Weaver in 'Pulitzer's revolution', in his *News and the Culture of Lying* (New York: Free Press, 1994).

39 Schudson, *Discovering the News*. See also Helen Douglas, *The Front Page* (Michigan: University of Michigan Press, 1938), for her imaginative restoration of how front pages evolved.

40 I take much here from a brilliant excursus on the way newspapers make our world, and the similarities with the experience of reading a novel, in Benedict Anderson's *Imagined Communities: Reflections on the origin and spread of nationalism* (London and New York: Verso, 1983), pp. 28–40.

41 By Jeffrey Tulis in his *The Rhetorical Presidency* (Princeton: Princeton University Press, 1987). But see also Weaver, *News and the Culture of Lying*, pp. 55–67.

42 See David Nasaw, *The Chief: the life of William Randolph Hearst* (New York: Houghton Mifflin, 2000). I have also used freely John Dos Passos's dazzling ten-page cameo 'Poor little rich boy' in his novel *The Big Money* (New York: Harcourt Brace, 1932).

CHAPTER THREE *Public Opinion and Mass Politics:*
Gentlemen of the Press

1 Jürgen Habermas, *The Structural Transformation of the Public Sphere: An inquiry into a category of bourgeois society*, first published in German, 1962 (Cambridge: Polity, 1989), pp. 181–90.

2 As it is by Benedict Anderson, *Imagined Communities*. See also Lucien Febvre and Henri-Jean Martin, *The Coming of the Book: The impact of printing 1450–1800* (London: New Left Books, 1976).

3 Habermas, *The Structural Transformation of the Public Sphere*, pp. 22ff.

4 The classic expression of its central place in jurisprudence is, in Britain, A. V. Dicey, *Law and Public Opinion in England*. (1905; London: Macmillan 1963), and in the USA, J. Bryce, *The American Commonwealth* (New York: Macmillan, 1888).

5 C. Wright Mills, *The Power Elite* (New York: Oxford University Press, 1968), pp. 303–4.

6 Knightley, *The First Casualty* (rev. edn, 2000), chapters 5, 6 and 7, 'The last war 1914–1918', 'Enter America', 'The remedy for Bolshevism'.

7 Knightley, *The First Casualty*, p. 84.

8 Quoted by Robert Graves, *Good-bye to All That* (1929; Harmondsworth: Penguin, 1960), p. 189.

9 Knightley, *The First Casualty*, p. 117.

10 Though I can find no legal or anecdotal evidence to support his saying (p. 105) that taking photographs at the front was a capital offence. In any case, thousands of such photographs remain extant.

11 A. J. P. Taylor, *English History 1914–1945*, vol. 15 of *Oxford History of England* (Oxford: Clarendon Press, 1965), p. 59n.

12 These four local papers, of varying status and readership (two dailies, two weeklies, north, east, west) happen to be the four archives which I could readily consult. I'm confident they serve my representative purpose.

13 Ernest Hemingway, *A Farewell to Arms* (1929; St Albans: Granada Publishing, 1977), p. 133.

14 Graves, *Good-bye to All That*, p. 188.

15 As A. J. P. Taylor says, see *English History 1914–1945*, pp. 26–7.

16 *Darlington and Stockton Times*, 13 Nov. 1916.

17 The phrase alludes to Paul Fussell's famous and remarkable book *The Great War and Modern Memory* (New York: Oxford University Press, 1975), much drawn on in these pages.

18 The phrase refers to my own book in which his novels have a central place, see Inglis, *The Promise of Happiness: Value and meaning in children's fiction* (Cambridge: Cambridge University Press, 1981).

19 The phrase was coined by the social psychologist D. W. Harding in his essay, of considerable importance to our understanding of newspaper audiences, 'The bond with the author', *Use of English*, 22, no. 4 (1971).

20 Arthur Ransome's prefatory note to *Swallows and Amazons* in the Puffin edition (Harmondsworth, 1972).

21 Arthur Ransome, *The Autobiography*, ed. Rupert Hart-Davis (London: Jonathan Cape, 1976), p. 161.

22 Ransome, *The Autobiography*, p. 187.

23 Ransome, *The Autobiography*, p. 207.

24 Ransome, *The Autobiography*, p. 216.

25 Ransome, *The Autobiography*, p. 262.

26 Arthur Ransome, *Six Weeks in Russia in 1919* (London: Unwin, 1919).

27 *Manchester Guardian*, 10 Feb. 1920.

28 *Manchester Guardian*, 22 Feb. 1920.

29 Arthur Ransome, *Racundra's First Cruise* (London: Unwin, 1923).

30 A bit puzzlingly, Knightley seems to think Ransome left Russia in 1918. See Knightley, *The First Casualty*, p. 163n.

31 Ransome, *The Autobiography*, p. 321.

32 Published and republished up to the present day as *Rod and Line.*

33 James Thurber, *My Life and Hard Times* (Harmondsworth: Penguin, 1948), author's blurb.

34 Konstantin Paustovsky, *Slow Approach of Thunder* (London: Harvill Press, 1965), p. 160.

35 Paustovsky, *Slow Approach of Thunder*, p. 174.

36 Paustovsky, *Slow Approach of Thunder*, p. 236.

37 Konstantin Paustovsky, *In That Dawn* (London: Harvill Press, 1967), p. 40.

38 Paustovsky, *In That Dawn*, p. 60.

39 Paustovsky, *In That Dawn*, p. 150.

40 Konstantin Paustovsky, *Years of Hope* (London: Harvill Press, 1968), p. 98.

CHAPTER FOUR *Walter Lippmann:* The Real Voice of America

1 Steven Lukes, *Power: A radical view* (Basingstoke: Macmillan, 1974), esp. p. 25 and ch. 7.

2 Canetti, *Crowds and Power*, pp. 35–51.

3 Clifford Geertz, 'Centers, kings and charisma: symbolics of power', in his *Local Knowledge: Further essays in interpretive anthropology* (New York: Basic Books, 1983), p. 124.

4 *Literary Digest*, 2 Feb. 1907.

5 I steal these phrases from Storm Jameson's autobiography *Journey from the North*, vol. 2 (London: Virago, 1984), p. 136 where they apply to a rather lesser figure than Lippmann.

6 As he is by John Patrick Diggins in his *The Promise of Pragmatism* (Chicago: University of Chicago Press, 1994), ch. 8.

7 Ronald Steel *Walter Lippmann and this American Century* (New York: Random House, 1981) p. 34.

8 *New Republic*, 21 Oct. 1916.

9 For an admirable and detailed account of this see J. Lee Thompson, *Northcliffe* (London: John Murray, 2000).

10 Lippmann to House, 11 Nov. 1918; quoted by Steel (1981) p. 150.

11 J. M. Keynes, *The Economic Consequences of the Peace* (1919), vol. 2 of *The Collected Writings* (22 vols), ed. Elizabeth Johnson and Donald Moggridge (London: Macmillan, 1956).

12 Walter Lippmann, *Public Opinion* (1922; New York: Macmillan, 1960), p. 196.

13 Walter Lippmann, *A Preface to Morals* (New York: Macmillan, 1929); these sentences are from Walter Lippmann, *The Essential Lippmann*, ed. C. Rossiter and J. Lare (New York: Random House, 1963), p. 229.

14 Steel (1981), p. 291.

15 *Herald Tribune* column, 29 June 1932.

16 *Herald Tribune*, 30 Oct. 1941.

17 Walter Lippmann, *US Foreign Policy: Shield of the Republic* (Boston: Little Brown, 1943).

18 Winston Churchill, *The Second World War*, vol. 6: *Triumph and Tragedy* (London: Cassell, 1954), p. 198.

19 Lippmann himself said he picked it up from conversations in France in the 1930s when it was used to describe Hitler's provocations. Lippmann's was certainly the first work to use 'cold war' in its title: see Walter Lippmann, *The Cold War* (Boston: Little Brown, 1947).

20 *Herald Tribune*, 11 Sep. 1945, but I follow Anwar Syed's treatment in his *Walter Lippmann's Philosophy of International Politics* (Philadelphia: University of Pennsylvania Press, 1963).

21 Here discussed in the version reprinted in George Kennan, *American Diplomacy*, expanded edn (Chicago: Chicago University Press, 1984).

22 The aphorism is in fact Kenneth Burke's, a pragmatist with Marxist sympathies, in his *Attitudes to History*, first published in 1937; see 3rd rev. edn (Berkeley: University of California Press, 1965), p. 315.

23 Quoted by the excellent David Yergin in his *Shattered Peace: The origins of the Cold War and the National Security State* (Harmondsworth: Penguin, 1980), p. 327.

24 Quoted by David Caute, *The Great Fear: The anti-communist purge under Truman and Eisenhower* (New York: Simon and Schuster, 1978), p. 305.

25 Quoted by Bruce Cumings and Jon Halliday, *Korea: The forgotten war* (New York: Pantheon, 1989), p. 128.

26 See Reston's essay in the collection he edited with Marquis Childs, M. Childs and J. Reston (eds), *Walter Lippmann and his Times* (New York: Harcourt Brace, 1959).

27 Cumings and Halliday, *Korea*, p. 197.

28 *Herald Tribune*, 26 June 1952.

29 In 1957 Kennan broadcast his Reith lectures for the BBC proposing reunification, see his *Memoirs 1950–63* (Boston: Little Brown, 1972).

30 Quoted in Steel, *Walter Lippmann*, p. 515, emphasis added.

31 *Thirteen Days* is Robert Kennedy's memoir of the episode (New York: Norton, 1969); in 2001 it was made into a successful film.

32 Arthur Schlesinger, *A Thousand Days: John F. Kennedy in the White House* (London: André Deutsch, 1965), p. 316.

33 *Herald Tribune*, 29 Oct. 1962.

34 With the help of her remarks to me and her autobiography Katherine Graham, *Personal History* (New York: Random House, 1998).

35 Just how key it was is the opening subject of Neil Sheehan's mighty book on his journalistic experience in Vietnam, *A Bright Shining Lie: John Paul Vann and America in Vietnam* (New York: Random House, 1988).

36 Quoted in Steel, *Walter Lippmann*, p. 548, observation made in one of his TV interviews, 6 Feb. 1965.

37 These remarks were echoed by Martin Kettle writing about the British Prime Minister, *Guardian*, 6 May 1997.

38 *Washington Post*, 17 May 1966.

CHAPTER FIVE *Ardour and Detachment:*
Fascism, Communism and Journalism

1 A paraphrase of a definition offered by Clifford Geertz in *The Interpretation of Cultures* (London: Hutchinson, 1975), pp. 444–5.

2 Knightley, *The First Casualty*.

3 Halberstam, quoted by Michael Parenti, *Inventing Reality: The politics of the mass media* (New York: St Martin's Press, 1986), pp. 52–3.

4 A condition in which the message system of growth is corrupted and the bone formation of ribcage and spine is compacted but not stopped, and chest and back grow laterally but not upwards.

5 Gramsci's sister Nennetta's words, quoted in Giuseppe Fiori, *Antonio Gramsci: Life of a revolutionary* (London: New Left Books, 1970), p. 16.

6 Quoted in Fiori, *Antonio Gramsci*, p. 107.

7 I take these points from Quintin Hoare in his edition of Antonio Gramsci, *Selections*

from the Prison Notebooks (London: Lawrence and Wishart, 1971), pp. xxxv–xlvi.

8 From *L'Ordine Nuovo*, 5 July 1921; reprinted in Gramsci, *Antonio Gramsci: Selections from political writings 1921–1926*, ed. Quintin Hoare (London: Lawrence and Wishart, 1978), p. 54.

9 *L'Ordine Nuovo*, 18 Dec. 1920.

10 Gramsci, *Antonio Gramsci: Selections from political writings*, p. 62.

11 Perry Anderson, 'The antinomies of Antonio Gramsci', *New Left Review*, 100 (Nov.–Jan. 1977), pp. 5–80.

12 Theodor Adorno, *Minima Moralia: Reflections from a damaged life* (London: New Left Books, 1974), p. 224.

13 In his autobiography, William Shirer, *Twentieth Century Journey, vol. 1: The Start, 1904–1930* (New York: Simon and Schuster, 1976), book 4.

14 Ernest Hemingway, *The Sun Also Rises* (New York: Scribner's, 1926), p. 11.

15 Shirer, *The Start, 1904–1930*, p. 488.

16 R. Anwar, *The Tragedy of Afghanistan: A first-hand account*, (London: Verso, 1989), pp. 41–4.

17 William Shirer, *Twentieth Century Journey*, vol. 2: *The Nightmare Years 1930–1940* (Boston: Little, Brown, 1984), p. 158.

18 Shirer, *The Nightmare Years 1930–1940*, p. 162.

19 Norman Finkelstein, *With Heroic Truth: The life of Edward R Murrow* (New York: Clarion Books, 1997), p. 58.

20 A hundred pounds sterling at the then exchange rate.

21 As we learn from Elias Canetti in *Crowds and Power*.

22 Shirer, *The Nightmare Years 1930–1940*, p. 322.

23 Shirer, *The Nightmare Years 1930–1940*, p. 363.

24 CBS, 23 Apr. 1939.

25 Shudson, *Discovering the News*, p. 319.

26 William Shirer, *Berlin Diary* (1940; London: Hamish Hamilton, 1947), which became a bestseller.

27 Shirer, *Berlin Diary*, p. 49.

28 Leo Tolstoy, *War and Peace*, trans. A. Maude (London: Macmillan, 1942), p. 1338.

29 Shirer, *The Nightmare Years, 1930–1940*, p. 591.

30 The phrase is Thomas Nagel's and the name of his book: *The View from Nowhere* (Oxford: Oxford University Press, 1985). It characterises the aspired-to but impossible position from which one sees *all round* a moral action.

31 William Blake, *Marginalia*, no. 516. 'What is the price of experience? do men buy it for a song? or wisdom for a dance in the street? No, it is bought with the price of all that a man hath, his house, his wife, his children.'

32 Edmund Wilson in *New Republic*, 9 Aug. 1933, reprinted in R. W. B. Lewis (ed.), *Malraux: Twentieth century views*, (New York: Prentice-Hall, 1969).

33 André Malraux, *La Tentation de l'Occident* (Paris: Grasset, 1926), p. 25.

34 David Wilkinson, *Malraux: an essay in political criticism* (Cambridge: Harvard University Press, 1967), p. 5.

35 These biographical details are taken from Jean Lacouture's classic and caustic *André Malraux. Une vie dans le siècle* (Paris: Seuil, 1973), one of the greatest biographies of the twentieth century, much helped by the author's intimacy with his subject. See also Olivier Todd, *André Malraux. Une vie* (Paris: Gallimard, 2001) for a bitterly incredulous perspective.

36 Leon Trotsky, 'The strangled revolution', (1931), reprinted in Lewis, *Malraux*, p. 13.

37 Translated as *Man's Hope* by Stuart Gilbert and Alistair MacDonald (New York:

Random House, 1983); the incident featuring Slade is on pp. 385–6.

38   *The Nation*, 20 Mar. 1937.

39   Malraux, *Man's Hope*, p. 258.

40   André Malraux, *Anti-memoirs* (London: Hamish Hamilton, 1968), pp. 152ff.; Lacouture, *André Malraux*, pp. 290ff.

41   Malraux, *Anti-memoirs*, p. 162.

42   Malraux, *Anti-memoirs*, p. 83.

43   *Combat*, 28 Jan. 1945.

CHAPTER SIX *Fascism and the English*

1   Richard Cockett, *Twilight of Truth: Chamberlain, appeasement and the manipulation of the press* (London: Weidenfeld and Nicolson, 1989), pp. 1–2.

2   Founded in 1877, see Cockett, *Twilight of Truth*, p. 10.

3   *Manchester Guardian* archive, 23 Mar. 1935; to the editor, W. P. Crozier.

4   *Observer*, 28 Feb. 1937.

5   Quoted from Halifax's diary by Cockett, *Twilight of Truth*, p. 40.

6   *Daily Express*, 17 Sept. 1938, quoted by Engel, *Tickle the Press*, p. 138.

7   On 24 January 1923; quoted by Donald McLachlan, *In the Chair: Barrington-Ward of The Times 1927–1948* (London: Weidenfeld and Nicolson, 1971), p. 99.

8   Cockett, *Twilight of Truth*, p. 111.

9   R. G. Collingwood, *An Autobiography* (Oxford: Clarendon Press, 1938), pp. 155, 166.

10 Francis Williams, *Dangerous Estate: The anatomy of newspapers* (London: Longmans Green, 1957), pp. 274–5.

11 *History of the Times* (London: Times Newspapers, 1952), p. 907.

12 This timetable summarised from McLachlan, *In the Chair*, ch. 10.

13 Quoted in McLachlan, *In the Chair*, p. 107.

14 A. G. MacDonnell, *England, Their England* (London: Macmillan, 1933).

15 Evelyn Waugh, *The Diaries of Evelyn Waugh*, ed. Michael Davie (Harmondsworth: Penguin, 1979), pp. 321–9. The date on which he first learned of his wife's adultery was 9 July 1930.

16 The reports appeared in *The Times* and Waugh then published them in 1931 with embellishments as *Remote People* (Harmondsworth: Penguin, 1985), this quotation p. 41.

17 Waugh, *Diaries*, p. 330.

18 Waugh, *Diaries*, p. 332.

19 Waugh, *Remote People*, p. 64.

20 Evelyn Waugh, *Waugh in Abyssinia* (London: Longmans Green, 1937), p. 48.

21 This story, suppressed in *Waugh in Abyssinia*, he told to his close friend and biographer, Christopher Sykes: *Evelyn Waugh: A biography* (Harmondsworth: Penguin, 1977), pp. 221–2.

22 Knightley, *The First Casualty*, p. 201.

23 Herbert L. Matthews, *The Education of a Correspondent* (New York: Harcourt Brace, 1946), pp. 48, 51, 53.

24 Iris Murdoch, *The Sovereignty of Good* (London: Routledge and Kegan Paul, 1970), pp. 70ff.

25 Claud Cockburn, *I, Claud: An autobiography* (Harmondsworth: Penguin, 1967), p. 212.

26 Cockburn, *I, Claud*, p. 57.

27 Cockburn, *I, Claud*, p. 74.

28 Cockburn, *I, Claud*, p. 133.

29 Cockburn, *I, Claud*, p. 139.

30 Knightley, *The First Casualty*, p. 213.

31 Milan Kundera, *The Book of Laughter and Forgetting* (Harmondsworth: Penguin, 1983), p. 62.

32 Cockburn, *I, Claud*, p. 234.

33 See Raymond Williams, *Politics and Letters* (London: New Left Books, 1979), p. 384. I take much in what follows from Bernard Crick's excellent *George Orwell: A life* (London: Secker and Warburg, 1980).

34 All articles available in George Orwell, *Collected Essays, Journalism and Letters of George Orwell*, ed. Sonia Orwell and Ian Angus (4 vols, Harmondsworth: Penguin, 1970).

35 Orwell, *Collected Essays* vol. 1, pp. 59–60.

36 George Orwell, *Homage to Catalonia* (1938; Harmondsworth: Penguin, 1962).

37 Orwell, *Homage to Catalonia*, p. 8.

38 Orwell, *Homage to Catalonia*, pp. 8–9.

39 Orwell's phrase in an essay on Yeats; Orwell, *Collected Essays*, vol. 2, p. 314.

40 Orwell, *Collected Essays*, vol. 1, p. 438. The article appeared in the *Adelphi*.

41 Camus writes in *La Chute*, 'Si l'on n'a pas un caractère, on a besoin d'une méthode.'

Chapter Seven *The Important Fact of Fictions about Journalism*

1 The aphorism belongs to Noam Chomsky in his great essay 'The responsibility of intellectuals', in Noam Chomsky, *American Power and the New Mandarins* (London: Chatto and Windus, 1969), p. 257.

2 Pilate is the joker according to Francis Bacon in his *Essays, or Counsels, Civil and Moral*; his original question is reported in St John's Gospel, 18:37.

3 A contrivance roundly dismissed by Sissela Bok in her *Lying: Moral choice in public and private life* (Hassocks: Harvester, 1978), pp. 165ff.

4 Gore Vidal, *The Golden Age* (Boston: Little, Brown, 2000), pp. 138–9.

5 P. G. Wodehouse, *Psmith Journalist* (Harmondsworth: Penguin, 1970).

6 Wodehouse, *Psmith Journalist*, p. 7.

7 Wodehouse, *Psmith Journalist*, pp. 32–3.

8 Wodehouse, *Psmith Journalist*, p. 73.

9 Wodehouse, *Psmith Journalist*, p. 58.

10 The 1920s stage play by Ben Hecht and Charles MacArthur, who turned it into a screenplay for Howard Hughes in 1931.

11 Stanley Cavell, *Pursuits of Happiness: The Hollywood comedy of remarriage* (Cambridge: Harvard University Press, 1981).

12 Cavell, *Pursuits of Happiness*, p. 25.

13 Cavell, *Pursuits of Happiness*, p. 164.

14 Cavell, *Pursuits of Happiness*, p. 170.

15 Cavell, *Pursuits of Happiness*, p. 177.

16 *Front Page Woman* (1935), directed by Michael Curtiz with Bette Davis and George Brent in the starring roles.

17 *The Sweet Smell of Success* (1957), directed by Alexander Mackendrick, written by Clifford Odets, starring Burt Lancaster, Tony Curtis, Émile Meyer.

18 These last phrases are in fact Raymond Williams's in his novel *The Volunteers* (London: Eyre Methuen, 1978), one of the most intelligent on the subject that you could wish for, and to which we return.

19   Robert Penn Warren, *All the King's Men* (1946; New York: Bantam Books, 1951).

20   Warren, *All the King's Men*, p. 261.

21   Warren, *All the King's Men*, p. 49.

22   Evelyn Waugh, *Scoop* (1938; Harmondsworth: Penguin, 1984).

23   Waugh, *Scoop*, p. 68.

24   Waugh, *Scoop*, p. 66.

25   Waugh, *Scoop*, p. 43.

26   Keith Kyle, 'Orders of empire', *London Review of Books*, 7 Mar. 1985, p. 8.

27   Waugh, *Scoop*, pp. 210, 220, 219.

CHAPTER EIGHT   *The Blessed Simplicity of Action*

1   Orwell, *Collected Essays*, vol. 1, p. 587.

2   Joseph Conrad, *The Shadow Line* (London: Dent, 1917).

3   Orwell, *Collected Essays*, vol. 2, p. 75.

4   Raymond Williams, *Orwell* (London: Fontana, 1971).

5   Orwell, *Collected Essays*, vol. 2, p. 88

6   Williams, *Politics and Letters*, p. 391.

7   Michael Walzer in *The Company of Critics: Social criticism and political commentary in the 20th century* (New York: Basic Books, 1988), ch. 7, 'George Orwell's England'.

8   This is a phrase implying its opposite as used by David Hare in his fine play *The Absence of War* (1993) in which his point is that without imminent political danger, like war, idealistic Labour politicians can make no progress.

9   *Partisan Review* (Mar–Apr. 1943). Orwell described the Beveridge Report (largely written by a Liberal peer but with ample help from the London School of Economics) as a 'very moderate reform' which 'no one believes will be adopted'.

10   Crick, *George Orwell*, p. 305.

11   Orwell, *Collected Essays*, vol. 3, pp. 72, 109, 174.

12   Nicholas Cull, *Selling War: The British propaganda campaign against American neutrality in World War II* (Oxford: Oxford Universty Press, 1995), pp. 85–6, 111.

13   There are several familiar photographs published of this group at work in the BBC studios, one in Crick, *George Orwell*, p. 258.

14   Cull, *Selling War*, p. 77.

15   Not quite how the official historian Asa Briggs puts it, but near enough; see Asa Briggs *History of the British Broadcasting Corporation* (5 vols., Oxford: Oxford University Press, 1970), vol. 2.

16   Biographical details come, variously, from Alexander Kendrick, *Prime Time: The life of Edward R Murrow* (Boston: Little, Brown, 1969); Joseph E. Persico, *Edward R Murrow: An American original* (New York: McGraw-Hill, 1988); Norman H. Finkelstein, *With Heroic Truth: The life of Edward R Murrow* (New York: Clarion Books, 1997) (this last a biography written for schoolchildren).

17   List in Kendrick, *Prime Time*, p. 122.

18   Edward Murrow, *This is London* (Simon and Schuster, 1941), on 8 September 1940.

19   Kendrick, *Prime Time*, p. 257.

20   Kendrick, *Prime Time*, p. 269.

21   The title of the extract which appears under Murrow's name in Samuel Hynes et al. (eds), *Reporting World War II: American journalism 1938–1946*, vol. 2: *1944–1946* (New York: Library of America, 1995), see pp. 681–5.

22   These examples are summarised from Andrew Sharf, *The British Press and Jews under Nazi Rule* (London: Oxford University Press, 1964), ch. 3.

23 The phrase is Kenneth Burke's coinage, see Kenneth Burke, *A Grammar of Motives* (1945; New York: Prentice Hall, 1974).

24 Finkelstein, *With Heroic Truth*, p. 122.

25 Finkelstein, *With Heroic Truth*, p. 11.

26 I imply here Clifford Geertz's theory of symbolic action and its application to politics conceived as a play of tableaux: see his *Negara: The theatre-state in 19th century Bali* (Princeton: Princeton University Press, 1981).

27 And given wonderful immediacy in Gore Vidal's novel *Hollywood* (New York: Random House, 1969).

28 Quoted in Peter Kurth, *American Cassandra: The life of Dorothy Thompson* (Boston: Little, Brown, 1990), p. 161.

29 Kurth, *American Cassandra*, p. 335.

30 Charles Fisher, 'Dorothy Thompson, cosmic force', in Charles Fisher, *The Columnists* (New York: Howell, Soskin, 1944).

31 Most of his wartime articles are posthumously collected in A. J. Liebling, *Mollie and Other War Pieces* (New York: Harcourt Brace, 1964).

32 Collected in Liebling, *Mollie and Other War Pieces*, reprinted in Hynes et al., *Reporting World War II*, vol. 2, pp. 80–9; *New Yorker*, 22 Apr. 1944.

33 Posthumously published as E. Pyle, *Home Country* (New York: Henry Holt, 1947); war reports published in E. Pyle, *Brave Men* (New York: Henry Holt, 1944 and 1947).

34 22 Aug. 1944, reprinted in Hynes et al., *Reporting World War II*, vol. 2, pp. 218–9.

35 John Hersey, *Hiroshima*, first published in the *New Yorker*, 31 Aug. 1946 (Harmondsworth: Penguin, 1980), p. 66.

36 Hersey, *Hiroshima*, p. 74.

37 Hersey, *Hiroshima*, p. 112.

Chapter Nine   *Cold War and Cruel Peace*

1 Figures in Engel, *Tickle the Public*, p. 179.

2 Figure in Williams, *Dangerous Estate*, p. 1.

3 Headlines quoted by Engel, *Tickle the Public*, pp. 173–4.

4 *Daily Mirror*, 23 Sept. 1946.

5 As testified by Hugh Cudlipp, *Publish and be Damned* (London: Hamlyn, 1967). Robert Connor, *Cassandra: Reflections in a mirror* (London: Cassell, 1969).

6 *Daily Mirror*, 6 Sept. 1939.

7 Connor, *Cassandra*, p. 65.

8 'Cassandra', *The English at War* (London: Secker and Warburg, 1941).

9 'Cassandra', *The English at War*, p. 128.

10 Collected in 'Cassandra', *Cassandra at his Finest and Funniest*, ed. Paul Boyle (London: Hamlyn for the *Daily Mirror*, 1967).

11 *Daily Mirror*, 7 Mar. 1953.

12 *Daily Mirror*, 22 May 1953.

13 Compare Hoggart, *The Uses of Literacy*, especially those pages where he characterises the voices of working-class newspapers and journals.

14 *Daily Mirror*, 2 May 1946.

15 Reported in the *Daily Telegraph*, 4 Apr. 1946.

16 *Daily Mirror*, 2 May 1946. See also Michael Foot, *Aneurin Bevan: A biography* (London: Four Square, 1966), vol. 2, pp. 80–129 and *passim*.

17 Engel, *Tickle the Public*, p. 178.

18 Although finely recollected for us of late in Michael Frayn's play, *Copenhagen* (1999).

19 Richard Rhodes, *The Making of the Atomic Bomb* (Harmondsworth: Penguin, 1988), p. 533.

20 *New York Herald Tribune*, 12 June 1947.

21 Joseph Alsop and Stewart Alsop, *The Reporter's Trade* (London: Bodley Head, 1958), p. 130.

22 Stewart Alsop, in the *New York Herald Tribune*, 23 June 1950.

23 Quoted in David Horowitz, *From Yalta to Vietnam: American foreign policy in the Cold War* (Harmondsworth: Penguin, 1967), p. 65.

24 I depend here on Alan Foster's summary of British press attitudes to the USSR in 1946. See his 'The British press and the coming of the Cold War', in Anne Deighton (ed.), *Britain and the First Cold War* (London: Macmillan, 1990).

25 *New York Herald Tribune*, 5 June 1950, reprinted in Alsop and Alsop, *The Reporter's Trade*, p. 144.

26 As Joseph Alsop happily acknowledges in *I've seen the Best of It: Memoirs with Adam Platt* (New York: Norton, 1992). Alsop died in 1989, aged seventy-nine.

27 As portrayed by Gore Vidal in *Pentimento: A memoir* (London: Abacus, 1996), pp. 200–1.

28 See S. J. Taylor, *Stalin's Apologist: Walter Duranty, the New York Times's man in Moscow* (Oxford: Oxford University Press, 1990).

29 Walter Duranty, *USSR: The story of Soviet Russia* (New York: Lippincott, 1944).

30 Bruce Cumings, *Origins of the Korean War* (2 vols, Princeton: Princeton University Press, 1989).

31 Cumings, vol. 1, pp. 201–10.

32 *Herald Tribune* 4 Dec. 1950.

33 Caute, *The Great Fear*, pp. 137–51.

34 Alsop and Platt, *I've Seen the Best of It*, pp. 232ff.

35 Alsop and Platt, *I've Seen the Best of It*, p. 411.

36 Alsop and Platt, *I've Seen the Best of It*, p. 415.

37 Alsop and Platt, *I've Seen the Best of It*, p. 432.

38 *New York Herald Tribune*, 1 Oct. 1963.

39 James Cameron, *Point of Departure: An experiment in biography* (London: Arthur Baker, 1967), p. 70.

40 Cameron, *Point of Departure*, p. 41.

41 He is misrepresented as such by Knightley, *The First Casualty*, p. 371; but see Cameron, *Point of Departure*, pp. 73–4, 127.

42 Cameron, *Point of Departure*, p. 72.

43 Cited in Nagel, *The View from Nowhere*, chapter 5, n. 30.

44 Cameron, *Point of Departure*, p. 80.

45 *The Times*, 11 Mar. 1950.

46 Cameron, *Point of Departure*, p. 217.

47 Cameron, *Point of Departure*, pp. 130–1.

48 Figure taken from Cumings and Halliday, *Korea*, pp. 200–1.

49 Cameron, *Point of Departure*, p. 146.

50 See René Cutforth, *Korean Reporter* (London: Allan Wingate, 1952), esp. pp. 49–50 and 174–5.

51 I have in mind the defence of this at times belittled value by Norman Geras, *Solidarity in the Conversation of Humankind* (London: Verso, 1993).

52 Reprinted as James Cameron, *Witness* (London: Victor Gollancz, 1966).

53 Cameron, *Witness*, p. 113.

54 Sam Tanenhaus, *Whittaker Chambers: A biography* (New York: Random House, 1997).

55 Making this decision, even with so deliberately biographical an approach as mine, cuts out the fascinations of psychoanalytical speculation or those small excesses of post-modernism which turn on the recovery of meaning from what the agents themselves could not be said to have intended.

56 Whittaker Chambers, *Witness* (New York: Random House, 1952).

57 Chambers, *Witness*, p. 454.

58 Victor Navasky, *Naming Names* (New York: Viking, 1980); Caute, *The Great Fear*; Alistair Cooke, *A Generation on Trial* (London: Rupert Hart-Davis, 1950).

59 Navasky, *Naming Names*, p. 7.

60 Chambers, *Witness*, p. 692.

61 Chambers, *Witness*, p. 695.

62 Cooke, *A Generation on Trial*, p. 341.

63 Chapman Pincher, *Their Trade is Treachery* (New York: Bantam Books, 1982), pp. 252–3; see also his *Traitors* (Harmondsworth: Penguin, 1987). All traitors are communists, it goes without saying.

CHAPTER TEN   *The Soloists:* Living History on our Behalf

1 *Daily Express*, 15 July 1956.

2 Anthony Nutting, *No End of a Lesson: The story of Suez* (London: Constable, 1967).

3 Christopher Hitchens, 'Mad dogs and others', *Grand Street*, 6, no. 1 (1986), p. 105.

4 Provided by Leonard Mosley in *Dulles: A biography of Eleanor, Allen and John Foster Dulles and their family networks* (London: Hodder and Stoughton, 1978), p. 409.

5 *Daily Express*, 5 Nov. 1956.

6 Anthony Shaw, *Eden, Suez and the Mass Media* (London: I. B. Tauris, 1996).

7 There are many insider accounts of these days. My version depends on Anthony Nutting's *No End of a Lesson*.

8 Charles Wheeler, 'You'd better get out while you can', *London Review of Books*, 19 Sept. 1996.

9 Reprinted in Leszek Kolakowski, *Marxism and Beyond* (London: Paladin, 1971), p. 164.

10 Timothy Garton Ash, 'Hungary's revolution: 40 years on', *New York Review of Books*, 14 Nov. 1996.

11 Robert C. Cottrell, *Izzy: A biography of I. F. Stone* (New Brunswick: Rutgers University Press, 1993), p. 116.

12 I. F. Stone, *Underground to Palestine and Reflections Thirty Years Later* (New York: Pantheon, 1978); I. F. Stone, *This is Israel* (New York: Boln and Garer, 1948).

13 I. F. Stone, in *PM*, 27 June 1946; quoted in Cottrell, *Izzy*, p. 141.

14 I. F. Stone, *The Hidden History of the Korean War 1950–1951* (New York: Monthly Review Press, 1952).

15 Stone, *The Hidden History of the Korean War*, pp. 124–50.

16 Stone, *The Hidden History of the Korean War*, p. 214.

17 Cottrell, *Izzy*, p. 8.

18 Cottrell, *Izzy*, p. 176.

19 *New York Review of Books*, 2 Jan. 1969; reprinted in I. F. Stone, *Polemics and Prophecies 1967–1970* (New York: Vintage Books, 1972).

20 *I. F. Stone's Weekly*, 18 May 1970.

21 Stone, *Polemics and Prophecies*, p. 481.

22 I am developing a powerful idea belonging to Krishan Kumar, 'Holding the middle ground', in James Curran (ed.), *Mass Communication and Society* (London: Edward Arnold, 1977).

23 Walter Cronkite, *A Reporter's Life* (New York: Ballantine Books, 1997).

24 George Kennan, *Memoirs 1925–1950* (Boston: Little, Brown, 1967).

25 Cronkite, *A Reporter's Life*, p. 161.

26 Cronkite, *A Reporter's Life*, p. 176.

27 He made this unselfconsciously clear in an interview given personally to me in New York on 24 Sept. 1999.

28 Cronkite, *A Reporter's Life*, p. 186.

29 William Manchester, *Death of a President* (London: Michael Joseph, 1967), pp. 224, 288.

30 Manchester, *Death of a President*, p. 291.

31 Manchester, *Death of a President*, p. 309.

32 Cronkite, *A Reporter's Life*, p. 220.

33 Quoted in Schlesinger, *A Thousand Days*, p. 251.

34 Cronkite, *A Reporter's Life*, p. 246.

35 Quoted in David Halberstam, *The Best and the Brightest* (New York: Ballantine Books, 1992), p. 272.

36 Quoted in Sheehan, *A Bright Shining Lie*, p. 699.

37 Cronkite, *A Reporter's Life*, pp. 257–8.

38 Cronkite, *A Reporter's Life*, p. 350.

39 Nick Clarke, *Alistair Cooke: The biography* (London: Orion Books, 2000).

40 From Cooke's notebooks, quoted in Clarke, *Alistair Cooke*, pp. 212–13.

41 Clarke, *Alistair Cooke*, p. 301.

42 *Manchester Guardian*, 12 May 1955.

43 Published by the *Manchester Guardian* in pamphlet form as *Ordeal of the South* (1956), p. 66, quoted also by Clarke in *Alistair Cooke*, p. 368..

44 Quoted in Clarke, *Alistair Cooke*, p. 370.

45 Kenneth Burke, *Attitudes towards History* (3rd edn, Berkeley: University of California Press, 1984), p. 42.

CHAPTER ELEVEN   *Adventurers and Constitutionalists:*
                 Vietnam and Watergate

1 Halberstam, *The Best and the Brightest*, first published in 1972, here quoted in the 1992 edition.

2 Halberstam, *The Best and the Brightest*, pp. 634–5.

3 Halberstam, *The Best and the Brightest*, pp. 32, 214–15, 162–3.

4 David Rudenstine, *The Day the Presses Stopped: A history of the Pentagon Papers case* (Berkeley: University of California Press, 1996), p. 53.

5 Neil Sheehan, 'Should we have war crime trials', *New York Times* Book Review, 28 Mar. 1971.

6 Chomsky's journalistic essays, notable for bringing high-density scholarly referencing to everyday political commentary, frequently appeared in the *New York Review of Books*, itself a key opponent of the war. The essays were collected as, variously, *American Power and the New Mandarins*; *At War with Asia* (New York: Pantheon, 1970); *For Reasons of State* (New York: Pantheon, 1973).

7 After serialising parts, the *New York Times* published the full series with explanatory contributions as *The Pentagon Papers: The secret history of the Vietnam War, based on investigative reporting by Neil Sheehan*, written by Neil Sheehan, Hedrick Smith, E. W. Kenworthy and Fox Butterfield (New York: Bantam Books, 1971).

8 Tom Wicker, *On the Press* (New York: Viking, 1978), p. 8.

9 Reprinted in full in Sheehan et al., *The Pentagon Papers*, pp. 652ff.

10 Rudenstine, *The Day the Presses Stopped*, pp. 99–216 passim.

11 Ben Bradlee, *A Good Life: newspapering and other adventures* (New York: Simon and Schuster, 1995), p. 311.

12 Bradlee, *A Good Life*, p. 316.

13 Knightley, *The First Casualty*, pp. 409–40.

14 All phrases are taken from Chomsky, *American Power and the New Mandarins*, chapters entitled 'Objectivity and liberal scholarship' and 'The responsibility of intellectuals'.

15 Noam Chomsky, 'On war crimes', in Chomsky, *At War with Asia*, pp. 225–44.

16 Michael Herr, *Dispatches* (New York: Bantam Books, 1969).

17 Michael Herr, *Reporting Vietnam* (New York: Library of America, 1998), p. 315.

18 *Reporting Vietnam*, p. 321.

19 *Reporting Vietnam*, pp. 323–4.

20 Gloria Emerson, *Winners and Losers: Battles, retreats, gains, losses and ruins from the Vietnam War* (New York: Harcourt Brace Jovanovich, 1978).

21 James Fenton, *All the Wrong Places: Adrift in the politics of the Pacific rim* (New York: Atlantic Monthly Press, 1988), p. 6.

22 Fenton, *All the Wrong Places*, p. xv.

23 Fenton, *All the Wrong Places*, p. xvi.

24 Fenton, *All the Wrong Places*, pp. 28–9.

25 Fenton, *All the Wrong Places*, p. 86.

26 James Fenton, 'In a notebook', in James Fenton, *The Memory of War* (Edinburgh: Salamander Press, 1982), p. 25.

27 For example, Someth May, 'The field behind the village', *Granta* 13 (1984).

28 Norman Mailer, *The Armies of the Night* (London: Weidenfeld and Nicolson, 1968), p. 21.

29 Original dustjacket blurb on Norman Mailer, *The Naked and the Dead* (New York: Rinehart, 1948).

30 Mailer, *The Armies of the Night.*.

31 Tom Wolfe (ed.), *The New Journalism* (London: Picador, 1990); originally published as Tom Wolfe, *The New Journalism, with an Anthology edited by Tom Wolfe and E. W. Johnson* (1973).

32 Mailer, *The Armies of the Night*, p. 262.

33 Norman Mailer, *Miami and the Siege of Chicago: An informal history of the American political conventions of 1968* (Harmondsworth: Penguin, 1969).

34 Mailer, *Miami and the Siege of Chicago*, p. 117.

35 Mailer, *Miami and the Siege of Chicago*, p. 140.

36 Mailer, *Miami and the Siege of Chicago*, p. 182.

37 Mailer, *Miami and the Siege of Chicago*, p. 197.

38 Bob Woodward and Carl Bernstein, *All the President's Men* (1974; London: Bloomsbury, 1998).

39 Bradlee, *A Good Life*, plate 33.

40 Bradlee, *A Good Life*, p. 329.

41 Woodward and Bernstein, *All the President's Men*, p. 3: 'Bernstein knew that Woodward couldn't write very well. One office rumour had it that English was not Woodward's native language!'

42 Bradlee, *A Good Life*, p. 337.

43 Graham, *Personal History*, p. 472.

44 Graham, *Personal History*, p. 468.

45 *Time*, 9 July 1973.

46 Thereby bequeathing to folklore the inimitable euphemism 'expletive deleted'.
47 Clive James, in the London *Observer*, 11 Aug. 1974.

CHAPTER TWELVE *Fictions (2):* The View from Somewhere

1 Max Weber, *The Theory of Social and Economic Organisation*, ed. Talcott Parsons (New York: The Free Press, 1947), pp. 324–40.
2 Jürgen Habermas, *The Theory of Communicative Action*, vol. I: *Reason and the Rationalisation of Society* (London: Heinemann Educational Books, 1974).
3 Alasdair MacIntyre, *After Virtue: A study in moral theory* (London: Duckworth, 1981), p. 201.
4 Henry James, letter to Grace Norton (1883), quoted in Leon Edel, *Henry James: The conquest of London* (London: Bodley Head, 1962), p. 505.
5 Saul Bellow, *The Dean's December* (London: Secker and Warburg, 1982).
6 Bellow, *The Dean's December*, pp. 151–2.
7 Bellow, *The Dean's December*, p. 67.
8 Bellow, *The Dean's December*, p. 124.
9 Bellow, *The Dean's December*, p. 244.
10 Bellow, *The Dean's December*, p. 118.
11 Williams, *The Volunteers*, pp. 32-3.
12 Williams, *The Volunteers*, p. 52.
13 Williams, *The Volunteers*, p. 64, already quoted, p. 159, above.
14 Williams, *The Volunteers*, p. 91.
15 Williams, *The Volunteers*, p. 107.
16 Williams, *The Volunteers*, p. 138, my emphasis.
17 Williams, *The Volunteers*, p. 138.
18 Williams, *The Volunteers*, pp. 148–9.
19 Williams, *The Volunteers*, p. 176.
20 Williams, *The Volunteers*, p. 179.
21 Written and directed by Oliver Stone (1986).
22 Joan Didion, *Salvador* (New York: Washington Square Press, 1982), pp. 29, 88.
23 Adapted from a journalist's article, 'The death and life of Dith Pran' by Sidney Schanberg; movie directed by Roland Joffe (1984).
24 Film version of the autobiographical story published as *Natasha's Story* by Michael Nicholson (an ITN reporter); the film (1997) was directed by Michael Winterbottom and produced by Mark Geraghty.
25 Particularly Misha Glenny, *The Balkans: Nationalism, war and the Great Powers 1804–1999* (New York: Viking, 2000), much depended upon below.
26 Directed by Alan Pakula (1976), written by William Goldman.
27 The offices were eventually reproduced in facsimile in California; see William Goldman, *Adventures in the Screen Trade* (London: Macdonald, 1984).
28 Made in Poland (1981) and written by Aleksander Scibor-Rylski, with advice from the well-known Polish journalist, Ryszard Kapucinski.
29 Certainly for the Polish-speaking Englishman, Timothy Garton Ash, who was there; see Timothy Garton Ash, *The Polish Revolution: Solidarity* (rev. edn, London: Granta, 1981).
30 *Cry Freedom* (1987), directed by Richard Attenborough, adapted by John Briley from Woods's autobiography of the same title.
31 Made in 2000, directed by Michael Mann, written by Mann and Eric Roth.

CHAPTER THIRTEEN   *Rights and the Right:*
Difficulties with Democracy

1   Harold Evans, *Good Times, Bad Times* (1983; 3rd edn, London: Orion Books, 1994), p. 465.
2   Nonetheless, I owe a debt to the attempts to do so by Noam Chomsky with E. S. Herman, *Manufacturing Consent: The political economy of mass media* (Boston: Beacon Press, 1982).
3   Compressed from, among others, David Cannadine, *Class in Britain* (New Haven and London: Yale University Press, 1998).
4   Evans, *Good Times, Bad Times*, p. 8.
5   This is Knightley of *The First Casualty*, a shining example of practitioner-journalist and historian.
6   The Insight team published their inquiries as Bruce Page, David Leitch and Philip Knightley, *Philby: The spy who betrayed a generation*, introd. John le Carré (London: André Deutsch, 1968).
7   Evans, *Good Times, Bad Times*, p. 58.
8   In the preface to his plays about the spies Anthony Blunt and Guy Burgess, Alan Bennett, *Single Spies* (London: Faber and Faber, 1988), p. ix.
9   Evans, *Good Times, Bad Times*, p. 60.
10 Evans, *Good Times, Bad Times*, p. 76.
11 Williams, *Politics and Letters*, p. 91.
12 Curran and Seaton, *Power without Responsibilty*, p. 101.
13 See D. Goodhart and P. Wintour, *Eddie Shah and the Newspaper Revolution* (London: Coronet, 1986); G. Munster, *Rupert Murdoch* (Victoria: Viking, 1985); J. Tunstall, *Newspaper Power* (Oxford: Oxford University Press, 1996); J. Keane, *The Media and Democracy* (Cambridge: Polity, 1991).
14 Evans, *Good Times, Bad Times*, ch. 7, 'Biffen's missing millions'; see also Curran and Seaton, *Power without Responsibility* 'The age of conglomerates', pp. 71–108.
15 Evans, *Good Times, Bad Times*, pp. 171–3.
16 Evans, *Good Times, Bad Times*, p. 314.
17 *New York Times*, 31 Jan. 1981.
18 As witness Evans, *Good Times, Bad Times*, p. 331.
19 Their last report on Maxwell's business affairs wasn't published until 30 March 2001.
20 See Seamus Milne, *The Enemy Within: MI5, Maxwell and the Scargill affair* (London: Verso, 1994).
21 This summary is taken from Roy Greenslade, editor of the *Mirror* 1990–1, in *Maxwell's Fall* (New York: Simon and Schuster, 1995).
22 Evans, *Good Times, Bad Times*, p. 439.
23 Harold Evans, *The American Century* (London: Jonathan Cape, 1998).
24 In understanding which I have been much helped by Godfrey Hodgson, *The World Turned Right Side Up: A history of the conservative ascendancy in America* (New York: Houghton Mifflin, 1996).
25 Elaborated, variously, in Pierre Bourdieu, *Outline of a Theory of Practice* (Cambridge: Cambridge University Press, 1978); Pierre Bourdieu, *The State Nobility* (Cambridge: Polity, 1996); Pierre Bourdieu, *The Rules of Art* (Cambridge: Polity, 1996), esp. pp. 337–48.
26 Norman Podhoretz, *Breaking Ranks: A political memoir* (London: Weidenfeld and Nicolson, 1979).
27 Podhoretz, *Breaking Ranks*, pp. 42–4, 316–18.

28 Podhoretz, *Breaking Ranks*, p. 317.

29 Podhoretz, *Breaking Ranks*, p. 320.

30 Podhoretz, *Breaking Ranks*, p. 350.

31 Podhoretz, *Breaking Ranks*, p. 349.

32 See, for example, J. B. Morton ('Beachcomber'), *Here and Now* (London: Hollis and Carter, 1947).

33 Norman Podhoretz, *Ex-Friends* (New York: Free Press, 1999), p. 117.

34 William F. Buckley, *Overdrive: A personal document* (New York: Doubleday, 1983).

35 William F. Buckley Jr, *Right Reason* (New York: Doubleday, 1985).

36 Buckley, *Right Reason*, p. 97; reprinted from an unidentified column dated 8 Sept. 1983.

37 R. W. Johnson, *Shootdown: The verdict on KAL 007* (New York: Doubleday, 1985).

38 It should be pointed out that Seymour Hersh, writing at the same time, found no corroborative evidence for Johnson's case from Washington sources and records, but agrees this in itself proves nothing. See Seymour Hersh, *The Target is Destroyed: What Really Happened to Flight 007* (London: Faber and Faber, 1986).

39 R. L. Garthoff, *Détente and Confrontation: American–Soviet relations from Nixon to Reagan* (Washington DC: Brookings Institution, 1985), p. 1016.

40 Later retitled *Arkansas Democratic Gazette*.

41 See Elizabeth Cobbs and Bernie Smith, *Longtime Coming: An insider's story, the Birmingham Church bombing* (Birmingham: Crewe Hill, 1964).

42 Details and quotations from personal conversations in September 1999.

43 These figures, and much else, are taken from David Halberstam, *The Children* (New York: Random House, 1998), see p. 53; see also Andrew Young, *An Easy Burden: The civil rights movement and transformation of America* (New York: HarperCollins, 1996).

44 Halberstam, *The Children*, p. 80.

45 Halberstam, *The Children*, p. 234.

46 *Nashville Tennessean*, 20 Apr. 1960.

47 Wolfe, *The New Journalism*, p. 25.

48 Tom Wolfe, *A Man in Full* (New York: Farrar, Straus and Giroux, 1998).

49 Joan Didion, *Democracy* (New York: Simon and Schuster, 1984).

50 Didion, *Democracy*, p. 85.

51 Didion, *Democracy*, p. 188.

52 All unassigned quotations are taken from conversations I had with Joan Didion in June 1989 and September 1999.

53 Didion, *Democracy*, p. 53.

54 Didion, *Salvador*, p. 16.

55 Didion, *Salvador*, p. 34.

56 Joan Didion, *Miami* (New York: Simon and Schuster, 1987), p. 36.

57 Didion, *Miami*, pp. 129–30.

58 First appearing as three articles in the *New York Review of Books*, reprinted as 'Washington' in Joan Didion, *Sentimental Journeys* (London: HarperCollins, 1993).

59 Didion, *Sentimental Journeys*, pp. 32–3.

60 Didion, *Sentimental Journeys*, p. 50.

61 Didion, *Sentimental Journeys*, p. 82.

62 Didion, *Sentimental Journeys*, p. 84

63 For instance, Michael Sandel, *Democracy's Discontent: America in search of a public philosophy* (Cambridge: Harvard University Press, 1996), pp. 317–52.

CHAPTER FOURTEEN   *Fame is the Spur:*
News without History since 1989

1   Geertz, *Negara*, pp. 135–6.
2   Cited in Milne, *The Enemy Within*.
3   Habermas, *The Structural Transformation of the Public Sphere*, pp. 181–95.
4   Manuel Castells, *The Power of Identity*, vol. 2: *The Information Age: Economy, society and culture* (Oxford: Blackwell, 1997), p. 337.
5   Nick Cohen, 'Hacking their way to a fortune', *New Statesman*, 22 May 2000, pp. 8–10.
6   Edward Luttwak, *Turbo-Capitalism: Winners and losers in the global economy* (London: Orion, 1999).
7   Cohen, 'Hacking their way to a fortune'; he concludes his article by recording his own salary in 1999–2000: £55,000.
8   Castells, *The Power of Identity*, p. 349.
9   Conversation with the author, September 1999.
10 Ryszard Kapucinski, *The Shadow of the Sun* (London: Allen Lane, 2001).
11 Kapucinski tells the story in *Shah of Shahs* (London: Picador, 1986), p. 127.
12 Ryszard Kapucinski, *The Emperor* (London: Picador, 1984).
13 John Simpson, *Strange Places, Questionable People* (London: Pan, 1999).
14 Simpson, *Strange Places, Questionable People*, p. 124.
15 Radio 4, *Six O'Clock News*, 14 May 1974.
16 Simpson, *Strange Places, Questionable People*, p. 249.
17 Simpson, *Strange Places, Questionable People*, p. 259.
18 I take most details from the recent, extraordinary and well-authenticated *The Tiananmen Papers*, compiled (and smuggled out) by Zhang Llang, ed. Andrew Nathan and Perry Link (Boston: Little, Brown, 2001).
19 John Simpson, 'Beijing Report', *Granta*, 28 (1989), pp. 12 and 21–2.
20 Simpson, *Strange Places, Questionable People*, p. 330.
21 A definition I take and applaud from Richard Rorty, *Contingency, Irony and Solidarity* (Cambridge: Cambridge University Press, 1989), part 3.
22 Forcefully rebutted by the dependable (and distinguished) Charles Wheeler, whom nobody, as we saw in 1956, could accuse of lacking radical credentials; See Charles Wheeler, 'Half the way with LBJ', *New Statesman*, 10 May 2000.
23 Quoted by Anthony Hayward, *In the Name of Justice: The television reporting of John Pilger* (London: Bloomsbury, 2001), p. 10.
24 Hayward, *In the Name of Justice*, p. 14.
25 François Ponchaud, *Cambodia: Year Zero* (Harmondsworth: Penguin, 1978).
26 Clive James, *Observer*, 14 Sept. 1980, reprinted in *Clive James on Television* (London: Picador, 1991), p. 488.
27 See Henry Kamm, *Dragon Ascending: Vietnam and the Vietnamese* (New York: Arcade, 1991); Duong Thu Huong, *Memories of a Pure Spring* (New York: Hyperion, 1999).
28 ITV, 6 Mar. 2000; text transcribed by Hayward, *In the Name of Justice*, pp. 270–2.
29 Hugo Young, *One of Us: A life of Margaret Thatcher* (London: Pan Books, 1993).
30 Hobsbawm, *Age of Extremes* (1994) pp. 558-86.
31 This list of the changing value-field has been adapted from Charles Taylor, *Philosophy and the Human Sciences* (Cambridge: Cambridge University Press, 1985), pp. 15–57.
32 John Cole, *As It Seemed to Me: Political memoirs* (London: Orion Books, 1996), p. 404.

33 Cole, *As It Seemed to Me*: 'I assume he thought Trotskyism was one of those unpleasant personal diseases that can happen to any of us', p. 346.

34 Reconstructed from Cole's notes for the broadcast; see Cole, *As It Seemed to Me*, pp. 381–2.

35 The script was also published as a book: Jonathan Lewis and Phillip Whitehead, *Stalin: A time for judgement* (London: Methuen and Thames TV, 1990).

36 See, for example, Neal Ascherson's collection of journalism, *Games with Shadows* (London: Hutchinson Radius, 1988).

37 He tells his version of the full story in Garton Ash, *The Polish Revolution*; his journalism about the end of Cold War is collected as *The Uses of Adversity* (Cambridge: Granta, 1989).

38 Timothy Garton Ash, *The Magic Lantern* (Cambridge: Granta, 1990).

39 Timothy Garton Ash, *History of the Present: Essays, sketches and dispatches from Europe in the nineties* (London: Allen Lane, 1999).

40 I follow much here of Perry Anderson's long review, 'A ripple of the Polonaise', *London Review of Books*, 26 Nov. 1999.

41 A point made frequently by another leading intellectual as well as journalist, Edward Said; see Edward Said, *Representations of the Intellectual* (London: Vintage, 1994), the 1993 Reith lectures.

42 Christopher Hitchens, 'On the road to Timisoara', *Granta*, 30 (1990).

43 The first volume of which is Christopher Hitchens, *Prepared for the Worst: Selected essays and minority reports* (New York: Hill and Wang, 1988).

44 Hitchens, *Prepared for the Worst*, p. 176.

45 Christopher Hitchens, *For the Sake of the Argument: Essays and minority reports* (London: Verso, 1993), p. 179.

46 Christopher Hitchens, *The Trial of Henry Kissinger* (London: Verso, 2001).

47 Christopher Hitchens, 'Let's not get too liberal', *Nation*, 21 Sept. 2001.

48 See Emily O'Reilly, *Veronica Guerin: The life and death of a crime reporter* (London: Vintage, 1998).

CHAPTER FIFTEEN   *Epilogue:* For Continuity

1 Roger Poole, *Towards Deep Subjectivity* (London: Allen Lane, 1972), pp. 31–43.

2 He charts the geography of the passion in his *Among the Believers: An Islamic journey* (Harmondsworth: Penguin, 1982). He coins the phrase in 'Our Universal Civilization', *New York Review of Books*, 31 Jan. 1991.

3 *Independent*, 20 Oct. 2001.

4 He began these for the *New York Times*, then published them as *The Price of Power: Kissinger in the Nixon White House* (New York: Simon and Schuster, 1983).

5 Seymour Hersh, a selection: 'King's Ransom', *New Yorker*, 22 Oct. 2001, pp. 35–9; 'Annals of National Security', 8 Oct. 2001, pp. 34–40; 'Escape and Evasion', 11 Nov. 2001.

6 Tim Judah's reports were collated and rewritten as *The Serbs: History, myth and the destruction of Yugoslavia* (New Haven: Yale University Press, 2000).

7 Tim Judah, 'War in the Dark', *New York Review of Books*, 29 Nov. 2001, pp. 14–17.

8 Michael Ignatieff, *Guardian*, 19 Oct. 2001.

9 See Emily O'Reilly, *Veronica Guerin: The life and death of a crime reporter* (London: Vintage, 1998).

Bibliography

Adorno, T., *Minima Moralia: Reflections from a damaged life*, London: New Left Books, 1974.

Alsop, J., *I've Seen the Best of It: Memoirs with Adam Platt*, New York: Norton, 1992.

Alsop, J. and Alsop, S., *The Reporter's Trade*, London: Bodley Head, 1958.

Anderson, B., *Imagined Communities: Reflections on the origin and spread of nationalism*, London and New York: Verso, 1983.

Anderson, P., 'The antinomies of Antonio Gramsci', *New Left Review*, 100 (Nov.–Jan. 1977.

Anderson, P., 'A ripple of the Polonaise', *London Review of Books*, 26 Nov. 1999.

Anwar, R., *The Tragedy of Afghanistan: A first-hand account*, London: Verso, 1989.

Ascherson, N., *Games with Shadows*, London: Hutchinson Radius, 1988.

Bacon, F., *Essays, or Counsels, Civil and Moral*, ed. B. Vickers, Oxford: Oxford University Press, 1999.

Baker, C., *Ernest Hemingway: A life story*, London: Collins, 1969.

Barth, G., *City People: The rise of modern city culture in 19th century America*, New York and Oxford: Oxford University Press, 1980.

Bellow, S., *The Dean's December*, London: Secker and Warburg, 1982.

Benjamin, W., 'The storyteller', in W. Benjamin, *Illuminations*, London: Jonathan Cape, 1970.

Bennett, A., *Single Spies*, London: Faber and Faber, 1988.

Blume, M., *Côte d'Azur: Inventing the French Riviera*, London: Thames and Hudson, 1992.

Bok, S., *Lying: Moral choice in public and private life*, Hassocks: Harvester, 1978.

Bourdieu, P., *Outline of a Theory of Practice*, Cambridge: Cambridge University Press, 1978.

Bourdieu, P., *The State Nobility*, Cambridge: Polity Press, 1996.

Bourdieu, P., *The Rules of Art*, Cambridge: Polity Press, 1996.

Bradlee, B., *A Good Life: Newspapering and other adventures*, New York: Simon and Schuster, 1995.

Briggs, A., *History of the British Broadcasting Corporation*, 5 vols, Oxford: Oxford University Press, 1961–1995.

Bryce, J., *The American Commonwealth*, New York: Macmillan, 1888.

Buckley, W. F., *Overdrive: A personal document*, New York: Doubleday, 1983.

Buckley, W. F., *Right Reason*, New York: Doubleday, 1985.

Burke, K., *Attitudes to History* (1937), Berkeley: University of California Press, 1965.

Burke, K., *A Grammar of Motives* (1945), 2nd edn, New York: Prentice Hall, 1974.

Cameron, J., *Witness*, London: Gollancz, 1966.

Cameron, J., *Point of Departure: An experiment in biography*, London: Arthur Barker, 1967.

Canetti, E., *Crowds and Power* (1960), Harmondsworth: Penguin, 1981.

Cannadine, D., *Class in Britain*, New Haven and London: Yale University Press, 1998.

'Cassandra', *The English at War*, London: Secker and Warburg, 1941.

'Cassandra', *Cassandra at his Finest and Funniest*, ed. P. Boyle, London: Hamlyn, 1967.

Castells, M., *The Power of Identity*, vol. 2: *The Information Age: Economy, society and culture*, Oxford: Blackwell, 1997.

Caute, D., *The Great Fear: The anti-communist purge under Truman and Eisenhower*, New York: Simon and Schuster, 1978.

Cavell, S., *Pursuits of Happiness: The Hollywood comedy of remarriage*, Cambridge: Harvard University Press, 1981.

Chambers, W., *Witness*, New York: Random House, 1952.

Childs, M. and Reston, J. (eds), *Walter Lippmann and his Times*, New York: Harcourt Brace, 1959.

Chomsky, N., *American Power and the New Mandarins*, London: Chatto and Windus, 1969.

Chomsky, N., *At War with Asia*, New York: Pantheon, 1970.

Chomsky, N., *For Reasons of State*, New York: Pantheon, 1973.

Chomsky, N. and Herman, E. S., *Manufacturing Consent: The political economy of mass media*, Boston: Beacon Press, 1991.

Churchill, W., *The Second World War*, vol.6: *Triumph and Tragedy*, London: Cassell, 1954.

Clarke, N., *Alistair Cooke: The biography*, London: Orion Books, 2000.

Clarke, T., *My Northcliffe Diary*, London: Gollancz, 1931.

Cobbs, E. and Smith, B., *Longtime Coming: An insider's story, the Birmingham Church bombing*, Birmingham: Crewe Hill, 1964.

Cockburn, C., *I, Claud: An autobiography*, Harmondsworth: Penguin, 1967.

Cockett, R., *Twilight of Truth: Chamberlain, appeasement and the manipulation of the press*, London: Weidenfeld and Nicolson, 1989.

Cohen, N., 'Hacking their way to a fortune', *New Statesman*, 22 May, 2000.

Cole, J., *As It Seemed to Me: Political memoirs*, London: Orion Books, 1996.

Colley, L., *The Britons: Forging the nation 1707–1837*, New Haven: Yale University Press, 1992.

Collingwood, R. G., *An Autobiography*, Oxford: Clarendon Press, 1938.

Connor, R., *Cassandra: Reflections in a mirror*, London: Cassell, 1969.

Conrad, J., *The Shadow Line*, London: Dent, 1917.

Cooke, A., *A Generation on Trial*, London: Rupert Hart-Davis, 1950.

Cottrell, R. C., *Izzy: A biography of I. F. Stone*, New Brunswick: Rutgers University Press, 1993.

Crick, B., *George Orwell: A life*, London: Secker and Warburg, 1980.

Cronkite, W., *A Reporter's Life*, New York: Ballantine Books, 1997.

Cudlipp, H., *Publish and be Damned*, London: Hamlyn, 1967.

Cull, N., *Selling War: The British propaganda campaign against American neutrality in World War II*, Oxford: Oxford University Press, 1995.

Cumings, B., *Origins of the Korean War*, 2 vols, Princeton: Princeton University Press, 1989.

Cumings, B. and Halliday, J., *Korea: The forgotten war*, New York: Pantheon, 1989.

Curran, J. (ed.), *Mass Communication and Society*, London: Edward Arnold, 1977.

Curran, J. and Seaton, J., *Power without Responsibility: The press and broadcasting in Britain*, 5th edn, London and New York: Routledge, 1997.

Cutforth, R., *Korean Reporter*, London: Allan Wingate, 1952.

Cutforth, R., *Order to View*, London: Faber and Faber, 1969.

Dicey, A. V., *Law and Public Opinion in England during the 19th century* (1905), ed. E. C. S. Wade, London: Macmillan, 1963.

Didion, J., *Salvador*, New York: Washington Square Press, 1982.

Didion, J., *Democracy*, New York: Simon and Schuster, 1984.

Didion, J., *Miami*, New York: Simon and Schuster, 1987.

Didion, J., *Sentimental Journeys*, London: HarperCollins, 1993.

Diggins, J. P., *The Promise of Pragmatism*, Chicago: University of Chicago Press, 1994.

Dos Passos, J., *The Big Money*, New York: Harcourt Brace, 1932.

Douglas, H., *The Front Page*, Michigan: University of Michigan Press, 1938.

Duranty, W., *USSR: The story of Soviet Russia*, New York: Lippincott, 1944.

Edel, L., *Henry James: The conquest of London*, London: Bodley Head, 1962.

Emerson, G., *Winners and Losers: Battles, retreats, gains, losses and ruins from the Vietnam War*, New York: Harcourt Brace Jovanovich, 1978.

Engel, M., *Tickle the Public: 100 years of the popular press*, London: Gollancz, 1996.

Evans, H., *Good Times, Bad Times*, 3rd edn, London: Orion Books, 1994.

Evans, H., *The American Century*, London: Jonathan Cape, 1998.

Evans, H., 'What a century!', *Columbia Journalism Review* (Jan.–Feb. 1999).

Febvre, L. and Martin, H.-J., *The Coming of the Book: The impact of printing 1450–1800*, London: New Left Books, 1976.

Fenton, J., *The Memory of War*, Edinburgh: Salamander Press, 1982.

Fenton, J., *All the Wrong Places: Adrift in the politics of the Pacific rim*, New York: Atlantic Monthly Press, 1988.

Finkelstein, N., *With Heroic Truth: The life of Edward R Murrow*, New York: Clarion Books, 1997.

Fiori, G., *Antonio Gramsci: Life of a revolutionary*, London: New Left Books, 1970.

Fisher, C., 'Dorothy Thompson, cosmic force', in C. Fisher, *The Columnists*, New York: Howell, Soskin, 1944.

Foot, M., *Aneurin Bevan: A biography*, London: Four Square, 1966.

Foster, A., 'The British press and the coming of the Cold War', in A. Deighton (ed.), *Britain and the First Cold War*, London: Macmillan, 1990.

Fussell, P., *The Great War and Modern Memory*, New York: Oxford University Press, 1975.

Garnham, N., *Capitalism and Communication: Global culture and the economics of information*, London: Sage Books, 1990.

Garthoff, R. L., *Détente and Confrontation: American–Soviet relations from Nixon to Reagan*, Washington DC: Brookings Institution, 1985.

Garton Ash, T., *The Uses of Adversity*, Cambridge: Granta, 1989.

Garton Ash, T., *The Magic Lantern*, Cambridge: Granta, 1990.

Garton Ash, T., *The Polish Revolution: Solidarity*, rev. edn, London: Granta, 1991.

Garton Ash, T., 'Hungary's revolution: 40 years on', *New York Review of Books*, 14 Nov. 1996.

Garton Ash, T., *History of the Present: Essays, sketches and dispatches from Europe in the nineties*, London: Allen Lane, 1999.

Geertz, C., *The Interpretation of Cultures*, London: Hutchinson, 1975.

Geertz, C., *Negara: The theatre-state in 19th century Bali*, Princeton: Princeton University Press, 1981.

Geertz, C., *Local Knowledge: Further essays in interpretive anthropology*, New York: Basic Books, 1983.

Gellhorn, M., *The Face of War*, New York: Atlantic Monthly Press, 1988.

Gellhorn, M., *The View from the Ground*, New York: Atlantic Monthly Press, 1988.

Geras, N., *Solidarity in the Conversation of Humankind*, London: Verso, 1993.

Glenny, M., *The Balkans: Nationalism, war and the Great Powers 1804–1999*, New York: Viking, 2000.

Goodhart, D. and Wintour, P., *Eddie Shah and the Newspaper Revolution*, London: Coronet, 1986.

Graham, K., *Personal History*, New York: Random House, 1998.

Gramsci, A., *Selections from the Prison Notebooks*, ed. Q. Hoare, London: Lawrence and Wishart, 1971.

Gramsci, A., *Antonio Gramsci: Selections from political writings 1921–1926*, ed. Q. Hoare, London: Lawrence and Wishart, 1978.

Graves, R., *Good-bye to All That* (1929), Harmondsworth: Penguin, 1960.

Greene, G., *The Honorary Consul*, Oxford: Bodley Head and Penguin, 1973.

Greenslade, R., *Maxwell's Fall*, New York: Simon and Schuster, 1995.

Habermas, J., *The Theory of Communicative Action*, vol. 1: *Reason and the Rationalisation of Society*, London: Heinemann Educational Books, 1974.

Habermas, J., *The Structural Transformation of the Public Sphere: An inquiry into a category of bourgeois society* (1962), Cambridge: Polity, 1989.

Halberstam, D., *The Best and the Brightest* (1972), New York: Ballantine Books, 1992.

Halberstam, D., *The Children*, New York: Random House, 1998.

Harding, D. W., 'The bond with the author', *Use of English*, 22, no. 4 (1971).

Harding, J., 'No one leaves her place in line', *London Review of Books*, 7 May, 1998.

Hare, D., *The Absence of War*, London: Faber and Faber, 1993.

Hart, H. L. A., *Punishment and Responsibility: Essays in the philosophy of law*, Oxford: Oxford University Press, 1968.

Hayward, A., *In the Name of Justice: The television reporting of John Pilger*, London: Bloomsbury, 2001.

Hemingway, E., *The Sun Also Rises*, New York: Scribner's, 1926.

Hemingway, E., *A Farewell to Arms* (1929), St Albans: Granada Publishing, 1977.

Hemingway, E., *By-line: Selected articles and dispatches of four decades*, ed. W. White, New York: Simon and Schuster, 1998.

Herr, M., *Dispatches*, New York: Bantam Books, 1969.

Hersey, J., *Hiroshima*, Harmondsworth: Penguin, 1980.

Hitchens, C., 'Mad dogs and others', *Grand Street*, 6, no. 1 (1986).

Hitchens, C., *Prepared for the Worst: Selected essays and minority reports*, New York: Hill and Wang, 1988.

Hitchens, C., 'On the road to Timisoara', *Granta*, 30 (1990).

Hitchens, C., *For the Sake of the Argument: Essays and minority reports*, London: Verso, 1993.

Hitchens, C., *The Trial of Henry Kissinger*, London: Verso, 2001.

Hirst, P. and Thompson, G., *Globalisation in Question*, Cambridge: Polity, 1996.

Hobsbawm, E., *The Age of Revolution: Europe, 1789–1848*, London: Weidenfeld and Nicolson, 1962.

Hobsbawm, E. *Age of Extremes: The short twentieth century, 1914–1991*, London: Michael Joseph, 1994.

Hodgson, G., *The World Turned Right Side Up: A history of the conservative ascendancy in America*, New York: Houghton Mifflin, 1996.

Hoggart, R., *The Uses of Literacy: Aspects of working-class life with special reference to publications and entertainments*, Harmondsworth: Penguin, 1958.

Horowitz, D., *From Yalta to Vietnam: American foreign policy in the Cold War*, Harmondsworth: Penguin, 1967.

Huong, D. T., *Memories of a Pure Spring*, New York: Hyperion, 1999.

Hynes, S., Matthews, A., Sorel, N. and Spiller, R. (eds), *Reporting World War II: American journalism 1938–1946*, vol. 2: *1944–1946*, New York: Library of America, 1995.

Inglis, F., *The Promise of Happiness: Value and meaning in children's fiction*, Cambridge: Cambridge University Press, 1987.

Inglis, F., *Raymond Williams*, London and New York: Routledge, 1995.

James, C., *Clive James on Television*, London: Picador, 1991.

Jameson, S., *Journey from the North*, vol. 2, London: Virago, 1984.

Johnson, R. W., *Shootdown: The verdict on KAL 007*, New York: Doubleday, 1985.

Juergens, G. W., *Joseph Pulitzer and the New York World*, Princeton: Princeton University Press, 1966.

Kamm, H., *Dragon Ascending: Vietnam and the Vietnamese*, New York: Arcade, 1991.

Kapucinski, R., *The Emperor*, London: Picador, 1984.

Kapucinski, R., *Shah of Shahs*, London: Picador, 1986.

Kapucinski, R., *The Shadow of the Sun*, London: Allen Lane, 2001.

Keane, J., *The Media and Democracy*, Cambridge: Polity, 1991.

Kendrick, A., *Prime Time: The life of Edward R Murrow*, Boston: Little, Brown, 1969.

Kennan, G., *Memoirs 1925–1950*, Boston: Little, Brown, 1967.

Kennan, G., *Memoirs 1950–63*, Boston: Little, Brown, 1972.

Kennan, G., *American Diplomacy*, Chicago: Chicago University Press, 1984.

Kennedy, R., *Thirteen Days*, New York: Norton, 1969.

Keynes, J. M., *The Economic Consequences of the Peace*, vol. 2 of *The Collected Writings* (22 vols), ed. Elizabeth Johnson and Donald Moggridge, London: Macmillan, 1956.

Knightley, P., *The First Casualty: The war correspondent as hero, propagandist and myth maker*, 4th rev. edn, London: Pan Books, 2000.

Kolakowski, L., *Marxism and Beyond*, London: Paladin, 1971.

Koss, S., *The Rise and Fall of the Political Press in Britain*, London: Hamish Hamilton, 1984.

Kundera, M., *The Book of Laughter and Forgetting*, Harmondsworth: Penguin, 1983.

Kundera, M., *The Unbearable Lightness of Being*, New York: Harper and Row, 1984.

Kurth, P., *American Cassandra: The life of Dorothy Thompson*, Boston: Little, Brown, 1990.

Kyle, K., 'Orders of empire', *London Review of Books*, 7 Mar. 1985.

Lacouture, J., *André Malraux. Une vie dans le siècle*, Paris: Seuil, 1973.

Lewis, J. and Whitehead, P., *Stalin: A time for judgement*, London: Methuen and Thames TV, 1990.

Lewis, R. W. B. (ed.) *Malraux: Twentieth-century views*, New York: Prentice Hall, 1969.

Liebling, A. J., *Mollie and Other War Pieces*, New York: Harcourt Brace, 1964.

Lindner, R., *The Reportage of Urban Culture: Robert Park and the Chicago School*, Cambridge: Cambridge University Press, 1990.

Lippmann, W., *A Preface to Politics*, New York: Mitchell Kennerley, 1913.

Lippmann, W., *A Preface to Morals*, New York: Macmillan, 1929.

Lippmann, W., *The Cold War*, Boston: Little Brown, 1947.

Lippmann, W., *Public Opinion* (1922), New York: Macmillan. 1960.

Lippmann, W., *The Essential Lippmann*, ed. C. Rossiter and J. Lare, New York: Random House, 1963.

Lukes, S., *Power: A radical view*, Basingstoke: Macmillan, 1974.

Luttwak, E., *Turbo-Capitalism: Winners and losers in the global economy*, London: Orion, 1999.

MacDonnell, A. G., *England, Their England*, London: Macmillan, 1933.

MacIntyre, A., *After Virtue: A study in moral theory*, London: Duckworth, 1981.

McLachlan, D., *In the Chair: Barrington-Ward of The Times 1927–1948*, London: Weidenfeld and Nicolson, 1991.

Mailer, N., *The Naked and the Dead*, New York: Rinehart, 1948.

Mailer, N., *The Armies of the Night: History as a novel, the novel as history*, London: Weidenfeld and Nicolson, 1968.

Mailer, N., *Miami and the Siege of Chicago: An informal history of the American political conventions of 1968*, Harmondsworth: Penguin, 1969.

Malraux, A., *La Tentation de l'Occident*, Paris: Grasset, 1926.

Malraux, A., *L'Esprit*, Paris: Plon, 1938; trans. by S. Gilbert and A. MacDonald as *Man's Hope*, New York: Random House, 1983.

Malraux, A., *Anti-memoirs*, London: Hamish Hamilton, 1968.

Manchester, W., *Death of a President*, London: Michael Joseph, 1967.

Matthews, H. L., *The Education of a Correspondent*, New York: Harcourt Brace, 1946.

Milne, S., *The Enemy Within: MI5, Maxwell and the Scargill affair*, London: Verso, 1994.

Morton, J. B., *Here and Now*, London: Hollis and Carter, 1947.

Mosley, L., *Dulles: A biography of Eleanor, Allen and John Foster Dulles and their family networks*, London: Hodder and Stoughton, 1978.

Munster, G., *Rupert Murdoch*, Victoria: Viking, 1985.

Murdoch, I., *The Sovereignty of Good*, London: Routledge and Kegan Paul, 1970.

Murrow, E., *This is London*, New York: Simon and Schuster, 1941.

Nagel, T., *The View from Nowhere*, Oxford: Oxford University Press, 1985.

Nasaw, D., *The Chief: The Life of William Randolph Hearst*, New York: Houghton Mifflin, 2000.

Nathan, A. and Link, P. (eds), *The Tiananmen Papers*, compiled by Zhang Llang, Boston: Little, Brown, 2001.

Navasky, V., *Naming Names*, New York: Viking, 1980.

Novick, P., *That Noble Dream: The objectivity question and the American historical profession*, Cambridge and New York: Cambridge University Press, 1988.

Nutting, A., *No End of a Lesson: The story of Suez*, London: Constable, 1967.

O'Reilly, E., *Veronica Guerin: The life and death of a crime reporter*, London: Vintage, 1998.

Orwell, G., *Homage to Catalonia* (1938), Harmondsworth: Penguin, 1962.

Orwell, G., *Collected Essays, Journalism and Letters of George Orwell*, ed. S. Orwell and I. Angus, 4 vols, Harmondsworth: Penguin, 1970.

Page, B., Leitch, D. and Knightley, P., *Philby: The spy who betrayed a generation*, London: André Deutsch, 1968.

Parenti, M., *Inventing Reality: The politics of the mass media*, 2nd edn, New York: St Martin's Press, 1993.

Paustovsky, K., *Slow Approach of Thunder*, London: Harvill Press, 1965.

Paustovsky, K., *In That Dawn*, London: Harvill Press, 1967.

Paustovsky, K., *Years of Hope*, London: Harvill Press, 1968.

Penn Warren, R., *All the King's Men* (1946), New York: Bantam Books, 1951.

Persico, J. E., *Edward R. Murrow: An American original*, New York: McGraw-Hill, 1988.

Pincher, C., *Their Trade is Treachery*, New York: Bantam Books, 1982.

Pincher, C., *Traitors*, Harmondsworth: Penguin, 1987.

Podhoretz, N., *Breaking Ranks: A political memoir*, London: Weidenfeld and Nicolson, 1979.

Podhoretz, N., *Ex-Friends*, New York: Free Press, 1999.

Ponchaud, F., *Cambodia: Year Zero*, Harmondsworth: Penguin, 1978.

Pyle, E., *Home Country*, New York: Henry Holt, 1947.

Pyle, E., *Brave Men*, New York: Henry Holt, 1944 and 1947.

Ransome, A., *Racundra's First Cruise*, London: Unwin, 1923.

Ransome, A., *Swallows and Amazons* (1930), Harmondsworth: Puffin, 1962.

Ransome, A., *Six Weeks in Russia*, London: Unwin, 1969.

Ransome, A., *The Autobiography*, ed. R. Hart-Davis, London: Jonathan Cape, 1976.

Rhodes, R., *The Making of the Atomic Bomb*, Harmondsworth: Penguin, 1988.

Rorty, R., *Contingency, Irony and Solidarity*, Cambridge: Cambridge University Press, 1989.

Ross, R., *Ladies of the Press*, New York: Norton, 1974.

Rudenstine, D., *The Day the Presses Stopped: A history of the Pentagon Papers case*, Berkeley: University of California Press, 1996.

Ryan, A. P., *Lord Northcliffe*, London: Collins, 1953.

Said, E., *Representations of the Intellectual*, (the 1993 Reith lectures), London: Vintage, 1994.

Sandel, M., *Democracy and its Discontents: America in search of a public philosophy*, Cambridge: Harvard University Press, 1996.

Schlesinger, A., *A Thousand Days: John F. Kennedy in the White House*, London: André Deutsch, 1965.

Schudson, M., *Discovering the News: A social history of American newspapers*, New York: Basic Books, 1978.

Shapiro, H. (ed.), *The Muckrakers and American Society*, Boston: Beacon Press, 1968.

Sharf, A., *The British Press and Jews under Nazi Rule*, London: Oxford University Press, 1964.

Shaw, A., *Eden, Suez and the Mass Media*, London: I. B. Tauris, 1996.

Sheehan, N., 'Should we have war crime trials', *New York Times Book Review*, 28 Mar. 1971.

Sheehan, N., *A Bright Shining Lie: John Paul Vann and America in Vietnam*, New York: Random House, 1988.

Sheehan, N., Smith, H., Kenworthy, E. W. and Butterfield, F., *The Pentagon Papers: The secret history of the Vietnam War, based on investigative reporting by Neil Sheehan*, New York: Bantam Books, 1971.

Shirer, W., *Berlin Diary* (1940), rev. edn, London: Hamish Hamilton, 1947.

Shirer, W., *Twentieth Century Journey*, vol. 1: *The Start, 1904–1930*, New York: Simon and Schuster, 1976.

Shirer, W., *Twentieth Century Journey*, vol. 2: *The Nightmare Years, 1930–1940*, Boston: Little, Brown, 1984.

Simpson, J., 'Beijing report', *Granta*, 28 (1989).

Simpson, J., *Strange Places, Questionable People*, London: Pan, 1999.

Steel, R., *Walter Lippmann and the American Century*, New York: Random House, 1981.

Steffens, L., *Autobiography of Lincoln Steffens*, New York: Norton, 1931.

Stone, I. F., *This is Israel*, New York: Boni and Gaer, 1948.

Stone, I. F., *The Hidden History of the Korean War 1950–1951*, New York: Monthly Review Press, 1952.

Stone, I. F., *Polemics and Prophecies 1967–1970*, New York: Vintage Books, 1972.

Stone, I. F., *Underground to Palestine and Reflections Thirty Years Later*, New York: Pantheon, 1978.

Syed, A., *Walter Lippmann's Philosophy of International Politics*, Philadelphia: University of Pennsylvania Press, 1963.

Sykes, C., *Evelyn Waugh: A biography*, Harmondsworth: Penguin, 1977.

Tanenhaus, S., *Whittaker Chambers: A biography*, New York: Random House, 1977.

Taylor, A. J. P., *English History 1914–1945*, vol. 15 of *Oxford History of England*, Oxford: Clarendon Press, 1965.

Taylor, A. J. P., *Beaverbrook*, London: Hamish Hamilton, 1972.

Taylor, C., *Philosophy and the Human Sciences*, Cambridge: Cambridge University Press, 1985.

Taylor, S. J., *Stalin's Apologist: Walter Duranty, the New York Times's man in Moscow*, Oxford: Oxford University Press, 1990.

Thompson, E. P., *Whigs and Hunters*, London: Allen Lane, 1975.

Thompson, E. P., *William Morris: From romantic to revolutionary*, London: Merlin Press, 1977.

Thompson, J. L., *Northcliffe*, London: John Murray, 2000.

Thurber, J., *My Life and Hard Times*, Harmondsworth: Penguin, 1948.

Todd, O., *André Malraux: Une vie*, Paris: Gallimard, 2001.

Tolstoy, L., *War and Peace*, trans. Maude, London: Macmillan, 1942.

Trotsky, L., 'The strangled revolution'. *Nouvelle Revue Française*, 211 (Apr. 1931), repr. in R. W. B. Lewis (ed.), *Malraux: Twentieth century views*, New York: Prentice Hall, 1969.

Tulis, J., *The Rhetorical Presidency*, Princeton: Princeton University Press, 1987.

Tunstall, J., *Newspaper Power*, Oxford: Oxford University Press, 1996.

Vidal, G., *Hollywood*, New York: Random House, 1969.

Vidal, G., *Pentimento: A Memoir*, London: Abacus, 1994.

Vidal, G., *The Golden Age*, Boston: Little, Brown, 2000.

Walzer, M., *The Company of Critics: Social criticism and political commentary in the 20th century*, New York: Basic Books, 1988.

Watt, I., *The Rise of the Novel*, London: Chatto and Windus, 1957.

Waugh, E., *Waugh in Abyssinia*, London: Longmans Green, 1937.

Waugh, E., *The Diaries of Evelyn Waugh*, ed. M. Davie, Harmondsworth: Penguin, 1979.

Waugh, E., *Scoop* (1938), Harmondsworth: Penguin, 1984.

Waugh, E., *Remote People* (1931), Harmondsworth: Penguin, 1985.

Weaver, P. W., *News and the Culture of Lying*, New York: Free Press, 1994.

Weber, M., *The Theory of Social and Economic Organisation*, ed. Talcott Parsons New York: Free Press, 1947.

Weber, M., *From Max Weber: Essays in sociology*, ed. H. H. Gerth and C. Wright Mills, London: Routledge and Kegan Paul, 1948.

Wheeler, C., 'You'd better get out while you can', *London Review of Books*, 19 Sept. 1996.

Wheeler, C., 'Half the way with LBJ', *New Statesman*, 10 May 2000.

Wicker, T., *On the Press*, New York: Viking, 1978.

Wilkinson, D., *Malraux: An essay in political criticism*, Cambridge Mass: Harvard University Press, 1967.

Williams, F., *Dangerous Estate: The anatomy of newspapers*, London: Longmans Green, 1957.

Williams, R., *The Long Revolution*, Harmondsworth: Penguin, 1963.

Williams, R., *Orwell*, London: Fontana, 1971.

Williams, R., *The Volunteers*, London: Eyre Methuen, 1978.

Williams, R., *Politics and Letters*, London: Verso, 1981.

Wilson, E., 'André Malraux's novels'. *New Republic*, 9 Aug. 1933, repr. in R. W. B. Lewis (ed.), *Malraux: Twentieth Century Views*, New York: Prentice-Hall, 1969.

Wittgenstein, L., *Philosophical Investigations*, Oxford: Basil Blackwell, 1953.

Wodehouse, P. G., *Psmith Journalist*, Harmondsworth: Penguin, 1970.

Wolfe, T., *A Man in Full*, New York: Farrar, Straus and Giroux, 1998.

Wolfe, T. (ed.), *The New Journalism*, London: Picador, 1990; originally published as T. Wolfe, *The New Journalism, with an Anthology edited by T. Wolfe and E. W. Johnson* (1973).

Woodward, B. and Bernstein, C., *All the President's Men* (1974), London: Bloomsbury, 1998.

Wright Mills, C., *The Power Elite*, New York: Oxford University Press, 1968.

Yergin, D., *Shattered Peace: The origins of the Cold War and the national security state*, Harmondsworth: Penguin, 1980.

Young, A., *An Easy Burden: The civil rights movement and the transformation of America*, New York: Harper Collins, 1996.

Young, H., *One of Us: A life of Margaret Thatcher*, London: Pan Books, 1993.

Index